Cultural Identity and Urban Change in Southeast Asia:
Interpretative Essays

Cultural Identity and Urban Change in Southeast Asia: Interpretative Essays

◆

Edited by Marc Askew and William S. Logan

DEAKIN ⏴⏴⏴ UNIVERSITY PRESS

Published by Deakin University Press
Geelong, Victoria 3217
First published 1994
© Deakin University Press 1994
Printed in Australia

National Library of Australia
Cataloguing-in-publication data

Cultural identity and urban change in Southeast Asia.

  Includes index.
  ISBN 0 949823 43 0

  1. Urbanization – Asia, Southeastern. 2. Asia, Southeastern – Civilization. I, Askew, M. R. (Marc Richard). II.
Logan, W. S. (William Stewart), 1942–

307.14160959

Contents

Foreword

T.G. McGee[1]

TRIUMPH OF THE PROFANE: SHIELDING THE SACRED IN SOUTHEAST ASIAN CITIES

It is now almost 30 years since my study of Southeast Asian cities was published (McGee 1967) and it drew upon earlier research carried out by many prominent researchers such as Ginsburg (1955), Hauser (1957) and Fryer (1953). In searching for the elusive essence of the cities of Southeast Asia as I travelled around the region in the early 1960s I came to see these cities as essentially a mosaic of ethnic quarters as Haryadi observes in his contribution to this volume. One hundred and fifty years of 'accelerated' colonial incorporation had created cities in which the 'indigenous urban tradition' in a cultural sense (and sometimes in the concrete manifestations of the built environment) was one of many layers of migration and developing economic functions frozen into particular locales by the *mission civilisatrice*. As Furnivall (1944) and others have pointed out this colonial practice, the creation of plural societies, reflected colonial priorities for a stable social order that reduced social tension and dampened potential political discontent.

At the economic level this frozen world of city locales was captured with the concept of 'dualism.' Long before the fad of 'informal sector' studies Boeke (1953) and others had conceptualised the economic structure of colonial economies as being divided between a 'traditional' sector primarily based upon subsistence production and a 'modern' sector using capital and 'modern' techniques of management and organisation. Essentially this concept was used to divide rural from urban areas. Geertz's (1963) insight into this formulation was a contribution that a similar 'dualism' existed in the cities of Indonesia and in the early 1960s. The cities of Southeast Asia seemed fossilised in this dualism with a slowly-growing modern sector and a proliferating informal sector of hawkers, *betjak* drivers and street hustlers living in continuing poverty.

This simple economic model was duplicated in the social structure of the cities, divided between a small elite of politicians, business people and military officers, and a mass of low-income poor people struggling for survival. In the early 1960s the middle class of Southeast Asian cities was minuscule, made up of civil servants, teachers and small business owners. Of course, it should be emphasised that these generalised models of economic and class divisions drew boundaries in a situation where the interactions were becoming increasingly important and the power of some institutions such as the army, the state and the banking sector was increasing rapidly.

While this frozen world of the built environment determined the contours of the morphology of these cities, the period since the end of the Second World War had seen a rapid growth of nationalism and the emergence of independent states. An overwhelming motif of the 1950s and 1960s was the political elites reaching back into indigenous history of their countries to create national ideologies. The large cities of Southeast Asia (particularly the political capitals such as Jakarta, Kuala Lumpur, Manila, etc.) were assuming some of the feel of the 'sacred cult centres' of the earlier Southeast Asian urban tradition. A concrete iconography of statuary was proliferating throughout the cities. Thirty years later, when social sciences, architecture and planning are caught in the 'elusive' ambience of 'post-modernity' such a simple world of synthesis and models seems inappropriate. This volume recognises that the cities of Southeast Asia, as the editors comment, are 'locales of complexity.' The extraordinarily rapid growth of many cities in the region (indeed the rapid urbanisation of the region) has broken down the 'frozen mosaic' and created more complex cities and now urban regions which in some cases are reaching populations in excess of 10 million in Jakarta, Manila and Bangkok today (McGee and Greenberg, 1992).

As the editors correctly recognise, the processes that are bringing about this transformation are diverse and the elaboration of their features is complicated by the current 'post-modern' dictate for 'meaning.' Despite these reservations it is clear that there are a number of processes that are producing the changes in Southeast Asian cities. Perhaps the totality of this process is best captured by the phrase 'the global-local dialectic' which suggests a continuing battle between global forces impinging upon the local.

What are these global processes? At the production level they are characterised by the emergence of the so-called New International Division of Labour at the global level which has involved the relocation and establishment of industrial activity in some of the developing countries. Taking advantage of advances in communications and production technologies, the major international investors (often in joint ventures with local capital) identified production niches in a world spanning the production system for exports. This was also characterised by the establishment of industries (often protected by tariffs) involving the production of consumer durables for local markets.

With the exception of Singapore and to a lesser extent Malaysia, Southeast Asian countries have entered into this global production system rather late, but in the 1980s countries such as Thailand and Indonesia have begun to accelerate their industrial production (fuelled to a large extent by investment by the other Asian NICs - Japan, South Korea, Taiwan and Singapore). In the next decade Vietnam will also emerge as the newest component of this system.

For a variety of reasons (state encouragement, access to transport nodes, and access to labour and markets) a large proportion of this industry has been located on the urban periphery of the largest Southeast Asian cities, contributing to the emergence of large extended metropolitan regions (Ginsburg et al, 1991).

A second global force which has led to radical changes in the Southeast Asian cities is the 'transactional revolution.' All societies are characterised by a constant series of transactions flowing through national space and to other parts of the globe. In a very general way these transactions can be grouped into four groups: people, commodities, capital and information. Because of technological developments, the 'transactional space' has been radically altered in the past three decades. The relaxation of regulatory environments, together with advances in information transactions, mean that the flows of capital and information are not now generally subject to the constraints of space. While transactions involving the flow of people and commodities still involve time-distance relationships the improvement in the technologies that service these transactions have increasingly collapsed space. Thus, for example, the development of 'just-in-time' delivery systems have reduced the order cycle times in developing countries by 400 per cent. Of course, this logistical management could only be made possible by improvements in telecommunications, computers and information systems.

A third element of these global forces relates to the 'consumption' of the end products. At one level there is the emergence of a 'common' set of lifestyles relating to dress, food, entertainment and the built environment, which for lack of a better phrase we will call 'global culture.' These components coalesce in the many shopping malls that proliferate in the urban landscape of Southeast Asian cities. Adolescents lounge outside the fast food outlets; 'Living Dead' tee-shirts and 'dreadlocks' merge into the neon-lit windows on the West.

Perhaps the most ubiquitous feature of this consumption is the growth of the middle class housing tracts, creating sprawling suburbs on the fringes of virtually all Southeast Asian cities. Each of these new homes becomes the container for the durable goods, the TVs, furniture and stereo systems that are part of this consumer revolution.

Virtually all observers of this global impact are convinced that it is an important factor contributing to increasing centralisation within the urban systems of Southeast Asian countries. These global processes are leading to the establishment of global mega-urban regions which become the major nodal points in the movement of capital, people, information and commodities. Within Southeast Asia there is continuing competition between countries and their major cities. For instance, Singapore-Thailand competition as a major air transportation node. Thus cities are engaged in intense competition to gain a share of the regional and global markets for business and tourists. This involves investment in the telecommunications networks, the airports and the hotels that will attract visitors.

In the face of these overwhelming global forces aided and abetted by the national state, the land developers and local capitalists (often in close liaison if not the same groups) the 'frozen mosaic' of the Southeast Asian cities are split, invaded, destroyed and reconstructed. Perhaps this is most obvious in the case of Singapore, incontestably the most 'global' city of Southeast Asia which in the 1960s and 1970s completely transformed its built environment with a high-rise landscape set in a sea of greenery. Localities were subsumed by the national space (De Koninck, 1992).

This issue of the survival of the local is the central motif of this collection. In particular the papers in the collection are concerned with the 'conservation' of the local in the face of these global forces. While the authors variously see the conservation of the lo-

cal as an appeal to tradition, most recognise that there are serious problems with establishing the authenticity of the 'traditional.' For example see Logan's discussion of the role of Chinese as opposed to Vietnamese architecture in the northern Vietnamese cities. Even more intriguing is the comic opera of Bugis Street where the attempt to package traditional (sexual) non-conformity in the midst of a national attempt to promote 'family values' created a doomed replica of the past. Throughout Southeast Asia today national and city governments are attempting to refashion the built environment but conservation is a hard concept to sell.

A useful way to think of this clash between the global and the local is to focus on the way that the 'political economy of space' generates architectural and urban forms in which the emphasis is upon consumption and spectacle cities are being increasingly placed in competition with one another as locales for tourism and consumption investment as much as production investment. Thus the urban centres have experienced a rapid growth of hotels and tourist zones, middle and upper income housing and polycentric patterns of commercial centres have developed. There is a push to create rapid transit systems to improve the efficiency of the cities. The result of these developments is to create a built environment in which regional identity is dominated by 'international images' that destroys or masks the rich cultural traditions of the cities.

Thus in the chinatowns of Singapore and Jakarta land values increase and the Chinese inhabitants of these areas lead the exodus to the new housing developments. But the cities of 'global spectacle' still have persistent elements of the old cities. Royal enclaves, 'sacred buildings,' squatter and low-income housing, open markets and small shops that cater to the 'traditional' sections of the city social structure. In this situation one often sees a layering of the built environment in which the modern 'high-rise' cities are connected by 'flyovers' for automobiles that pass over the 'lower-order' cities, reminding one of the architectural fantasies of a Buck Rogers science fiction movie.

Unlike the colonial period when the social order was concerned with the preservation of a 'stable' mosaic of land use, the contemporary Southeast Asian cities have become contested terrains in which developers, the state and local groups struggle for urban space. While some of us see this contest as most uneven it is the virtue of this collection that the 'local' components of this three-sided contest are explored. The preservation of Kuala Lumpur's Central Market and the pressure to preserve Hanoi's colonial 'quarter' are efforts which are duplicated in many cities. But as yet this process of the 'local' asserting itself above broader market and political forces is very embryonic. Even Bali, with its rich cultural tradition is struggling to preserve its cultural identity. Townsend's beautifully-written dirge to Denpasar and the surrounding tourist region is evidence enough of the difficulties of maintaining the 'sacred landscape' in the face of the profanity of globalism. The future Southeast Asian cities (particularly the largest of each country) will probably look a lot more like Los Angeles or Sydney than the sacred cities of early Southeast Asia. As Townsend's image suggests, this will be the triumph of the profane.

The essays in this book carry a common message concerning the Southeast Asian cities. The built environment is a rich historical element of the past; from a materialistic and cultural point of view there are strong arguments to 'preserve' and 'conserve' some of the elements of this built environment. Whether the planners, politicians and developers concerned with shaping the contemporary Southeast Asian cities are willing to engage in this task is uncertain, but it is through such studies that are represented here that their awareness can be cultivated.

ENDNOTE

1   T. G. McGee is Professor of Geography at the University of British Columbia, Canada. He is a leading academic in the field of human settlements research in the Asian region. He has produced a number of seminal works on cities and development in Southeast Asia, including the *Southeast Asian Study: a Social Geography of the Primate Cities of Southeast Asia* (1967), and collaborated in the writing of key collections such as *Theatres of Accumulation: Studies in Asian and Latin American Urbanisation* (1985) and *The Extended Metropolis: Settlement Transition in Asia* (1991).

REFERENCES

Boeke, J.H. (1953), *Economics and Economic Policy in Dual Societies*. New York: Institute of Pacific Relations.

De Koninck, R. (1992), *Singapore. An Atlas of the Revolution of Territory*. Montpellier: Reclus.

Fryer, D.W. (1953), 'The Million City in Southeast Asia,' *Geographical Review*, October, pp. 474-94.

Furnivall, J.S. (1944), *Netherlands India: A Study of Plural Economy*. Cambridge: Cambridge University Press.

Ginsburg, N.S. (1955), 'The Great City in Southeast Asia,' *American Journal of Sociology*, March, Vol. 60, No. 5, pp. 455-62.

Ginsburg, N.S., B. Koppel and T.G. McGee (eds.) (1991), *The Extended Metropolis: Settlement Transition in Asia*. Honolulu: University of Hawaii Press.

Geertz, C. (1963), *Peddlers and Princes: Social Change and Economic Modernisation in Two Indonesian Towns*. Chicago: Chicago University Press.

Hauser, P.M. (ed.) (1957), *Urbanisation in Asia and the Far East*. Calcutta: Tensions and Technology Series, UNESCO.

McGee, T.G. (1967), *The Southeast Asian City: A Social Geography of the Primate Cities of Southeast Asia*. London: G. Bell & Sons Ltd.

McGee, T.G. and Greenberg, Charles (1992), 'The Emergence of Extended Metropolitan Regions in ASEAN: Towards the Year 2000', *ASEAN Economic Bulletin*, Vol. 9, No. 1, pp. 22-44.

NOTES ON THE EDITORS

Marc Askew is a lecturer in the Department of Asian Studies and Languages, Victoria University of Technology, Melbourne, Australia. Trained as a historian at Melbourne and Monash Universities, he has been particularly interested in the study of urban groups and their socio-ecological settings. His doctoral and published work has focussed upon the historical relationships between communities, institutions and the built environment. He has been active in the field of urban conservation for many years and edited the Australia ICOMOS journal *Historic Environment* from 1989 to 1993. For the past 4 years he has been engaged in research on the question of urban change in Bangkok, both as an individual scholar and together with other researchers at a number of universities in Bangkok on issues of urban research and interpretation. At the time of the final preparation of this book, he was teaching in the graduate program of the Department of Urban and Regional Planning, Chulalongkorn University, Thailand, and conducting research on socio-spatial change in Bangkok. He recently published *Interpreting Bangkok: the Urban Question in Thai Studies*

William S. Logan is Professor of Geography and Head of the Graduate School of Arts at Deakin University in Melbourne, Australia. He has taught at the University of Melbourne, Footscray Institute of Technology and Deakin University. A member of the Royal Australian Planning Institute and author of books and articles on urban history, geography, planning and heritage conservation, his research currently focuses on heritage protection in Asia, notably Vietnam. He has acted as consultant to UNESCO's Division of Physical Heritage since 1986, conducting evaluations of its heritage campaigns in Bangladesh, Sri Lanka and Nepal, updating its Moenjodaro campaign master plan in Pakistan, and preparing its Hanoi campaign. He is currently involved in a major Australian Government – sponsored planning project in Hanoi

NOTES ON THE CONTRIBUTORS

Christiane Blancot is an architect. She has worked for the last 10 years as an 'urbaniste' (architect/planner) in the Atelier Parisien d'Urbanisme and has carried out numerous town-planning projects in Paris. She also teaches planning history and theory at the Institut d'Etudes Politiques de Paris. During the last 2 years, as part of a co-operative endeavour between the City of Paris and the City of Phnom Penh, she has been specifically responsible for the preparation of building regulations and the implementation of planning projects for the City of Phnom Penh.

Annette Hamilton has been Professor of Anthropology and Comparative Sociology at Macquarie University since 1983. She has carried out field research among Aboriginal communities in remote Australia for many years before turning to research in Thailand, working on aspects of mass media and the consequences of globalisation with a special focus on cinema, television and tourism. She has published a number of papers based on this research and is currently preparing a book on Thai media and popular culture. Her current research concerns the circulation of culture in the Asia-Pacific region.

Haryadi is a lecturer in the Department of Architecture at Gadjah Mada University, Yogyakarta, and a member of the research team in the University's Centre for Environmental Studies. His chapter in this book is based on his Ph.D. which dealt with *kampung* (village) residents' strategies for coping with environmental stress in Yogyakarta. The thesis was written at the University of Wisconsin-Milwaukee under the supervision of Professor Amos Rapoport. He has previously published reports on development and conservation in *kampung* for the United Nations Centre for Regional Development and the Aga Khan Program in Architecture.

Kuah Khun Eng is currently teaching anthropology at the University of Hong Kong. Before her present appointment, she was a research fellow at the Institute of Southeast Asian Studies in Singapore and a lecturer in anthropology at the University of Melbourne. Her current research is focussed on Chinese identity and cultural reproduction, the relationship between state and religion, and conservation, environment and development.

Jimmy Cheok-Siang Lim is an outspoken professional with strong personal convictions about architecture and the environment. An architecture graduate from the University of New South Wales, he is the Principal of CSL Associates in Kuala Lumpur. He was a founding member of the Heritage of Malaysia Trust (BWM) and its first Vice-President from 1964-68; he is also the immediate past President of Friends of the Heritage of Malaysia and is currently the President of the Malaysian Institute of Architects (PAM). His professional work is widely recognised and featured in international and local publications and he has received numerous awards for his contribution to Malaysian architecture.

Guy Lubeigt studied History and Geography at the Sorbonne University, Paris, and was Cultural Attaché at the French Embassy in Rangoon before teaching at Chulalongkorn University, Bangkok, from 1971-74. In 1976 he became, and still remains, a member of the Centre National de Recherches Scientifiques in Paris. He has written numerous books, articles and reports dealing with the economic and administrative systems, rural industries, urban development and ethnogeography of Burma and Thailand. The thesis for his Ph.D. in Tropical Geography was on 'The Exploitation and Culture of the Sugar Palm (Borassus flabellifer) in Central Burma' and was published by the Sorbonne Geography Department in 1979. He is currently studying the urban changes in Burma and writing a Doctorat d'Etat titled 'Ethnogeography of Buddhism in Burma'.

Michael Pinches is a Senior Lecturer in the Department of Anthropology at the University of Western Australia. He received his B.Arch. from the University of Melbourne in 1973 and a Ph.D. in anthropology from Monash University in 1985. He has conducted extensive research on the Philippines and is joint editor with Salim Lakha of the book *Wage Labour and Social Change: the Proletariat in Asia and the Pacific.*

Doosadee Thaitakoo is an architect and planner. She is currently Assistant Professor in the Department of Urban and Regional Planning at Chulalongkorn University, Bangkok, Thailand, where she teaches courses in urban design and urban history in the Masters degree program. She has worked as a consultant planner for the National Housing Authority and as an urban design consultant. Her current projects include a use and perception study of Sukhothai Historical Park and research into the sense of place and identity in the Khlong Toey community, Bangkok.

Don Townsend trained as a geographer and regional planner, with special interests in transport planning and development studies. He has worked as a consultant in development planning projects in Papua New Guinea, Australia, Indonesia, Thailand, China, the Maldives and Philippines. He is active in training, curriculum development and institutional development projects, mainly for the major donor agencies, including the Australian International Development Assistance Bureau. He recently completed two assignments in the Bali Tourism Management Project and is now engaged on a master plan project in Palau.

Mohammed Hussain Sahib is a lecturer in Geography at Deakin University, Rusden Campus, where he has been teaching cartography for twenty seven years. He has provided consultancy service in cartography to authors of books, journal articles and reports. Since 1966 he has also provided consultancy service to several publishing firms in Melbourne.

Introduction:
urban tradition and
transformation

Marc Askew and William S. Logan

THE STUDY OF URBAN CHANGE IN SOUTHEAST ASIA

The process of urbanisation, its causes and its impact on the environment and the quality of life of people are important features in the current pattern of change in Southeast Asia. Levels of urbanisation in the region vary - in 1990, from 43 per cent in Malaysia and 31 per cent in Indonesia to 23 per cent in Thailand, 22 per cent in Vietnam and 12 per cent in Cambodia (United Nations 1993, pp.2-11). But the trend of increasing urbanisation of the population of the region is clear, particularly for those countries presently experiencing high rates of economic growth. The region is home to three of the world's 'mega-cities' - Bangkok, Jakarta and Manila - and these are predicted to experience further population growth of between 2 to 3 million each by the end of this century. The ratio of population of these mega-cities to other urban centres has been increasing markedly over the last decade and will continue to the point where, by the year 2000, some 25 per cent (around 90 million) of all Southeast Asia's urban dwellers will reside in the region's largest cities (United Nations 1986). The well-documented impacts of such change on the environment and the problems associated with providing adequate shelter for the poor, urban services and infrastructure are sub-

jects of concern for agencies at the local, regional and international levels (United Nations 1990).

Urban growth has been the conspicuous partner of industrialisation and structural economic change over the past twenty years in particular, both reflecting and promoting internal transformations in the demography and government of the countries of Southeast Asia, as well as responses to an increasingly globalised economy. Indigenous entrepreneurs, in partnership with overseas investors, particularly from Japan, have been encouraged by international funding bodies such as the International Monetary Fund, World Bank and Asian Development Bank, as well as by national governments such as those of Singapore, Thailand and Indonesia, to expand export-oriented industrial activities. Such changes have encouraged sectoral shifts in national economies towards manufacturing, with the largest shifts over the past five years being recorded in Malaysia and Thailand, as reflected in figures on the contribution of that sector to Gross Domestic Product. To an even greater extent, all countries of the region have registered a significant decline in the contribution of agriculture to GDP over the same period.

The wider effects of such changes are reflected in corresponding shifts in employment patterns across economic sectors (Asian Development Bank 1992;

United Nations 1993; World Bank 1992). The growth of the urban areas and their peripheries is a fundamental part of this restructuring process: the urbanising regions of Southeast Asian countries are playing a decisive role in economic growth, largely by virtue of the expansion of manufacturing and allied activities.

Until quite recently there were few restrictions on the location of manufacturing industries, so not surprisingly, firms capitalised on economies of scale and sited their plants near existing industrial concentrations in urban areas. Added to existing centralisation tendencies and metropolitan primacy in government and services, this trend has further consolidated the dominance of capital cities and spurred growth in some provincial centres. Other, smaller settlements in the Southeast Asian region, on the coasts or islands, have been a favourite target of the tourism industry.

The striking regional variations within Southeast Asia not only make for an extraordinary cultural richness attractive to tourists and indigenous peoples alike, but also adds complexity to the discussion of urban transformations. Tourism in the Southeast Asian region has expanded rapidly over the last decade, with tourist numbers multiplying threefold from an estimated 7 million to over 21 million per year between 1981 and 1990 (United Nations 1992). These figures do not include Vietnam, which is beginning to experience significant growth in tourism. A conspicuous facet of globalisation, international tourism has manifested a range of transforming effects 'on regions and localities, in terms of culture, economies and the natural environment.

Of the capitalist Association of South East Asian Nations (ASEAN) countries, Thailand and Malaysia see themselves becoming the next 'economic tigers of Asia'; Singapore has probably achieved this status already. By contrast the three nations of Indochina - Vietnam, Cambodia and Laos - have trodden a different, socialist path since independence and are only now beginning to implement capitalist economic ideas in order to secure greater material wellbeing for their citizens. Although they could learn much from the experience of their neighbours as they move into the cycle of economic, social and environmental transformations, unfortunately their rush to de-

velop economically may well lead them to repeat many of the same mistakes. Thus Hanoi, Ho Chi Minh City and Phnom Penh are already threatening to become as polluted as Bangkok, Jakarta and Manila, and sharpened economic inequities between urban groups and neighbourhoods may follow soon after.

However much the problems of the Southeast Asian cities attract World Bank support in addressing infrastructural tasks and projects, and however much the occasional documentary exposé about sweated workers or exploited prostitutes shocks TV viewers or newspaper readers, it would be true to say that the urban environment has attracted less attention than the rural or the natural environment in current debates surrounding the nature of 'development' in the region. Why is this, given that leading academics in Asia predict (such as Bandaranayeke 1992) that within the next generation they expect to see the destruction of 90 per cent of the continent's traditional cultural landscapes? Is it that images of urban change do not evoke the required stereotype of traditional society, so well reflected in the rural village? Is it assumed somehow that, given the right policy directions, the continuing wave of rural-urban migration will be reversed? Or that village societies, denuded of their young people for so long because of the concentration of work opportunities in the cities, will become magically reconstituted when a well-balanced economic framework has been devised? Or is it that there is a division of labour in development thinking, a simplistic duality with the question of 'culture' concentrated on rural 'tradition' while urban environments are the necessary but less significant or appealing sites of cultural meaning in changing modern societies? On the other hand, the most recent Ministerial Conference of ESCAP (October 1993), by resolving to promote 'economically efficient, environmentally sustainable, socially just, politically participatory and culturally vibrant urbanisation in the region', perhaps signals that 'the urban' is coming to be regarded as a culturally meaningful site (ESCAP 1993). The production and definition of that meaning remains, however, a major issue.

Are there urban traditions in Southeast Asian cities and towns? A prominent argument among academics has been that most of these countries had no significant urban base prior to colonisation and thus 'the city', at least in the Western sense of being an economic and administrative centre and the focus of capital accumulation, was seen to be an alien implant in Southeast Asian cultures and societies (King 1976). Yet others contend that, not only do some urban areas maintain great significance nationally and regionally, but also that this has been a longstanding role of urban centres in the history of the region. The question arises as to how modernisation has transformed social and spatial patterns in these urban places and, in the process, has also transformed the significance of 'the urban' in cultural terms, as a site for transmitted symbols, inherited lifestyles and lived spaces.

The above statement of course begs the question of the definition of 'modernisation' and 'modernity'. We use 'modernisation' here to refer to that process of economic, social and cultural change which, through transformations in communications and economic relations, gives rise to transformations in geographical and social patterns, leading to a condition - 'modernity' - which is characterised by the conspicuous extraction of time from space and 'place' from space. By 'place' we refer to the meaning conferred on particular spaces by groups of people through sustained association at various levels (following Giddens' notion of 'disembedding', 1990). Simultaneous with this is a general trend towards more homogenous characteristics in lifestyles and patterns of consumption, in dress, in food, in housing and leisure. We would contend here that the process of modernisation (some might prefer the less loaded expression 'cultural and social change') is inextricably connected to the historical development of world capitalism and the incorporation of the non-Western societies into a system which, propelled by the impulses of capitalist accumulation and production, set these societies on courses of structural change which were irreversible.

By the same token, however, the character of socio-cultural change has not been uniform among these societies, even though capitalism must be seen as a primary impulse in the process which induced changes in traditional social orders (Eisenstadt 1987, pp.4-7).

The complementary processes, entailing at once the dissolution of locality systems and the increasing

uniformity of patterns of life, are simultaneously economic and cultural in nature and clearly inform the character of change in the Southeast Asian region. This is why so much of the discussion in the following chapters will, in various ways, address the question of locality - more precisely, the local identification with place or community at various levels - as an increasingly fragile basis for meaningful identification by people in the region. Paradoxically, it is 'the local' which is increasingly seen as the alternative basis for development aspirations and goals in the international debate between governments, international agencies and non-government organisations.

Given the nature of contemporary global interdependencies and existing balances of economic power (which are focussed as much on Asia as they are on the West), identifying a source of contemporary change in geographical terms is an empty task: it is not now a 'Western' bogey that threatens what one scholar has dubbed 'the post-traditional' developing societies (Eisenstadt: ibid); it is a global economic process which induces not only changes in economic structures and relationships, but also transforms the socio-cultural foundations of these societies. Marx's famous characterisation of the transforming power of materialist bourgeois ideology over the values which supported the structure of traditional European society is still appropriate, particularly the emphasis on the breakdown of local identification with custom and place in the face of a disinterested economic process. Globalisation is a process with wide cultural ramifications for traditional societies.[1] So the enemy is not outside: the impulses to change are generated from among groups within the region's societies, albeit often groups which control a disproportionate share of wealth and power. Modernity is a global state. Post-colonial societies in Asia are inextricably embedded in this context.

Nevertheless, it must be admitted that the urban arena clearly represents what can be regarded as foreign and alien in these societies. Urban areas have always been the entry point for new commodities and technologies as well as the sites where new social groups have been introduced or emerged: places of complexity within overwhelmingly agricultural and peasant societies. Urban areas, open to outside influence, are the conduits and representations of change in traditional societies. Notwithstanding in-digenous urban traditions which can be traced to an early period, the urbanism of the nineteenth century particularly, which did so much to create the urban landscape of Southeast Asia, was often introduced through the process of colonisation and the conse-quent unequal relationships generated by that proc-ess. In cultural terms, in reacting to changes expressed through urbanisation, should Southeast Asian socie-ties then repudiate the urban past completely as a source of authentic cultural symbols and representa-tions? Pol Pot's regime in Kampuchea took such an approach to Phnom Penh, virtually ordering its de-struction as a non-indigenous form of habitat.[2] That solution was as superficial as it was radical.

It should be acknowledged that most urban settle-ments of any size in the region were always 'differ-ent' by virtue of the contrast between their relatively complex social and ethnic composition and the pre-dominantly rural societies within which they were situated. Plurality has been a marked characteristic of these settlements from an early period, with the settlement of these groups having different causes and consequences. The conflict and hostility gener-ated by the presence of Chinese merchant commu-nities in some societies (for example, Indonesia) can be contrasted with peaceful coexistence in other so-cieties (for example, Thailand). Within the histories of particular settlements different groups have man-aged to develop their own niches and areas, main-tain customs and produce their own traditions, for example, Singapore's 'Little India', Bangkok's Sampeng and Pahurat, or Yogyakarta's Chinese quarters.

Of course 'tradition' is itself problematic as a bench-mark of authenticity and legitimacy, particularly on a national level (Anderson 1983). But it is tradition - in the form of a body of symbols and practices chosen to represent cultural and social continuity in-herited from the past - which is summoned as a bul-wark of certainty in an ever-changing world, despite the fact that it often needs to be mass produced for consumption by an increasingly urbanised popula-tion in the region. In addition, of course, the pack-aging of identity for Western tourists, most often a mixture of the 'traditional' and the 'exotic', is now well established and a vital income earner for coun-tries such as Indonesia, Malaysia and Thailand. The re-fashioning of tradition is part and parcel of the process of contemporary change.

The contributors to this volume address the con-tested nature of traditions and meanings in the chang-ing contexts of urban and urbanising areas of the region. In dealing with the multifaceted process of urbanisation which takes its shape and trajectory from inherited local factors as well as regional, national and global influences, we see conflicts and tensions emerging on a number of levels. We see the state embracing development goals which propel socie-ties towards a destination where old cultural mean-ings and contexts have little function; we see icons of tradition being absorbed within a complex of im-ages which commodify the past as a consumable tradition (while the groups which actively produced such traditions in their everyday life have been marginalised); we see old images being re-configured to fit the quotable vocabulary of post-modern archi-tectural style; we see groups surviving in urban ar-eas where old patterns of allegiance and identity still help such groups persist. The categories of 'tradi-tional' versus 'modern' or 'indigenous' versus 'West-ern' are highly simplified dichotomies, particularly when we are trying to understand changes in the complex plural environments of urban areas. Such dichotomies nevertheless are generated in situations of conflict which are increasingly emerging at vari-ous levels as a result of rapid socio-economic change, of which urbanisation is the most conspicuous product.

THE CULTURAL DIMENSION OF DEVELOPMENT

This book is offered as a part of the wider discus-sion about development and the role of urban places in it, picking up on those themes of 'cultural re-sources' and 'identity' which have become recog-nised as integral to the debate and to the thinking of those engaged in formulating development strate-gies and policy responses to economic change in Southeast Asia. In addressing the urban and urbanis-ing context of change in Southeast Asia, this collec-tion of interpretative essays does not make claims to a particular disciplinary distinctiveness - rather, it is a recognition both of a gap in current literature on cultural transformation in the region and of the importance of marshalling a range of perspectives in order to understand its manifestations and implications in urban settings.

Central to the difficult and conflict-bound process of re-conceptualising development - by whom? for whom? - is the question of maintaining or dealing with the issue of cultural meaning and the direction of change. Governments within the region are now aware of the severe dislocation that economic modernisation has left in its wake. A common response has been to re-emphasise tradition. As the Secretary General of the National Culture Commission of Thailand noted in 1989:

> As most of the people, a silent majority, [have] lost confidence in their own cultural base, the government must try, in many possible ways, to restore the folk dignity and wisdom. This does not mean to simply retain the traditional mode of production and traditional way of life. It is simply to make people aware of their own confidence in their cultural roots and become readily adaptable to new values and behaviours so that they may be ready to stride forward amidst changes (NCC 1989, p.145).

Such official responses, tinged with the traditional concerns of governments in the region for social order and stability in the face of widening income disparities and inequalities, have been regarded critically by coalitions of non-government organisations with their strong focus on locality and community as the real base of authentic and sustainable development. We need to ask in what way do such discussions and propositions, concerning principally the national or rural levels, implicate or reflect - perhaps even ignore -transformations in urbanised and urbanising settlements?

The changing urban landscapes of the countries of Southeast Asia are a tangible feature of contemporary change in the region. In referring to the transformations of the cultural landscapes of urban settlements, we do not here assume that the unit of analysis is an abstracted physical environment. Cultural and urban landscape here means those sociophysical environments which have emerged from the dynamic interplay of activity, society and culture over time. In dealing principally with lived environments,

we are seeking to identify and argue for the protection of a people's cultural heritage as reflected and played out in urban environments. We are not focussing on the curatorial issues which may be specific to those great ancient sites of former civilisations (for example, Borobudur, Sukhothai, Angkor) which are justly the concern and pride of the peoples of the region. Our framework of discussion is the socio-cultural, spatial and physical environment of urbanised and urbanising areas of Southeast Asia, the ways in which they are being transformed, the significance of their spaces, and the responses and predicaments of local people and the agencies which play a part in their management and control.

Again, in thus using the terms 'heritage' or 'the past', we do not offer a technical definition as advanced by global agencies such as the United Nations Educational Scientific and Cultural Organisation (UNESCO) or the International Council on Monuments and Sites (ICOMOS) which from time to time have promulgated statements regarding the significance of the physical legacies of 'historic' places in Asia and the world. The urban settlements of Southeast Asia are interacting socio-spatial systems which have generated cultural values throughout their respective histories. Such values are embedded in lifestyles and reflected in localities, social structures and artefacts. The wider significance of these urban systems and spaces is itself determined by patterns of change, often imposed from without - such as by colonialism - as much as generated from within societies. In most of the societies under discussion in this book, the 'great traditions', determined by the traditional elites and longstanding institutionalised belief systems, have established a pattern of clear urban significance read into icons and rituals focussing on the capital cities or centres of power. In addition there are what may be referred to as the 'little traditions' of the society defined as 'folk society' by the anthropologists Redfield and Singer (1954). According to this model, such a 'little tradition' is characterised by popular customs, attitudes and practises largely spawned in the rural areas; yet it is arguable that the 'little tradition' manifests itself in older localities amidst the spaces of the burgeoning cities where it is embodied in the activities and everyday survival strategies of the inhabitants.

So, the culture and cultural heritage of the places discussed in this book derive importance because of the variety of their expressions in both artefact, activity and values. But we are concerned as well with culture as a production, and while the essays in this collection discuss issues of preservation and protection, they do not do so in relation to some unproblematic view of cultural traditions. For this reason a stress is placed on the negotiated and contested meanings of the various elements in the urban cultural landscape. In Southeast Asia, the State and the private sector continue to play a key role in the reconstitution of urban culture, expressed in symbolism, iconography, historical interpretation and the uses of urban space. This process of creating culture in urban settlements is expressed in tourist promotion, preservation of structures or re-creation of precincts. In addition to this, there is an accelerated level of change and destruction of the urban fabric. The latter process occurs both on the level of reorientating and re-forming economic relations in urban space through the planned location of industry and infrastructure (effectively furthering the separation of functional areas in cities of traditionally mixed land uses) and in the redevelopment of areas for modern service, commercial, recreational and residential uses, exemplified in shopping malls, five-star international hotels, resorts, conference centres and golf courses. The cultural landscape, expressed in one sense as changes to shapes-on-the-ground, reflects clear patterns of power holding and influence in urban settlements, revealing in turn the nature of national and regional power structures as well as the influence of international corporate investors.

The spatial transformations of urban settlements in Southeast Asia have been viewed primarily as expressing international economic transformations in regional perspective. To the now-conventional focus of political economists on the post-colonial economies of Southeast Asia and the relationships between indigenous (or *comprador*) capitalists and their senior partners in the West and Japan, has now been added the radical post-modern geographers' perspective on the reconstitution of space under post-Fordist capitalism and the New International Division of Labour (for example, Harvey 1990; Giddens 1990). Matching the paradigm of the multi-centred, multi-

layered, sprawling global city of Los Angeles, favoured by the critical post-modernists who, incidentally, have all but ignored Asian trends (Soja 1989), another school of critical geographers advances the proposition that in Asia there is developing an economic and spatial formation known as the 'metropolitan mega-region', characterised by expanding spatial linkages between sub-centres, forming a growing urban sprawl of coexisting industry and commercialised farmland, sustained by export-driven economies (Ginsburg, Koppel & McGee 1991). Less ideologically-driven than the former, this second group of scholars is essentially focussing on the growth of the outer areas of Asian cities and their contribution to the recent expansion in economic growth.

Does this spatial trend, whatever it is to be called, have implications for urban culture? Clearly the growth in the urbanised territories of such megacities as Bangkok and Jakarta reflects new economic dynamics and spatial configurations which differ markedly from the older patterns of urban growth. So far one can note that it has spurred changes in the lifestyles of rice farmers and gardeners, formerly on the urban fringes, interposing an increasingly heterogeneous landscape between suburbia and countryside. It is a trend unlikely to abate as long as the mechanisms of land use and development continue to be fuelled by overseas and local investment. This landscape of change overshadows societies whose middle classes - the great beneficiaries of modernisation - seem to be groping for some form of identification with the past, whether this be in the form of replicas of traditional houses or the consumption of traditional textiles in new dress fashion.

What landscapes do these new configurations replace, and what sort of urban societies did they formerly sustain? The essays in this volume view this, the socio-spatial historical dimension, as one element in the production of an older urban culture now being lost. In the West, the process of packaging, designing, reconstituting and reinventing the urban and 'historical' past as a compensation for its previous destruction has been in progress for at least 20 years. Fuelled by the loss of that sense of place, locality and community which had been at the basis of earlier urban life, the Western heritage and tourist industries (sponsored by a host of organisations, in addition to national and local government) have produced an iconography of place which, some have argued, signals, in its ultimate shallowness, the demise of the lived and livable past (Giddens 1990, pp.19-26; Lowenthal 1985, chs 6-7; Eco 1986, pp.151-157). The reconstituted main streets, the gentrified inner suburbs, the open-air historical museums, the overblown claims of localities to uniqueness, and the manufacture of civic ceremony are testimony to modernity's striking tendency to separate time and space and the voracious ability of capitalist institutions to destroy the unique by mass production and commodification. Urban designers, formerly given to an obsession with the application of abstract universal elements, have now returned to seek the 'genius loci' of 'place', in order to find some meaningful context for creating livable environments (Lozarno 1990). Is there any reason to suggest that such a process may occur in Southeast Asia? Feature history parks already exist in Singapore and Thailand. Do they echo Western responses to a similar loss of the past? And what, anyway, is the alternative? Are the well-intentioned attempts to conserve the 'lived and livable past' in Southeast Asian cities in fact poorly directed, out of line with the needs and aspirations of the people actually living in those environments, and merely representing the romanticised views of middle class and often Western outsiders?

In the two decades after World War Two, the clearest expression of modernity on the urban skyline was the skyscraper in the 'international' style of functional concrete box design with glass curtain walls. In the prospering cities and precincts of the Asian urban regions, the emergence of this architecture reflected the pretensions of national elites and the technical-aesthetic internationalism that marked the values of the largely overseas-trained architects and planners. The blatant disregard of architectural modernism for indigenous sources of inspiration had its early critics, such as Ernest Hébrard in Indochina in the 1920s; but the hold of modernity as an image for the elites and developers of postwar cities was such that considerations of local identity or regionalism were swept aside in the enthusiasm for the construction of new government buildings, corporate headquarters and hotels. Today there are stronger voices

in favour of an architectural 'regionalism' which recognises such aspects of tradition as design adaptations to climatic conditions or the application to design and structure of enduring symbolic 'substructures' (for example, Yeang 1987).

One might argue, however, that the professional discourse of architects will have little effect unless their clients are likewise persuaded of the importance of design as an environmentally and culturally necessary exercise. But architects themselves are divided over what constitutes a meaningful regionalism of style and structure, and their own professional identities will not take kindly to stylistic stipulations unless such are legitimised by a more universal principle of building. Moreover the profession of architecture is a Western invention, exalting individual creativity over the less heroic tasks of craftspeople, who, in Asia, reproduced traditional built forms. Some Western architects have fallen back on the anthropological understandings of urbanisation in order to promote appropriate forms of building and urban design for Southeast Asian and other Third World cities (Robin 1992, p.9). Others have argued that nationalist forms of architecture pursued with a principal aim of projecting local or regional identity will produce crassness and superficiality. Whatever the merits of such efforts, it is clear that this has to be *new* architecture, a new reconciliation, as Hublin (1992 p.24) points out, between the elitist knowledge of the architect and the more humble expressions of popular building impulses:

> The protection of ancient heritages, no more than research into the adaptation of traditional building materials, cannot aspire to achieve a real revival of the processes of vernacular production. The taking up again of traditional building forms and modes will occur with the aid of modern techniques, combining customary know-how with contemporary procedures....

The challenge is new, too, needing to confront population growth on a vast scale, a generally rising standard of living and, especially, rising housing expectations. The role of the media, printed and audiovisual, in awakening such expectations is a study in itself. These expectations are now apparent even in the Indochinese countries where an anarchic flurry of 'do-it-yourself' building extensions is rapidly changing the face of historical precincts in the cities. Regional architecture may have some of the answers to the dilemma of balancing the protection of cultural heritage with the provision of modern facilities but, as Hublin (*ibid*) again points out, the task is formidable and, because of the sheer scale of housing shortages in developing countries, will require types of architectural intervention which are without precedent.

On the other hand, the freedom that post-modern quotation has brought to the profession has resulted in a meaningless 'pastiche' architecture, or, in the words of one critic (Sumet 1986), a 'punk architecture' which aims to deconstruct all meanings and symbols. The trend of post-modernism, it has been argued, expresses the collapse of meaning among arbiters of taste, fashion and intellect in the West, but it also has its effects in the cityscapes of Asia (Kuban 1983; Curtis 1986; Saliya, 1986).

Global influences thus pressure architects as professional shapers of the urban landscape in ways that they cannot escape - indeed, which they generally embrace. As Brian Bruce Taylor points out, the transformation of the architectural appearance of Southeast Asian urban areas in the postwar years has its roots in 'the effects upon the designers of new buildings and the clients of their numerous, continuing encounters with differing civilisations' (Taylor 1986, p.19). Technological problems and modern engineering solutions aside, the stylistic choices made in the postwar period have often aimed at impressing with a monumentalism designed to reflect the claims to power of new urban and national elite groups. Current fashions for the neo-classical 'pastiche' in office and residential design, on the other hand, highlight the process whereby the European 'fragment' is being absorbed within a system of wealth and power which ignores - indeed celebrates - the juxtaposition of dissimilar styles; it is a reflection of the complex globalisation of economic and cultural forces taking place today.

But who and what really has control of the shaping of the urban landscape in Southeast Asia? The architects are merely one, and probably a quite powerless group, among the agents interacting to determine the ways urban environments are created, and

this extends to style as well as space. Architects operate within an environment determined essentially by the power relations and economic interests which are responsible for the reproduction of the urban environment as a whole. They are not independent actors, and can be categorised, indeed, as 'urban managers', with a role of introducing elements of an aesthetic, design and planning culture into activities that support the power and values of dominant groups in urban society (Knox 1987, p.366). It is the clients of the architects, in addition to other developers (supported by local and overseas capital) and the State, that have been main players in the game of producing modern urban space in Southeast Asia. This applies as much to the production of housing estates in the suburbs as it does to the building of commercial complexes, plazas and shopping malls in city centres. In the former case the intervention of the government of Singapore in the housing market is a clear example; in the latter the transformation of Silom-Suriwong commercial precinct in Bangkok is a conspicuous case. In the socialist states of Southeast Asia, the State's monopoly over housing provision is only now being opened up to private enterprises using foreign and local capital. While the State in Vietnam produced some of the most monstrous 'modern' living conditions, it is to be seen whether private enterprise will more successfully solve that country's chronic housing shortage.

Urban growth and development in the contemporary period have introduced dramatic physical change in Southeast Asia, fuelled by changes in land use and building functions and transformations in transport and industrial infrastructures. The tearing down of the old built fabric to make way for the new, the imposition of a new spatial logic of planning, and the juxtaposition of the 'new' with the 'old' urban lifestyles and locales, moves us beyond the territory of the solely aesthetic and arcane into the realm of considerations of the meaning of 'place', 'locality' and the significance of the past as a cultural ecology for urban dwellers. The question then becomes, why is this or that area worth keeping? Why prevent change? Why promote it? How does a society set about determining its 'heritage', its 'significant cultural landscapes'? How does it arbitrate between the protection of traditional features and the promotion of modern, albeit internationalised, buildings and places?

Treated variously as texts, functional spaces, symbols, systems and habitats, urban settlements have attracted a multitude of discipline-based studies using discrete concepts particular to academic and professional fields and subfields. This is a natural reflection both of the organisation of academia and of the multi-faceted nature of human settlements and the ways we understand and manage their various subsystems; but in terms of understanding them as places, such analytical separation can be counterproductive and tears apart naturally interacting dimensions. Although there are indications that practitioners of different fields are accepting the need for interdisciplinary approaches to understanding urban culture (see Agnew, Mercer & Sopher 1984), so far the recent effort which has gone under the banner of research into urban and social space has been disappointing in delivering little more than a further indictment of capitalism as a process transforming spatial relations. More significantly, the paradigm had been drawn from the contemporary Western experience. Aside from geographers and a few bold anthropologists, research on socio-cultural change in urban Southeast Asia has been fairly thin on the ground (see O'Connor 1983; Clammer 1987; Askew 1993).

ABOUT THIS COLLECTION

The contributors to this collection are drawn from a variety of disciplines and professions, and although their interpretations differ as a result in 'style' and topical emphasis, all share a concern for understanding the relation between societies and their built environment in the context of change and modernisation. All address questions about the meaning of the past in these societies, in socio-cultural, physical and spatial terms. In the changing societies and environments of the region, the themes of tradition and identity commonly emerge as questions for exploration in the face of the contrasts between past and present. This applies as much to 'culture' defined as a national construction or invention, as it does to culture conceived as a local inheritance of customs, lifestyles and links with locality on a smaller scale.

Each of the essays presented in this collection seeks to describe and analyse the issue of the nature of change in the built and social environments of urban areas large and small. A number of them dwell on the way in which governments - traditional imperial and colonial imperial, post-independence socialist and paternalistic right-wing alike - have used the city environment as a stage upon which to demonstrate their political and cultural control. Anthropologist Michael Pinches analyses the recent impact of the 'New Society' regime under Ferdinand and Imelda Marcos on the modernisation of Manila's townscape. He makes the point that the Marcos regime, being obsessed with its and the country's global standing, especially vis-à-vis the West, borrowed Western architectural and planning models but pretended to the populace that this showcase creation was part of a uniquely Filipino cultural heritage. Geographer William Logan, in his chapter on Hanoi, outlines the re-interpretation of city features and the construction of new icons that occurred as one set of rulers and ideologies was replaced by others over the last 120 years. The significance of this environment in contributing to identity can be debated in terms of the contemporary aspirations of people. Why preserve colonial architecture or precincts if they are reminiscent of a period of foreign domination? Should those parts of the built environment in Vietnam's Hanoi, for example, where the heavy influence of the Beaux Arts architectural and urban design traditions universalised by French colonialism overlie an older indigenous pattern, be devalued and demolished because of their colonial connotations? Is the issue so simple? Do the French precincts have a claim to an 'international significance' status overriding local evaluations? In his essay Logan highlights some of the difficult decisions ahead for Hanoi's leaders in assessing the scope of environmental change which is likely to accompany economic advancement and tourism.

Architect and urban designer Christiane Blancot also outlines the work of the French colonists in her essay on Phnom Penh, but focuses especially on their struggle to impose urbanistic principles devised in metropolitan France on a difficult site on the banks of the Mekong. She notes that their response was not, in the end, markedly different from the traditional methods of controlling the environment which the indigenous Khmer had used. Hers is a story of a city's continuing struggle with nature and, increasingly, with people, whether this be Pol Pot and his genocidal actions or the property speculators and developers who have set up shop in the city in the wake of the United Nations sponsored peace treaty. By contrast, although with the exception of the brief race riots of 1968, the development of Kuala Lumpur has progressed relatively calmly from its British colonial origins, through the independence period until, today, it stands as one of the more 'environmentally friendly' modern Asian cities. Here, as architect Jimmy Lim shows in his essay on Kuala Lumpur, governments, concerned professionals and members of the public have joined forces to ensure that the best of both the British and Asian urban heritage survives, that historic and modern precincts and buildings will continue to coexist as part of a 'new city image'.

But modernisation inevitably impacts on urban environments by transforming the uses and meanings of space. The Indonesian examples provided by Don Townsend and Haryadi highlight the contrasts of older spatial patterns and the impact of change in, respectively, Denpasar in Bali and Yogyakarta in central Java. Bali, only a generation ago, was one of the most exotic, mysterious and, despite being on Australia's doorstep, 'faraway' places on the earth's surface. Tourists from Australia, the North Asian region and elsewhere have undercut the mystery and introduced powerful outside influences which threaten the Balinese cultural traditions. The scale of Don Townsend's inquiry is broad: a geographer-planner, he looks at the momentous changes which have transformed an island's distinctive culture and asks whether and how it will survive the onslaught. In a study inspired by the work of Amos Rapoport, architect Haryadi works at a more detailed scale, making a special plea for the preservation of small *kampung* in the modernising Indonesian city, not as areas shamefully degenerating into slums, but as neighbourhoods with their own systems of symbols and meanings, the essential settings for the activities and culture of the majority of the nation's urban dwellers. As such they represent critical living environments and among the most prominent of Yogyakarta's visual images. His essay, like most of

the contributions in this book, shows the need for understanding that 'cultural heritage' and 'cultural identity' are essentially issues of perception, and it raises key ethical questions for city planners: whose heritage are we talking about and whose heritage should be protected?

The realisation that the 'cultural landscape' includes both physical and non-physical elements - that is, buildings, monuments and artefacts on the one hand, and activities, meanings and symbols on the other - is taken up again by historian Marc Askew in his essay on Bangkok. He describes how various Thai governments have attempted to address the impacts of change on Bangkok's cultural landscape through a variety of development plans and conservation strategies. Bangkok's changing built environment and spatial transformations reflect forces of change within urban society which have been generated by broad trends in the regional and national economies and have been channelled by inherited power structures and values. He shows that Bangkok has always been the centre of change in Thai society, yet the communities of the city developed a pattern of coexistence (both between themselves and the environment) which seemed to be workable until 50 years ago. The sweeping aside of small-scale society in Bangkok in recent years coincides with a period of anxious searching for satisfying symbols of earlier styles of life and environment. He argues that the persistence of culturally significant urban spaces and artefacts in Bangkok at the local and metro wide levels has been ensured not primarily through policy, but through the persistence of strong cultural dispositions which reflect concepts of power and the sacred in Thai society.

In the Thai town of Phuket, as outlined by urban planner Doosadee Thaitakoo, the threat to the physical fabric of the township is symptomatic of a range of changes which have swept that island, a process driven by economic changes consequent on the decline of traditional economic activity (notably tin-mining) and the dramatic rise of tourism over the last decade. In this case, control is taken from the hands of local people and delivered into those of outside investors who, not content with ringing the island with resorts (with disastrous environmental consequences), capitalise on local culture, which is commodified and transformed in the process. Identity is thus bound up not only in the appearances of architecture, but also in the communities' conceptions of their history and habitat - in this case, the Hokkien Chinese. Annette Hamilton's anthropological study of another Thai seaside town, Hua Hin, bears many similarities but has the additional element of royal patronage and, hence, symbolism. Here, too, tourism and property speculation have dramatically reshaped the physical and cultural environment in the last 20 years. She interweaves descriptions of Hua Hin's physical elements (buildings, shrines) with narratives demonstrating the symbolic significance of the town's cultural landscape to its various inhabitants and Thai, Chinese and Western visitors. In Chiang Mai in Thailand's North, property speculators from Bangkok and other Asian centres, seeking to profit from the city's massive tourist boom, have undermined many attempts by local planners and ecologists to balance the protection of the city's heritage with economic development. Guy Lubeigt describes the dramatic impact on Chiang Mai's morphology and streetscapes, concluding that the city's residents have been forced to accept a way of life for which they were little prepared and which they perhaps did not want. Significantly, all three cases show the importance of Bangkok, the primate city, as an influence on provincial life in Thailand.

Singapore is in many ways the most advanced of the Southeast Asian nations and this is especially true with regard to the impacts of economic development, tourism growth, property speculation and environmental transformation. Indeed, so successful has this island state been in modernising that many Singaporeans and tourists began in the 1980s to regret the loss of traditional cultural elements in an increasingly sanitised cityscape. The State's response here has recently been to seek to bolster the tourist trade by re-inventing Bugis Street, one of Singapore's notorious nightspots destroyed less than a decade earlier as part of a plan to clean up the city. Kuah Khun Eng traces these events from an anthropological point of view, evaluates their results in terms of cultural and environmental authenticity, and raises important questions about the philosophical and economic bases of city planning and conservation. Her essay, like Jimmy Lim's on Kuala Lumpur, also dem-onstrates once again the potent role of city symbolism in the ideological framework developed by the State to maintain social cohesion and to create a sense of nationhood; in both the Singapore and Kuala Lumpur cases, this has meant using invented and re-invented 'heritage' to foster a feeling of belonging to a cohesive multiracial and multicultural nation.

As editors, we have chosen to encourage this variety of disciplinary approaches, to leave the authors' individual styles intact and to permit a range of essay lengths. The chapters are 'interpretations', each author bringing to the task her or his own intellectual baggage of understandings and attitudes. All of the chapters have been written specifically for this book, with the exception of Guy Lubeigt's paper on Chiang Mai which was first published in *Péninsule indochinoise: Etudes urbaines* (1992) and is here reproduced, in translation, with kind permission of the publisher L'Harmattan, Paris. While some of the authors are from the Southeast Asian region, all have worked extensively there. The book is, nevertheless, conscious of the need to avoid imposing alien Western views on to the Southeast Asian experience. Though recognising the methodological difficulties involved in - indeed, the impossibility of - attempting to produce 'objective' or 'culturally-free' analysis, the book's aim is simply to reflect on the challenges posed by the urban transformations taking place, on the policy dilemmas being or likely to be faced by these rapidly changing societies, and on the implications of action, whether this be the protection, enhancement, destruction or re-invention of the urban environment and the cultural heritage it contains.

ENDNOTES

1   For an application of the concept of globalisation to religious changes in Southeast Asia, see Lee 1993.

2   Another paradox: the political ideas on which his vision of Cambodian society was based were equally non-indigenous.

REFERENCES

Anderson, B. 1983, *Imagined Communities: Reflections on the Origin and Spread of Nationalism.*, Verso, London.

Asian Development Bank 1992, *Key Indicators of Developing Asian and Pacific Countries.*, Oxford University

Press, London.

Askew, M. 1993, *Interpreting Bangkok: The Urban Question in Thai Studies*, Chulalongkorn University Press, Bangkok.

Bandaranayeke, S. 1992, *World Heritage Convention: Testing the Limits - Management Debate: Relevance to the Asia-Pacific Region.*, Paper presented to ICOMOS Australia Conference, Sydney.

Clammer, J. 1987, 'Urban anthropology in Southeast Asia: A brief overview', *Contributions to Southeast Asian Ethnography*, vol.6, pp.3-11.

Curtis, W.J.R. 1986, 'Towards an authentic regionalism', *Mimar*, vol.19 (Jan.-Mar.), pp.24-31.

Eco, U. 1986, 'Culture as show business' in his *Travels in Hyper-Reality*, Picador, London, pp. 151-7.

Economic and Social Commission for Asia and the Pacific (ESCAP) 1993, *Draft Regional Action Plan on Urbanisation in Asia and the Pacific: Preparatory Meeting of Senior Officials*, ESCAP, Bangkok.

Eisenstadt, S.N. 1987, 'Historical Traditions, Modernisation and Development' in Eisenstadt, S.N. (ed.) *Patterns of Modernity*, Howard Pinter, London, vol.2, pp.1-11.

Giddens, A. 1990, *The Consequences of Modernity*, Stanford University Press, Stanford, California.

Ginsburg, N., Koppel, B. & McGee, T.G. (eds) 1991, *The Extended Metropolis: Settlement Transition in Asia*, University of Hawaii Press, Honolulu.

Harvey, D. 1990, *The Condition of Postmodernity: An Inquiry into the Origins of Cultural Change*, Blackwell, Cambridge, UK.

Hublin, A. 1992, 'Construction populaire et architecture savante', *Cahiers de la recherche architecturale*, no.27/28, 1st trimester, pp.15-24.

King, A. D. 1976, *Colonial Urban Development: Culture, Social Power and Environment*, Routledge & Kegan Paul, London.

Knox, P.L. 1987, 'The social production of the built environment: architects, architecture and the post-modern city', *Progress in Human Geography*, vol.11, pp.354-78.

Kuban, D. 1983, 'Modern versus traditional: a false conflict?', *Mimar*, vol.9, Jul.-Sept., pp.54-8.

Lee, R.L.M. 1993, 'The Globalisation of Religious Markets: International Innovations, Malaysian Consumption', *Sojourn*, vol.8, no.1, pp.35-61.

Lozarno, E. 1990, *Community Design and the Culture of Cities*, Cambridge University Press, Cambridge.

Lowenthal, D. 1985, *The Past is a Foreign Country*, Cambridge University Press, Cambridge, UK.

National Culture Commission (NCC) 1989, *Towards New Dimensions of Culture and Development*, Office of the National Culture Commission, Bangkok.

O'Connor, R. 1983, *A Theory of Indigenous Southeast Asian Urbanism.*, Institute for Southeast Asian Studies, Singapore.

Redfield, R. & Singer, M. 1954, 'The cultural roles of cities', *Economic Development and Cultural Change*, vol.3, pp.53-73.

Robin, C. 1992, 'De l'ethno-architecture aux anthropologiques de l'espace', *Cahiers de la recherche architecturale*, no.27/28, 1st trimester, pp.7-14.

Saliya, Y. 1986, 'Notes on architectural identity in the cultural context', *Mimar*, vol.19 (Jan.-Mar.), pp.32-33.

Soja, E.W. 1989, *Postmodern Geographies: The Reassertion of Space in Critical Social Theory*, Verso, London.

Sumet Jumsai 1986, 'The West Pacific Region versus punk architecture', *Mimar*, vol.19 (Jan.-Mar.), pp.22-23.

Taylor, B.B. 1986, 'Perspectives and limits on regionalism and architectural identity', *Mimar*, vol. 9 (Jan.-Mar.), pp.19-21.

United Nations 1986, *Global Report on Human Settlements*, U.N. Centre for Urban Settlements, Nairobi.

—— 1990, *State of the Environment in Asia and the Pacific 1990*, U.N. Economic and Social Commission for Asia and the Pacific, Bangkok.

—— 1992, *Statistical Yearbook for Asia and the Pacific*, U.N. Economic and Social Commission for Asia and the Pacific, Bangkok.

—— 1993(a), *Urbanisation and Socio-economic Development in Asia and the Pacific*, U.N. Economic and Social Commission for Asia and the Pacific, Bangkok.

—— 1993(b) , *State of Urbanisation in Asian and the Pacific 1993*, U.N. Economic and Social Commission for Asia and the Pacific, New York.

World Bank 1992, *Trends in Developing Economies 1992*, The Third World Bank, Washington, D.C.

Yeang, K. 1987, *The Tropical Verandah City: Some Urban Design Ideas for Kuala Lumpur*, Longman Malaysia, Petaling Jaya, Selangor.

1 Modernisation and the quest for modernity: architectural form, squatter settlements and the new society in Manila

♦

Michael Pinches

INTRODUCTION

This essay examines some of the ways in which modernity and the pursuit of modernity have found expression in the urban landscape and architecture of Manila. More specifically, it considers the relationships and tensions between the popular housing of Manila's squatter settlements and the state's 'rational planning' and 'showcase architecture', in an environment where commercialisation and rapid urban growth have put control over the city's built form beyond the reach of any single interest group. The discussion focuses on the post-colonial period, with particular reference to the New Society regime of Ferdinand and Imelda Marcos.

When the author first visited Manila in 1976, two recent pieces of state-sponsored building construction were particularly impressive. The most visually striking was the multi-million dollar Cultural Centre Complex, constructed on land newly reclaimed from Manila Bay along Roxas Boulevard, within close proximity of the city's tourist belt. Of the several large public buildings that made up the complex, the first and most imposing was the Cultural Centre of the Philippines, designed by 'prize-winning' architect Leandro Locsin (Chesnoff 1978, p.121).[1] Fronted by a large pool and spectacular fountain, it rose as a huge white concrete monolith cantilevered out over

a glazed entrance hall and raised semi-circular vehicular ramp (Figure 1.1). The imposing character of the structure owed much to the flat, empty expanse of park land that surrounded it, particularly given the contrasting high density of building along the streets nearby and through most of the city. On one occasion the author approached the main entrance of the Cultural Centre and was met by a security guard who inspected my attire before allowing me inside. A sign on the door greeted the casual visitor with the information that entry would only be permitted to those wearing suitable footwear. Inside the foyer hung a larger than life full length portrait of the First Lady, Imelda Marcos, alongside which - in

Figure 1.1   Cultural Centre of the Philippines

bold lettering - was printed 'Sanctuary of the Filipino Soul'. Apart from myself and the security guard, the building and its immediate surrounds were empty. Like the Cultural Centre, the other two major buildings in the complex - the Folk Arts Theatre and International Convention Centre - were grand concrete structures built in a style indicative of a modern, uncluttered, monumental architecture associated with prestige state constructions in the industrial West.

The grandiose, long-term plan for this part of Manila was to reclaim about ten kilometres of land along the foreshore and on it to create:

> a modern city complete with a financial centre, an area for hotels and restaurants, an embassy enclave, high class residential areas, a yacht basin and other appurtenances of luxury living Florida style (*Far Eastern Economic Review (FEER)* Jan 2 1976, p.39).

Both functionally and symbolically, this whole complex seemed to address the affluent West as a statement of progress, national identity and state power under the regime of Ferdinand Marcos. Just as the Cultural Centre is said to have been inspired by the likes of Carnegie Hall (Pedrosa 1987, p.106), so was the Folk Arts Theatre erected as the venue for the 1974 Miss Universe Beauty Pageant. The Philippine International Convention Centre, described in one Government publication of the time as 'one of the largest and most modern in the world' (Gaddi 1976, p.144), was constructed for the 1976 International Monetary Fund and World Bank Conference, and in 1994 will be used for yet another Miss Universe Beauty Pageant. In 1981, in preparation for the Manila International Film Festival, another imposing concrete structure - the National Film Centre - was erected as part of the same complex. Anxious to have the building completed in time for the festival, and the celebrities who would be visiting Manila, the First Lady and Patron of the Arts, Imelda Marcos, ordered such haste in the construction that part of the building collapsed reportedly killing over 100 workers, many of whom were left buried in the setting concrete, so the opening of the festival would not be delayed (Manapat 1991, p.51). Nearby on the highly polluted shore of Manila Bay, tons of imported white sand were used to create a beach scene intended to rival Cannes as a setting for celebrity photographs.

Responding to criticisms of the Film Centre, Imelda Marcos affirmed its national cultural significance with these words:

> ...we brushed aside the catcalls convinced that the Filipino people wanted to affirm their identity and searched for a venue where the creative artists could allow their talents to blossom and for our own people and those of other lands to apprehend the Filipino soul (*South China Morning Post* Jan 31 1982, p.9).

In an earlier response to criticism of the Cultural Centre and other such buildings, Imelda Marcos amplified these sentiments:

> For 500 years we didn't know who we were... Now we have taken off our mask and we see that our face is beautiful too (*FEER* February 13 1976, p.33).

The form, function and location of the Cultural Centre Complex suggested a strong desire by the Marcos regime to win recognition from the affluent industrial West by emulating its forms of architectural modernism.[2] Yet, there is also an important sense in which the Cultural Centre and Folk Arts Theatre, in particular, sought to encapsulate, dignify and display a cultural heritage that was uniquely Filipino. A similar concern motivated the restoration of the old Spanish walled city of Intramuros a few kilometres away (Zaragosa 1990, pp.55–65), a project also under the public patronage of Imelda Marcos. Though colonial and Castilian in origin, the medieval architecture of the walled city represented one of the Filipino elite's few tangible claims to an ancient aristocratic heritage.[3] Recasting this heritage in late twentieth century Manila seemed to be as much a quest for respectability within a global community of modern nations as it was a claim to tradition.

The second piece of state building construction that struck me in 1976 was not designed to display, but rather to conceal. The occasion was the International Monetary Fund and World Bank Conference that year. In preparation for the hundreds of foreign dignitaries who would be attending the conference, strategically placed whitewashed fences were erected along roadways throughout Manila in order to hide the most visible of the city's numerous squatter settlements. In some cases the settlements were bulldozed and their inhabitants forcibly evicted so as to offer the city's foreign guests a favourable perspective of the Philippines and its credentials as a modernising society. The same measures were also adopted on other occasions of international exposure, such as the 1975 visit by US President Ford and the Papal visit of 1981. What was striking was not just the inhumanity of the Marcos regime in its dealings with the squatters, but also the ineffectiveness of these measures as a strategy for dealing with the city's squatter settlements, which by this time housed over a million people, or 25-30 per cent of metropolitan Manila's population (*FEER* Feb 13 1976, p.32; Freeman Fox 1976, pp.143-154).

These two architectural emblems - the Cultural Centre Complex and the white washed fences - offer a valuable insight into the character of modernisation in the Philippines under the Marcos regime. Both communicated an aesthetic of development, state power, and national pride, in a style modelled on the contemporary architectural fashions in the West. The first, like many other Government projects, also conveyed something of the mystique of patronage the country's leaders sought to fabricate around themselves and their New Society; the second showed the ruthless dehumanisation with which the same leadership treated that sector of the population whose very existence challenged the sensibilities of the country's modernising elite. While the Cultural Centre Complex was something apart from the rest of the city, located on almost uninhabited, newly created land jutting out into the sea, the dwellings of the urban poor were more clearly enmeshed into the overall fabric of the city's landscape.

When the Philippines' First Lady addressed the International Monetary Fund and World Bank Conference delegates at the Cultural Centre Complex in 1976, she had this to say about the relationship between the two architectural forms:

You have come to our country at a most exciting time, though at a somewhat awkward stage, when we are negotiating the challenging transition from a traditional order to a progressive humanist society. This new complex of buildings erected on land reclaimed from the sea stands in dramatic contrast to the slum areas that blight our city. The contrast of

shrine and shanty symbolises the shining future against our impoverished past (*FEER* Oct 15 1976, p.20).

MANILA BEFORE MARCOS: *LAISSEZ-FAIRE* AND STATE PLANNING

Located at the mouth of the Pasig river, adjacent to an established Malay *barangay* settlement, Manila was founded in 1571 as the seat of Spanish colonial government and entrepot in the galleon trade between Mexico and China (Figure 1.2). Since that time Manila has been the Philippines' major urban centre: it has served as the seat of national government and ecclesiastical power, has been home to the nation's most privileged and prosperous people, and has been the country's focal point for economic and cultural exchange with the West.[4] By the late nineteenth century, as Spain's economic and political hold over the islands waned, Manila had become a significant centre for international trade and the location of the country's first factories. When the United States assumed colonial authority at the turn of the century, Manila's population had reached about 220 000 people (NCSO 1980, Table 1).

As the commercial, service and manufacturing hub of a national economy, centred on cash crops and primary exports, the centre of an expanding state bureaucracy, and the major point of cultural contact with American affluence, Manila's power and prosperity assumed increasing symbolic influence in the countryside. Home to the country's most powerful elite and centre of a developing national labour market, Manila became the destination of more and more rural migrants, discontented with conditions in the countryside and attracted by the prospects of advancement in the city.

Commenting on Manila's power to attract migrants in the 1960s, Hollnsteiner had this to say:

Manila ... represents to the masses the centre of excitement, freedom from the dullness and confining pressures of village or small-town life, and advantages which through luck and effort will accrue to those in search of them (1969, p.148).

While internal migration had contributed to Manila's pre-World War Two population of about

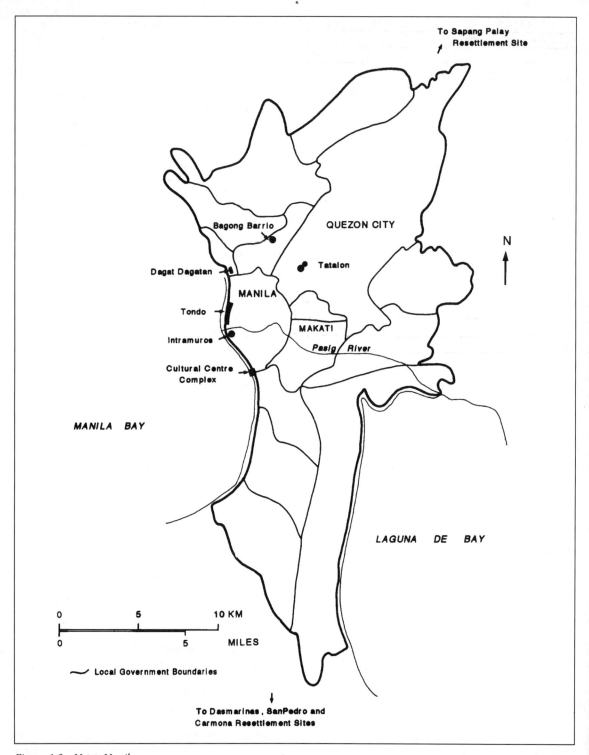

Figure 1.2   Metro-Manila

994 000, the most dramatic impact of rural-urban migration came after the war. Between 1948 and 1960, the number of people living in metropolitan Manila increased from about 1.6 million to 2.5 million (NCSO 1980, Table 1). In 1960, about half of the metropolitan population had been born elsewhere (Hollnsteiner 1969, p.157).

Originally organised in accordance with Spanish racial ideology and Italian renaissance urban planning, Manila's landscape developed around the spatial separation of the Spanish, Chinese and indigenous Malay Filipinos (Reed 1978). It also developed around the symbolic order of the Plaza complex, first established in the Spanish walled city of Intramuros, then replicated in Manila's expanding suburbs, as well as in other parts of the archipelago (Reed 1978; Hart 1955). While this heritage continues to be evident, the spatial pattern of Manila's growth since the Spanish colonial era has rested more in private hands, particularly those of the elite, than it has in the authority of the state or the church. A master plan prepared for Manila in the early American colonial period by the famous Chicago modernist planner Daniel Burnham (Caoili 1988, pp.6,52,130; Harvey 1989, pp.27,40) served as a guide to urban development, but it was largely overlooked in favour of laissez-faire growth. With the total devastation of large areas of the city through bombing at the end of World War Two, a number of planners and politicians saw this as an ideal time to prepare a detailed plan for Manila and its future growth, since massive rebuilding was inevitable. An Urban Planning Commission and a Real Property Board were established almost immediately, but it was not until 1954, after much rebuilding and urban expansion had already taken place, that another master plan was produced. But this was not adopted and nor were the planning and zoning ordinances of the pre-war era seriously implemented (Ramos 1961, p.94).

Abueva describes the outcome of Manila's *laissez-faire* growth as follows:

> No other city in the country shows unguided development as glaringly as Manila. Slum and squatter areas conglomerate in Tondo; universities and boarding houses are ubiquitous in Sampaloc; hotels and tourist shops dot the Malate landscape; Quiapo, Binondo and Sta Cruz are sites of mongrel buildings whose ground floors are stores and upper storeys are living quarters - mostly Chinese-owned and inhabited; Paco, Sta Ana, and San Miquel abound in factories and warehouses. And interspersed with all these in various sections of the city are apartment buildings, *accesorias*, single dwellings, shops and stores and neighbourhood markets, shanties and condominiums, growing in indiscriminate fashion like seeds carelessly sown. This pattern, or lack of it, reaches out in all directions and repeats itself, in varying degrees, in the adjoining areas (Abueva et al 1972, p.28).5

The major exception to Manila's *laissez-faire* development, was Quezon City, originally conceived by the Commonwealth period's President Quezon as a place to house factory workers and labourers from the inner city (Ramos 1961, p.92). The major impetus for the establishment of Quezon City after World War Two was its designation as the new seat of national government and symbolic centre of the country's efforts at 'nation building' (Lopez 1973). The Arellano Commission that prepared plans for Quezon City, described its vision in the following terms:

> In planning the new Capital City, the Commission took into initial account the role that the city is destined to play; politically, as the seat of the national government; aesthetically, as the show place of the nation, a place that thousands of people will come to visit as an epitome of the culture and spirit of the country; socially as a dignified concentration of human life, aspirations, endeavour and achievement and economically as a self-contained community... This new Capital City where our constitutional offices will function in an atmosphere of dignity, freedom and human happiness will rise as the citadel of democracy in the Orient (cited in Lopez 1973, p.10).

The growth of Quezon City, as well as the other cities and municipalities that came to make up metropolitan Manila, initially centred on a process of suburbanisation as Old Manila's elite and growing middle classes sought to escape inner city congestion and 'blight' for homes in new, subdivisions on the urban fringe (Hollnsteiner 1969, pp.57-59; Stinner

& Bacol-Montilla 1981). In Quezon City, some of this growth was accommodated in a number of specially planned Government housing estates for public servants, teachers and other state employees. Today, what most distinguishes Quezon City's planned development is that in all of metropolitan Manila it is the only place to possess substantial symmetry in its road layout: a large quadrangle of intersecting avenues and boulevards, at one corner of which is located an elliptical road centred on the 20 to 30-storey high Quezon monument. Around the elliptical road and along the quadrangle were to be erected new buildings housing new or relocated Government offices and other state institutions. While the sheer size of the Quezon monument is impressive, and while some building and relocation took place, the planned development of Quezon City faltered. Many commentators, who visualised the development of Quezon City in the terms quoted above, were disappointed. In 1973, the President of the University of the Philippines, one institution that relocated most of its activities to Quezon City, complained bitterly of the city's failure, contrasting it to what he saw as the outstanding success of such planned cities as Brasilia, Chandigarh and Canberra. Among other things, he despaired that the park surrounding the Quezon monument had been closed off to the public and 'was abandoned to the weeds' (Lopez 1973, p.10).

Although state building regulations and authorities responsible for roads, drainage and other infrastructural provisions, exercised some influence over the physical form of Manila's urbanisation, the spatial pattern of post-war metropolitan growth has reflected much more a modernity of private wealth and mobile labour than a modernity of rational state planning. For the most part, the massive suburban expansion of Manila since World War Two has been directed by the private capital of leading elite families, such as the Ayalas, Ortigases and Aranetas, who accumulated large tracts of fringe land destined to become valuable urban real estate as Manila expanded. Rather than being constrained by the state, such families frequently used privileged access to state power in order to accumulate their private land holdings (Pinches 1986).

The most successful project of privately developed urban real estate was carried out in the 1950s by the

Ayala Corporation on its 958 hectare property in Makati. Anticipating the suburban expansion of Manila's post-war growth, and particularly the movement of the rich out of the congested inner city, the Ayala Corporation established Forbes Park on what was then unsettled fringe land. This soon became the country's most prestigious luxury housing estate. Other similar housing estates and luxury apartment buildings followed. With their success, Makati also became a thriving business centre, as the country's leading banks and business houses relocated from the old American business district of Escolta. Five-star hotels and foreign businesses followed suit. Significantly, part of the Ayala Corporation's success is said to have been due to its ability to impose strict zoning and site development regulations (Guttierez 1979). If Quezon City brought disappointment, Makati aroused celebration and pride. In 1979, the editors of a popular magazine had this to say:

> Any foreign visitor prospecting for business opportunities in the Philippines is bound to look towards Makati, that gleaming, smart-looking town southeast of Manila. Makati, after all, has emerged as the business and financial mecca of the country beckoning investors in the enticing fashion of Hong Kong and Singapore...Today, Makati is both boom town and financial hub where...90 per cent of the country's top 1000 corporations have congregated. It has been variously described, but Makati's charm probably lies in its being an interesting study in urban development, which has made it the Philippines' showcase to the world (*Nation's Journal II* (2) 1979, p.3).

The image of Makati's success is most evident in its architectural form, regarded throughout Manila as the image of progress and prosperity. Most famous is Ayala Avenue, sometimes likened to Wall Street, not only for its economic function, but also for its canyon of modern international style multi-storied office blocks (Figure 1.3). Though it is far too expensive for most people in Manila to live in or nearby the Makati business district, many thousands work there and many more sample its prosperous 'stateside' aura as shoppers or sightseers. More concealed and protected, but equally well-known, are the American bungalow style mansions in the exclusive residential subdivisions, such as the original Forbes Park,

Figure 1.3   Ayala Avenue, Makati

which one Filipino journalist favourably likens to Beverly Hills (Banaag 1979, p.32). Though closed off to the general public, the thousands of resident maids, drivers, gardeners and security guards who tend the needs of those who can afford to live in these estates, report widely on the houses and life-styles within.[6]

In Manila's post-war urbanisation, Makati may have been a 'showcase to the world' as well as to many Filipinos in search of progress, but it was an exceptional case. While there were other pockets of affluence, most of the rebuilding of Old Manila, and the construction of the city's suburban expansion was carried out cheaply, quickly and frequently without reference to building regulations, zoning ordinances or overall urban planning principles. This applied to all forms of building: shops, eating houses, factories and workshops, offices, places of entertainment, residential apartments and houses. Most of this represented not the *laissez-faire* of the Ayalas or the Ortigases, but the initiatives of much less prosper-

Figure 1.4   Downtown, Old Manila

ous Filipinos. Public buildings - schools, universities, hospitals, government offices and church properties - were also, for the most part, constructed under conditions of poor funding. What most of the new building had in common and what separated it from much of the pre-war construction, was the extensive use of reinforced concrete. Thus much of the city's commercial and institutional roadside development took the form of low or medium rise, rectilinear, concrete slab construction, minimally decorated and cheaply furnished. Makati may well have provided the Philippines with a vision of the future, but set against the rest of the urban landscape, it also offered poignant testimony to the contrasting experiences of modernity in the urbanisation of Manila.

SQUATTER SETTLEMENTS: THE ARCHITECTURE OF INTIMACY AND IMPROVISATION

Most alarming for many of those planners, journalists and wealthy Filipinos who celebrated the vision of Makati, or mourned the unfulfilled promise of Quezon City, was the proliferation of urban slums and squatter settlements which resulted predominantly from the massive movement of rural poor into Manila (Figure 1.5). While many migrants found accommodation in the subdivided, run-down inner city houses that had been vacated by the well-to-do, growing numbers from Manila's poor labouring classes had little alternative but to squat. The development of a privately controlled urban real estate market, coupled with vast income differences, and the practice of land hoarding and speculation by members of the urban elite, made access to legal accommodation, either through ownership or rent, impossible for large numbers of people. However, it did not stop the flow of migration or the belief among migrants that Manila offered better opportunities for income and advancement than most other parts of the country.

Thus, in pursuing these opportunities, increasing numbers of people chose to squat on land that was accessible to employment and offered a degree of security: often on the banks of the city's estuaries, along railway sidings, on flood prone land, in bombed-out building sites or simply on land that was not ruthlessly protected by the legal owners.

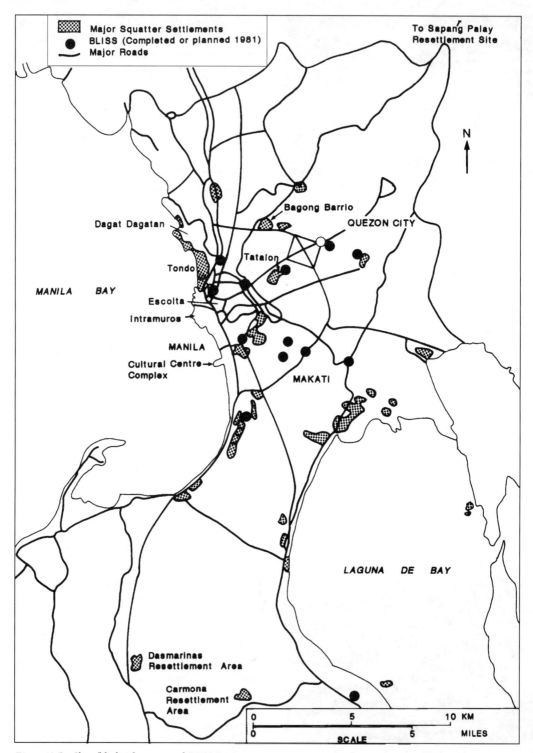

Figure 1.5   Slum/blighted areas and BLISS Project

There, under the threat of harassment or eviction, they built their own dwellings or, in some cases, rented from others who had done so before them. By the end of the 1960s, squatter settlements were to be found throughout the metropolitan area, in some cases in small clusters of only a few households, but more often in bigger groupings, mainly because of the mutual protection offered by greater numbers. In contrast to the large overnight invasions that characterised squatting in many Latin American cities, the growth of individual squatter settlements in Manila generally occurred more incrementally as kin, provincemates, friends or fellow workers assisted each other in finding a suitable place to live (Pinches 1987(a), 1992(a)). The biggest single concentration of squatters in Manila had settled in the Tondo Foreshore, on land reclaimed from Manila Bay for port development at the end of World War Two (Figure 1.6). By 1974, about 170 000 people lived as squatters on the Tondo Foreshore (Sembrano et al 1977, p.13), making of this reclamation a dramatic contrast to that which accommodated the Cultural Centre Complex only a few kilometres further south.

In 1968 a Special Committee Report from the Office of the President recorded the number of squatters and slum dwellers living in metropolitan Manila at over one million people or nearly one third of the whole metropolitan population. Well over two thirds were classified as squatters and 93 per cent were reported as rural migrants (Bernido 1968). While the whole metropolitan population during this time was growing at 4 per cent annually, the number of squatters and slum dwellers in Manila was reported to be growing at 12 per cent (Hollnsteiner 1969,

Figure 1.6   Estuary squatters, Tondo

pp.155,157).

A striking feature of almost all first-hand accounts of Manila's squatter settlements is that, along with their high residential densities, they were characterised by extensive interpersonal relations of familiarity and mutual help at the local neighbourhood level (Hollnsteiner 1971, 1972; Laquian 1964, 1969, 1971(a); Stone and Marsella 1968; Goss 1990). While Manila's legal subdivisions and housing compounds also often display extended relations of interpersonal familiarity, this is rarely so marked as it is in the squatter neighbourhoods, where localised patterns of mutual help are usually much more crucial in the conduct of daily life. This familiarity, combined with the relative absence of roads and the local control over pedestrian circulation, often made for a distinctive spatiality.

The author first travelled to Manila in 1976 and visited a number of the city's squatter settlements. In each case it was necessary to be directed by a guide who came from or was familiar with the particular neighbourhoods. Even the author's Filipino companions - in one case another anthropologist, in another a Catholic priest, and in another a person who turned out to be a military informant - had to rely upon someone with local knowledge in order to find their way. By contrast, finding the way to, and around, neighbourhoods in legal housing estates was relatively easy: they could be clearly located on a map, they had simple street patterns, the streets had names and individual houses usually had numbers. Their spatial form was decipherable through an impersonal language of bureaucratic order. The squatter neighbourhoods, on the other hand, could only be navigated through the possession of particularistic local knowledge. For the stranger, their alleyways, pedestrian underpasses, stairways, narrow footbridges and small courtyards seemed a mysterious, even forbidding, maze. In large part, it was the very spatial intimacy of the squatter neighbourhoods that forbade the outsider: one really needed to live there in order to know them. While entry to the streets of Manila's elite residential subdivisions, like Forbes Park, was for most Filipinos also forbidden, their exclusivity relied principally on high walls, barbed wire and armed security guards: their spatial form posed little mystery.[7]

For about 18 months during the period 1979-1980,

the author lived in a neighbourhood in one of Manila's largest squatter settlements, Tatalon, and has since stayed there for shorter periods on a number of occasions (Figure 1.7).[8] After several weeks of confusion, the author eventually became familiar with the spatial form of this neighbourhood, but only by simultaneously becoming familiar with its social form, as particular openings, closures, rises, falls, twists and turns in the spaces between dwellings came to be associated with particular families, households or neighbours. While people spent their nights indoors, much of their daily life was spent immediately outside their houses with friends, neighbours or other family members, talking, joking, playing, washing clothes, drinking and so on. These were the main places in which the people of Tatalon pursued and enjoyed sociability. Indeed, for most of the day, the main indoor living spaces merged with the walkways and open areas immediately outside, as neighbours moved relatively freely in and out of each other's houses. Conversely, interpersonal or intergroup conflicts usually resulted in people avoiding each other's domestic space, extending to the walkways near their houses. Pedestrian movement was thus rarely impersonal or anonymous: all unusual comings and goings were noted and commented upon. Thus, the author came to learn about social life in Tatalon through its spatial configuration.

What wealthy outsiders frequently interpreted as both spatial and social chaos turned out to be something quite different and a good deal more complex. Not only did insiders develop a mental map through which they could locate each other spatially, but the spatial configuration of their neighbourhood also displayed a complex historical logic, variously reflecting the patterns of migration of particular residents from the countryside, the fusion and fission of different families over the course of their domestic cycles, variable and fluctuating incomes, the acquisition or loss of employment by particular individuals, the closeness or otherwise of kin and ethno-linguistic relations between households, and so on. The spatial order of this neighbourhood was thus steeped in, and reflected, an intimate and complex interpersonal order in a far more profound way than what one could find in Manila's legal housing estates, where state bureaucratic controls, rational planning, and a legal real estate market based on private landed property, took precedence over locally generated spatial form.

Though these latter forces were not directly evident in the internal social and spatial fabric of squatter neighbourhoods, such as those in Tatalon, together they constituted the major external parameters governing the development of Manila's squatter settlements. For Manila's poor labouring classes, they were basically forces of exclusion and danger. Given their exclusion from legal residential property, squatters have had to provide not only their own dwellings, but also to develop their own systems of pedestrian access, drainage, water supply, waste disposal, and lighting. Moreover, they have had to provide as best they could for themselves in the face of often strenuous opposition from landowners and state authorities. The intimacy of squatter settlement spatiality thus developed as much out of the residents' mutual response to exclusion and danger, as it did out of a preferred mode of social existence, although, in my experience, the two reinforced each other (Pinches 1986; 1992(a)(b)).

The landscape of Manila's squatter settlements is certainly an architecture of material hardship: of cheap, often flimsy, building materials, of minimal living space, of open drains and contaminated water, and of vulnerability to fire and flood. Overwhelmingly, this is the way in which it is portrayed by outsiders; but it should also be read as an architecture of popular innovation and resourcefulness. Firstly, as noted, the city's squatter settlements are commonly constructed on sites that are inhospitable to other land use. Many of the steep banks of the

Figure 1.7   Tatalon squatter housing

Pasig River, and the tributaries that run into it, are lined with relatively sturdy squatter houses carefully erected on timber stilts and platforms; similar construction can also be found on low-lying marsh land where a grid of raised timber walkways provide access between houses. In the case of houses erected along infrequently used railway lines, unused land between and immediately adjacent to the tracks is often employed for play, meeting and temporary market space, while specially fashioned push-carts fitting the railway line are sometimes used for local transport.

Secondly, an almost endless array of materials is used in construction, in many cases materials that have been discarded by others, such as disused scaffolding, packing cases, broken-down automobiles, old hoardings, flattened oil cans and materials gathered from demolition sites. In the squatter settlement in which the author lived for some time, there were a number of small businesses which recycled scrap metal and auto parts from old cars, jeeps trucks and buses. While most of the metal and auto parts were sold to outsiders, the families in one cluster of houses made extensive use of materials made available through these businesses: flattened car roofs were used for walls and roofing, and so too the disused upholstery; tyres were used to help secure the roofs; good quality car seats were recycled as household furniture; and the wire mesh from within poor quality car seats was used for fencing around garden beds adjacent to the houses.

Thirdly, squatter houses are generally constructed with a degree of speed and adaptability not matched in most legal domestic architecture. In part this is made possible by the extensive use and re-use of timber, nails and galvanised iron as the basic construction materials. Speed of construction is often crucial in evading the authorities who are generally more inclined to notice and stop a building during construction, than one that is already complete. Thus many squatter houses in Manila are erected on Sundays, the official day of rest, when security guards and officials are most likely to be off duty. Furthermore, once houses have been standing for some time, and thus assume some *de facto* legitimacy, they become the nuclei for extensions or the erection of adjacent dwellings to provide living space for new households. As families expand, as kin and provincemates settle in the city, so whole neighbourhoods emerge. Thus the architecture that follows this expansion is one that assumes continually changing spatial form as new rooms, floors, alcoves, verandahs, stairways, windows, doors, alleyways, underpasses and courtyards are created or displaced. Not only is the spatiality of Manila's squatter settlements one of intimacy; it is usually also one of unusual flux.

A crucial dimension to the improvisation that is practised in Manila's squatter settlements is the co-operative pattern of inter-household or inter-family relations through which a range of amenities are provided and maintained for collective use: walkways, waste disposal and drainage systems, bath houses and toilets, water and power supplies, basketball or volleyball courts and, in some cases, neighbourhood chapels. The form that these amenities take and the extent to which they rely on collective effort varies considerably, but, in the absence of provision by the state or private developer, they usually rely to some extent on co-operative labour, local group decisionmaking processes and collective funding between households. Neighbourhood co-operation often extends not only to the mere physical production and maintenance of amenities, but to their production and maintenance in the face of state or private landlord repression. Indeed, Manila's squatters have frequently proved to be highly organised and politically effective in warding off depredations by the state and landowners (Laquian 1964, 1965; Hollnsteiner 1971, 1976; Makil 1983; Pinches 1985, 1986; van Naerssen 1989; Murphy 1990, pp.39-50).

While Manila's squatter settlements may be at variance with the spatiality and architecture of the Ayalas' Makati, they have, nevertheless, been just as integral to the experience of modernisation in the Philippines. Firstly, in general terms, their presence in Manila reflects a process of proletarianisation as more and more Filipinos have been uprooted from landholdings and incorporated, albeit precariously, into a developing national labour market which offers economic and cultural incentives for rural-urban migration (Pinches 1987, 1989).

Secondly, Manila's squatter settlements demonstrate the growth of an urban real estate market whose very success has been such as to exclude large numbers of urban workers from legal accommodation. However, this marginalisation is qualified. In some cases, construction and workshop employees in Manila are permitted, even encouraged, by employers to build on-site dwellings which are occupied rent-free as an indirect wage and which are indistinguishable from those houses found in many illegal settlements. Indeed, there is a good deal of ambiguity and contention surrounding the legal status of much housing in Manila. Many 'squatters', for instance, pay rent to legal landowners even though their dwellings do not meet legal building requirements. Furthermore, most squatter settlements themselves contain an internal real estate market in rental accommodation, albeit an illegal one.[9]

Thirdly, the construction of squatter settlements is usually integral to the same construction industry that produces office blocks and houses in Makati and other more affluent parts of Manila. In those squatter settlements familiar to me, most of the house building is directed or carried out by workers or tradesmen with experience in the construction of large expensive buildings. Often the building process combines both wage and co-operative (*bayanihan*) labour. Furthermore, the materials used for squatter houses frequently come from large construction sites or from other so-called modern sector industries. But beyond this, squatters frequently purchase at least some of their building materials, either new or second-hand, from building suppliers, hardware stores or other commercial outlets, such as the small recycling businesses mentioned earlier (cf Ward and Macoloo 1992).

In short, Manila's squatter settlements are integral to the process of modernisation in the Philippines because they are integral to the process of commodification: of labour, land and construction. But there are also two other ways in which Manila's squatter settlements can be read as 'modern'. Firstly, though the design of squatter houses owes something to the 'traditional' rural domestic architecture of the *bahay kubo* (nipa hut), the spatiality and architecture found in places like Tatalon is characterised by a social intimacy and an improvisation that have themselves largely been generated in the city by the contemporary conditions of danger and ex-

clusion.[10] While it is useful to contrast, as Stone (1973) and Hollnsteiner (1969, pp.162-168) do, the personalism of space in Manila's squatter settlements with a spatial order that is rational-bureaucratic, there is a significant sense in which the former is produced by the imposition of the latter. The pattern of improvisation that marks squatter housing in Manila has largely come about in this way and is indicative more of the constant flux of modernity than the relative stability of pre-modern architectural forms (cf Berman 1983; Harvey 1989).

Secondly, the variable and changing character of squatter houses, apparent in their size, quality of materials and interior decoration, commonly evidence a desire for symbols of progress and 'modern' living standards, as families or individuals compete with each other for status or respectability through conspicuous consumption (see Pinches 1992(a); 1992(b)). These symbols of progress may only be small, such as a timber rather than earthen floor, a painted rather than unpainted timber wall, windows with louvred shutters or glass rather than simple horizontally hinged panels, or the possession of a radio or sideboard display featuring such items as imported Johnny Walker whiskey bottles. But they may also be more substantial, involving, for instance, the building of larger houses using hollow block concrete construction, with multiple rooms and relatively expensive furnishings and electronic equipment. Much of this principally reflects a desire for affluence and respectability in the context of impoverishment and stigma, rather than a wish to emulate the most recent architectural fashions of Forbes Park.

A concern with fashion among people in Manila's squatter settlements is much more evident in their tastes for household appliances, clothing, music and dance. For many, the ideal house was a contemporary, scaled down variation on the 'traditional' two storey wood and stone ancestral homes of the old Philippine elite (cf Zialcita 1991). But architectural tastes and opinions were also divided. People often commented critically on the modern mansions of Forbes Park, in particular on the personal isolation entailed in the high walls and separate bedrooms. In some instances, critical comment turned to scathing ridicule, as was the case with a woman who had worked as a maid in one Forbes Park house where it was necessary to sleep with an electric blanket because the air conditioning was always kept on.[11] On the other hand, there were sometimes clear indications that progress and affluence were associated with modern architectural form. Such was the case with one of my neighbours in Tatalon whose interior wall featured a large magazine photograph of the expansive interior of a luxurious American house upon which were pasted suitably scaled photographs of two of her children. Despite the obvious and continuing overall material poverty of Manila's squatter settlements, and the varied tastes and opinions of their residents, the quest for status, conceived through visions of progress and moneyed prosperity, is a vitally important feature of daily life. Even though it is rarely achieved, and then only partially, this quest evidences part of Manila's common, yet variable and contradictory experience of modernity.

VOICES OF ALARM: SQUATTERS AS MODERNITY'S 'OTHER'

The above rendering of squatter settlement architecture and spatiality suggests a different picture to those that are commonly painted by outside commentators in Manila and elsewhere, according to whom squatters are the very anathema of modernity, either because they adhere to some traditional or rural way of life, which they reproduce in the city, or because they represent a state of material, moral and aesthetic impoverishment.

Most of Manila's rich are able to live an enclaved existence removed from the city's squatter settlements, and are largely impervious to the daily hardships of the urban poor. Moreover, for much of the period since independence, individual politicians have often simply dealt with squatter neighbourhoods through particularistic relations of patronage, exchanging some degree of protection for electoral support (Laquian 1964, 1965, 1971(a)). To a large extent, despite periodic harassment and *ad hoc* evictions, this pattern has generally amounted to official inaction. However, the rapid growth of slums and squatter settlements during the 1950s and 1960s began to generate widespread concern and, increasingly, fear and revulsion among sections of Manila's middle classes and elite. This is particularly so amongst the growing layer of professionals, planners, journalists and academics whose job it was to intervene in, or comment on, the city's growth and the nation's development. These sentiments found expression in the popular press, in political speeches and in academic writings. Thus, Lopez's lament over the fortunes of Quezon City, was not only that it had been abandoned to weeds, but also to growing numbers of squatters (Lopez 1973, p.10). In their major work on Philippine history, originally published in 1960, two nationalist academics, had this to say about squatters and inactive politicians:

> The 'immigrant' squatters have posed a problem to the community, for their houses are fire hazards and their surroundings a threat to public health. More than the problem of safety and sanitation, however, is the moral problem involved, for some squatters' areas have been transformed into a paradise for women of easy virtues...The squatters are a class by themselves, for they are the only ones who have the temerity to defy the government and get away with it - thanks to the peanut politicians (Agoncillo & Guerrero 1987, p. 579).

In 1967, commenting on Manila City, an administrative subdivision of metropolitan Manila, one journalist noted the following:

> In Manila alone, no fewer than 150 000 people live in slums and squatter areas, the spawning ground of immorality, criminality and disease...In many a barong-barong (shanty) there, families live, eat, sleep and mate in the same room. If there is hell on earth, it can be found in the barong-barong or jerry built shanties or slums where people live no better than animals (*Philippines Free Press* Jan 7 1967, p.63).

Around the same time, another journalist echoed similar sentiments:

> To live in a slum or squatter area is punishment enough; but worse punishment is that which is inflicted not on the body alone, but also on the psyche. Slums are breeding places of crime, immorality, vice, disease and juvenile delinquency. They are a menace to society and a drain on the national economy (*Philippines Free Press* April 29 1967, p.7).

A few years earlier President Macapagal had warned that:

To remain apathetic to this is to encourage the creation of a social ferment which bottled into violence, can blow up bomb-like and rock the very foundations of the free institutions of this Republic (*Philippines Free Press* August 7 1965, p.14).

These views were also expressed by some Western academic observers such as Geographer Donald Fryer, according to whom:

Politically one of the most intractable, and certainly among the more obvious, of the problems of rapid urban growth is the infestation of large areas of the city with a scab-like crust of illegal squatter settlements, built with whatever materials come to hand. These urban sores have proliferated throughout the underdeveloped world in the postwar period, and in Southeast Asia they have often invaded the very heart of the city itself...The removal of squatter camps, however, is a matter of the greatest difficulty, for politically squatters are well organised and are often the subject of considerable attention by communist or extreme left-wing groups...When squatters are eventually cleared from an area they promptly occupy the nearest vacant sites; landlords who make vigorous efforts to rid their property of squatters are liable to find themselves threatened with physical violence by militant left-wing thugs (1970, p.91).

The main message was clear: that the presence of growing numbers of squatters and slum dwellers posed both a moral and physical threat to social well-being, stability and development in Manila, and, indeed, in the Philippines at large. They, along with their *barong-barong* houses, constituted the 'other' of Makati's modernity. On the one hand, they were thought to be out of place, a visible symptom of 'over-urbanisation' (Ramos 1961); on the other they provided, in stark visible form, the underside of Makati's modernity, a measure against which progress could be delineated, an alternative future into which the whole country could slide unless its leaders took decisive action. Alongside the opposition between modernity and its 'other', stood a more fundamental pairing of civilisation and savagery. Thus, to Makati's prosperity, order and modern architectural refinement was counter-posed the poverty, chaos and crude animal-like existence of the slums and squatter settlements. In another sense, the recognition that lay behind these sentiments was of modernity's rapidly expanding class of labouring poor, dislodged from the countryside and accumulating in the city in ways that were largely beyond the established patronal institutions of elite power. On the one hand, the intimacy and improvisation of spatial form in Manila's squatter settlements represented a response to exclusion and danger. But on the other, it communicated to the wealthy a solidarity and capacity for independent action, rephrased as moral disorder, that needed to be stopped. This reading of Manila's landscape in the 1960s was not the only reading, but it was highly influential among Manila's elite and middle classes, both at that time and in the present.

Though this reading embraced divergent sentiments of contempt and charitable or humanitarian concern, its concrete expression in state programs of urban renewal unambiguously called for eradication. The first and less significant form involved the rehousing of squatters in inner city medium-rise tenement buildings (Hollnsteiner 1977, pp.311-313). Only a few were built and they made virtually no impression on what was widely described, in the technocratic language of the time, as Manila's 'housing backlog'. In large part this failure was simply due to the fact that state revenues and preparedness for income redistribution were severely limited. The second response was the wholesale relocation of squatters to resettlement sites outside the city, or alternatively their repatriation to the provinces (Juppenlatz 1970, pp.89-147; Viloria 1971, p.147; Abesamis 1974-75).

The first major instance of relocation occurred over a four month period in 1963, involving the forcible eviction of about 80 000 squatters from Tondo, North Harbour and the old Spanish walled city of Intramuros. In what was described as a military operation, about 25 000 of those evicted were carried by Manila City garbage trucks to the distant and inadequately prepared relocation site of Sapang Palay where they were left to fend for themselves, far away from any sources of livelihood (Laquian 1966, pp.151-169; Juppenlatz 1970, pp.117-147). While many Filipinos suffered great hardship from this ordeal, others treated it as a victory for national pride. In 1977, two authors writing on the changing fortunes of the Spanish walled city of Intramuros, had this to say:

After the war, hordes of what sociologists call the dispossessed, poor provincial folk seeking employment in the city, swarmed into the stone nooks and tufa crannies of the bombed-out ancient walls to form a squatters' hive. It was the ultimate degradation of the once proud city from whose surrounding moat drawbridges were pulled up at night so that during the slumber hours only pure Castilian exhalation filled the air. The squatters were moved out twenty years ago and the place disinfected (Ira & Medina 1977, p.5)

As the 1960s and early 1970s proceeded, more houses were demolished, more squatters evicted and more relocation sites established. While this program was successful in freeing particular sites for real estate development by legally recognised owners, large numbers of relocated squatters, who were predictably unable to make a living away from the city, simply returned to squat elsewhere (Viloria 1971, p.147; Makil 1983, p.6). And in practice, eviction and resettlement occurred on a largely a*d hoc* basis depending on the political power of landowners, the particularistic interests of politicians, and the size and political organisation of specific squatter settlements or neighbourhoods. In the meantime hundreds of thousands of other poor working people were filling vacant land elsewhere in the city. Despite the Government-sponsored programs of demolition, eviction and resettlement, more and more of the city's privileged residents believed that Manila was being swamped. Even Makati seemed as if it was being inundated with squatters; however fast they could be evicted, more would return and with them came a growing sense of alarm.

Against this perspective came another reading of Manila's 'squatter problem' which was to be found among a minority of the city's planners, administrators and academics, a number of whom, unlike most of the alarmists, had first-hand experience with people in the squatter settlements. This was not so much a reading of alarm, as a reading of optimism that placed faith in self-help and the process of modernisation as the pathways to human well-being for both rich and poor. Influenced in part by community development programs in urban North America and the self-help arguments of British architect John

Turner in relation to urban housing in Latin America, some planners and commentators began to see in Manila's squatter settlements the potential for popularly initiated development and social integration.[12] Proponents of this view argued that squatters and slum dwellers were advancing themselves and their neighbourhoods as best they could, and should be assisted in this process through state housing policies more appropriate to their circumstances and capacities for self-help. The proponents of this reading basically argued that the perceived blight of Manila's squatter settlements and slums would effectively disappear as the state facilitated the self-help efforts of the urban poor, thereby allowing them to become integrated into urban life and the upward trajectory of modernisation. Their principle criticisms were levelled at the state for not recognising and acting on this (Laquian 1969, 1971(a), 1971(b); Poethig 1969; 1971; Hollnsteiner 1972, 1976, 1977; Keyes & Burcroff 1976).

The one thing these negative and positive readings of the slum and squatter settlement phenomenon had in common was their call for decisive and comprehensive state intervention in the form and process of Manila's urbanisation. Indeed, as the 1960s and early 1970s advanced, many of the Philippines' growing numbers of technocrats took this position on a wide range of perceived forms of urban blight: inadequate waste disposal, water supply and sanitation; traffic congestion, poor roads and inadequate public transport; clogged and polluted water-ways and insufficient flood control (Ramos 1961; Laquian 1966; Viloria 1971; Abueva et al 1972; Caoili 1988). In 1971, Viloria warned that without decisive and far-reaching state intervention, metropolitan Manila could become a 'colossal slum' (Viloria 1971, p.148).

NEW SOCIETY, RATIONAL PLANNING AND THE ARCHITECTURE OF DISPLAY

The impetus for more centralised planning and greater state intervention in the shaping of Philippine society came from a number of directions and culminated in the declaration of martial law in 1972, under the banner of what the Marcos regime called the 'New Society'. The principal bases upon which the regime sought to justify itself were the promises of development, and social and political order, the latter in part presented as a precondition for the former.[13] In various speeches and writings, President Marcos identified, as some of the major impediments to modernisation and national prosperity, the political particularism, conservatism and lack of discipline which he said characterised the 'Old Society', especially its highly privileged landed oligarchy (Marcos 1978, pp.17-22). What was called for he said, was a 'revolution from the centre', a 'master plan' that would bring 'rational' solutions to the country's problems of poverty and disorder thereby preparing the Philippines for 'industrial take-off' into a future 'modern agro-industrial state' (Marcos 1973, 1978; Magno 1983, pp.9,31-32,40). While Marcos invoked a modernist vision and language consistent with the American colonial and neo-colonial cultural tradition (cf Constantino 1978), he also appealed to a nationalist mythology that would see the Philippines construct its own particular brand of modernity through the recalling of such ancient traditions as 'ba*rangay* democracy' and completion of the 'unfinished revolution' of 1898 (Marcos 1973, pp.77-79, 83-88; 1978, pp.39-41).

As in the neighbouring countries of South-east Asia, the promise of modernity found strenuous support within the Philippine elite and middle classes, and increasingly among lowland peasants and workers, making it a powerful political symbol for the Marcos regime to champion (Magno 1983; McCallus 1989; Turner 1990). While previous regimes had sought appeal on a similar basis, Marcos took this to new symbolic heights. Despite some opposition, many people, believing that drastic measures were needed to propel the Philippines along the road to modernity and prosperity, supported Marcos's 'developmental authoritarianism'. Thus, a central feature of the regime was the substantial increase in state power and centralisation of authority in the hands of the President and his family. Like a number of other countries in the region, the quest for modernity was to be pursued through the might of the iron fist.

Apart from the various written and verbally delivered propaganda of the Marcos regime, nowhere was there more obvious evidence of an effort to both communicate and implement the vision of the New Society than in the built environment. In the countryside, this was principally in the form of roads,

highways and bridges, frequently cited by local officials as proof of the advances made under martial law. But more than anywhere else, it was in Manila that the Marcos regime attempted to construct an edifice of modernity and national pride. This had begun before martial law, in what the Marcoses called the 'New Epoch', with a number of building projects, none more spectacular than the Cultural Centre of the Philippines. But it was in the New Society era that the Marcos regime engaged in its most thoroughgoing attempt to transform Manila. Two tendencies were evident in this refashioning: the first, an architecture of display, exemplified by the Cultural Centre, and associated with a visionary language of utopian humanism; the second, rational planning which concerned itself with problem-solving through the re-ordering of Manila - both physically and administratively - along technical-bureaucratic lines. The first was associated most with Imelda Marcos, the powerful First Lady, and the second with a newly influential layer of state technocrats occupying positions in a number of new or restructured state instrumentalities. Of these instrumentalities, the most significant were the National Housing Authority, the Metro Manila Commission and the Ministry of Human Settlements.

Many economic and physical planners within the Philippines, and in such bodies as the World Bank, believed that much of the ineffectiveness of the Philippine state in dealing with the country's development problems, including Manila's urbanisation, lay in the weakness and confused multiplicity of government agencies (*FEER* Jan 2 1976, pp.38-41; Caoili 1988). They called for bureaucratic rationalisation and legislation that would give greater institutional power to bodies engaged in the planning and implementation of development programs. The World Bank exercised considerable pressure on the Philippines Government to bring about these changes (Bello *et al* 1982, pp. 101-125).

Several of Manila's problems were seen as a consequence of the fact that land use planning and building codes, together with the provision of water, sanitation, health services and police forces, lay in the hands of 17 separate municipal or city authorities (Figure 1.2). Under such conditions, it was argued, an efficient and comprehensive system of

ARCHITECTURAL MODERNISM

urban development was impossible. In 1975, these pressures and arguments led to the creation of a new urban administrative, service and planning body: the Metro Manila Commission under the appointed Governorship of Imelda Marcos. Similar arguments were advanced in relation to housing and, in the same year, the National Housing Authority was created, replacing numerous agencies that were previously responsible for housing and resettlement. It was headed by a retired army General, but later was also formally presided over by Imelda Marcos. Most far reaching of all was the Ministry for Human Settlements, formed in 1978 out of the earlier Task Force and Commission on Human Settlements. It, too, was headed by the First Lady who assumed the role of Minister. On paper, the Ministry of Human Settlements had responsibility for nearly all facets of development planning and implementation in the Philippines and did so with an explicit brief to transform or create local communities throughout the Philippines. It was to do so in reference to what it defined as 'man's eleven basic needs': water, power, food, clothing, livelihood, medical services, education, ecology, sports, shelter and mobility (MHS 1978; Benitez 1981-82; Mathay 1981-82; Serrote 1987-88). Through her headship of these bodies, particularly the Commission and the Ministry, Imelda Marcos and her immediate advisers played a key role in the reshaping of Manila, though one that was often in conflict with, or resented by, the technocrats who worked under her, particularly those in the National Housing Authority where World Bank influence was most marked. While showcase architecture principally drew its power from the First Lady, the major force behind rational planning was the World Bank, though it should be added that in practice there was not always a clear divide between the two tendencies.

The projects and plans emanating from the Ministry of Human Settlements and associated with Imelda Marcos were grandiose. Through voluminous reports, studies, brochures, drawings, scale models and insignia, they were presented in a distinctive rhetoric which combined technocratic jargon with a particular brand of utopian humanism. While there were certain local idiosyncrasies to the rhetoric, it was derived in part from the ekistics design tradition associated with Greek architect C. A. Doxiadas. This

tradition, which also traced back through Geddes and Le Corbusier, professed an 'integrated' and 'humanistic' approach to urban design in that it attempted to consider the multiple ways in which 'man' was connected to the physical habitat. This 'science of human settlements', as it was called, enjoyed substantial influence in planning and architectural circles in the West during the 1960s and 1970s. It found expression through the establishment of the United Nations' Commission on Human Settlements which in turn promoted the formation of a local counterpart in the Philippines.[14] Much of the language used in Imelda Marcos's speeches, often dismissed as highly idiosyncratic, appears to be an embellishment on the jargon of this tradition.

Under the auspices of the Metro Manila Commission, and later, the Ministry of Human Settlements, Manila started to be referred to as the 'City of Man'. In 1977, in an address to the Rotary Club of Metropolitan Manila, the First Lady described her vision for Manila in the following terms:

> Our metropolis then must be a new frontier of the human spirit. For, indeed, why do we create a city, a metropolis that is to be the crown of civilisation? We do not create it for ourselves alone nor for the city dwellers. We create it for an entire people. As with all the great cities of the world - New York, Moscow, Peking, Paris, London, Rome or Tokyo - Metro Manila is for everyone, for every human being of whatever nationality who craves for that community which is in rhythm with the universe (*Manila* Feb 1-28 1978, p.5).

Three years later in characteristically sweeping, but more prosaic language, Mrs Marcos outlined the objectives of the Metro Manila Commission as follows:

> ...to uplift the City of Man with the cleaning and dredging of rivers and esteros, the planting of trees, the relocation of squatters, the creation of new food supply, a comprehensive shelter program, improvement of health and educational facilities, of the garbage collection system, providing employment and roads, and improving police capability (*Ibon* 68, 15 June 1981, p.2).

Through the joint preparations of the Metro Manila Commission and the Task Force that later became the Ministry of Human Settlements, a Manila master plan was released in 1976 for the growth and re-organisation of the city and its immediate hinterland (Metro Manila Commission 1976). This 'structure plan', as it was officially called, provided for an overall rationalisation of land use to be achieved, in part, through new zoning regulations, the development of new or existing radial highways and ring roads and a new public rail and waterway transportation system. In addition there was to be an expansion and modernisation of port facilities, the creation of 'special activity districts', the integration of residential subdivisions, new industrial and agro-industrial sites, the construction of a series of peripherally located 'new towns' as alternative growth centres, a number of 'special projects' and a range of other proposals. The plan was given substantial publicity in the Government controlled mass media, different components of it received backing from the World Bank and other international financial agencies, and, for once, the Philippine state seemed powerful enough to overcome particularistic or other local interests which might have opposed such a plan.

As new legislation was enacted and as work was carried out on a number of fronts - in the cleaning of streets and waterways, and in the construction of highways, overpasses, light rail transit and public housing estates - so were the people of Manila given tangible evidence of centrally planned urban development in action. This attempt to plan and build metropolitan Manila as a modern metropolis consumed the time and energy of thousands of planners, economists, architects, engineers, propagandists, clerical staff, construction workers, building contractors and lawyers. Among the state's growing workforce of technocrats, it contributed significantly to a sense of collective commitment to the goals of modernisation and nation building. It also offered substantial financial benefits to a number of business people with close connections to the Marcoses, notably Rodolfo Cuenco, head of the Construction and Development Corporation of the Philippines which was awarded many of the major infrastructural contracts (Manapat 1991, pp.274-292).[15] Yet the whole program also engendered dissatisfaction among many of the technocrats who believed that too much of the attention and money was being devoted to what

were known as the 'Projects of the First Lady'.

In addition to the various buildings found in the Cultural Centre Complex, Imelda Marcos was responsible for the construction of a number of prominent, highly expensive public buildings which many local critics believed were oriented to the narrow interests of the nations's elite rather than to solving problems that faced Manila or the nation as a whole. These included the Philippine Heart Centre, the Lung Centre of the Philippines, the Kidney Centre Foundation, the Coconut Palace and Children's City (a national hospital for children complete with beds designed as modern automobiles). Indeed, in contrast to the rational planners, who sought to have a direct impact on the city's whole population, the First Lady saw herself more as a visionary whose task it was to symbolise and inspire the nation's developmental program. Thus, when asked to justify her showcase projects, she responded:

> Why do I build a Heart Centre or Convention City instead of urban mass housing...I believe we just can't do that. I don't believe in building houses for everyone because I don't want our people to be mendicant...(Bello et al 1982, p.107).

THE NEW SOCIETY AND MANILA'S SQUATTER SETTLEMENTS

A major feature of the Marcos regime's effort to transform Manila into a City of Man was its attempt to solve the 'squatter problem'. Although failing in terms of its own definition of this problem, it nevertheless had a far more profound impact on Manila's squatters than had any regime before it. This was due both to its more ambitious vision and to its political and bureaucratic restructuring which made decisive state intervention more possible. Yet despite this vision, which was to deal with the 'squatter problem' throughout the metropolis rather than in the *ad hoc* manner of the past, it pursued divergent programs, tending over time to lurch from one to another.

One of these went under the rubric of 'beautification' and was most closely associated with Imelda Marcos and her advisers.[16] Thousands of Metro Aides wearing bright yellow and red uniforms were recruited from among the urban poor to clean the streets. In the early years of the New Society they became a highly visible feature of city's major thoroughfares. On the other hand, thousands of other urban poor, also mainly women but who worked the streets as vendors, were the object of periodic eviction drives, particularly in the vicinity of five-star hotels or other large prestigious buildings, the claim being that they were an 'eyesore' and blocked traffic. However the beautification program's attempt to remove 'eyesores' was most profoundly associated with the removal of slums and squatter houses from public vision, again primarily in areas frequented by foreigners or members of the Manila elite. In some cases this was attempted through the erection of white washed fences, but it also occurred through massive campaigns of demolition and eviction, frequently in preparation for visits by foreign dignitaries. Conducted more systematically and on a grander scale than had been possible before, the full force of martial law was used to drive squatters away from the city. In preparation for the 1974 Miss Universe Pageant, 100 000 people were reported to have had their houses demolished; for the state visit of US President Ford in 1975, 200 000 squatters are said to have been evicted; and for the IMF-World Bank Conference in 1976, about 60 000 lost their houses to state demolition teams (Jimenez *et al* 1986, p.52; Bello *et al* 1982, p.107). Between 1973 and 1980 the Marcos regime is said to have evicted or resettled a total of 400 000 families (Ruland cited in *Ibon* 100 1982, p.1).

These measures were combined in 1975 with a new draconian Presidential Decree which made squatting a criminal offence subject to imprisonment and directed a number of state authorities 'to remove all illegal constructions including building on and along esteros and river banks, those along railroad tracks and those built without permit on public and private property' (Presidential Decree No 772). Though the magnitude of this task raised questions as to the viability of the decree, the known power and ruthlessness of martial rule, coupled with the experience of the demolition drives, generated a great deal of fear and apprehension among squatters throughout the city.

Yet at the same time, Manila's beautification also addressed the 'squatter problem' in another way. Just north of the Tondo Foreshore, in Dagat-Dagatan, on reclaimed fishpond land, Imelda Marcos directed the construction of a cluster housing project for approximately 500 squatter families who were to be relocated from the Foreshore. Named *Kapitbahayan* (neighbourliness), this project was supposed to embody the Filipino traditions of *bayanihan* (mutual help) and *barangay* (pre-colonial local community) and to become a prototype for community housing throughout the country (Marcos n.d.). In one Government document the project was described as showing 'what can be done to upgrade the quality of life of slum dwellers' (cited in Jimenez *et al* 1986, p.57). However, many squatters in Tondo questioned the general significance of the project. Not only was it restricted to relatively high income squatters, it was also an extremely expensive project which they believed would not be repeated. One story circulating in Manila at the time was that the original plan to use comparatively cheap galvanised iron roofing was overturned after the First Lady realised that the flight path of some aeroplanes coming into Manila passed over the area. What galvanised iron roofing had already been attached was duly removed and replaced with costly Spanish style terra cotta tiles (Figure 1.8). The significance of Kapitbahayan, it seems, was similar to the significance of the Cultural Centre Complex: it was a showcase for local and foreign consumption. Apart from its symbolic appeal to a domestic audience, *Kapitbahayan* was presented as the First Lady's and the Philippines' contribution to the United Nation's Vancouver Habitat conference of 1976. This also coincided with an associated and highly publicised international architectural competition, sponsored by the Philippine Government and

Figure 1.8 Kapitbahayan, *Navotos*

the International Architectural Foundation, in which entrants were called on to design housing and community facilities for some of the 100 000 squatters who were to be relocated from Tondo.[17]

The Tondo Foreshore Dagat-Dagatan Development Project was also the vehicle through which an alternative program aimed at Manila's squatter settlements was initially developed. Prompted by a concerted political campaign by the squatters themselves (Hollnsteiner 1976; Pinches 1977; Murphy 1990, pp.39-50) and the considerable loan-based influence of the World Bank, the redevelopment of Tondo was to be carried out through a program of 'upgrading', the stated intention being that most squatters would thereby not have to be relocated. Additional accommodation for the minority who would be displaced was to be provided through a program of 'sites and services' on a nearby resettlement site in Dagat-Dagatan, adjacent to Imelda Marcos's *Kapitbahayan*. 'Upgrading' involved the subdivision of most of the Tondo Foreshore into small residential plots, often roughly corresponding to the existing configuration of houses, but rationalised so that individual plots could be clearly demarcated for private mortgage sale and for the provision of drains, piped water, pathways, electricity and better vehicular access. 'Sites and services' resettlement would be similar, except that in this case relocated squatters were to be provided with small serviced plots which they would then build on. In both cases households would become involved in individual, long-term mortgage contracts, thereby removing their illegal status.

Domestically, the rationale behind this program - minimal displacement, self-help house building, state provision of urban services, and relatively affordable home ownership - arose not only out of the pressures mounted by squatters themselves but also out of the argument developed by academics and planners such as Laquian, Hollnsteiner and Keyes, noted earlier for their positive developmental reading of Manila's squatter settlements. Partly through the auspices of the World Bank, such programs were being developed in the cities of many third world countries, including a number in the region of Southeast Asia where they were receiving substantial support among housing technocrats. In 1977 two Presidential Letters of Instruction were issued declaring a nationwide program of squatter settlement upgrading, and sites and services, on the grounds that:

> ..a large number of our people are living in an environment of filth and degradation in slums and blighted communities - a situation incompatible with the New Society

and that

> ..the traditional approach to the housing need...is exceedingly expensive and can be undertaken by the Government only on a limited scale (Letter of Instruction No 557, 1977).

In light of past programs, one of the most significant provisions of these letters, contradicting the still valid anti-squatting decree of two years earlier, was that:

> Relocation and resettlement of families shall be undertaken only to complement a slum improvement program in the locality or where the families are staying in areas considered dangerous to public safety or are needed for infrastructure program (sic) of the Government (Letter of Instruction No 557, 1977).

Made possible by loan funds from the World Bank, which by 1980 totalled US$136 million (Mathay 1981-82, p.43), a range of national and local state authorities, and hundreds of state employees were put to work. The state authority principally responsible for the implementation of this program - the National Housing Authority - conducted a survey of all known squatter settlements in metropolitan Manila, designating those that would be upgraded and those that would have to be subject to resettlement. While the Tondo project was still in progress, the National Housing Authority set up office and began 'upgrading' programs in a number of other large settlements. At the same time existing resettlement sites, 40 or more kilometres out of the central city, were developed according to the sites and services model, and some attempt was made to establish local industries as sources of employment. For the first time Philippine state housing and planning bodies were attempting to deal with Manila's squatter settlements in terms of a rational master plan that could embrace the whole metropolitan area.

Undoubtedly much of the Marcos regime's interest in the upgrading/sites and services housing strategy, lay in its potential to win support from, and gain greater control over, a major sector of the city's population whose political capabilities were regarded with apprehension (Bello 1982, pp.101-125). Both the Tondo and Tatalon projects were presented to the people of these settlements as acts of personal generosity by the First Couple. They received much attention along these lines through public ceremony and the mass media and were used in a well-worn tradition of political patronage to win support at elections, notably the fateful presidential elections of 1986, after which the Marcoses were forced from office (Pinches 1987; 1992(a)). In his early manifestos on the New Society, President Marcos had spoken at length about the way his regime represented a continuation of the revolution against Spain and an answer to the 'rebellion of the poor'. In launching the Tondo Foreshore upgrading project he again drew this connection with the statement:

> If there was a Cry of Balintawak for the Revolutionaries of 1896 which rallied the people to the rebellion against political servitude, let there be today the cry of Tondo...a cry against impoverishment, indignity and degradation of the poor (TFDA n.d.).

According to Government brochures circulating in Manila in the mid 1970s, 'the Cry of Tondo' was at last being answered (TFDA n.d.).

While it is not the place here to look in detail at the outcome of this program, the World Bank is reported to have regarded the Tondo project as a great success (Makil 1983, p.8).[18] Most of the people in the squatter neighbourhood of Tatalon generally agreed, principally because of their new-found sense of security and because of the removal of the stigma associated with squatting. Despite claims made by some critics of these projects (Bello et al 1982, pp.111-113) that mortgage repayments were prohibitively high, this was not the case for the people the author worked with in Tatalon, and nor was it the case in parts of Tondo where repayments were even lower (Viloria & Williams 1987, p.20). In both instances many fell behind in their repayments, but this was also the case in some middle class state housing schemes. In Tatalon and Tondo, the coincidence of an increased sense of security of land tenure and a

growth in the number of workers employed on relatively lucrative contracts overseas, resulted in the building of a significant number of comparatively large and expensive houses (Figure 1.9). In both places too, legalisation resulted in a substantial growth of the internal market in rental accommodation (for Tondo, see Llewelyn Davies Kinhill 1977, pp.10-11). In Tatalon it also brought about a degree of social atomisation as households now found themselves private mortgage holders, and as the recruitment of residents was now circumscribed by formal bureaucratic rules of eligibility, as well as the larger, more open rental market. With these changes, so the architecture of intimacy and improvisation was undermined in the direction of the conventional housing subdivision. As argued elsewhere in this paper, one of the chief benefits for the state of squatter settlement upgrading is the provision it makes for bureaucratic incorporation of a population hitherto regarded as politically dangerous: principally through mortgage provisions based on the privatisation of residential property and the creation of formal impersonal rules governing residential access (Pinches 1985, 1986).

However, in the mid 1980s squatter settlement upgrading effectively came to a halt, even in projects that were only partially complete. In part this was due to the mounting national political and economic crisis which culminated in the overthrow of the Marcos regime in 1986, but there were also other reasons. One of the lending conditions of the World Bank for upgrading and sites and services projects was full cost recovery, but this did not occur as ex-

Figure 1.9   Overseas worker's house after squatter settlement upgrading, Tatalon

penses went over budget and as large numbers of former squatters fell behind in their mortgage repayments, effectively casting themselves back into the legal status of squatter. The state's use and acquisition of highly priced, often centrally located urban real estate for Manila's poor also aroused significant opposition, both from within Government circles and from powerful private real estate interests outside. Though martial law provisions made land acquisition easier, the state could not afford to alienate influential sections of the urban business elite (cf. Keyes 1976).

Secondly, this program did not arrest the steady growth of Manila's squatter population; it may even have speeded it up as more migrants entered Manila in the hope of benefiting from Government support.[19] Without a massive redistribution of wealth, the state simply did not have the resources to incorporate the whole squatter population through its upgrading and sites and services program. These two factors, multiplied by similar experiences elsewhere, help explain the World Bank's effective abandonment of squatter upgrading and sites and services in favour of a more free market, private enterprise orientation (Ward & Macoloo 1992).

A third factor working against the upgrading/sites and services program in Manila, stemmed from the fact that squatter settlements, whether 'upgraded' or not, were mostly inhabited by lowly paid, often unemployed workers most of whom could do little more than construct the dwellings that had for a long time characterised these settlements. Thus, they continued to offend the aesthetic and social sensibilities of many within the city's elite and middle classes who still saw living conditions within urban poor neighbourhoods as contrary to their vision of modernity and national identity. In large part their architectural sensibilities were an expression of the antagonistic class relations that prevailed in much of Manila (Pinches 1992(a)), but they were also shaped, as was painfully evident in the case of Imelda Marcos's projects and pronouncements, by a modernist sense of national pride which constantly sought affirmation from the affluent West.

Not surprisingly then, the showcase architecture exemplified by the Cultural Centre and *Kapitbahayan* persisted. In relation to the urban poor it did so un-der the rubric of BLISS, an acronym for *Bagong Lipunan* (New Society) Integrated Sites and Services, though in practice it had little to do with sites and services. From the late 1970s BLISS became the cornerstone of the Ministry of Human Settlements program. BLISS was not only to be a key component in the Ministry's reconstruction of Manila as the 'City of Man', but according to Government documents, was also to be a nationwide movement for the creation or transformation of human settlements throughout the country. Promoted as an embodiment of the 'integrated approach' to human settlements, it was supposed to provide not only for housing, but for all of 'man's eleven basic needs', thereby making these settlements 'self-reliant' and 'self-sufficient' (MHS 1978; Maramag 1979). Thus, a widely publicised component of BLISS was a livelihood program known as KKK (Movement for Livelihood and Progress) which aimed at promoting entrepreneurship through the provision of cheap small business loans (Benitez 1981-82).[20]

BLISS projects in Manila (Figure 1.5) and in other parts of the country were announced by prominent hoardings featuring the name of the First Lady and the distinctive Ministry logo: an eleven pointed star with the silhouetted figure of a man in the centre, each point standing for a 'basic need'. Over the period 1980-1981, when the program had most impact, nine medium rise BLISS apartment complexes were built in Manila (Makil 1983, p.10), including one in the squatter settlement of Tatalon. While their layout and designs differed, they were typically *in situ* concrete constructions with the same red Spanish terra cotta tiles that were used in the *Kapitbahayan* project

Figure 1.10   Urban BLISS Project

(Figure 1.10). Though they became prominent landmarks in various parts of the city, their number did not match the images of urban renewal indicated in the grandiose plans and glossy reports of the Ministry, and, despite the claims that they would provide for 'basic needs' and 'self-sufficiency' they amounted to little more than apartment buildings.[21] In each one of these apartment complexes was constructed a KKK livelihood centre, but they generally benefited few residents and were frequently closed.

Furthermore, though ostensibly addressed to the needs of the urban poor, Manila's BLISS projects provided accommodation for middle income earners, in particular state employees, and were looked upon by squatters with derision and resentment. If the National Housing Authority's upgrading/sites and services program ultimately failed to reach the majority of Manila's squatters, the impact of BLISS on the urban poor was purely symbolic. As the acronym itself suggests, BLISS housing represented a remote fantasy. But the fantasy was not so much that of the squatters as of Imelda Marcos and her advisers. It was a fantasy that the whole of Manila could somehow be transformed architecturally into a state of comfort and affluence, independently of significant societal and economic transformation (Figure 1.11).

Given the ultimate failure of BLISS and other examples of the Marcos regime's showcase architecture to eradicate what politicians, planners and journalists popularly described as Manila's urban blight, it was not surprising that, in 1982, the various authorities under the jurisdiction of the Ministry for Human Settlements and the Metro Manila Commis-

Figure 1.11   Imelda Marcos' vision of the transition to Manila's 'City of Man'

sion launched a massive demolition drive in what they called the 'Last Campaign Against Squatting'. In some respects this constituted a return to the eviction campaigns that marked the early years of authoritarian rule, a principal objective of which was the removal of the city's 'eyesores'. One version of this aesthetic rationale was expressed by prominent Filipino economist:

> Slums and dilapidated communities...should be cleared and beautified, not necessarily because they are inhuman, but because they are a social sore, unpleasant to the eyes of tourists and visiting executives, and conducive to social unrest, which always frightens foreign business (A. Lichauco cited in *Ibon* 100, 15 Oct 1982, p.4).

Yet the Last Campaign Against Squatting was also conducted according to another rationale which concerned not so much the wholesale eradication of the city's 'eyesores', but rather the selective removal of squatter settlements in favour of rational planning principles that justified displacement in terms of the needs of urban infrastructural development, flood control and public safety. This is the view that was expressed in the 1977 Presidential Letters of Instruction which set up the upgrading/sites and services program. It is in these terms that Head of the National Housing Authority, General Tobias, explained the Last Campaign Against Squatting in 1982. In his rendering of the campaign, the very term 'squatter' excluded nearly all of those people who had long standing residence or who were not inhabiting sites that were either dangerous or required for state infrastructure. Furthermore, his stated understanding of the evictions was that they would only occur where alternative accommodation could be established through serviced lots on state resettlement sites (Tobias 1982). Often public pronouncements did not match state practices, but this rationale was at variance with the push by some other officials not to discriminate in the eradication of squatters.

Thus it was often the case that both aesthetic and rationalist arguments were invoked in favour of squatter settlement demolition under the Marcos regime. While the most publicised demolitions were associated with the First Lady's beautification drives, others were conducted in accordance with a master plan for Manila's redevelopment and future growth. Thousands of squatters were removed from river banks and estuaries, not just because they were believed to be eyesores, but also because they were believed to have contributed to the city's flood and health problems. Thousands more were removed for the construction of port facilities and highways as well as the building of the new National Government Centre in Quezon City. In this case the ruthlessness of destruction was that of rational planning rather than of an architecture of display. In one case, a major radial highway leading north out of the city was built straight through the centre of one of Manila's largest and most densely populated settlements, Bagong Barrio, which like Tatalon and Tondo was the site of an upgrading project. The outcome of building this highway through the settlement, rather than around it, was that a number of families were physically divided so that their members regularly had to run a gauntlet of automobiles in order to maintain family life.

While the campaigns of eviction, demolition and resettlement under the Marcoses were waged with a ferocity and on a scale hitherto unexperienced in Manila, the number of squatters living in the metropolitan area continued to grow as the disparities in wealth and opportunity between the city and the countryside remained. Not only was there a steady stream of migrants from the countryside, but various studies indicate that a high proportion of people removed from the city returned to squat elsewhere, despite Government claims that it had remedied this problem through better serviced relocation sites and the provision of new job opportunities outside the urban area (Makil 1983, pp.5-6). By 1982 the number of people living in squatter settlements in metropolitan Manila was recorded by the National Housing Authority to be about 1.65 million or about a third of the city's total population (Makil 1983, p.2). By 1985 the National Housing Authority figure had grown to over two million (Gregorio-Medel 1989, p.1) and by 1990 another source suggested a figure of about 3.5 million (*Anawim* IV (4), p.2). For all the rhetoric and power of authoritarian rule under the Marcoses, their regime, like those before, could not stem the flow of people entering Manila in search of a better life.[22]

CONCLUSION

In contrast to those dualist analyses which use the idea of modernity as the ideal type counterpart to that of tradition, this essay has attempted to show how an analysis of Manila's changing built environment can be better served through a perspective that stresses contradiction and contention as fundamental qualities of modernity itself.[23] Manila's post-colonial urbanisation is testimony to a process of modernisation that might be conceived of in two ways: as something that is encountered and as something that is strived for.

Firstly, modernity in Manila concerns the changing circumstances that Filipinos have experienced, both in the cities and the countryside, as their lives are increasingly circumscribed by the flux and uncertainty of commodity production, commercialisation and a nation-state whose political economy orientates them to a global market in goods, labour and cultural values. Spatially positioned at the centre of this vortex, Manila has undergone rapid urban expansion. The building of the city since World War Two has seen the establishment of numerous factories, warehouses, banks, office buildings, hotels, markets, shops and residential areas for the city's growing population of workers, professionals, state officials and business people. To a large extent, the process of post-war urbanisation in the Philippines has been one of *laissez-faire* in the context of an increasingly mobile population, a growing national labour market and a spatial concentration of private capital and state expenditure in Manila. These developments have been characterised by massive inequalities in wealth, political power and social status. The associated growth of an urban real estate market, dominated by property developers from the country's established landed oligarchy, has catered only to a narrow segment of the urban population.

On the one hand this *laissez-faire* growth has produced significant enclaves of prosperity, most notably in the business district and exclusive housing estates of Makati, characterised by an international modernist architectural style largely indistinguishable from that found in many North American cities. On the other hand, it has resulted in the massive growth of squatter settlements which house many from within Manila's swelling class of labouring poor, drawn heavily from the countryside through rural-urban migration. In contrast to the rational order and modernist aesthetic of the city's affluent enclaves, Manila's squatter settlements can be described as displaying a spatiality and architecture of intimacy, improvisation and flux. These qualities are not so much a consequence of tradition, as a particular manifestation of modernity, resulting primarily from the exclusionary and hostile stance of the Philippine state and propertied classes towards the city's disinherited.

The second way in which Manila's modernity might be conceived is in terms of the ideals of progress and development which almost everywhere have influenced or captured popular, elite and official imaginations. Furthermore, as Filipinos have increasingly been set free in the markets of labour, goods and capital, so has the attainment of progress been experienced as self-willed. Thus, modernity has not simply become an ideal but also a basis for identity construction as individuals and groups have increasingly come to understand themselves through the degree to which they have achieved progress.[24] These ideas of progress and development have been equated generally with a romantic and largely unproblematic reading of the industrial West and have been associated particularly with life in the United States.

This essay has examined some of the ways in which the quest for progress have been given expression in Manila's built environment, in particular by the state and by the city's squatters. State intervention in the urban landscape of Manila has tended to take on two forms: rational planning and showcase architecture based on an international modernist aesthetic.[25] While both have to some extent been evident since 1946, it was the New Society regime of the Marcoses that attempted the most thoroughgoing modernisation of Manila's built environment through these forms of intervention. Both attested not only to a desire for power and legitimacy within the Philippines, but also to a pre-occupation with the regime's and the country's standing in the global arena, especially with reference to the West. Yet tensions were also generated between these two tendencies as different elements within the state fought for ascendancy and as each approach proved unable to harness the dynamic and complexity of Manila's urbanisation.

Although the forms of modernist aesthetic and rational planning practised by the Marcos regime evidenced a conformity to Western and North American traditions of modernity, they were also, to some extent, deliberately embedded in a rhetoric of cultural heritage that was presented as uniquely Filipino.[26] This uneasy combination is indicative of the deeply divided and ambiguous way in which members of the Philippine elite and civil servants have approached the construction of national identity.

In contrast to the efforts of the state, a high proportion of Manila's poor working classes have pursued the ideas of progress and prosperity through migration into the city and through the creation of squatter settlements. While it is obvious that such settlements are a monument to material hardship when considered alongside the residences of the middle classes and rich, their residents have almost everywhere been found to be motivated by a desire for advancement, and, for the most part, they see themselves as having made tangible gains, even if these have only been modest. Although their houses and neighbourhoods have taken shape in a less contrived way than the state's architecture and physical planning, the presence and changing material form of squatter housing, particularly where there is a relatively high security of tenure, are indicative of a common commitment to the pursuit of progress.

Despite the general coincidence of commitment to the idea of modernity found within the Philippine state and among Manila's squatters, the two parties have pursued this idea in sharp conflict. For their part, the politicians, planners and state officials, along with most of Manila's elite and middle class, have mounted much of their quest for modernity on the backs of the cheap labour offered by Manila's squatters. Yet simultaneously they have viewed the squatters and their settlements as the very anathema of modernity and progress. Accordingly, much of the Marcos regime's modernisation project in Manila entailed various attempts to obliterate, rationalise and control the city's squatter settlements. For Manila's squatters, therefore, the state and elite have been experienced as a major obstacle to the pursuit of progress. Some see themselves as having gained through the state sponsored squatter settlement upgrading, and sites and services program, but many more have suffered the hardships of demolition and eviction. Yet through their various forms of resistance and sheer numbers, they have prevented the state from realising its goal.

The encounter with and pursuit of modernity in Manila, evident in the variable character of the city's architecture and spatial form, attests to a phenomenon and ideology that are highly contradictory. While the ideals of progress, rational order and modernist aesthetics inform and animate Manila's urbanisation, they have also proved both illusory and destructive.

ENDNOTES

1 Locsin, who was patronised by the Marcoses, designed a number of monumental public buildings during this era.

2 These buildings, and others like them, are certainly suggestive of Imelda Marcos' peculiar obsession with reproducing the grandeur and opulence of life among the Western world's elites (Pedrosa 1987; Ellison 1989), but they are also indicative of a much wider pre-occupation in the Philippines with Western, particularly North American, artefacts and lifestyles (see Constantino 1978).

3 Unlike the other major nations in the region, pre-colonial Philippine societies, for the most part, did not have a tradition of statecraft, including monumental architecture. The concern for establishing aristocratic heritage led Imelda Marcos to construct a Spanish styled 'ancestral home' in her home town in Leyte. For the wedding of one of the Marcos daughters, President Marcos' birthplace, Sarret, was reported to have been transformed into a medieval Spanish town (Pedrosa 1987, pp.189-192, 222-223). Of course there is also an obvious pecuniary side to the creation of the Cultural Centre Complex and the restoration of Intramuros which concerns the development of the Philippine tourist industry.

4 For a detailed description of early colonial Manila see Reed (1978).

5 *Accesoria* means apartment house.

6 This, at least, was the case in the squatter settlements that are familiar to me, where there are many people who work or have worked as domestic servants in these exclusive housing estates.

7 Not all of Manila's squatter neighbourhoods displayed the same apparent spatial disorder: some were organised around pre-existing rectilinear roadways, but even most of those that I came across quickly turned to narrow, twisting alleyways immediately one left the roadway. Newer, more sparsely occupied settlements displayed less of this character, but as they grew the same pattern generally followed.

8 The author have also spent time conducting research in Tondo and a number of other squatter settlements in Manila.

9 For one attempt to differentiate the various forms of low income housing in Manila, see Tekie (1989). The question of legality of land title in many parts of Manila is an extremely contentious one. Indeed, land that is subject to legal dispute frequently attracts squatters (see Pinches 1986).

10 For one of the growing number of recent studies of traditional domestic architecture in the Philippines, see Zialcita (1991).

11 Elsewhere (Pinches 1992(a), 1992(b)), the author has tried to explain these contradictory perspectives in terms of class experience and class resistance.

12 For the fullest statement of Turner's argument, see Turner (1976). The anthropologist William Mangin, who collaborated with Turner, offers a similar argument (1967).

13 For these and other matters concerning the character of the Marcos regime's New Society see Rosenberg (1979), Magno (1983), McCallus (1989) and Turner (1990).

14 Some of the writing in the Doxiadas tradition can be found the edited collection by Bell and Tyrwhitt (1972) and the journal *Ekistics*. See also Marcos (1981-82).

15 Serrote (1987-88) argues that the Ministry of Human Settlement's responsibility over 'man's eleven basic needs' enabled the Marcoses and their crony capitalists to capture vital areas of the national economy which they used to enrich themselves.

16 Anderson (1978, p.304) also notes for Indonesia a 'contemporary vogue for beautification work by presidential wives'.

17 Commentary on the competition and presentation of the highest placed designs was provided in a special issue of the prestigious American architectural journal *Architectural Record* May 1976. For critical discussion of the competition see Robertson *et al* (1977). To some extent the competition backfired on the Marcos regime

when the winning entrant, who had been contacted by squatters in Tondo, refused to allow the use of his design unless the Philippine authorities complied with the stated requirements of the squatters. This did not happen and the results of the competition quickly gave way to the plans of the National Housing Authority.

18 For further detail and assessment of the Tondo/Dagat-Dagatan Redevelopment Project see Sembrano *et al* (1977, pp.8-126); Llewelyn Davies Kinhill (1977); Bello *et al* (1982, pp.101-125); Swan *et al* (1983, pp.6-18); Munarriz 1987; and Viloria & Williams (1987).

19 This was the case in the neighbourhood where the author worked in Tatalon.

20 As with many of the acronyms and logos used by the Marcos regime, there is a referent here to the symbols of the Philippine revolutionary movement, in this case against Spain: the KKK stood for the Katipunan secret society which took up arms against Spanish colonial rulers at the end of the last century.

21 BLISS in part suffered because of the lack of financial support from the World Bank, which favoured the upgrading/sites and services program (*Philippine Times* March 3-9 1979, p.60), and was sceptical of projects initiated by the First Lady.

22 In 1989, Government sources estimated that about 70 per cent or more of the urban poor are rural migrants (Gregorio-Medel 1989, p.2). According to ESCAP (1993, p.18), 60 per cent of city dwellers in the Asia Pacific Region will be living in slums and squatter settlements by the year 2000.

23 The classic ideal type statements, of course, come from Weber, Durkheim and Tonnies. For one Philippine sociological text which uses a dualist perspective, see Espiritu *et al* (1976). This essay draws more on the tradition of Marx and Baudelaire through Berman (1983) and Harvey (1989).

24 For general discussion of this matter see Lash & Friedman (1992).

25 For further discussion of the way in which architectural form in third world cities is linked to global political, economic and cultural processes, see King (1990 (a), (b)).

26 The desire to promote an architectural form that is indicative of the Philippines national heritage has become more pronounced since the ousting of the Marcoses, as is evident in the recent publication of several books on vernacular architecture.

REFERENCES

Abesamis, F. 1974-75 'Squatter-Slum Clearance and Resettlement Programs in the Philippines', *NEDA Journal of Development* I and II (2-4), pp.300-311.

Abueva, J. Guerrero, S, & Jurado, E. 1972 *Metro Manila: Today and Tomorrow*, Institute of Philippine Culture, Ateneo de Manila University, Quezon City.

Anderson, B. 1978 'Cartoons and Monuments: The Evolution of Political Communication under the New Order' in Jackson, K. & Pye, L. (eds), *Political Power and Communications in Indonesia*, University of California Press, Berkeley, pp. 282-321.

Agoncillo, T. & Guerrero, M. 1987, *History of the Filipino People*, R.P. Garcia, Quezon City.

Architectural Record (Special Issue on Human Settlements focused on Manila) May 1976.

Banaag, C. 1979, 'Makati: Showcase of Little Wonders', *Nation's Journal* February 21, pp.30-34.

Bell, G. & Tyrwhitt, J. (eds), *Human Identity in the Urban Environment*, Penguin, Harmondsworth.

Bello, W. Kinley, D. & Elinson, E. 1982, *Development Debacle: The World Bank in the Philippines*, Institute for Food and Development Policy, San Francisco.

Benitez, J. 1981-82, 'KKK: Livelihood for Every Filipino', *Fookien Times Philippines Yearbook*, Fookien Times Philippines Yearbook Pub Co, Manila, pp. 40-41.

Berman, M. 1983, *All That Is Solid Melts Into Air: The Experience of Modernity*, Verso, London.

Bernido, E. et al 1968, 'Squatting and Slum Dwelling in Metropolitan Manila', *Philippine Sociological Review* 16 (1-2), pp.92-105.

Caoili, M. 1988, *The Origins of Metropolitan Manila: A Political and Social Analysis*, New Day, Quezon City.

Chesnoff, R. 1978 *Philippines*, Harry N. Abrams Inc, New York.

Constantino, R. 1978, *Neocolonial Identity and Counter-Consciousness: Essays on Cultural Decolonisation* New York, M.E.Sharpe Inc

Economic and Social Commission for Asia and the Pacific (ESCAP) 1993, *State of Urbanisation in Asia and the Pacific 1993 (Executive Summary)*, United Nations, Bangkok.

Ellison, K. 1989, *Imelda: Steel Butterfly of the Philippines*, McGraw Hill, New York.

Espiritu, S. et al 1976, *Sociology in the New Philippine Setting*, Phoenix, Quezon City.

Far Eastern Economic Review (*FEER*)

Freeman Fox and Associates 1976 *Metroplan: Metro Manila Transport, Land Use and Development Planning Project - Interim Report*, Republic of the Philippines, Manila.

Fryer, D. 1970, *Emerging Southeast Asia: A Study in Growth and Stagnation*, George Philip and Son Ltd, London.

Gaddi, E. 1976, *Manila 1571-1976*, City of Manila, Manila.

Goss, J. 1990, *Production and Reproduction Among the Urban Poor of Metro Manila: Relations of Exploitation and Conditions of Existence*, Unpublished PhD, University of Kentucky.

Gregorio-Medel, A. 1989, *The Urban Poor and the Housing Problem*, Centre for Social Policy and Public Affairs, Ateneo de Manila University, Quezon City.

Guttierrez, J. 1979, 'Exit Manila; Enter Makati', *Nation's Journal* February 21, pp.10-14.

Hart, D. 1955, *The Philippine Plaza Complex: A Focal Point in Cultural Change*, Yale University Press, New Haven.

Harvey, D. 1989, *The Condition of Postmodernity*, Blackwell, Oxford.

Hollnsteiner, M. 1969, 'The Urbanisation of Metropolitan Manila' in Bello, W. & de Guzman, A. (eds), *Modernisation: Its Impact on the Philippines*, Ateneo de Manila University Press, Quezon City, pp. 147-174.

Hollnsteiner, M. 1971, 'Inner Tondo as a Way of Life' in Gowing, P. & Scott, W. (eds), *Acculturation in the Philippines*, New Day, Quezon City, pp. 235-245.

Hollnsteiner, M. 1972, 'Becoming an Urbanite: the Neighbourhood as a Learning Environment' in Dwyer, D. (ed), *The City as the Centre of Change in Asia*, Hong Kong University Press, Hong Kong, pp. 29-40.

Hollnsteiner, M. 1976, 'People Power: Community Participation in the Planning and Implementation of Human Settlements', *Philippine Studies* 24, pp.5-36.

Hollnsteiner, M. 1977, 'The Case of the "People versus Mr. Urbano Planner Y Administrator' in Abu-Lughod, J. & Hay, R. (eds), *Third World Urbanisation*, Maaroufa Press, Chicago, pp. 307-320.

Ira, L. & Medina, I. 1977, *Streets of Manila*, GCF Books, Manila.

Juppenlatz, M. 1970, *Cities In Transformation: The Urban Squatter Problem of the Developing World*, University of Queensland Press, St Lucia.

Keyes, W. 1976, 'Land Use - and Abuse' *Philippine Studies* 24, pp.381-398.

Keyes, W. & Burcroff, M. 1976, *Housing the Urban Poor: Non-Conventional Approaches to a National Problem*, Institute of Philippine Culture, Ateneo de Manila University Press, Quezon City.

Keyes, W. 1977, 'Freedom to Build' in Pama, R. *et al* (eds), *Low Income Housing - Technology and Policy*, Asian Institute of Technology, Bangkok, pp. 455-465.

Keyes, W. 1980, 'Case Study: Metro-Manila, Philippines' in Sarin, M. (ed), *Policies Towards Urban Slums*, United Nations, Economic and Social Commission for Asia and the Pacific, Bangkok, pp. 44-59.

King, A. 1990(a), 'Architecture, Capital and the Globalisation of Culture' in Featherstone, M. (ed), *Global Culture*, Sage, London, pp. 397-411.

King, A. 1990(b), *Urbanisation, Colonialism and the World-Economy: Cultural and Spatial Foundations of the World Urban System*, Routledge, London.

Laquian, A. 1964, 'Isla de Kokomo: Politics Among Urban Slum Dwellers', *Philippine Journal of Public Administration* 8 (2), pp.112-122.

Laquian, A. 1965, 'Politics in Metropolitan Manila', *Philippine Journal of Public Administration* 9 (4), pp.331-342.

Laquian, A. 1966, *The City in Nation-Building: Politics and Administration in Metropolitan Manila*, School of Public Administration, University of the Philippines, Manila.

Laquian, A. 1969, 'The "Rurban" Slum as Zone of Transition', *Comparative Local Government* 3, pp.16-27.

Laquian, A. 1971(a), *Slums Are For People: The Barrio Magsaysay Project in Philippine Urban Community Development*, East-West Centre Press, Honolulu.

Laquian, A. 1971(b), 'Slums and Squatters in South and Southeast Asia' in Jakobson, L. & Prakash, V. (eds), *Urbanisation and National Development*, Sage, Beverly Hills, pp. 183-203.

Lash, S. & Friedman, J. 1992, 'Introduction: subjectivity and modernity's Other' in Lash, S. & Friedman, J. (eds), *Modernity and Identity*, Blackwell, Oxford, pp. 1-30.

Llewelyn Davies Kinhill Pty Ltd 1977, *The Second Feasibility Study of Dagat Dagatan and Regional Centres (Draft Final Report)*, National Housing Authority, Manila.

Lopez, S. 1973/1974, 'Quezon City: Cinderella Capital of the Philippines', *Philippine Planning Journal* IV (2), V (1, 2), pp.9-13.

Magno, A. 1983, *Developmentalism and the 'New Society': The Repressive Ideology of Underdevelopment*, The Philippines in the Third World Papers Series No 35, Third World Studies, University of the Philippines, Quezon City.

Makil, P. 1983, *Slums and Squatters in the Philippines*, Series No 3, Concerned Citizens for the Urban Poor, Intramuros.

Manapat, R. 1991, *Some are Smarter than Others: The History of Marcos Crony Capitalism*, Aletheia Publications, New York.

Mangin, W. 1967, 'Latin American Squatter Settlements: A Problem and a Solution', *Latin American Research Review* 2 (3), pp.65-98.

Manila 1978, Feb 1-28, p.5.

Maramag, I. 1979, 'BLISS', *Fookien Times Philippines Year book,* Fookien Times Philippines Yearbook Publishing Co, Manila, pp. 52-53.

Marcos, F. 1973, *Notes on the New Society of the Philippines*, Marcos Foundation, Manila.

Marcos, F. 1978, *Revolution From the Centre*, Raya, Hong Kong.

Marcos, I. 1981-82, 'A Universal View of Human Settlements', *Fookien Times Philippines Yearbook*, Fookien Times Philippines Yearbook Publishing Co, Manila, pp. 38-39.

Marcos, I. n.d., *Kapitbahayan* (brochure), Republic of the Philippines, Manila.

Manuel, M. 1978, 'Human Settlements: the Metro Manila Experience', *Fookien Times Philippines Yearbook*, Fookien Times Philippines Yearbook Publishing Co, Manila, pp. 50-57.

Mathay, I. 1981-82, 'Metro Manila: The City of Man', *Fookien Times Philippines Yearbook*, Fookien Times Philippines Yearbook Publishing Co, Manila, pp. 42-49.

McCallus, J. 1989, 'The Myths of the New Filipino: Philippine Government Propaganda During the Early Years of Martial Law', *Philippine Quarterly of Culture and Society* 17(2), pp.129-148.

Metro Manila Commission (MMC) 1976, *Manila: Toward the City of Man*, Republic of the Philippines, Manila.

Ministry of Human Settlements (MHS) 1978, *Bagong Lipunan Sites and Services* Vol 1: Program Proposal Makati, Republic of the Philippines.

Munarriz, M. 1987, 'Tondo Foreshore 1974 and 1984: An Evaluative Study of Socioeconomic Impacts', *Philippine Sociological Review* 35 (1-2), pp.59-68.

Murphy, D. 1990, *A Decent Place to Live: Urban Poor in Asia*, Claretian, Quezon City.

National Census and Statistics Office (NCSO) 1980, *Census of Population and Housing: Metro Manila*, Republic of the Philippines, Manila.

Pedrosa, C. 1987, *The Rise and Fall of Imelda Marcos*, Bookmark, Manila.

Philippines Free Press

Pinches, M. 1977, 'Squatters, Planning and Politics in Tondo, Manila' *Asian Bureau Australia Newsletter* 32, pp.11-18.

Pinches, M. 1985, 'The Urban Poor' in May, R. & Nemenzo, F (eds), *The Philippines after Marcos*, Croom Helm, London, pp 152-163.

Pinches, M. 1986, *A Rocky Road to the Promised Land: Squatters, Oligarches and the State in the Philippines - A Case Study*, unpublished paper.

Pinches, M. 1987(a), '"All that we have is our Muscle and Sweat": the Rise of Wage Labour in a Manila Squatter Community' in Pinches, M. & Lakha, S. (eds), *Wage Labour and Social Change: the Proletariat in Asia and the Pacific*, Centre of Southeast Asian Studies, Monash University, Clayton, pp. 103-140.

Pinches, M. 1987(b), 'People Power and the Urban Poor: The Politics of Unity and Division in Manila' in Krinks, P. (ed), *The Philippines Under Aquino*, Development Studies Network, Australian National University, Canberra, pp. 85-102.

Pinches, M. 1989, 'Sending People Up: Industrial Structure and Primordial Sentiments in the Making of Philippine Elevator Workers', *Anthropological Forum* VI (1), pp.7-26.

Pinches, M. 1992(a), 'The Working Class Experience of Shame, Inequality and People Power in Tatalon, Manila' in B.Kerkvliet & R.Mojares (eds), *From Marcos to Aquino: Local Perspectives on Political Transition in the Philippines*, University of Hawaii Press, Honolulu, pp. 166-186.

Pinches, M. 1992(b), 'Proletarian Ritual: Class Degradation and the Dialectics of Resistance in Manila', *Pilipinas* 19, pp.69-92.

Poethig, R. 1969, 'An Urban Squatter Policy for Metropolitan Manila', *Solidarity* 4(11), pp.20-32.

Poethig, R. 1971, 'Two Views: Roofing the Urban Squatters', *Solidarity* 6(6), pp.15-28.

Ramos, C. 1961, 'Manila's Metropolitan Problem', *Philippine Journal of Public Administration* 5 (2), pp.89-117.

Ramos-Jimenez, P. Chiong-Javier, M. & Sevilla, J. 1986, *Philippine Urban Situation Analysis*, UNICEF, Manila.

Reed, R. 1978, *Colonial Manila: The Context of Hispanic Urbanism and Process of Morphogenesis*, University of California Press, Berkeley.

Robertson, C. et al 1977, 'Professional Elitism or Community Control? The Manila Housing Competition', *Australian and New Zealand Journal of Sociology* 13 (1), pp.75-81.

Rosenberg, D. (ed) 1979, *Marcos and Martial Law in the Philippines*, Cornell University Press, Ithaca.

Sembrano, M. Imperial, S. & Felix, N. 1977, *Case Studies on the Improvement of Slums, Squatter and Rural Settlements: the Philippines*, Institute of Philippine Culture, Ateneo de Manila University, Quezon City.

Serrote, E. 1987/1988, 'Urban Planning and State Corporatism: The Philippine Experience Under Martial Law', *Philippine Planning Journal* XIX (1, 2), pp.59-69.

South China Morning Post Jan 31 1982, p.9.

Stinner, W. & Bacol-Montilla 1981, 'Population Deconcentration in Metropolitan Manila in the Twentieth Century', *The Journal of Developing Areas* 16 (1), pp.3-16.

Stone, R. & Marsella, J. 1968, 'Mahirap: A Squatter Community in a Manila Suburb' in Bello, W. & de Guzman, A. (eds), *Modernisation: Its Impact in the Philippines* (vol 3), Ateneo de Manila University Press, Quezon City.

Stone, R. 1973, *Philippine Urbanisation: The Politics of Public and Private Property in Greater Manila*, Centre for Southeast Asian Studies, Northern Illinois University, DeKalb.

Swan, P. Wegelin, E. & Panchee, K. 1983, *Management of Sites and Services Housing Schemes: the Asian Experience*, John Wiley and Sons, Chichester.

Tekie, M. 1989, 'Low Income Housing in Metropolitan Manila, the Philippines' in Swindell, K. et al (eds), *Inequality and Development: Case Studies from the Third World*, Macmillan, London, pp. 201-222.

Tobias, G. 1982, 'Interview: G.V.Tobias On the "Last Campaign" Against Squatting', *Pananaw* 5(5), pp.18-21.

Tondo Foreshore Development Authority (TFDA) n.d., *'The Cry of Tondo' - The Beginning of the Fulfilment* (brochure), Republic of the Philippines, Manila.

Turner, J. 1976, H*ousing by People*, Marion Boyers, London.

Turner, M. 1990, 'Authoritarian Rule and the Dilemma of Legitimacy' *The Pacific Review* 3 (4), pp.349-362.

van Naerssen, T. 1989, 'Continuity and change in the urban poor movement of Manila, the Philippines' in Schurrman, F. & van Naerssen, T. (eds), *Urban Social Movements in the Third World*, Routledge, London, pp. 199-219.

Viloria, J. & Williams, D. 1987, 'Evaluation of Community Upgrading Programs in Metro Manila' in Skinner, R. *et al* (eds), *Shelter Upgrading for the Urban Poor: Evaluation of Third World Experience*, Island Pub., Manila, pp. 11-37.

Viloria, L. 1971, 'Manila' in Laquian, A.(ed), *Rural Urban Migrants and Metropolitan Development*, Intermet, Toronto, pp. 135-150.

Ward, P. & Macoloo, G. 1992, 'Articulation Theory and Self-Help Housing Practice in the 1990s', *International Journal of Urban and Regional Research* 16 (1), pp.60-80.

Zaragoza, R. 1990, *Old Manila*, Oxford University Press, Singapore.

Zialcita, F. 1991, 'The Wood and Stone House and its Southeast Asian Cousins', *Solidarity* No 131–132, pp.32–45.

ACKNOWLEDGMENTS

The collection of material presented in this essay was made possible through support from a range of institutional sources: the Department of Architecture and Building, University of Melbourne; the Department of Anthropology and Sociology, Monash University; the Institute of Philippine Culture, Ateneo de Manila University; and the Department of Anthropology, University of Western Australia. Particular thanks to Charles Robertson and the late Michael Swift, who long ago encouraged the author to combine interests in architecture and anthropology. Thanks also to Al McCoy who more recently urged the author to return to this combined interest. Special thanks to the National Housing Authority personnel who assisted in the Philippines. Most of all the author is indebted to his wife Lenny, and to friends and informants in Tatalon and Tondo who remain the main source of inspiration.

2

Hanoi townscape: symbolic imagery in Vietnam's capital

◆

William S. Logan

FIRST IMPRESSIONS

In January 1990 the author set out on a first visit to Hanoi, capital of the Socialist Republic of Vietnam, on a consultancy 'mission' for the United Nations Educational Scientific and Cultural Organisation (UNESCO). The purpose of the visit was to assist the local planners prepare a strategy to attract international financial and technical support for the protection of the city's 'Old Sector'[1]. At the time the author's mental picture of Hanoi was of a city largely destroyed by American bombers during the Vietnam War (1955-75) or by the earlier war against the French (1946-54). It was puzzling why UNESCO should be showing such interest in Hanoi and a preliminary library search had provided few clues, there being almost no details of Hanoi's urban environment in print in English. However, far from being a city destroyed, it was found on arrival to be a fascinating city with an Old Sector still substantially intact, much of it dating from the nineteenth century but with a scatter of ancient pagodas and temples often dating back more than 800 years (Figure 2.1).

The highly politicised role of the media reporting on the Vietnam War - on both sides of the conflict - is well recognised[2]. Nevertheless, the extent to which the images of the capital city, its life and environment were distorted was unexpected. Hanoi had es-caped devastation; indeed, it stands as a remarkable monument to the perseverance of an urban culture against terrible odds. Another equally striking testimony to the ability of the Vietnamese to adapt and survive is the multilayered character of Hanoi's cultural environment, each layer the legacy of a period of political and cultural domination by an external power, notably China, France and the Soviet Union. With extraordinary flexibility and resilience, the Vietnamese have been able to incorporate these alien influences into their own culture and cultural landscapes - indeed, to such an extent that, to the outsider at least, the contribution of authentically Vietnamese cultural factors to the creation of Hanoi's landscape is difficult to discern.

Since the Australian ambassador of the time, Graham Alliband (1988-91) had played a large part in encouraging the Vietnamese planners at the National Institute for Urban and Rural Planning (NIURP) to take action to protect the Old Sector, an early visit was made to the Australian Embassy in Ly Thuong Kiet Street (Figure 2.2). The area in which the embassy is located is known as the 'French' or 'Western Quarter' and forms the southern half of Hanoi's Old Sector. Designed by the French colonial authorities, who controlled northern Vietnam as the Protectorate of Tonkin from the 1880s until the battle of Dien

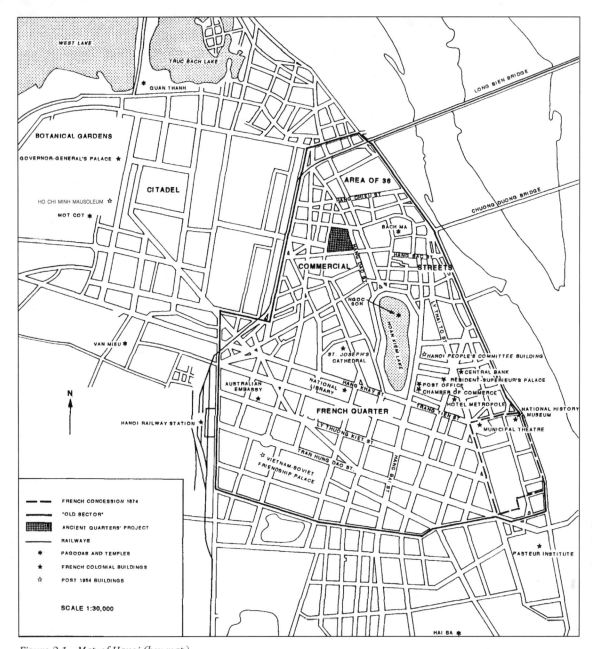

Figure 2.1   Map of Hanoi (key map)

Bien Phu in 1954, the area's streets follow a pattern typical of French town planning of mid-to-late nineteenth century - broad boulevards, neatly cobble-stoned and kerbed, and lined with trees, wide footpaths, decorative iron or masonry fences and stuccoed villas and office buildings.

In contrast within a short block or two of the Australian Embassy are other landmark buildings, including several dating from far more distant eras. The Quan Su ('Ambassadors') pagoda stands diagonally opposite - one of the most colourful and well-patronised Buddhist complexes in Hanoi (Figure 2.3).

Figure 2.2   *The Australian embassy in Hanoi bears all of the hallmarks of early twentieth-century French provincial architecture. Its restoration under the direction of David Abotomey is one of the better examples of Vietnam's opening up to modern architectural approaches. On the other hand, fifty-six Vietnamese residents had to be rehoused -presumably in suburban housing estates - when the building was allocated to the Australian Government.* (Source: W.S. Logan)

Built in the twelfth century, it is a significant monument representative of the precolonial period when Vietnam enjoyed independence - but is it culturally Vietnamese or is it merely Chinese, a reflection in the landscape of the earlier 1000-year period of incorporation within the Middle Kingdom (111 BC - 939 AD) and the longer period of suzerainty over northern Vietnam?

At the end of Quan Su Street, just beyond the turn-

Figure 2.3   *The Quan Su Pagoda, comprising main worship hall and multiple altars, teaching and dormitory buildings on three sides and front courtyard and entrance gate surrounded by flower and Buddha stick sellers.* (Source: W.S. Logan)

of-the-century offices built to house the French Indochinese Union Railways headquarters (Figure 2.4), stands yet another contrasting building - the Vietnam-Soviet Friendship Palace (Figure 2.5). This was built in the modern international style as interpreted by a team of Soviet architects headed by Garony Isakovitch. Like others built during the period 1955-90 when the former Union of Soviet Socialist Republics (USSR) was Vietnam's main source of foreign aid and expertise, its architecture owes little to the local culture; rather, it was based on a prototype project for an exhibition and sporting hall developed in Moscow for replication around the Soviet Union and its dependencies. The United States, the Soviet's rival on the world stage and here in Vietnam, had a far more hostile impact at the end of adjacent Tran Hung Dao Street where Hanoi's main

Figure 2.4   *The French Indochinese Union Railways building, like most colonial buildings in Hanoi now suffering severe physical deterioration due to poor maintenance.* (Source: W.S. Logan)

Figure 2.5   The Vietnam-Soviet Friendship Palace, a reinforced concrete monument overpowering surrounding buildings. (Source: W.S. Logan)

railway terminal - the Ha-Noi Ga (the word itself deriving from the French 'gare') - closes off the vista (Figure 2.6). The only major building in the Old Sector obviously to have suffered from aerial attacks during the war years, its main pavilion was destroyed by a laser-guided 'smart bomb' during an American B52 raid in December 1972. The two wings were left standing, their French architecture still intact, and now are connected by a concrete brick building of little architectural significance.

To the observer, fragmented impressions soon gelled, making it apparent that Hanoi's townscape was not the product of chance forces, nor even merely the result of architectural and town-planning fashions changing over time; rather, each of the successive political regimes set out deliberately to impose on Hanoi its own set of beliefs about the way in which urban centres should function. Each regime proceeded to design buildings, streetscapes and

whole districts to demonstrate those beliefs, and, by so doing, also to demonstrate its mastery of the city and its people. As a result, and perhaps more explicitly than in most other Southeast Asian cities, Hanoi's environment is strewn with political icons. Beyond this, each regime attempted to define, for the people, which elements of the urban environment were to be regarded as symbolically significant, treasured as part of the city's 'heritage' and protected against physical damage.

This case study draws on the literature in the fields of geography, sociology and anthropology dealing with urban iconography, that is, the theoretical and historical study of symbolic imagery and the symbolic meanings of places (Cosgrove & Daniels 1988, p.1)[3]. The paper attempts to explore the urbanistic intentions of these various regimes controlling Hanoi and to describe the resulting impacts on the cultural landscape. For the purposes of this analysis, Hanoi's political history has been divided into three broad periods: the long precolonial Vietnamese era from its nomination as capital city by Ly Thai To, the first king of the Ly dynasty, in AD 1010 to the first French territorial claims in 1873; the French colonial period from 1873-1954; and the period since 1955 when the Vietnamese regained independence but came under the tutelage of the Soviet bloc countries, especially the Russians who did not finally quit Vietnam until 1990.

In addition the case study also investigates the attitudes and actions of Hanoi's decision-makers in the

Figure 2.6   Hanoi Railway Station, rebuilt since the December 1972 blitz and always the scene of frenetic activity. (Source: W.S. Logan)

current period which, overlapping with the period of Soviet influence, dates from the Sixth National Congress of the Vietnamese Communist Party in 1986. It was at this congress that Vietnam embarked upon a process of economic renovation, called *Doi Moi* (renovation), and began opening up to Western economic and social (though not yet political) ideas. The final section of the study asks three main questions: what political icons, if any, will be built in the 1990s to herald these new 'Doi Moi' policies? how will the politicians and planners of this new age treat the icons of previous periods? is it inevitable that Western aesthetic, architectural and heritage protection ideas and ideals will infiltrate the Vietnamese setting?

Other important issues are also raised: How is the cultural heritage of the city to be defined? Who by? Will the process of definition continue to be politically motivated or is 'grass-roots' lobbying beginning to have an impact on environmental decision-making? What is the role of professional town planners and architects in this process? To what extent will a new twenty-first century Hanoi, including a conserved 'Old Sector' (if, indeed, it is conserved) come to reflect the power structures and socio-political attitudes of the 1990s? On a more theoretical level, is Hanoi about to demonstrate once again that 'instability of meaning', which Cosgrove & Daniels (1988, p.7) describe as both an inherent feature of cultural history and a main preoccupation in today's post-modern apprehension of the world?

THE CHINESE BASIS OF FEUDAL HANOI PRE-1873

As its name suggests, Indochina lies between Asia's two major blocks, India and China, a shatter belt both geographically and culturally, bearing the impacts of Indian and Chinese expansion on the indigenous peoples and their civilisations. Although almost contemporary, the processes of expansion of these two powers, and their effects, contrast strikingly. Groslier (1961, p.39) described the differences well: India's stay was short-lived and merely sowed the seeds of cultural change, particularly among the peoples who formed the Champa kingdom (third to seventeenth centuries) in the middle and southern parts of Vietnam, later known as Annam and

Cochinchina respectively, whereas China's dominance was total.

In 214 BC China simply annexed Tonkin (the northern section of Vietnam based on the Red River delta) and proceeded to expand down the coastal plain into Vietnam's middle section, Annam. Over the next 1000 years, Vietnam was transformed into one of China's own provinces, indistinguishable politically from the many other provinces in its vast empire. China imposed its civilisation by wiping out most of the cultural heritage of the dominant class so that, even though independence was regained in AD 938, the Vietnamese urban elite remained sinicised and its art, architecture and other cultural forms continued to follow Chinese models. A key point, therefore, in understanding the history of Hanoi's transformation is that the townscape basis onto which the colonists in the nineteenth and twentieth centuries grafted their architectural and planning influences was largely Chinese. Indeed, it is astonishing that, despite two millennia of foreign cultural dominance, the people's own sense of being Vietnamese, rather than Chinese, miraculously survived. The crucial fact that China was unable to supplant the Vietnamese spoken language helps explain the survival of the Vietnamese identity and the regaining of independence[4].

With the annexation of Tonkin, the Chinese incorporated it administratively into the province of Giao-Chi and destroyed the traditional Vietnamese ruling class. Despite brief periods of revolt under the Trung sisters (AD 39-43) and Ly-Bon (AD 544), the territory remained Chinese until AD 938. The previous capital of Co-Loa, 20 kilometres from Hanoi, was destroyed and its Dong-son culture crushed under the Han culture of the north. Tonkin was reorganised in Chinese style: its administrative structure became that of province, military command and prefecture, and Chinese administrative codes were imposed. Chinese ideographs became the official script - indeed the first form of writing known to the Vietnamese. It is usually claimed that the Chinese taught the local people how to control river flooding and reclaim land for production by building dykes. The reclaimed compartments established the geographical pattern of villages that soon formed, and the peasants were tied to the land thereafter in a constant struggle with

Figure 2.7   The Van Mieu temple of literature, a vast Confucist complex of religious, teaching and residential buildings within an enclosing wall. (Source: W.S. Logan)

nature. However Duiker (1986, p.2) challenges this view on the basis of recent archaeological evidence which suggests that the earlier Vietnamese civilisation had mastered irrigation and wet rice cultivation techniques already, as well as bronze casting and other economic and artistic skills.

The local rulers and intelligentsia quickly adopted Chinese ways, a political act, bending with the political wind, as well as a recognition of the 'superiority' of Chinese culture. A command of Chinese literature and script became the key to the mandarinate, to wealth and fame, and was insisted upon by the Vietnamese themselves as much as by the Chinese: it was the chief way in which the Vietnamese elite was able to maintain its position of power. The special status of Chinese meant that the intellectual life of urban Vietnam was sinicised and remained such long after Chinese political control ended. Imposing buildings were constructed to house the mandarin examination system - in Hanoi, the Confucist Van Mieu temple in the eleventh century (Figure 2.7) and the Thi Huong Examination Site where the gruelling triennial examinations were held. While the first remains as a major symbol of this period of Chinese dominance, the latter was demolished during the early French years to make room for a new Chamber of Commerce building, now the National Library of Vietnam.

According to Groslier (1961, p.232), Vietnamese cultural achievements - whether in literature, art or architecture - were 'never more than a mediocre reflexion of China'. In architectural terms, he argued,

only the 'dinh', or communal house, stands out (Figure 2.8). Built in each village, often on timber piles, they are said to resemble the houses represented on drums from the Dong-son period found during the excavations of Co-Loa. Many of the villages around Hanoi were engulfed by the expanding city in the late nineteenth and the twentieth centuries and their 'dinh' swallowed up by shops and houses. Now that the traditional social structures have succumbed to a century of change - firstly, Westernisation along French lines and then socialisation since 1954 - some 'dinh' have been turned into multifamily dwellings and have lost their original significance as places of religious and communal ceremony.

Other religious buildings - notably Buddhist pagodas or 'chua' and Taoist dynastic temples or 'den' - are almost entirely Chinese in character. Built in timber with cross beams and typically supported by columns standing *on* rather than being inserted *into* stone plinths set in the ground, these often look older than they in fact are - or, at least, while they may have existed on their sites for upwards of 800 years, their fabric usually dates from more recent times as the result of renovation or rebuilding[5]. The famous Mot-Cot Pagoda (Figure 2.9), for instance, has stood since AD 1049 but was completely restored in 1922. The Bach Ma ('White Horse') Temple (Figure 2.10) has been renovated six times since it was erected in the eleventh century, the last time being in 1930. By comparison with architecture in the West, Chinese

Figure 2.8   A dinh in Pho Hang Bac ('Silver Street'), now housing a score of families. (Source: W.S. Logan) The 'dinhs' served to preserve old social structures and were closer to the people than the Confucian temples built for the scholars.

Figure 2.9   The badly-weathered Chua Mot-Cot (One-Column Pagoda) before being restored by the École Française d'Extrême-Orient in 1922. (Source: Archives Photographiques Musée National des Arts Asiatiques - Guimet. © R.M.N.)

styles varied little over time, making the visual dating of heritage buildings more hazardous: to the untrained eye, the Ngoc Son Pagoda, on Jade Island in central Hanoi's Hoan Kiem Lake, is deceptively like the Hai Ba ('Two Sisters') Temple dedicated to the Trung sisters on the southern edge of Hanoi's Old Sector but, in fact, the former was built in 1864 whereas the latter is older by half a millennium.

North of Hoan Kiem Lake is the 'Area of the 36 Commercial Streets', known as the 'Native Quarter' in French colonial times. Here the street pattern and street names hark back to feudal times although most of the building fabric postdates the arrival of the French. Traders appear to have lived in this area since Hanoi's establishment and the irregular pattern of narrow streets, called 'hang', was well developed by

the fifteenth century. Each of the various craftspeople guilds and traders corporations came to control its own length of street, separated from the others by gates which were sealed off at night. The names borne by the streets today refer to these guilds and corporations - Hang Bac (Silversmith Street), Hang Dao (Silk Street), Hang Duong (Sugar Street), Hang Bo (Basket Street) - even though the functions carried out in them have changed and new functional groupings have emerged. Masson (1929) described the area in the 1870s as having a very dense population, three-quarters occupied by small Vietnamese artisans and stall-keepers and one-quarter by large traders of Chinese origin. The central axis appears to have been Hang Chieu (Plaited Mat Street), now a minor commercial street leading to the only remaining gate in the feudal city's walls (see Figure 2.11).

In 1883, when the French forced the Vietnamese to sign a treaty making Tonkin a French 'protectorate', the town was in a state of chaos: indeed the whole province of Hanoi had been the scene of murder, looting and arson by a group of Chinese pirates and irregulars known as the Black Flags[6]. The Chinese traders' houses had been built of brick and survived the fires; less lucky were the Vietnamese houses most of which were bamboo huts, covered with straw, reeds and leaves. Essentially the commercial town had to be built again and this took place under the French, only to suffer once again severe damage from artillery fire, bombs and fire in the period after World War Two when the Vietnamese and French fought bitterly for control of the city.

The building type which characterises the com-

Figure 2.10   Den Bach Ma with adjacent modern hotel. (Source: W.S. Logan)

Figure 2.11   1880 Lithograph of the Jean Dupuis Gate in Pho. Hang Chieu (Source: L'Illustration. Journal Universel*) Saved by the EFEO in 1905 from demolition when the street was being widened to improve traffic flow and clean up the area, it remains today as the sole surviving city gate.*

mercial quarter is the 'shop-house', or 'tube house'. No doubt having their origin in makeshift stalls on the street line, these houses have widths of around 3 metres, a limit set by the maximum length of available timber beams; but their depths ranged from 60 to 100 metres. Until recent years, shop-houses were rarely more than two storeys in height: indeed, until at least the middle of the nineteenth century, there was strict adherence to Article 156 of the royal 'Annamite Code' prohibiting commoners from erecting buildings in brick or of more than a single storey (Azambre 1958, p.281). Royal decree also prohibited the external decoration of houses. The design of shop-houses gives as many families as possible a room fronting onto the street from which to conduct business; behind this are storage spaces, workshops and residential spaces, interspersed with courtyards which provide access to light, ventilation and rainwater. One of the most distinctive features of Hanoi's commercial quarter is the repetition of stepped parapet walls between tiled shop-house roofs, most easily seen in nineteenth-century illustrations (eg. Figure 2.11) but now obscured by the street trees which have matured over the ensuing period.

However the building form itself is far from unique, being found in cities throughout Southeast Asia. Viaro (1992) refers to the numerous recent studies insisting on the critical role of Chinese immigrant communities in the development of Southeast Asian cities and seeks to determine whether the shop-house can be said to be a Chinese architectural creation. His conclusion is that, even if there are Chinese elements in the building techniques and especially the decor of shop-houses in Southeast Asian cities, the shop-house as an architectural type owes its expansion and manner of grouping into terraces to the influence of the European colonial authorities, notably the Dutch in Indonesia and the British in Singapore, Malaysia and Burma. His explanation does not work well for Hanoi where shop-houses clearly predated the arrival of the French authorities as illustrations of the time indicated (see Figure 2.11). If Viaro's explanation is followed, the Chinese immigrant community in feudal Hanoi must have brought with it notions of architectural design and knowledge of building technology already established under the colonial regimes in place in China. Whatever its origin, the French colonial authority accepted the design sense of the shop-houses and only sought to impose regulations on building materials, amount of ventilation and other performance standards.

Here one begins to see that it is the grouping of urban features rather than the individual elements themselves that makes Hanoi specially significant: the pagodas and shop-houses taken individually have limited architectural value on a world scale, but, together, they form a rich urban complex of undoubted heritage significance. Moreover, Hanoi's heritage is not restricted to monuments alone, but also includes the spatial relations between them - 'the way things are together in space', as prominent French architect Henri Gaudin calls it[7] - something that architectural historians have generally overlooked in their interpretation of cultural heritage.

So far the religious and commercial areas and buildings have been described. To complete the picture of the spatial features which constituted feudal Hanoi as the first French colonists found it, now must be added the citadel or walled palace, the symbol of military power and political control, the prime movers behind Hanoi's existence.

Chinese cities typically performed military and internal security functions, as symbolised by the citadel at their centre. With the introduction of Chinese political control and administrative organisation (especially taxation) into Vietnam, it was inevitable that citadels would be needed and cities would develop along the same lines as in southern China. And, indeed, a number of citadels were established, many of them - Co-Loa, Thang-Long or Ha-Noi, Dong-Do, Hue - playing the role of Vietnamese capital as successive rulers chose from time to time to relocate their court and build anew. Thus the king Ly Thai To chose for the site of his new royal residence an area of swampy ground in the bend of the Red River[8] and in 1014 surrounded it with a 4700-metre earthen wall (Azambre 1958, p.265).

Three sets of factors would have dictated the king's choice, according to Bézacier (1952, p.190). The first two - political and military considerations - are clearly seen: the site was at the centre of the area to be administered, was on productive soil, well populated and accessible, and was in a flat delta location where advancing enemies could be seen at a fair distance. But the third set of factors - the ancient Chinese sciences of geomancy and astrology - was always present in royal building, often outweighing the other two or at least causing a modification of choices based on them. A combination of climate and geomantic principles, for instance, set the orientation of citadels towards the south: to avoid the cold north winds and the penetrating rays of the rising and setting sun and to provide a spatial arrangement unfavourable to evil spirits (Phan 1986, p.44). In Hanoi's case, the orientation is in fact displaced to north-north-east/south-south-west. Geomantic principles also determined the precise site chosen: a 'royal screen' of hills or forest to the south was required to protect the citadel and especially the royal palace from pernicious influences; the topography of the site had to allow the citadel's plan to take the propitious form of a White Tiger ('Bach Ho') and Blue Dragon ('Thanh Long'); and a winding river, the To Lich, tributary to the Red River, was needed to irrigate the 'magnetic field' (Bézacier 1952, p.191). When one of these elements was lacking, it was for people to improve upon nature and to erect screens for protection, raise mounds to provide better surveillance or dig ditches to create streams.

The architectural plan, too, was tightly controlled by these principles so that a citadel constructed for a Chinese governor looked exactly the same as one built for a Vietnamese king: it comprised the royal palace surrounded by high walls -the 'Forbidden City' - and several sets of outer walls, forming a rectangle or square and, complete with towers and moats, acting as lines of military defence. At Hanoi, a series of tumuli were built up to provide high points. The highest, the 'Nung-son' or 'hill where the dragon sits', was the site chosen by Ly Thai To for his palace. Observers in the seventeenth century noted that the solid walls, ramparts and moats had disappeared, probably reflecting the relative political stability of the time (Azambre 1958, p.269). On the south side of the citadel, however, on another artificial tumuli, this one dedicated to the planet Mars and the element of Fire which governed the South, the Le kings had built a large 'mirador' or 'flagstaff' tower. A tower still stands on this site, although the current one was not completed until as recently as 1912.

The shape of Vietnam's citadels was only modified at the start of the nineteenth century when Emperor Gia-Long, founder of the Nguyen dynasty, under the influence of French army engineers, introduced Vauban-style fortified walls. It was also Gia-Long who shifted his court from Hanoi to Hue, re-modelling the pre-existing citadel at Hue into a new capital, once again in Chinese style replete with Forbidden City, ceremonial buildings and enclosures but surrounded by Vauban fortifications. Hanoi maintained much of its importance as a regional capital and its citadel survived intact until late in the century when it was demolished by the French colonial authorities. The motive for this act of vandalism was not the desire to eliminate a military threat to France's hold on Hanoi. Vauban walls had in fact been rendered ineffective long ago by advances in military technology, particularly the invention of cannons firing explosive shells. The citadel was destroyed now because it represented the wrong symbolism - the old Vietnamese regime - and it was to be replaced by other landscape icons heralding and soon celebrating France's civilising mission to its Asian colonies.

THE FRENCH 'MISSION CIVILISATRICE' 1873-1954

The first Europeans - Portuguese, Dutch and English traders seeking to buy silk and spices in return for European goods - arrived in Vietnam in 1626, but, finding the markets poor and the location too distant from major shipping routes, disappeared again by the end of the century. It was left to the French to colonise this part of Southeast Asia in any permanent sense. In the case of the French in Vietnam, missionaries - starting with Alexandre de Rhodes at Hanoi in 1627 - preceded traders. Despite Vietnamese imperial bans on proselytising, the priests had considerable impact, including the introduction of the unique *quoc ngu* romanised system of writing the Vietnamese tonal language. It was harassment of the missionaries which, only much later, led France to intervene militarily in Cochinchina in 1858-59 and Tonkin in 1873. After taking the Hanoi citadel, the French troops had withdrawn the following year under the *Philastre Agreement* to a 2.5-hectare Concession on the banks of the Red River southeast of the commercial quarter where they began to create a settlement along European organisational and architectural lines. Ten years later, the citadel was reoccupied, the French commandant taking up residence in the old royal palace and turning the Thi Huong Examination Site into a military post. The Protectorate of Tonkin was established with Hanoi as its capital and, in 1887, Hanoi became capital of the French Indochinese Union comprising Tonkin, Annam, Cochinchina, Cambodia and Laos, a status it enjoyed until after World War Two.

Masson (1929) calls the first phase of French settlement the *période héroïque*, characterised by bold steps to tame the place they had acquired, to subdue the population and overcome the most urgent of Hanoi's many environmental problems, both social and physical. Later, from the 1890s, they turned to improvements of a more sophisticated nature, much more a reflection of the ideas current in metropolitan France or adopted in other French colonies than a reflection of Hanoi's specific characteristics. Both periods left distinctive marks on the townscape, sets of icons that say much about the prevailing attitudes of the colonial authorities and the architects, town planners, engineers and builders who worked for them.

France's military power was quickly demonstrated by the development of its Concession and, in the 1870s, buildings were constructed to accommodate the army headquarters and barracks, military hospi-

tal, mapping and other units. The first consulate was built here, soon to be enlarged to house the first *Résident-Supérieur* of Tonkin and the Governor-General of the French Indochinese Union. A drastic remodelling of the citadel further showed who held the reins: not only were the walls and moats removed to make way for a new grid of road reservations (see Figure 2.12), but, in the years 1886-87, the artillery headquarters was constructed on the site of the royal Kinh Thien Palace itself (Nguyen Quoc Thong 1988, p.42). A well-protected road was established to link the Concession and citadel, thus setting in place Hanoi's key east-west axis, today's Trang Tien Street. Called the Pearl-Inlaid Tray Street by the Vietnamese but renamed Rue Paul Bert by the French in honour of the first *Résident-Supérieur* of Tonkin, it was widened in 1886 from its original 3-metre width to 18 metres, at the cost of the original Vietnamese houses along it and the historic gate at its eastern end, and soon became Hanoi's main commercial thoroughfare. Railway lines and improved roads to the interior were opened up, the fluvial port dredged, and customs house and railway station constructed.

In the 1880s the administrative buildings on the Concession were relocated in a new government complex at the south-eastern corner of Hoan Kiem Lake on the east-west axis. Old symbols of authority were demolished in the process: the imposing Chua Bao An complex of religious buildings erected in 1842 gave way to the post office, treasury buildings and Resident's palace and adjacent offices designed by architect Henri Vildieu; while to construct the Town Hall - Hanoi was proclaimed a municipality in 1888 - the Champa-style Chua Tao, or Temple of Supreme Reason was torn down. The Bank of Indochina's first head office, the Hotel Métropole and several private mansions completed the rebuilding of this once-sacred precinct. A new Governor-General's palace was constructed on one corner of the botanical gardens, necessitating the demolition of the Mieu Hoi Dong Pagoda claimed by the Vietnamese elders to be over 1000 years old (Hanoi Archives, RST Files 56.735, 58.806). The architecture of the new buildings was *Beaux-Arts*[9] in form and decoration, the Renaissance classical building forms and baroque ornamental details straight out of provincial France: it had no connection with the Vietnamese culture

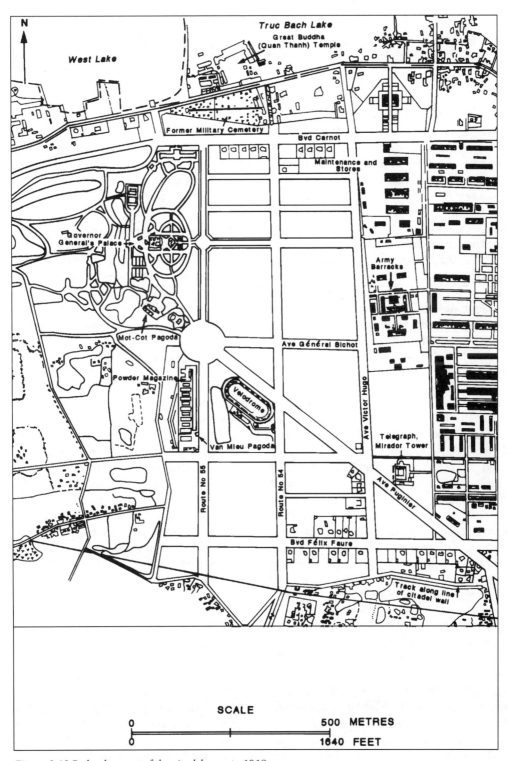

Figure 2.12 Redevelopment of the citadel area to 1918

and was in many ways quite ill-suited to Vietnamese climatic conditions.

The French missionaries' early efforts to tend to the spiritual health of the *indigènes* seemed to bear fruit in 1886 when Monseigneur Puginier inaugurated the square-towered St Joseph Cathedral (on the site of the Bao Thien Pagoda which the French demolished). The physical health of the colonists and local population was also of concern and subsequently Hoan Kiem's banks were freed of the ring of shambling stilt huts and its waters cleansed by the diversion of household wastes. The filling-in of the hundreds of swamps and ponds in and around Hanoi, generally with sands from the Red River, and the construction of water channels and pumping stations helped reduce the problems of malaria and dysentery. Work started on a system of fresh water supply and major streets were lit with gas, then electricity. In the built-up Area of 36 Commercial Streets, roads were straightened and widened, the residents being forced to comply with planning orders to conform to the new street alignments with no form of compensation. The gates between the various guild areas were removed and the old wall, at that time still running along the east side of the city and used to protect the city from floods, was dismantled. The French Quarter was laid out with its rectangular pattern of avenues 20 to 30 metres wide and large housing blocks to take villas and gardens, the healthy suburban lifestyle by then in coming into vogue in the affluent Western cities. Within 20 years these blocks were filling up with ornate villas with white and ochre lime-washed walls and green timber trim.

By the turn of the century, more substantial public amenities were being built. Of these, the municipal theatre (known often as the 'opera house') was the most extravagant: not completed until 1911, it was very French in inspiration - an attempt to replicate the Garnier opera house in Paris. And, just as Garnier's opera continues to be viewed as a window onto the Second Empire France, 1852-70 (Woolf, in Cosgrove & Daniels 1988, p.214), Hanoi's opera reflects the swelling cultural ambitions of the colonial authorities during the *période héroïque*. Also characteristically French, it was sited in baroque town-planning style at the convergence of important roads and closing off a key vista along Rue Paul Bert, by now lined

with fashionable shops and cafes. An ornamental bandstand in Paul Bert Square near Hoan Kiem Lake had become a social meeting point for the warm evenings and a Philharmonic Society built an impressive edifice further along the lakeside. Hanoi began to see itself as the *Paris de l'Annam*. The colony celebrated its growing status in style in 1902 with a major 'exposition', for which the race course was commandeered for the construction of a major complex of buildings, later converted to the Maurice Long Museum. But, in the long run, the establishment of the École Française d'Extrême-Orient (EFEO) by Governor-General Paul Doumer in 1898 was a more important event in Hanoi's cultural life - for this organisation quickly became an effective documenter and protector of the city's precolonial cultural heritage, enabling the Vietnamese residents of Hanoi to maintain their cultural links with the past, or, at least, with those elements which the French deemed worthy of maintaining as Vietnamese heritage.

The French authorities' activities in Hanoi during the *période héroïque* support Gwendolyn Wright's (1987, p.298) representation of the nineteenth-century colonial period as one of fairly naked 'assimilationist' policies: if the indigenous people were to 'progress', they were expected to adopt French behavioural patterns and cultural mores, use the French language and build in the French architectural style. But gradually the attitudes of politicians back home and of Tonkin's rulers - or at least of reformist Governor-Generals like Albert Sarraut (1911-14 and 1916-20) and Maurice Long (1920-24) - seem to have shifted. In the years before World War One, controversy raged in France over the conduct of the Indochinese colonies. Criticism was on both economic and social grounds: production in the colonies had failed to cover expenditure (a situation that only changed in the 1930s) and the Indochinese authorities had acquired a reputation of insensitivity in its dealings with the indigenous peoples.

In April 1909 the Chamber of Deputies called for new policies in all colonies based on giving more visible attention to the needs, wishes and cultures of the colonised peoples (Wright 1991, p.190). In the face of this, the Governor-Generals were determined to continue their modernisation programs but to do so in ways that would win greater support from the indigenous population as well as the colonists. Some improvements in schooling for the Vietnamese were made and educated Vietnamese were admitted to the public service[10]. Architecture and town planning were part of this effort. Modernisation included the development of the first comprehensive and co-ordinated 'master plans' for Hanoi and other major cities, with attention being given to town extensions to cope with population and economic growth, to land-use zonation and to traffic circulation. Governor-General Long set up a Town Planning and Architecture Service within the Public Works Ministry in 1923. Greater sensitivity to the local peoples translated into attempts to preserve the traditional cultures, from bolstering the communal leadership structures to historic monument preservation (through the work of the EFEO) and the use of indigenous motifs in architectural decorations. Wright (1987, p.292) calls this a shift from assimilation to policies of association embodying a greater tolerance of indigenous cultures. 'Such officials', Wright says:

> hoped to preserve an established sense of hierarchy and propriety, buttressing it with what they perceived to be traditional rituals, spatial patterns, and architectural ornament, believing that this would reinforce their own superimposed power.

In Hanoi, this attitude and policy shift had its impact mainly through the work of Ernest Hébrard, outstanding *Beaux-Arts*-trained urbanist who had worked on the rebuilding and modernisation of Thessalonika and a number of futuristic 'World City' projects (Gresleri & Matteoni 1982). Invited by Governor-General Long to advise the Indochinese authorities, his work there mainly consisted of master plans for the main cities and for the hill town of Dalat which Doumer had decided would become Indochina's new administrative capital replacing Hanoi. Hébrard's influence was felt in two main ways - architecturally and in terms of town planning. He was responsible for the design of a number of significant buildings which incorporated Indochinese decorative elements based on his extensive field research and which, by the use of verandahs, window canopies and ventilation devices, were better suited to the local climate. Three buildings stand out,

Figure 2.13   The Ministry of Finance Offices designed by Ernest Hébrard incorporates Indochinese decorative elements as well as better means of coping with Hanoi's climate. The building is now occupied by the Ministry for Foreign Affairs. (Source: W.S. Logan).

landmarks still in Hanoi today: the Ministry of Finance (1925-27), now the Ministry of Foreign Affairs (Figure 2.13); the Louis Finot Museum (1925), now the National History Museum (Figure 2.14); and the Pasteur Institute (1925-30), now the Hanoi Microbiology Institute. He organised the Town Planning Service which Long had created and prepared the first Hanoi master plan with extensions to cover the suburban zones to the west and south. The plan sought to keep incompatible land uses apart. This included the continued separation of European from 'Annamite' residential areas and the shifting of industry to Gia-Lam on the left (eastern) bank of the Red River to reduce air pollution problems in the town.

The advances should not be overstated. Hébrard only stayed in the colonies until 1929 and much of his incorporation of traditional cultural elements has

Figure 2.14   Hébrard's Louis Finot Museum, now the National History Museum. The architecture plays with a variety of Asian elements - Chinese/Vietnamese, Japanese, Thai - as befitting a building designed to house the EFEO's Asian artefact collections. (Source: W.S. Logan).

been criticised as being superficial decoration. His master plan was only partially implemented and several other major ministerial buildings did not proceed. While he was relatively enlightened in terms of aesthetics, it is not clear that he was any more politically enlightened than his masters. He continued to advocate racial and class segregation in his planning[11] and, according to Wright, he never saw the Vietnamese architects and planners developing a national style for themselves. He had no interest in designing cheap housing for the poor majority of Vietnamese residents, mostly living in the suburbs. Despite his use of traditional design elements, he was essentially a modernist concerned to develop rational approaches to architecture and planning and he was still imbued with the Haussmannian planning ideals of the nineteenth-century as in his 'World City' projects. Wright (1991, p.217) sums him up in these terms:

> As a traditional Beaux-Arts trained architect, Hébrard could never see his true mission in Indochina as the development of industry or the provision of mass housing. He envisioned his role as that of a master urbanist, giving artistic form and efficient overview to the morphology of entire cities.

Thus when Governor-General Long suggested to him that Hanoi needed new buildings and open spaces 'worthy of a great colony', both the Governor-General and Hébrard had in mind an axially sym-

metrical plan of wide tree-lined boulevards intersecting to create building islands ('îlots'), green spaces and vistas to be enclosed by imposing monuments. This can be seen in his design for the new governmental quarter, one of the main tasks Long had invited Hébrard to Indochina to undertake (Figures 2.15 and 2.17). Wright (1991, p.202) claims that Long detested the Lycée Sarraut recently constructed opposite his Governor-General's palace and decided to build himself a new palace further south and give the existing one to the Colonial Council. Whatever the origin of the plan, it was soon designed by Hébrard and approved by Governor-General Martial Merlin in 1924. Commandeering more of the botanical gardens and old citadel grounds, the plan placed the Governor-General's new palace at the apex of three radiating roads which were to be lined with new ministerial buildings, such as the Ministry of Finance.

Hébrard's mission in Hanoi ground to a halt for a number of reasons: budgetary constraints in the mid-1920s under Merlin and his successor Varenne; the opposition of the engineers in the Public Works Ministry; criticism from the old *colons*, who had previously attacked government expenditure on the *Beaux-Arts* administration buildings as unnecessarily extravagant and who were no less convinced by Hébrard's cultural-relativist works; and finally by the Depression in 1929. His work was, by then, also out of line with the Modern International architecture and urbanism that was sweeping the Western world with its universalist principles. When the next major phase of development in Hanoi got under way in the late 1930s, the Chief of the Town Planning and Architecture Service, Henri Cérutti-Maori, and his deputy, Louis-Georges Pineau, were more attuned to this new thinking. After the French capitulation in 1940 and the occupation of Indochina by the Japanese (1940-45), they were able to continue working for the Vichy-installed Decoux Administration under a pact with Japan which left the French nominally in charge of day-to-day life in the colonies. It was during this time that Cérutti did his most productive architectural and planning work in Hanoi: the sleekly functional Chamber of Commerce building (Figure 2.16) and the 1942 Hanoi master plan with its important extension to the Bay Mau district and the Cité

Figure 2.15   The Governor-General's precinct c.1920. (Source: *Hanoi Archives, National Archives Centre No.1)*

Universitaire in the south. There was little reference to local cultural traditions here - but this was a key point of the Modern International movement.

Figure 2.16   The Chamber of Commerce Building designed by Cérutti and erected in Dinh Tien Hoang Street (formerly Boulevard Francis Garnier) in 1941; now part of Hanoi's central post office. (Source: *W.S. Logan)*

Governor-General Decoux was keen to show that Indochina was progressing and, in architecture and planning, abreast of Europe. The result was a sharp break with the Hébrard line and, in building forms at least, closer to the Soviet-inspired monuments of the next period in Hanoi's cultural history. However, the blending of indigenous with Western design features, for which Hébrard had fought, was taken up by a first wave of professionally trained Vietnamese architects and was not entirely a lost cause (Nguyen Quoc Thong 1988, p.49).

INDEPENDENT SOCIALIST VIETNAM, 1954-86

As with Hébrard's work, events on the international stage got in the way of the full implementation of Cérutti's plans. Although Vietnamese resistance had existed from the first colonial days, now the nationalists made the most of the political turmoil of World War Two - the March 1945 Japanese *coup de*

Figure 2.17 Ernest Hébrard's new governmental district (approved 1924)

force which put an end to the French administration, the fall of Japan shortly after, and the vacuum left in Indochina. In August 1945, the Viet Minh took control of the city. Ho Chi Minh occupied the Resident's palace and declared Vietnam's independence from the steps of 38 Ly Thai To Street. The last days of the Japanese withdrawal had seen much damage by American bombing raids in Hanoi, including the razing of the Maurice Long Museum which had been used by the Japanese as barracks. But this was nothing compared with the death and destruction following France's recapture of Hanoi, with the help of the British and Chinese, in March 1946. 'The sole intellectual bond between Annamites, Cambodians, Laotians is the French culture', declared Saigon-based architect Leo Craste in 1945, 'and Urbanism is one of its elements' (1945, p.97). In fact, 'Urbanism' as well as French intellectual influence generally suffered rather badly in this period: according to Public Works figures, more than 21 per cent of Hanoi's houses were completely destroyed and nearly 8 per cent partially destroyed during 1946 fighting (Hanoi Archives, MR File 803). But these were mostly in Hanoi's suburban zone and the Vietnamese and French public buildings in the old city once again survived.

There ensued another 35 years of wars, first against the French (1946-54) and then the Americans and their Australian, South Korean and other allies (1955-75). In July 1954 the Geneva Accords brought the First War of Independence against the French to a close. Ho Chi Minh's united Vietnam was divided along the 17th parallel and Hanoi became for the next 20 years the capital of the Democratic Republic of Vietnam. The Second War of Independence brought American bombers across Hanoi skies on two main occasions - 1965 and, worse, Christmas 1972. The 1965 bombs struck the French embassy housed in a recycled distillery complex. The Christmas 1972 American bombing raids did little damage to the centre of Hanoi, although the Long Bien (ex-Doumer) bridge and the railway station were damaged and rogue bombs hit suburban Bach Mai Hospital and a residential area behind the station. The number of deaths is difficult to determine: according to Than (1984, p.78), 283 people in the city as a whole were killed and a similar number wounded, but Turley (1975, p.387) gives much larger

figures - 200 in the 1966-67 Operation Rolling Thunder and over 2000 in the December 1972 blitz. After the fall of Saigon in 1975, Hanoi became the capital of a reunited Socialist Republic of Vietnam and the government set about the enormous task of reconstruction. The main tasks confronting independent and united Vietnam were - and still remain -strengthening the national economy and upgrading the people's living conditions, particularly housing. In Hanoi the latter was particularly severe given a massive influx of population from rural areas since World War Two. Progress on reconstruction was delayed by two further wars: the invasion of Cambodia in 1978 and the border war with China in 1979. Peace gradually returned in the 1980s.

Meanwhile Hanoi was expanding rapidly, despite the official registration controls which were supposed to limit internal migration. From around 120 000 in 1943, the number of residents rose to 650 000 in 1960 and, following a redrawing of the municipal boundaries, to 900 000 in 1961 and 1.4 million in 1974. At the 1974 census, Hanoi's inner city held 736 211 people (Turley 1975, pp. 377-9). Municipal Hanoi's population today is estimated to be well over 3 million.

In their planning and construction activities to cope with the exploding city, the socialist Vietnamese authorities rejected Western approaches associated with their colonial enemies and borrowed new ideas from the world revolutionary leader, the Soviet Union. This new cultural alliance had been developing for some time: Ngo Huy Quynh (1991), in his socialist interpretation of Vietnam's architectural history, recalls that the fledgling Vietnamese Communist Party drafted at the time of the unsuccessful uprising of August 1930 was a 'Cultural Revolution' statement which 'made way for a new culture and the liberation of art and architecture from the feudal and colonial periods' (*ibid.* p.160). By the creation of a socialist state in 1954, extended to the South in 1975, art, architecture and town planning became subservient to Party policy: 'Learning from experience, our new architects must carry out the Party's resolutions, developing in our country a national and modern socialist architecture' (*ibid.* p.167). Thus, a new townscape began to be created, with icons demonstrating the brotherly links between Vietnam and the Soviet bloc countries. These socialist links were further entrenched in 1978 when America, to support Beijing in its argument with Hanoi over the Khmer Rouge, organised an economic embargo against Vietnam which saw most Western foreign aid dry up and prevented Vietnam from seeking loans from the World Bank, the Asian Development Bank and the International Monetary Fund. Serving the geo-political interests of the major world powers, the embargo ensures that Vietnam's misery continues to this day[12].

Among the new icons that emerged in Hanoi's townscape in this period, the most striking is the mausoleum of Ho Chi Minh on Ba Dinh Square (Figure 2.18). Despite Ho's dying wish that his ashes be sprinkled over the country he loved, his successors in the Party wanted a shrine to match Lenin's. Nguyen Ngoc Chan (1990) gives an insight into the process of designing the mausoleum which followed the Party's 1969 decision. Two competitions were conducted and at one stage 300 Vietnamese architects and engineers were working on the design. Assistance was requested from the Soviet Union and an agreement signed which gave the Soviets control over the preliminary design, labour management, organisation of the construction equipment and general direction of the project; the Vietnamese were relegated to providing most of the raw materials and the labour. But a battle of wills followed between the Soviet team, headed by architects Medenxep, Director of the Special Projects Design Institute, and Garony Isakovitch, Chief of the Institute's Design Office, and the Vietnamese team headed by Vuong Quoc My and Nguyen Ngoc Chan. The Soviets assumed they had the expertise and ventured to lecture the Vietnamese on what makes good 'national architecture': 'it must be majestic, symmetrical and solemn' (*ibid.* p.16). The Vietnamese, however, stubbornly stuck to their own ideas, arguing that the monument had to fit the Vietnamese Communist Party's guiding principles - 'modern, cultured, dignified and simple'. Eventually Chan's original plan prevailed with minor concessions to keep the Soviets happy. The mausoleum was opened to the public in 1975.

The mausoleum was placed on a key symbolic site: on Ba Dinh Square at the apex of Hébrard's three grand boulevards, the very point at which the

Figure 2.18   Ho Chi Minh's Mausoleum - neat lines but sterile architecture in Ba Dinh Square. (Source: W.S. Logan)

French had planned the entrance to the new Governor-General's palace and the place where the podium had stood from which Ho had inaugurated independent North Vietnam in 1954. Figure 2.19 shows the way in which this section of Hanoi has been redesigned in line with the new principles. A concrete parliamentary assembly building sits alongside Hébrard's office building, now the Ministry for Foreign Affairs, on the east side of the square, while the Mot Cot Pagoda continues to rest amid lotus lilies on its single pillar to the south and Ho's house on stilts hides behind the old Governor-General's palace to the north. In 1990, to mark the 100th anniversary of Ho's birth, a Ho Chi Minh Museum was opened. Designed and built between 1978 and 1990 with technical assistance from Soviet and Czech architects and engineers and under the direction of Garony Isakovitch, it adhered to the same requirements of being 'modern, cultured, dignified and simple', although it is now criticised for its 'heavy feel' and lack of refinement (Nguyen Truc Luyen 1990, p.12).

Elsewhere similar developments were occurring. On the empty space which had once been the site of the 1902 Hanoi Exposition and Maurice Long Museum, the Soviet Union financed and helped construct the imposing reinforced concrete Friendship Palace containing theatres, lecture halls and meeting rooms (Figure 2.5). Numerous new administrative buildings in Soviet versions of the modern international style were built in the 1970s and 1980s and are marked by uninspired design, poor materials and, worse, disastrous siting decisions, having been un-

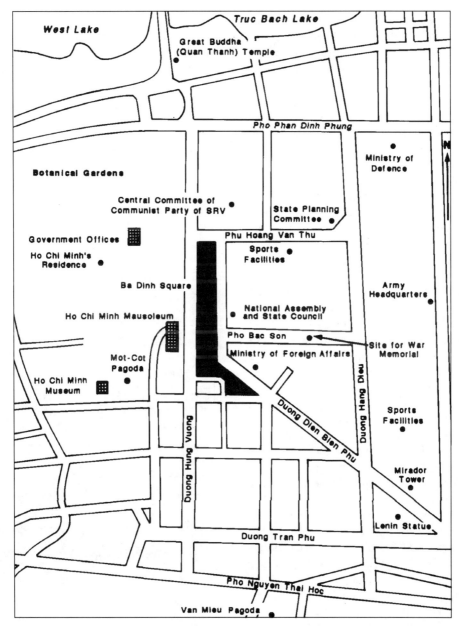

Figure 2.19   Redesign of Ba Dinh Square in the 1970-90 period

sympathetically constructed alongside, behind or in front of significant buildings of earlier times and architectural styles. The municipal authority, the Hanoi People's Committee, wins the prize for lack of cultural and visual sensitivity: it knocked down the old town hall, described by Palazzoli (1981, p.4) as having a 'very Louis XVth daintiness' and replaced it with an uninviting modern block that now towers over Hoan Kiem and clashes with surrounding French colonial buildings. Other townscape changes reflecting the ideological change happened earlier: a simple move, the streets were renamed to honour revolutionary leaders, past and present; near the town hall, Paul Bert Square became Indira Gandhi Square to acknowledge her pro-Soviet leanings and its old ornamental band stand was converted into a monkey cage. Across the road, a State Government Guest House was erected in the rear garden of the former Resident's palace and the Hotel Métropole became the Thong Nhat [Reunification] Hotel. Lenin's name was particularly prominent: his statue, again designed by Garony Isakovitch, stands opposite the mirador tower and the large recreation area enclosing Lake Bay Mau was renamed Lenin Park.

In the suburbs, industrial and residential developments sought to ease Vietnam's and Hanoi's economic and housing problems. These outlying areas, like these urban developments, had had low priority under the French; by comparison, in the period 1955-90, these involved most of Hanoi's construction activity. The new housing provided by the State is almost entirely in high-rise apartment blocks, minimising the use of land and infrastructure costs. Already in the 1940s some French engineers had been calling for such an approach, citing the more efficient cities being developed in Hong Kong and Manila (Craste 1945, p.97); but they would have been aghast at the tired rows of prefabricated concrete slab blocks that have been built. From a distance, the blocks could be in Moscow, Beijing or even New York or Melbourne; closer up the poverty of materials and poor quality of labour become more apparent. The concrete is often too soft, partly due to the pilfering of its cement ingredient in the making, and so 'rots' in the humid Hanoi climate.

In 1973 the Soviets were also called upon to lend their expertise to draw up a new town plan for Hanoi to the year 2000. The Leningrad Scientific Research Centre for Town Planning and Construction had completed master plans for cities in Siberia and Kazakhstan but this was its first effort in tropical Asia. Even though Vietnamese planners were involved in the process, the results as outlined in Sokolov's 1983 paper are fantastic, being based on a false understanding of Hanoi's history and demography and totally divorced from both the local culture and the economic realities of an impoverished government. A new city centre was to be built on the southern and south-western banks of the West Lake (Ho Tay), with a new set of radial boulevards, green spaces, high-rise public buildings and pedestrian overpasses

(see Figure 2.20). Standard Soviet planning techniques were used, such as the planning of residential communities as 'micro-rayons'; that is, planning units of residential and associated facilities theoretically based on a fixed population formula and replicated around the city outskirts. In Hanoi's case, the size of the micro-rayon was to be set by the number of people required to provide a viable base for a senior high school - 60 000 to 70 000. Five industrial districts were planned, each with its own specialisation. Growth was to be channelled to the north-west, west, south-west and across the river to Gia-Lam and beyond. A ring railway and a new airport at Noi Bai were planned and the latter constructed, although not the major highway that was planned to run from it to the city centre, carving a swathe through the Old Sector. But the population predictions on which

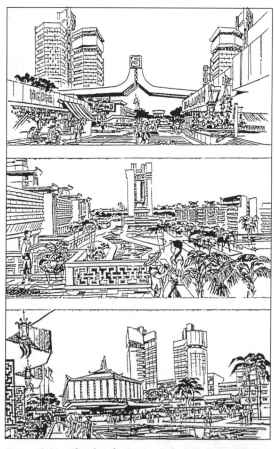

Figure 2.20   Sketches from Soviet plan (Source: *Sokolov 1983)*

the plan was based were unrealistic, as was the prediction that Hanoi's area would need to expand three times. As a result the Noi Bai Airport stands in wide open countryside, an unnecessary hour's drive from the city centre. The Vietnamese Government approved the first stage of the plan in 1976, no doubt in the first heady days of peace and unity. Today, in retrospect, it is clear that the optimism underlying the plan was ill-founded: Hanoi would not become the bustling metropolis envisaged by the planners - during this century at least.

Indeed, conditions in Hanoi, especially in the Old Sector, continued to deteriorate. Overcrowding had become intense: 95 per cent of the Old Sector's buildings were, by now, two or three storeys; people had an average of 1.5 square metres of living space, compared with the government regulation of 6 square metres. It was not much better in the new estates: even a Party member living in an apartment in Kim Lien shared four rooms with eight other family members although, unlike most Old Sector residents, the member did have bathroom facilities. The building stock was worn-out, its maintenance not helped by the temperature variations - 45°C in summer, 5°C in winter - and 90 per cent humidity. The city's patrimony was in a state of decay which, without an injection of extensive amounts of capital, would probably have been terminal. The poverty was overpowering. Fashionable Rue Paul Bert was now depressed Pho Trang Tien, the private shops gone, replaced by the State store - a *palais de la désolation* (Palazzoli 1981, p.17).

By the mid-1980s it was becoming clear to Vietnamese leaders that the centrally controlled economic system was not performing well; indeed, with inflation running at 700 per cent annually, it was on the verge of collapse. Pressures to liberalise the State's economic organisation came to a head at the Sixth Party Congress in Hanoi in 1986 and emerged as the new Doi Moi (renovation) policy. In 1990 the Soviet Union officially withdrew from Vietnam: the period of Soviet socialist urbanism was over. Probably the last urbanistic act in the Soviet mould still to be played out is the erection, in Ba Dinh Square, of the war memorial approved by the Ministerial Council in August 1990. The design chosen in competition is by Trinh Hong Doan; it comprises four 25-metre high intersecting walls of reinforced concrete topped by a pagoda-like decorative roof and is described by the local press as 'architecturally majestic enough...to blend in with the other features in the area'. It will complete the Soviet-inspired redesign of Ba Dinh Square that has taken place since 1955.

DOI MOI, HANOI AND HERITAGE REDEFINITION

In April 1992 the Vietnamese Communist Party agreed to remove the enormous portrait of Ho Chi Minh from the top of the State Bank in central Hanoi. A sign of the times: as Vietnam opens up to Western economic thinking, old symbols give way to new and Hanoi's townscape begins to undergo yet another politically-driven transformation.

Doi Moi's success has already been considerable: inflation was down to an annual 25 per cent by 1990, prices have stabilised, new profit incentives have made Vietnam a significant rice exporter for the first time since the 1930s, and foreign investments have escalated. These changes are easily seen in Hanoi's streets as each day more shops open, a wider range of goods appears and fresh advertisement hoardings are erected. Unemployment due to the demobilisation of troops is still very high but little thought is given to those worse social disasters which have already struck other Southeast Asian cities coming in the wake of Westernisation and, especially, large-scale foreign tourism - prostitution and AIDS. For the moment the population is enjoying this rapidly rising, if still relatively low, prosperity and the townscape is feeling the impact. Motorcycles are quickly replacing the bicycle. A major shift to motorcars requires far greater capital and has not yet begun to occur; nevertheless Hanoi now boasts a fleet of motor taxis headquartering adjacent to the National Library. Traffic laws remain rudimentary and traffic lights few in number, but these will soon be needed as traffic increases. Already the congestion is so great at the downtown intersection of Trang Tien and Hang Bai Streets that the bicycle-driven taxis - the ubiquitous 'cyclos' - have been banned.

The internationalisation of the economy and privatisation of property, including real estate, which *Doi Moi* entails, requires fundamental changes to Vietnamese law and to the way in which Vietnamese cities are to be planned and administered. Already some important new pieces of legislation have been enacted: land laws in 1988, 1989 and 1993, housing laws in 1991 and town planning laws in 1992 (Logan forthcoming). The protection and use of historic buildings has been controlled by state legislation since 1984, although the list of buildings is still relatively small and historic precincts are not covered[13]. This catalogue of new legislation may give a misleading appearance of decisiveness on the part of Vietnamese planning authorities, whereas, if the pages of the Vietnamese Architect's Association (VAA) journal *Kien Truc* and conversations with Hanoi planners are any measure, attitudes to planning generally and ideas about Hanoi's future planning specifically are in a state of some confusion.

Earlier planning efforts are being reappraised. For many years after 1954, the French work was characterised as 'really more propaganda for the superiority of French culture than anything else', but it is now being recognised that:

> To its credit [that is, Hébrard's 1920s plan], this was the first time all the collective and complex issues often associated with the city were addressed and analysed in a 'master plan' (Nguyen Quoc Thong 1988, p.46).

Now the work of the Soviet bloc architects and planners is being reconsidered and generally found wanting. For example, the Director of the NIURP, Nguyen Ngoc Khoi (1992), Nguyen Lan, now Hanoi's Chief Architect (1990) have both written highly critically of the Soviet master plan and the methods used to develop it: it was too spread out, involved too much demolition, too much high-rise construction, only envisaged using Government funds (rather than those of the citizens themselves or of foreigners), and was based on inaccurate mapping. Pham Han (1991) goes further, using the term 'rural urbanisation' to describe the results of planning in Hanoi since 1954: new residential zones compartmentalised into separate housing estates which look in on themselves like rural villages rather than opening out to be part of the greater Hanoi, and deteriorating building and infrastructure standards with above-ground sewerage pipes. Hanoi's ancient lakes, like Van Chuong opposite the Van Mieu Pagoda, are eaten up

by the encircling houses and polluted by household wastes - just like Hoan Kiem Lake had been in the nineteenth century.

What does this redesigning and reconstruction mean for the definition of Hanoi's 'heritage' in these days of *Doi Moi*? In the nineteenth and early twentieth centuries, the French authorities discriminated between various relics of Vietnam's past, restoring some, knocking others down, and generally preferring Champa to Chinese. The 1951 EFEO list of only 31 classified monuments in Hanoi included 17 pagoda or temple complexes, nine communal houses, the citadel and several gates and smaller buildings - a very selective view of Hanoi's heritage in which no allowance was made for precincts, as distinct from buildings, or for buildings connected with recent Hanoi events. In the period after 1955, the heritage was redefined to include some humble Hanoi dwellings linked with the nationalist movement and French architectural achievements were dismissed as merely representing a colonial period best forgotten.

But it is the Soviet monuments which now receive the harshest criticism. In 1991, for example, the VAA wrote:

> A feature of the architectural heritage from the last 30 years of urban development in Hanoi is the high-rise apartment blocks such as Kim Lien and Nguyen Cong Tru built in the 1960s, and Thang Cong, Nghia Do and Thanh Xuan built in the 1970s and 1980s; these were once regarded as the image of the socialist city. Today, at these high-rise flats, the hopelessly unorganised and indiscriminate practice of residential construction is evident (p.19).

Glass curtain-wall office buildings - part of the 1970s and 1980s Modern International array of architectural techniques - are a main target of VAA rebuke, while the heaviness of most of the larger reinforced concrete structures is the subject of Nguyen Truc Luyen's criticism (1990, p.23). A few professionals can still be found who still appear to espouse the use of architectural and planning policies based on 'sound socialist principles'. Architect Hoang Phuc Thang is one example: as recently as 1989 he continued to argue in respect to heritage areas that architects and planners should set their plans within the social context and develop them through a dialectical process involving traditional and modern values:

> In the process of seeking a solution to the restoration of ancient Hanoi, it is to be noted that we do not opt for a nostalgic and dogmatic tendency seeking to patch up at will the remaining pieces of a dead past. Neither do we choose to put up an exhibition of archaeological findings following a modern pattern of arrangements. The problem is to have a correct analysis and a profound understanding of the complexity of the present society, of the structure and form inherent in traditional values in order to develop them logically and dialectically in the future (Hoang 1989, p.4).

But perhaps events in Eastern Europe will have led him to revise his views since 1989. Certainly the city fathers are now talking of changing Lenin Park to Central Park - from Moscow to New York in the slash of the official pen. Most architects and planners are reflecting this shift, too, by adopting a more flexible professional outlook, prepared, like Nguyen Ngoc Khoi (1992), to strike a balance between Western and indigenous architectural forms in order to develop a distinctive Vietnamese style, to achieve first-class architecture in harmonious townscapes and to protect heritage precincts.

If there is still, in the mid 1990s, a variety of opinion about what heritage elements should be protected in Hanoi, it is quite clear that, given the slow pace of political as distinct from economic change occurring in Vietnam, the decisions will remain 'top down' and driven as much by political and ideological as by aesthetic considerations. Although there is some involvement in shaping the concept of Hanoi's heritage by the planning and architectural professions, and also by university academics in their occasional urban history colloquia and writings, there are no signs of awakening grass roots interest or action amongst the general Hanoi citizenry. A major task, therefore, will be to convince the political leaders that heritage protection and high architectural and planning standards, like environmental protection generally, are important. At the moment these issues are not high on the government's agenda, caught up as it is in economic restructuring.

To date, a small number of projects, both local and international, have tried to take practical steps to protect either the whole of the Old Sector or key precincts within it (Logan forthcoming). Thus, during 1991, the VAA assisted the Ministry of Construction in the restoration of shop facades in Hang Khay Street, while other architects, starting in 1990, have drawn up the more ambitious 'Ancient Quarters' project to restore and redevelop part of the Area of 36 Commercial Streets. Neither local exercise has shown interest in the French and Soviet monuments and areas. UNESCO's 1990 Hanoi project covers the entire Old Sector but has not proceeded for lack of funds, while the French Government has funded small legal and design projects associated with the protection of the Hoan Kiem lakeside and a handful of prominent colonial buildings. But these projects have achieved very little and there remains no official heritage plan for Hanoi as a whole.

In the meantime, new threats to the city's cultural landscape have emerged as the result of *Doi Moi*. Encouraged by Vietnam's legal code changes, foreign investors are waiting in the wings to speculate in property development. The lifting of the United States' trade embargo, which occured in February 1994, will provide a further impetus for central city redevelopment. High-rise business centres and hotels could well be the major icons of the *Doi Moi* period. But, up to this point, the worst damage to Hanoi's cultural landscape is being inflicted by the Vietnamese themselves - either through the poorly sited offices or through the current 'do-it-yourself' building boom that has hit the Area of 36 Commercial Streets. The VAA is particularly concerned by the

Figure 2.21   Typical 'do-it-yourself' construction in the Area of 36 Commercial Streets. (Source: *W.S. Logan*)

latter, estimating that half the renovation work under way in Hanoi and 30 per cent of the investment is now coming from private residents rather than the state and seeing this leading to an 'unorganised, irregular and hybrid urban architecture' (1991, pp.17-19) (Figure 2.21).

What is needed more than ever now, if the accumulated heritage of the city is to be saved, is a master plan for Hanoi with tight heritage controls on key areas and buildings and a strong resolve on the part of government and planners to implement the controls rigorously. However, as Dunoyer de Segonzac notes, the implementation of *Doi Moi* has led the state to withdraw from a number of fields of activity in order to devote itself to broad economic management (notably reducing the external debt) leaving other fields open to unrestrained action by public bodies and individuals (in France, Ministry for Culture and Ministry for Foreign Affairs 1990, p.7)[14]. The government seems to have missed the point that Hanoi's Old Sector is a tourist goldmine and potentially a major contributor both to Vietnam's economy and, through the establishment of a flourishing cultural tourism industry, to the creation of new jobs to alleviate the massive unemployment and under-employment rates.

The planners - accustomed to following directions from their political masters and now finding none coming - seem unable to make a serious move on the problem even though to document the heritage and draw up protection schemes are steps quite within their power and capability. The planning system appears to be out of control insofar as the 'do-it-yourself' building activity is concerned: there is an impossible backlog of building applications and much building is done either without official approval or with approval given by under-the-counter methods. The Deputy Director of the Hanoi municipal department of construction, Trinh Hong Trieu (in Hiebert 1991, p.45) openly admits that the current regulations 'exist mainly on paper':

> Often when people apply for a building licence, they have already built the house according to their wishes. After they're caught, they have to pay fines, but it's so low that they're willing to pay it.

But Trinh Hong Trieu (in Hornik 1992, p.28) rationalises that in any case:

> People would just make changes to the State-approved design during the implementation process. In reality, that's less troublesome than asking for official permission to alter the design.

It also seems that not all planners and architects think controls are necessary and the view is often expressed that people should have the right to decide for themselves what to do with their properties. This is seen, for instance, in the aphorism used by Professor Truong Tung - until June 1992 the Deputy Chairman of the Hanoi People's Committee and the city's Chief Architect - 'Previously the State used to build for the people; henceforward the people will have to build for themselves' - and also in his published opinion that people in the 36 commercial streets should be able to rebuild up to four storeys if they wish. While he saw a need for some controls to maintain the integrity of traditional streetscapes, he advocated a flexible rather than purist approach to protecting the cultural heritage, telling Hanoi's *Xay Dung* newspaper shortly before he left his municipal post that:

> To me culturally relevant architecture is not different from architecture which is appropriate to people's lives... Culturally relevant architecture does not have to be tiled and eaved roofs. The thatched roof and the tiled roof cannot replace concrete and iron in this day and age. Advanced materials bring people close to modern technology, and advanced technology will lead people to seek modern architecture in order to suit their present lives. Today, we also need to preserve our historic buildings as reminders of the past. However, we cannot follow only the old style to preserve Hanoi...

The ambiguity of such statements plays into the hands of those in authority who place little value in cultural traditions and who fail to see that conserving the cultural environment makes good economic sense, not only directly through providing a mainstay of Hanoi's tourism industry, but also through generating other social improvements such as job creation and housing improvements. Unfortunately it would seem that, not only do senior politicians need to be convinced of the economic as well as

Figure 2.22   Called the Thong Nhat ['Re-unification']
Hotel during the independence period, the Hotel
Métropole resumed its original name when restored in
1992 as Hanoi's first luxury hotel. (Source: W.S. Logan)

environmental value of protecting Hanoi's Old Sector, but so too do some senior planning professionals.

Hanoi's heritage is rich and many layered; each layer contributes to the city's current character and the best elements of each should be protected. Western aesthetic and architectural ideas will inevitably influence the development of Hanoi as the society and its access to newspapers, literature, television and travel is liberalised. Vietnamese planners and architects would do well to take advantage of *Doi Moi* and adopt, or adapt, the best of these Western ideas and techniques for use in protecting their heritage and planning for the future. In this way one might hope that the icons of the *Doi Moi* period will turn out to be recycled and sensitively restored buildings, new architecture that bridges the modern and the traditional, and areas whose planning makes them aesthetically attractive, environmentally safe and socially sensitive (see Figure 2.22).

ENDNOTES

1 The definition of 'Old Sector' used in this paper is broad (see Figure 2.1) and covers the citadel area, the 'Area of 36 Commercial Streets' and the 'French Quarter'. Note that the term 'Ancient Quarter' is sometimes used by other authors and generally refers to the Vietnamese part of old Hanoi, that is, excluding the French Quarter. For an outline of the UNESCO Hanoi project see Logan 1991 and Logan forthcoming.

2 See, for example, Alf Louvre & Jeffrey Walsh 1988, *Tell Me Lies About Vietnam: Cultural Battles for the Meaning of the War*, Open University Press, Milton Keynes, UK; Jeffrey Walsh & James Aulich 1989, *Vietnam Images: War and Representation*, MacMillan, Basingstoke, UK; and Jeffrey Grey & Jeff Doyle (eds) 1992, *Vietnam: War, Myth and Memory*, Allen and Unwin, Sydney. It was also very easy for the Westerner, unfamiliar with Vietnam, to confuse the devastation scenes in Nam Dinh and other cities with Hanoi.

3 For example, Cosgrove, D. 1982, 'The myths and stones of Venice: an historical geography of a symbolic landscape', *Journal of Historical Geography*, vol.8, pp.145-69; Cosgrove, D. & Daniels, S.(eds) 1988, *The Iconography of Landscape*, Cambridge University Press, Cambridge; Domosh, M. 1992, 'Controlling urban form: the development of Boston's Back Bay', *Journal of Historical Geography*, vol.18, pp.288-306; Harvey, D. 1979, 'Man and myth', *Annals of the Association of American Geographers*, vol.69, pp.362-81.

4 The way in which the Vietnamese cultural identity has survived such long periods of foreign domination must be the subject of more intensive study. Other keys to the answer lie in the maintenance of a popular culture based on language and legend in Vietnam's 'countryside, the reinjection of this culture at various points into the educated culture of the cities and its reinforcement by the communist nationalists during the present century. There are, in any case, a number of Vietnamese scholars - such as Nguyen Phi Hoanh 1984 (1969), *Vietnamese Art* (in Vietnamese), Nha Xuat Ban Thanh Ho Chi Minh, Ho Chi Minh City; and Nguyen Huu Thong (ed.) 1992, *Fine Arts of the Nguyen Dynasty in Hue* (in Vietnamese), Nha Xuat Ban Hoi Nha Van, Ho Chi Minh City - who argue strongly that the visual arts and architecture, such as the major buildings at Hue, were clearly Vietnamese, rather than Chinese, having evolved from indigenous construction techniques.

5 Ngo Huy Quynh (1991, pp.166-7) claims that the technique of standing columns, whether thick timbers or flimsy bamboos, on the surface of plinths or on the ground was a traditional Vietnamese, as distinct from Chinese, form of construction - the movable frame. This structure allowed buildings to be moved quickly in time of flood or attack, in the case of houses and pagodas, or of change of capital, in the case of royal palaces. The distinctiveness of the technique requires

further exploration.

6 Some sources say the Black Flags worked in league with the Vietnamese authorities against the French.

7 Henri Gaudin, 'La façon d'être ensemble des choses', *Le Monde*, Paris, 22 Mar. 1989; for further discussion, see Christelle Robin 1992, 'De l'ethno-architecture aux anthropologiques de l'espace', *Les Cahiers de la recherche architecturale*, no.27/28, 1st trimester, pp.7-14.

8 Literally *Ha-Noi* means in the bend of the river.

9 The term *Beaux-Arts* is used to identify a form of architecture based on classical architecture and characterised by a rigid adherence to design rules, including symmetry, and the use of ornate decoration. It is associated with the teaching of the *École des Beaux-Arts* in Paris, founded in 1671 and frequently seen to oppose innovation in architectural design thinking.

10 Governor-General Long's efforts to replace some French with Vietnamese public servants were undermined (Wright 1991, p.203). The best he could achieve was to establish parallel positions (lateral cadres) for the Vietnamese. This added to the already heavy burden on colonial and metropolitan taxpayers but generated a demand for more administrative buildings in Hanoi.

11 See Hébrard (1928, p.33) where he argues that 'The specialisation of residential districts is necessary in them [the urban agglomerations], especially in relation to the native districts which must not be mixed with the European districts for a variety of reasons'.

12 For recent summaries of the impacts of the Vietnam War, see Brazier 1992 and the particularly evocative Sheehan 1992.

13 In moving towards Western legal structures, Vietnam has missed an opportunity that would have been cherished by Western city planners - to introduce wider heritage controls before handing back private property rights to the citizenry.

14 The response of the Vietnamese authorities, such as the Ministry of Tourism, has been to look to neighbouring Thailand - and especially Bangkok - as the model for achieving rapid development of international tourism. This is tourism development at almost any cost and would destroy Hanoi's heritage which is not based on a few monuments but the integrity of the whole Old Sector. I have argued with officials in Hanoi that they should take a lesson from their former colonial masters and adopt a Paris, rather than Bangkok, approach under which the Old Sector would be tightly regulated and high-rise offices and hotels displaced to nominated zones outside Old Sector.

REFERENCES

Azambre, Georges 1958, 'Les origines de Hanoï', *Bulletin de la Société des Etudes Indochinoises*, New Series, vol.33, no.3, 3rd trimester, pp.261-300.

Bézacier, Louis 1952, 'Conception du plan des anciennes citadelles-capitales du Nord Vietnam', *Journal Asiatique*, no.140, pp.185-95.

Brazier, Chris 1992, *Vietnam: the Price of Peace*, Oxfam, Oxford.

Cosgrove, D. & Daniels, S. (eds) 1988, *The Iconography of Landscape*, Cambridge University Press, Cambridge.

Craste, Leo 1945, 'Urbanisme et architecture en Indochine', *L'Architecture d'aujourd'hui*, vol.3, pp.97-102.

Duiker, William J. 1986, *China and Vietnam; the Roots of Conflict*, Institute of East Asian Studies, Berkeley, California.

de Segonzac. P. Dunoyer & Le Cuong 1990 (unpub.), *Premiers contacts en vue d'évaluer les possibilités de préservation du patrimoine architectural et urbain du centre de Hanoi*, Ministry For Culture and Minstry For Foreign Affairs, Paris (report of mission to Hanoi Aug.-Sept. 1990).

Gresleri, Giuliano & Matteoni, Dario 1982, *La Città Mondiale. Anderson, Hébrard, Otlet, Le Corbusier*, Polis/Marsilio Editori, Venice.

Groslier, Bernard Philippe 1961, *Indochine. Carrefour des Arts*, Editions Albin Michel, Paris.

Hanoi Archives, National Archive Centre No.1, Fonds de la Mairie-Résidence, Service du Cadastre et des Domaines de Hanoi (MR), File 8030.

——— Fonds du Résident-Supérieur du Tonkin (RST), Files 56.735, 58.8060.

Hébrard, Ernest 1928, 'L'Urbanisme en Indochine', *L'Architecture*, vol.41, no.2, pp.33-48.

Hiebert, Murray, 'Going down the tubes. Will new money destroy buildings the bombers spared?', *Far Eastern Economic Review*, 8 August 1991, pp.44-5.

Hoang Phuc Thang, 'On the problems of tradition and modernity in the planning and construction of Hanoi (in Vietnamese), *Hanoian Journal*, no.122, 14 October 1989, p.4.

Hornik, Richard, 'Protecting an imperilled legacy' (in Vietnamese), *Kien Truc*, vol.35, no.1, 1992, pp.27-28.

Logan, William, 'Planning for the protection of the Old Sector of Hanoi, Vietnam', *Journal of Vietnamese Studies*, vol.1, no.4, 1991, pp.78-81.

Logan, William (forthcoming), 'Heritage palnning in post - Doi Moi Hanoi: the national and international contributions', *Journal of the American Planners' Association.*

Masson, André 1929, *Hanoï pendant la période héroïque (1873-1888)*, Librairie Orientaliste Paul Gueuthner, Paris; trans. Jack A. Yaeger 1987 (1983), The *Transformation of Hanoi 1873-1888*, (edited and abridged by Daniel F. Doeppers),Wisconsin Papers on Southeast Asia no.8, Center for Southeast Asian Studies, University of Wisconsin-Madison, Madison, Wisconsin.

Ngo Huy Quynh 1991, *Understanding Vietnamese Architecture* (in Vietnamese), 2 vols, Nha Xuat Ban Xay Dung, Hanoi.

Nguyen Lan 1990, 'On improving urban planning' (in Vietnamese), *Kien Truc*, vol.30, no.4, pp.29-30.

Nguyen Ngoc Chan 1990 (in Vietnamese), 'The process of designing the Ho Chi Minh Mausoleum', *Kien Truc*, vol.27, no.1, pp.13-23.

Nguyen Ngoc Khoi 1992, 'Building management in Hanoi' (in Vietnamese), *Kien Truc*, vol.35, no.1, pp.17-18.

Nguyen Quoc Thong 1988, 'Morphological changes in the spatial planning of Hanoi under French colonialism' (in Vietnamese), *Kien Truc*, vol.31, no. 2, pp.40-9.

Nguyen Truc Luyen 1990, The Ho Chi Minh Museum on Ba Dinh Square (in Vietnamese), *Kien Truc*, vol.27, no.1, pp.19-23.

Palazzoli, Claude 1981, *Le Vietnam entre deux mythes*, Economica, Paris.

Pham Han 1991, 'Is this the way to build Hanoi?' (in Vietnamese), *Kien Truc*, vol.34, no.4, p.29.

Phan Thuan An 1986, 'Quelques traits de l'architecture de Hué', *Etudes vietnamiennes*, vol.13, New Series, pp.31-46.

Sheehan, Neil 1992, *Two Cities. Hanoi and Saigon*, Jonathon Cape, London.

Sokolov, S.I. 1983, 'Town on the Red River: in Leningrad a general plan has been formulated for the development of the capital of Vietnam' (in Russian), *Leningradskaya Panorama*, no.8 Aug, pp.26-9.

Than, Gabriel Thien 1984, 'Vietnam: vivre en ville aujourd'hui', *Habitat Social. Revue de l'Habitat Social*, no.97, June, pp.75-85.

Turley, William S. 1975, 'Urbanization in war: Hanoi, 1946-1973', *Pacific Affairs*, vol.48, pp.370-397.

VIARO, Alain 1992, 'Le compartiment chinois est-il chinois?', *Cahiers de la recherche architecturale*, no27/28, 1st trimester, pp.139-50.

Vietnamese Architects Association (VAA) 1991, 'Residential architecture and construction by individual resident investors' (in Vietnamese), *Kien Truc*, vol.32, no.2, pp.17-22.

Woolfe, Penelope 1988, 'Symbol of the Second Empire: cultural politics and the Paris Opera House', in D. Cosgrove & S. Daniels (eds), *The Iconography of Landscape*, Cambridge University Press, Cambridge, pp.214-35.

Wright, Gwendolyn 1987, 'Tradition in the service of modernity: architecture and urbanism in French colonial policy, 1900-1930', *Journal of Modern History*, vol.59, pp.291-316.

Wright, Gwendolyn 1991, *The Politics of Design in French Colonial Urbanism*, University of Chicago Press, Chicago

ACKNOWLEDGMENTS

This paper was prepared under an Australian Research Council grant although background material was gathered during visits to Hanoi in 1990-91 funded by UNESCO and Deakin University. The author wishes to express appreciation for the assistance given in Hanoi by Mrs Diem, Ms Vu Thi Minh Huong and Mr Ton at the National Archives Centre No. 1; Drs Nguyen Ngoc Khoi, Le Hong Ke, Ha Van Que, Nguyen Dan Kiem and Lai Thinh at the NIURP; Mr Luyen, editor of *Kien Truc*; Professor Pham Huy Le, Head of the Department of History at Hanoi University; the historian and author Nguyen Vinh Phuc; and David Abotomey, Eve Colebatch and Margaret McCulloch at the Australian Embassy. Translations from the Vietnamese are the work of the author's research assistants Nguyen Minh Phuong and Ton That Luyen; translations from the Russian are by Rae Mathew and those from the French are the author's. Ton That Quynh Du's comments on an earlier draft of the paper are much appreciated.

3

Phnom Penh: defying man and nature[1]

Christiane Blancot

Arriving in Phnom Penh from Paris, a French national is immediately struck by a sense of familiarity - a familiarity with the broad avenues running straight as an arrow, their footpaths, rows of trees and heavily shaded ground; a familiarity with the solid villas which could have been transplanted from French seaside resorts, with the square fronting the station, post office or market; a familiarity with the institutional buildings in Third Republic style[2], their pediments and pilasters only needing the inscription 'Liberty, Equality, Fraternity' to make one think one is in the most ordinary of French prefectures; a familiarity with the way of locating major public amenities at the end of the main avenues as a focus point and of opening up new streets in the axis of the existing monuments so that, no matter how far away from the observer, the buildings will be shown up to advantage; a familiarity with the grid street pattern, taken straight from the manuals written by French engineers at the École Polytechnique and adapted perfectly to suit this flat, featureless landscape and the shapeless village that Phnom Penh still was in 1866, a settlement where everything was still waiting to be done.[3]

And then, once the first impression has passed and as the observer moves through the town into areas well beyond its colonial period limits, another realisation takes over and the town emerges as what it fundamentally is: an amazing machine providing protection against the annual flood, a piece of land wrested by humans from the waters of the Mekong delta and the monsoons; an infrastructure of dykes and pumping stations, of pipes and sluice-gates, of harnessed lakes and water courses, an immense network of stormwater drains, built up little by little over the years.

Once a year from July to October, the level of the Mekong rises by 8 metres and reaches the height of the river banks. At the same time, the heaviest monsoon rains beat down on Phnom Penh. Established in this strategic location where the river divides into two additional arms - the Bassak, towards the south and part of the delta, and, in the north towards the lake situated south of Angkor, the Tonle Sap, a vast outlet for the over-full Mekong - the town is built on flood-prone land, a vast swamp composed of lakes (*beng*) and natural channels (*prek*) which the water invades when the river rises.

The way in which the town developed is thus subject to its topography, of the constantly renewing necessity to protect itself from the river waters, to hoist itself above them and to establish a durable town on soils of clay and sand and no really solid foundation until depths of at least 30 or 40 metres

Figure 3.1   Traditional lakeside village.

are reached. If looking for a European parentage for this town, one would have to say it was intrinsically Dutch: Phnom Penh is a large 'polder'.

ON THE USE OF EMBANKMENTS AND LANDFILL

The colonial engineers were incredible chameleons: capable of understanding not only the way a French villa and the neo-Romanesque cathedral should look - features so necessary to the French administration in staking their claim to *supériorité civilisatrice* - but also of understanding the logic of water control for centuries rooted in the Khmer civilisation and such a fascinating aspect of Angkorian capital cities. This method of harnessing water was more effective than the supposedly authoritative imported Western models and determined the way in which the town was to develop.

To survive, the colony had to fit in with the site's environmental constraints and it found no better method than the local techniques for draining the waters. Thus the first colonial town, drawn up in the 1890s, was established around the only point in the settlement standing above water, the Phnom, a small hill surmounted by a four centuries old *stupa* or Buddhist temple, the locality's symbol, and along the natural river levee where a village of traders and fisherpeople already existed, organised around a single street (see Figures 3.1 and 3.2).

Around this single monument, the colonial administration appropriated a piece of land which, while still not very large, was sufficient for its institutions, bureaucrats and military personnel. It filled in the area up to the level of the river levee and surveyed

street blocks which were soon lined with villas and official buildings; in doing this, it was as if the administration felt compelled to create a small town which disregarded the river, to push the water back as it also pushed away the pile houses, the Chinese merchants and even the king himself and his palace, beyond the boulevard and the encircling canal towards the south, and into what was to be called, until the 1950s, the Chinese town and the Cambodian town.

However in order to create this reserved quarter, the only solution the administration could find was to dig out the neighbouring ponds to bring in clay and sand, and to construct an encircling canal capable of collecting the run-off from this town which now sat above river-level. The system experimented with at this stage was to become the model: each new extension would be made by filling in a section of the marshland, filling up ponds and canals. The phenomenon was to accelerate after the 1920s and 1930s with dredges making possible the use of the river's alluvial deposits as landfill material.

But what differentiated the French colonist from the Chinese or the Cambodian was not simply the embankments and landfill but the particular way in which they made use of them and of the occupied territory created.

For the Chinese merchant who needed, for trading activities, houses in terraces 3.5 to 4 metres wide and fronting directly onto the street, shop-houses were built. These were rows of attached buildings constructed on piles (long columns driven into the ground), strictly aligned along the streets and comprising a room for commercial purposes at ground-

Figure 3.2   The French town at the turn of the century.

floor level with rooms behind and above for the family living quarters. The dimensions of these buildings could be directly inferred from the mode of construction (a grid of piles a beam's length apart, that is, 3.5 to 4 metres, linked and held together by a floor serving as a foundation) which was in turn a response to the nature of the land and the high economic return which could be obtained from this artificial ground. This subdivision into shop-house plots began towards the end of the nineteenth century on the initiative of private investors and with royal authorisation. (There was no private ownership of land at this time, all land belonging to the king who bestowed leaseholds for construction purposes, but private property rights were very quickly introduced by the colonial administration). A building form imported into Cambodia from China and said by some authorities to have been previously imported into China by Dutch colonialists in the seventeenth century (Viaro 1992), the so-called 'Chinese shop-house' became, in less than a century the most widespread urban building type in those sectors of Phnom Penh which developed around the markets and the main avenues.

The landfill system was also and above all an ancestral mode of organising the Khmer territory, but it was used sparingly in those days, being confined to religious buildings and sometimes palaces whereas dwellings were exclusively constructed on piles above the natural ground level. The main Buddhist compounds, when they were not engulfed by the landfill-based town, indicated clearly this use of embankments and landfill only for the symbolic elements of the religious complex. Within a single compound was found the in-filled area in which the temple was built, generally linked to a levee road by a path at the level of the levee or by a bridge situated in line with the temple. Around this, the living quarters of the bonzes (Buddhist priests or monks) and the communal rooms fitted the pattern of domestic architecture - wooden houses on piles or built of landfill materials. The ponds and dams assured drainage within the compound.

It was in this way that the Angkorian towns used to function traditionally: stone temples on landfill and houses on piles, with canals and lakes to collect and hold the waters. The town of Phnom Penh, in its

Figure 3.3   Royal palace on the banks of the Mekong (Source: © SIRPA/ECPA France)

southern part, around the Royal Palace (see Figure 3.3), functioned like this too until the end of the French colonial period (1954). Only the palace and the pagodas were constructed in masonry and fronting directly onto a levee road; only a few main streets were lined with shop-houses and villas, while the rest of the land, further out, was occupied by houses on piles and surrounded by gardens. The ponds and natural canals survived, used for growing aquatic plants. The lands belonged to the king who allowed families to settle there freely and to construct their houses made of wood and bamboo. And so the two systems sat side by side: a combination of embankments and landfill, dug-out water reservoirs and encircling drainage channels.

Thus, three towns were juxtaposed: a French town encircled by a canal, with public gardens, avenues planted with trees, large plots of land, neo-renaissance architecture and public institutions; a Chinese town, on a grid pattern, with narrow and deep subdivisions, divided into regular plots around the market, with its shop-houses lining the streets and opening onto rear lanes 3 or 4 metres in width; a Cambodian town (see Figure 3.4) growing over the water, in the water, on the edge of the water, crossed by rectilinear paths and focussed on its royal and religious institutions.

Even if this set of immediately identifiable urban areas survived to the end of the colonial period, a number of sharp breaks in the colonial capital's architectural development were going to take place. The influence of the Angkorian monuments and the Khmer civilisation which the *École Française*

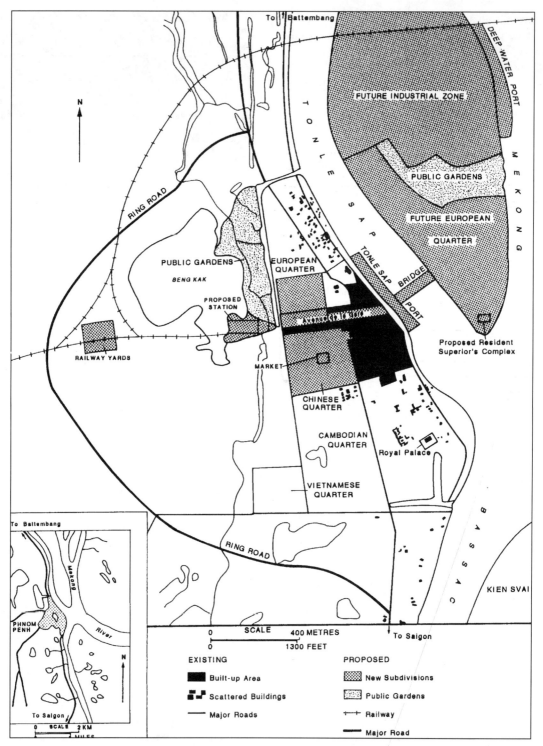

Figure 3.4   Phnom Penh, 1922 (after E. Hébrard)

d'Extrême-Orient (EFEO) had been studying for several decades was to influence urban architectural thought and encourage the invention of the new style inspired by Angkor. However, the experimentation involved in the construction of the Cambodian Fine Arts School and the Albert Sarraut Museum (1917-20) built next to the Royal Palace by the eminent *EFEO* member, Georges Groslier, remained without a follow-up. Nevertheless, it was symbolic of the attempt made to move beyond the colonial style which was ostensibly indifferent to the Cambodian culture.

THE MODERN TOWN AND THE PILE HOUSES

In 1921 the *Service d'Urbanisme de l'Indochine* (Indochinese Town Planning Service) was created. Within this framework, Ernest Hébrard was responsible for expansion plans for the whole set of Indochinese towns. Hébrard was a member of the *Société Française des Urbanistes* (French Town Planners' Society) which had just been created in Paris and which brought together a series of brilliant individuals who, before and during World War One, had formulated a method for designing expansion and beautification plans for urban areas. They wanted to make use of these plans to reconstruct the towns destroyed by the war and to anticipate the urban extensions which the rapid urban population growth resulting from the industrial revolution would make necessary. Their goal was both social and political. It was political in that they fought alongside others - doctors, engineers, municipal technicians - to persuade the French government to take responsibility for the problem of workers' living conditions, to put in place a public policy of state-owned housing and to regulate town planning. It was social in that they included as a basic necessity in their concept of planning the improvement of urban infrastructure, sanitation and public health, air and light, the creation of sewerage, drinking water and electricity systems, the creation of a network of parks and promenades, the widening of roads and so on. In order to be rational and coherent, the combination of these essential elements of urban existence had to be included in a global plan which organised, using the same logic, both the existing town and its new extensions by applying to one as to the other the same principles

of modernity, sanitation and beautification.

It was in this context that Ernest Hébrard left France for Indochina. The towns of the colony were actually very favourable for experimentation, far from the dead weight of the metropolitan administration. The towns were still small, easily controllable, with low populations (there were scarcely 50 000 residents in Phnom Penh in 1920) and little infrastructure. All seemed possible. Hébrard set down the basic ideas for the extension of Phnom Penh and prepared the program of major works which were to unfold from 1928 to 1939, necessitated notably by the arrival of the railway (Hébrard 1928; Hébrard 1931).

Between 1928 and 1932, the canal which encircled the first colonial town was filled in. It was transformed into a broad boulevard which ran from north to south along the edge of the town until, in the extreme south, it met the new bridge which straddled the Bassak River in the direction of Saigon; while from east to west, it became a huge esplanade framed by two tree-lined promenades and two lanes of traffic. To the south-west of the colonial town, the new railway station was established within the town boundaries, facing the Mekong, in a monumental position at the end of this new '*avenue jardin*'. The administrative sector came out of its isolation. From now on, it was linked to the northern suburban district and the Chinese commercial quarter in the south.

But the planning scheme and its projected extensions drawn up by the Indochinese Planning Service before 1928 had broader ambitions: starting from the main axes of the existing town, it set out to organise a vast territory extending equally to the north and south, east and west. The Chrui Changvar Peninsula (to the east of Tonle Sap) and the northern suburbs of Russei Keo were engulfed, as were also the villages, the Cambodian town and Beng Kak (a lake to the west of the first colonial town). This plan proposed a new network of public thoroughfares, opening up the town's main access roads and new, modern and extensive infrastructure. It made provision for the transformation of the Chrui Changvar Peninsula, linking it to the town by the creation of a bridge over the Tonle Sap and the installation there of a large commercial port composed of basins opening onto the principal arm of the Mekong and the new residence of the governor facing the junction of the four river arms. But the bridge was not to be constructed and the peninsula was to remain agricultural.

Similarly, to the north of the colonial town, a new district was proposed behind the riverside road. It was composed of 'a variety of street blocks: houses, commercial establishments, public institutions, open spaces, provisions and reserves for the hospitals, colleges etc.'[4] This subdivision was also to remain on the drawing board, doubtless because of the prolongation of the railway towards the north leaving only a narrow strip which could be built up along the river and which was steadily occupied by port installations that attracted small industries and warehouses to the area.

But by its inclusion of the new central market subdivision, Ernest Hébrard's extension plan oriented the development of the town principally towards the west and south. The new market was situated at the centre of a vast open square surrounded by shophouses. Around this, a regular and symmetrical grid of street blocks stretched from the North-South avenue, which was the town's boundary in the west, as far east as the Chinese town which was already becoming densely populated, and from the colonial town in the north to the Cambodian town in the south.

The layout of the most important thoroughfares in this vast subdivision led to the west becoming the main direction for development. This occurred especially through the creation of a road junction with three branches linking the Kampot road in the northwest to the market, making a start towards the west on a first main avenue lined up with the market, and towards the south-west, a second avenue which joined an existing road at whose side the racecourse had been established on a former military site. It was the same in the south where an avenue had been drawn in line with the market. To the east and north on the other hand, the new streets extended the streets of the first colonial town and the Chinese town as far as the river.

Thus the centre of the modern town grew up around a monumental market building, a completely novel architectural conception, built in reinforced concrete, in a cruciform plan which went with the layout of the new avenues towards the west. Sur-

Figure 3.5 *The new market building* (Source: Le génie civil, no.113, 1938, p.536)

mounted by a vast cupola 45 metres in height, it amounted in fact to an immense roof on piles. This vast shelter through which the air circulated freely, with numerous fretted screen walls that filtered the violent tropical light and allowed the hot air to escape, became the emblem of the commercial district. Between the arms of this cross, small market stalls were soon set up to the west, north and south, but to the east the esplanade was laid out as a garden, in order to show that the street leading to the Mekong was the most important (see Figures 3.5 and 3.6).

Here there was no trace of neo-renaissance or Khmer decoration, but rather a rational design without excessive ornamentation, the truthfulness of the construction constituting its aesthetic truthfulness. The architecture of the central station built 4 years earlier expressed the same idea. From this time on, the

Figure 3.6 *The market forms a major focus in sprawling Phnom Penh, 1992* (Source: © SIRPA/ECPA France)

architecture of the town was to be modern, avoiding pastiches, and the beauty of the buildings was to come from the way they adapted to the climate and from the arrangement of the beams, the posts and the arch vaults or cupolas. Pile buildings, until then neglected in colonial architecture, regained their position of acclaim. They no longer served to provide protection from the water but to allow the air to circulate.

This wave of major works which had commenced in the late 1920s came to an abrupt halt with World War Two and did not resume until after Cambodia's independence in the late 1950s. Then, given impetus by Prince Norodom Sihanouk and made both necessary and urgent by the new status of Phnom Penh as the national capital, the next wave of major urban development was implemented by a great Khmer architect, Vann Molyvann. Having returned to Cambodia after his studies at the *École des Beaux Arts* in Paris, and under the influence of modern architecture whose symbolic figure at the time was Le Corbusier, Molyvann was commissioned by the prince for a new expansion plan and for the construction of major public institutions for the new state. With architect V. Bodiansky, who had worked extensively with Le Corbusier, they were to find in Phnom Penh a political context and a location well suited to architectural and planning experimentation.

Once again, the public amenities and institutional buildings shaped the town's growth. Kampot road, the route which led to the new airport (1959) and to Sihanoukville City (Cambodia's new port), became a wide avenue with a central open strip along which the new ministries and universities were built. Shortly after, in the south-west, the racecourse was replaced by the Olympic stadium constructed for the Asian Games of 1965 (Vann & Hanning 1964). This was to be the occasion for creating a vast subdivision of shop-houses, two markets and two pagodas to the north and south of the stadium and a new district of detached houses. This subdivision was achieved by filling in a zone almost as large again as the existing town, the boundaries of which were then three concentric *boulevard digues* (dykes surmounted by boulevards) designed for protection against flooding.

Similarly, to the south of the Royal Palace, the sacred pond was filled in and transformed into a garden just as the *prek* which drained water towards the Mekong at the extreme south of the reclaimed zone had been. The Independence Monument was later built on the axis of this esplanade. New lands were won from the river and on them were established housing blocks for middle-managerial families and the national theatre. Finally to the west of Beng Kak, to the north of the railway, a new residential quarter called Toul Kork slowly took shape. This was a sort of garden city protected by a peripheral dyke and with broad avenues converging on a circular open space in the centre of which the new telecommunications tower was erected. Here the subdivision was into larger allotments, some being 15 to 20 metres wide, which were destined to accommodate detached houses.

The extension of Phnom Penh's built-up area soon made it necessary to rethink the stormwater and domestic drainage system. As long as the town was confined to a narrow strip of land running north-south along the river, and as long as ponds, *prek* and unfilled lands capable of collecting the river spill-over inside the dykes survived, it was relatively easy to let the water flow quietly away. But this natural drainage had now become impossible. The enlargement of the town towards the west necessitated casting back large quantities of water outside the peripheral dyke by means of pumping stations equipped with motors powerful enough to lift the water up and over the road dyke. The water no longer flowed towards the Mekong but towards the surrounding swamps. Those *beng* and *prek* which remained inside the dykes were no longer mere ponds but vast reservoirs each equipped with a series of pumps. Eight pumping stations were constructed in this way.

Until 1970, this exterior dyke seemed like an overcoat which was too big for Phnom Penh's population, and vast unfilled sectors within it were used for agriculture. The subdivisions which had started were still far from being completely built up, but the structure of a great capital was in place. In locations where future subdivisions were planned, the residents who until then had lived there in pile houses found themselves being offered plots of reclaimed land in exchange for their existing land. In this way, many swapped their houses of bamboo and straw for villas or shop-houses made of concrete.

The official architecture of this period (1954-70) skilfully combined the doctrines of modern architecture and Khmer tradition. It should be said that pile houses, so dear to Le Corbusier and inscribed in the Charter of Athens as one of the principles of 'modern movement', found here a very particular response. The conception of the high-rise university buildings, the Olympic village (created for the Asian Games athletes), the complex of luxury flats built on the section of river bank designated the '*Front de Bassac*', all stemmed from the same model: the cross-beam on piles set in the middle of a green space.

But here the use of green space was not ordinary, it was in fact a system of gardens within which were dug ornamental ponds which collected the rainwater and contributed to the sector's drainage. In the Olympic stadium, these ponds, which also received liquid wastes, flowed into a purification plant before being linked back into the network leading to the *beng* and the pumping station. It was therefore a question of a modern reinterpretation of the ancient system of artificial ponds in the Khmer towns or, more recently, the systems in the pagoda compounds. It was not a question of hiding the water, of denying the town's site but of making use of it for a goal that was at the same time aesthetic and practical. This adaptation to the Khmer culture was also revealed in the conception of the stadium itself, set in a large grass-covered embankment slope reminiscent of the lower slopes of the artificial hills of Angkor's mountain-temples. Thus piles, mounds and human-made ponds came together to make up a distinctive landscape, reinterpreting the most profound elements of Khmer civilisation and integrating them at the same time into an uncompromising modernity.

These great works of the Sihanouk period came to a brutal stop in 1970. Cambodia was thrown into war, and the works carried out between 1970 and 1975, notably the extensive dykes built several kilometres from the town, had strictly military objectives. In 5 years, the population of Phnom Penh doubled, growing from one to two million inhabitants with city-bound refugees chased from the countryside by bombing raids. Refugee camps were set up. This sudden population increase had immediate effects: the pace of building construction accelerated; the subdivisions initiated under Sihanouk became more densely populated; and the old two-storey shop-houses from colonial times were extended upwards, reaching four or five storeys in height. This intensification of shop-houses was soon to transform profoundly the patterns of physical access to dwellings. The shop-houses began to be built one on top of the other. From this period, entrances at the ground-floor level, resulting from shops opening directly on to the street or main rooms opening on to a lane, began to double up as second entrances. A staircase leading from the lane allowed direct access to the dwelling situated on the second floor. Ground-floor rooms kept their original function. The shop-house thus became a residence for two families and moved away from its initial function as a single family dwelling/commerce unit.

This evolution got under way from the middle of the 1960s in the Olympic stadium neighbourhood where the shop-houses were built five storeys high. This period would see also the appearance of the large 'western-style' blocks of flats served by a staircase and often by a gangway at the rear. These new shop-houses, like the blocks of flats, became symbols of modernity. In the most densely built-up parts, the shop-houses reached 25 metres in depth while the lanes remained 3 to 6 metres in width. Today some shop-houses are occupied by a separate family on each floor. As no allowance for private access to the first floor was included in the ground-floor plan, the upper floor occupants entered by a ladder or by a staircase rising directly from the footpath.

Of the period 1975-79 there is little to say. In April 1975, in just three days, the city was emptied of its inhabitants, most (about 80 per cent) being killed and a small number leaving the country without hope of returning. For 3 years, Phnom Penh's only occupants (about 30 000 persons in all) were the soldiers, part of the 'Khmer Rouge' leadership and a number of workers. The system of urban services no longer functioned, some infrastructure being wrecked and those materials which could be used for other purposes being dismantled; even trees planted in the streets were cut down. What can one say in the face of such furious determination to destroy the city, the culture of its inhabitants, the books in its libraries, the administrative documents, its history and its future?

After 1979, life slowly began again, little by little

people re-entered the city, the soldiers first then the public service workers. Initially, as the people were not given permission to live there, they set up along the access roads - to the north on the road to Kom Pong Cham, and in the south-east, on the opposite bank of the Bassak, along the road to Ho Chi Minh City (formerly Saigon). Next, the new inhabitants installed themselves in the shop-houses and villas situated near their work. None of the Phnom Penh residents from before 1975 were able to resume possession of the houses they owned previously. Private property was abolished. For everyone, a new and very different life commenced - in another neighbourhood, with another occupation and in poverty. While some public buildings could be returned to their former functions, others were allocated to new ministries or new administrations. The universities remained closed, the schools started up again one by one - but in the most extreme conditions of deprivation.

The population of the city was estimated at 400 000 inhabitants in 1989, 500 000 at the end of 1990 and 800 000 at the end of 1992. This rapid regrowth was essentially due to the Cambodians being given back the right to move about the country, as well as to the arrival of dollars accompanying the Peace Accords which had been signed at the end of 1991, although prepared 3 years previously. With the re-establishment of private property at the end of 1989, the urban transformation accelerated. One could now buy and sell real estate. The inhabitants began by repainting, and then building construction started up again and gathered a more and more frenetic pace with the arrival of foreigners (notably from the United Nations) and embassy staff who had to be housed. Gradually the Chinese shop-keepers also returned and commerce began to flourish.

But the population installed in Phnom Penh since 1979 is not the same as that of the pre-1975 years. Of rural origin, the new residents cannot be expected to understand overnight the rules of urban life: for them, public space has no meaning, nor does the keeping of animals outside the house. Also the problems of city management multiplied in the first years, but the same reflex reactions of extending and transforming the city are being seen now as they were in the 1960s. Shop-houses are shooting up again, tim-

ber houses line the dyke roads on unfilled lands. New walls are being constructed, the piles are being closed in to create living rooms, while pile houses are being turned into villas.

Some colonial institutional buildings no longer have an official function and Phnom Penh's inhabitants are therefore authorised to occupy them; the buildings are transformed into residences; several dozen families install themselves in the extensive gardens of these former administrative complexes and construct houses there. Designated *terrains de la population*, their inhabitants cannot obtain property titles but can sell their occupancy right to others. Thus a new urban law is in fact organising urban life but it is by definition transitional. The former division into neighbourhoods has been totally swept away by the tumultuous events of the past 20 years.

PHNOM PENH, CAMBODIAN CITY 1993

Phnom Penh is a beautiful city, built on an exceptional site at the junction of the four arms of the Mekong (see Figure 3.7). The great monuments of the city, the Royal Palace, the great pagodas, lying close to the river, create a townscape of unique quality. Phnom Penh is a city based on sweeping and majestic tree-lined avenues. It spreads across a vast area organised on the base of a extremely well-arranged and hierarchical network of public walkways. Phnom Penh is a green city, most of its urban area comprising villas surrounded by trees. It has, therefore, a low density and is perfectly adapted to the climate. The trees are in fact an important element in protecting the dwellings and streets against the extreme heat.

But another essential component of Phnom Penh's beauty is its fragility. This is seen in the fragility of its infrastructure and notably of its network of drains, drinking water and electricity supply systems that are now obsolescent, damaged, indeed non-existent over half the urbanised area. Phnom Penh's fragility is also caused by its site which is susceptible to flooding, where the network of drains and the system comprising open canals, *beng* and *prek* must store up and eliminate large quantities of water during the monsoon season, and where permanent maintenance and protection from being over-run by constructions of various sorts is needed.

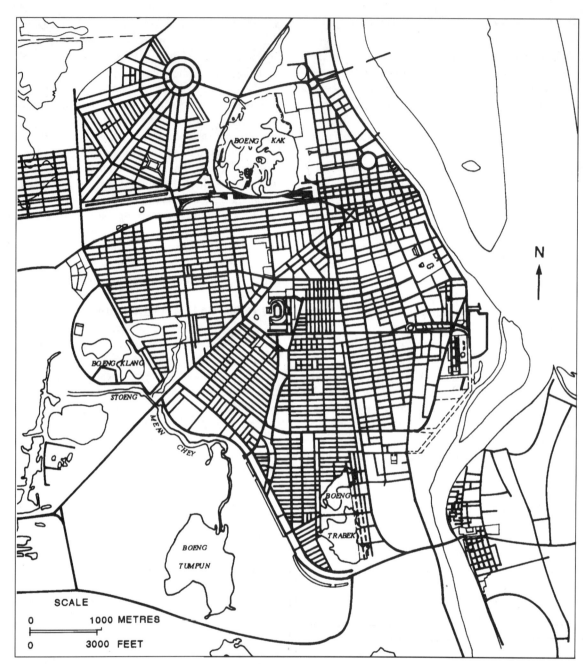

Figure 3.7   Phnom Penh, 1992 (after Service de l'Urbanisme de Phnom Penh and Atelier Parisien d'Urbanisme, December 1992)

The city's fragility also is due to the greed of speculators and investors whose only dream is to construct to the maximum extent on any pieces of land to the detriment of the gardens, tree plantings, open spaces and sometimes even the streets, *beng, prek* and canals. In fact, landowners tend to consider that, because a piece of land belongs to them, they have the right to build on it without regard to building height or the rights of neighbours, without any constraints whatsoever. They regard any restriction as an attack on property rights and that any constraint imposed by public authorities as unwarranted. Fragility also derives from the increase in the urban population which has accelerated in the last 2 years and to which has to be added the massive number of foreigners arriving with their capital, a major factor explaining the current level of property speculation. This phenomenon has led notably to the rapid transformation of shop-houses into hotels, the construction of new hotels and the restoration and extension of villas.

The transformations taking place are leading to an increase in building density, extensions upwards and outwards, new constructions in courtyards and gardens. This results in a removal of trees in the gardens and above all an increase in the volume of waste waters seeping into basements, septic tanks and the drains. The way things are going, in a few years Phnom Penh may well become an uninhabitable city where concrete will have replaced trees, raising the air temperatures, where water pollution will endanger the health of the residents (already not very sound today), where the quality of life will have deteriorated beyond redemption. This slightly apocalyptic vision is not just imagination; it has become a reality in some other cities, notably in Bangkok where traffic movement has become impossible, pollution is severe and life in the centre of the city is extremely difficult.

This frightening future is difficult to imagine, for a city's quality of life is lost little by little, without anyone taking note. Buildings are constructed one by

Figure 3.9   Law courts in January 1992

one, their pernicious effects not being realised at the start; it is only later after the buildings have multiplied, historic monuments obliterated (Figures 3.8, 3.9, 3.10) and whole quarters of villas concreted over that the sanitary and climatic effects of these transformations appear. But it is then too late to go back; the damage is done.

Today, in Phnom Penh, constructions are multiplying at a lively pace (Figure 3.11), but it is not their rapid construction which poses problems; rather, it is the very dense nature of the buildings, especially the five-storey and six-storey hotels being constructed in the city centre, on minimal areas of land, which threaten the quality of life of Phnom Penh's inhabitants by producing cubic metres of liquid waste without the infrastructure necessary for proper drainage. Problems stem also from the extensive building sites that lack protective fences: cement and sand is stored on the footpath, and building materials and rubble are allowed to wash into the drains, causing further deterioration in the underground drainage network. Furthermore, trees are cut down because they get in the way of the building. Construction work also gives rise to activities that defy all the rules of health and hygiene. In fact, one can see today the wholesale suppression of natural ventilation systems in favour of air-conditioning in hotels: plans propose that half the rooms be without windows opening onto the exterior. This means that the way the building functions is determined by the air-conditioner and is dependent therefore on the supply of electric energy which everyone knows is unreliable in Phnom Penh. Similarly it is not the pile houses which pose problems on the *beng* and the *prek* but

Figure 3.8   Law courts in 1905

Figure 3.10   Law court being demolished in April 1992

the unauthorised filling-in of land which is now out of control.

Today in Phnom Penh, the boundaries between public space and private land have become blurred, but, here too, it is necessary to see the problems in terms of their relative gravity. The flimsy constructions which are being erected on the footpaths are not very serious, even if they disrupt pedestrian movement. It becomes more important when people construct huts across the streets and transform streets into cul-de-sacs because traffic becomes impossible; nevertheless such obstructions can be shifted. The irremediable is created when the masonry constructions fail to respect the boundaries of the street and extend onto the footpath.

But other phenomena are shaping the city's future growth. Take, for example, the Cambodiana Hotel and the recently filled land along the river to the south of the hotel. From the square situated in front of Wat Onalom as far as the Cambodiana Hotel, the embankment is an immense esplanade punctuated by gardens, a place for promenades intended for all the inhabitants of Phnom Penh to enjoy. Now the Cambodiana Hotel extends down to the river bank and the esplanade cuts through it. The hotel's generators and the purification plant are installed on the square. In this place, no-one can enjoy the magnificent view of the four arms of the Mekong. And what can be done to the south of the hotel? The current projects are planning a public walkway along the river bank extending as far as the infill actually completed, but what will happen beyond that, between the current infill and the Monwong Bridge? Here a choice has to be made and made quickly because it

will influence the sale of land along the river's edge: a choice between public space, open to all, along the river and a succession of private landholdings mirroring the Cambodiana Hotel in that they, too, would prevent all access by the public to the river banks. Here the quality of life for all Phnom Penh residents is at stake and is today being hotly debated.

Another less localised example is that of the trees in the private gardens around the villas. Today, when a villa is restored or constructed, the owners tend to lay concrete over the garden so they can park vehicles; and most often this is accompanied by the cutting down of existing trees or the absence of plantations of young trees around new constructions. This trend, if it continues, will have very harmful effects on the urban environment. In fact, making the garden soils impermeable in this way prevents much of the rain water from soaking into the ground, accentuates the volume of water carried into drains which are already barely coping, and will therefore increase the floods. The chopping down of trees removes the shade and coolness, essential factors needed to make a building comfortable to live in. One might think that this is no longer of importance since the houses are now increasingly air-conditioned, but it is still the case that the houses are uninhabitable during periods of electricity failure.

Another example which relates to the preceding one but which concerns more particularly the shop-houses is that of permits to erect buildings overhanging public thoroughfares. In Phnom Penh, the facades are generally fitted with canopies, balconies

Figure 3.11   Upward growth of shop-houses in central Phnom Penh (Source: C. Blancot)

and loggias (covered and partitioned balconies giving shelter from the sun and overhanging the public thoroughfare by a width of about 1.2 metres). The ground-floor facade is protected by a wider canopy which generally juts 2 metres onto the footpath and which is situated at a height of 4.5 metres above the pavement. This system of sunshades, sometimes completed by a fretted partition, is designed to filter the light, to stop the sun reaching the facade and, by creating a zone of shadow, to cool the air which flows into the interior spaces through the ventilators situated above the doors and windows. Now when owners are carrying out work on a building these days, they are tending to close in the loggias and balconies in order to enlarge the floor space of the internal rooms and they are also shutting off the raised ventilators. The logic underlying their belief that the air-conditioning allows them to jettison the devices protecting them from the sun's rays and heat, also leads them to do away with the natural ventilation.

Today in Phnom Penh, the hydraulic infrastructure, the system of surface water drainage (canals, prek, beng, dykes, pumping stations), and the sites of public utilities (schools, hospitals, public administration, public gardens) are in danger of choking to death. The hydraulic infrastructure is in a poor state; the drains are old, partially blocked off and cover only half of the urbanised area. The same applies to the old septic tanks which are often out of use due to the lack of maintenance or because of their great age. Now when a property owner erects a high density building, a hotel for example, which is going to produce much waste water, too often the buildings are transformed without the tanks being remade and enlarged, an action which can only accentuate the pollution of the subsoil and therefore have negative effects on the already poor condition of the population's general health.

The system of stormwater drainage is also very important in the wet season, notably at times when the Mekong floods. Today, the floods in the city are increasing. One of the main reasons for this is the lack of dredging of the canals, the prek and the beng; however the unauthorised filling-in of sites in the flood-free zones also contributes to the problem. In general, only pile houses are authorised on unfilled sites and it is forbidden to cut the water run-off systems by landfilling.

In short, what is emerging today is a resumption of urban expansion plans: already new subdivisions are being created, but, in the absence of major works due to the country's poverty and the weakness of its public services, urbanisation is occurring before the construction of infrastructure necessary for harmonious development. The filling-in of land by private constructors or by owners is taking place in defiance of the logic of the drainage network. The easiest areas are being filled, the prek and beng, with all the risks of blocking the hydraulic system that this entails. Land speculation and population growth are accelerating this phenomenon.

Similarly, the city's architectural heritage is in danger of being largely destroyed. This is notably true for the buildings of the colonial period, coveted by speculators greedy for large well-located sites on which to build tourist hotels. Here, as in other cities in France's former colonies, the realisation barely exists that these colonial buildings will in the future form part of the national heritage, that they have a historical value, that they are on the whole solidly constructed and can therefore be put to new uses. Here again, one has to remember however that most of the city's population today are still working through their apprenticeship in urban living. The reappropriation of the city, of the entire city by its inhabitants, their attachment to its townscape, its monuments, its rhythm and its history cannot be achieved in a day. One hopes that it will not be achieved too late.

ENDNOTES

1 Translated from the French by W.S. Logan.

2 The Third Republic was the French governmental system established in 1870 after the fall of Napoleon III in the Franco-Prussian War and lasting until the German Occupation of 1940.

3 For a fuller description of the establishment of the colonial city than appears in this chapter, see Collard 1925; Goulin 1966; Lamant 1991; and Igout 1993.

4 Quoted from the key to the Phnom Penh expansion plan presented by E. Hébrard at the time of the International Congress on Urbanism in the Colonies and Tropical Countries, Paris 1931.

REFERENCES

Collard, Paul 1925, *Cambodge et cambodgiens. Métamorphoses du royaume khmer par une méthode française du protectorat*, École Française d'Extrême-Orient, Paris.

Goulin, Christian 1966, *Phnom Penh: étude de géographie humaine*, Doctorat de Troisième Cycle dissertation, Phnom Penh.

Hébrard, Ernest 1928, 'L'Urbanisme en Indochine', *L'Architecture*, vol.41, no.2, pp.33-48

Hébrard, Ernest 1932, 'L'Urbanisme en Indochine' in Royer, Jean (ed.), *L'Urbanisme aux colonies et dans les pays tropicaux. Communications et rapports du congrès international*, Delayance, La Charité-sur-Loire, vol.1, pp.278-89.

Igout, Michel 1993, *Phnom Penh Then and Now*, White Lotus, Bangkok.

Lamant, Pierre Lucien 1991, 'La création d'une capitale par le pouvoir colonial: Phnom Penh', in Lafont, P.B. (ed.), *Péninsule indochinoise. Études urbaines*, L'Harmattan, Paris, pp.59-102.

Vann, Molyvann & Hanning, Gérard H. 1964, 'Complexe olympique de Phnom Penh', *Architecture Aujourd'hui*, no.116, pp.30-3.

Viaro, Alain 1992, 'Le compartiment chinois est-il chinois?', *Les cahiers de la recherche architecturale*, no.27/28, 1st trimester, pp.139-50.

4

Bangkok: transformation of the Thai city

Marc Askew

URBANISATION AND NATIONAL DEVELOPMENT

The noted Thai social commentator Sulak Sivaraksa recently dismissed Bangkok simply as 'a second rate Western city' (Sulak, 1990, p.323). While clearly inadequate as a description of the Thai metropolis, implied in this shorthand slur is a much broader critique of the place of Bangkok, urbanisation and 'Westernisation' in the recent history of socio-cultural and economic change in Thailand. Summarised as 'modernisation', the transformation in Thailand has been expressed in many ways, but none so conspicuously as in the changing socio-cultural and physical environment of Thailand's great primate city. In terms of population alone, Thailand's metropolis dwarfs the large provincial towns: forty-one times the size of the second largest urban centre of Nakhon Rachasima and fifty-nine times the size of the third largest city of Khon Kaen (National Statistical Office [NSO] 1991). With little over a million people in 1947, Bangkok has expanded to over 5.5 million inhabitants by 1991. This estimate only covers the population in the thirty-six *ket* (urban administrative districts) which comprise the area controlled by the Bangkok Metropolitan Administration (BMA). If the provinces outside the 1 568 737 square kilometre BMA (which comprises the adjoining expanded Metropolitan Re-

gion of Bangkok [BMR]) are included, the population (official estimate) amounts to over 8.5 million, and is projected to reach 9.9 million by the year 2001 (National Economic and Social Development Board [NESDB] 1986, p.50; BMA, 1991, p.11). The populations and workforces of these outer provinces (officially part of the designated Bangkok Metropolitan Region) are growing at a faster rate (in absolute and proportional terms) than the inner and intermediate areas, and in fact the oldest districts of the city continue to experience population decline (NESDB 1986, p.49). The BMR's population represents at least 10 per cent of the national population and will continue to grow proportionately, representing nearly 45 per cent of the nation's population living in urban areas. The territorial expansion of the built-up area since the end of World War Two has been dramatic. Between 1947 and 1956, the built-up area expanded from around 67 square kilometres to some 90 square kilometres; by 1980 this had reached over 239 square kilometres. Bangkok's primacy, expressed in population figures, is corroborated in a range of further indices; from the metropolitan region's powerful contribution to the Gross National Product (GNP) (nearly 50 per cent) to its dominant role as the focus of administration and government, education, business and transport networks (Sternstein

1984; Rigg 1991, ch.7).

Located on the low-lying deltaic plain of the Chao Phaya River valley only 0-1 metres above sea level, Bangkok has always been prone to flooding; but changes over the last 30 years to the city's ecology through the filling of its old canals, the pumping of groundwater by industry, and the sheer weight of new high-rise buildings and traffic has led to the sinking of urban land and greatly exacerbated flooding. Today, ecologically-minded critics claim that nature has had its revenge on this transformed Thai city which apparently coexisted in greater harmony with its surroundings (Nid 1989). Yet setting the contemporary Westernised Bangkok against an earlier indigenous settlement can lead to oversimplified and overly romanticised images of the quality of urban life in the past.[1] In the nineteenth century, Bangkok's unique landscape and 'waterscape' of floating houses and temples set amidst lush greenery, a mighty river and labyrinthine canals was a source of continuing fascination to foreign visitors. This 'oriental' city of mystery and difference, gradually changing through this very contact with the West, was both quaint and anachronistic to the foreigner's gaze. Just as suburbanites who in their lifetime often witness the demise of the surroundings which once drew them to their domestic paradise, the Western visitors were soon lamenting the physical signs of change taking place in Bangkok - the rise of the street and the disappearance of the floating houses of old.

The simplified image of the old city embraced by Thais and foreigners alike is nevertheless indicative of a wider sense of loss and transformation in Thai society. So as images of the placid canalside lifestyle of Bangkokians of yesteryear are increasingly used in the popular media, the reality of contemporary Bangkok becomes more and more intolerable as a living environment. Thailand's modernisation has been held up as a masterpiece of controlled change from above, at least with regard to the last century. Yet the fundamental economic transformation which was wrought by closer connection to a capitalist world economy became increasingly obvious in the changing face of the city. Bangkok was the economic and physical space on which such change became inscribed. Just as the state polity changed to accommodate the aspirations of rising elites (seen in the

fall of the absolute monarchy in 1932), Bangkok was acting as the site where different groups competed for power and survival. Following World War Two, pressures on the Thai capital as a living space and environment mounted as it acted both as the conduit for economic change and modernisation in the Western mould as well as the magnet for the rural poor in search of economic opportunity.

To the problems generated by sheer demographic pressures and economic changes in the post World War Two years, a Western planning paradigm was imposed on Bangkok. While the model proposed by the consultants Litchfield, Bowne and Associates in 1961 was never, and could never be, fully implemented (largely because it assumed the possibility of co-ordinating the activities of agencies so that land-use controls could be possible), the idea of boosting a Western-styled transport infrastructure was embraced wholeheartedly by administrators. This locked the Thai elite into further dependence on Western technological expertise. The advice of succeeding waves of foreign experts since the late 1950s, while well intentioned and professionally proffered, has never been co-ordinated effectively, due both to circumstance (continued high rates of urban growth driven by demographic pressures and the imperatives of capital accumulation) and the persisting characteristics of the Thai power structure.[2] Transport problems, massive as they are, are only one part of a complex of forces which are making urban life at times almost intolerable for Bangkokians. Pressures on individuals and communities vary to some degree, depending on the locational choices available for work, residence and recreation. This is the same everywhere. In a socio-cultural sense, the material and environmental pressures in Bangkok are also threatening to eliminate older patterns and community resources which, paradoxically, could provide the best key to survival (Anuchat & Ross 1992).[3]

This discussion deals with the question of Bangkok's urbanism and urban identity from the perspective of the making and construction of Bangkok as a place, a site, a habitat and a symbol. How do the elements of urban Bangkok's social and spatial environment interact in a framework of rapid change? In what manner do local and global influences operate in the physical landscape? What is the role of the

Thai state (so critical in development planning) in influencing such processes? These themes are dealt with in the context of the socio-cultural changes and continuities that have marked Thai history since the nineteenth century, and development issues of the current decade. In addition to the many commentaries and studies which have stressed Bangkok's situation as an urban management problem and an engineering nightmare (Thailand Development Research Institute [TDRI] 1991), there are other perspectives on the meaning of urban change as represented in Bangkok, even though the city's pervasive environmental and traffic problems invariably influence the way 'the urban' is experienced at first hand by native urban dwellers and visitors alike. Critiques and discussions grounded on a socio-cultural base are taking place in Thailand, increasingly so in relation to urban experience and urban communities, even though the transformation of rural life attracts most attention from this perspective (Kwansuong 1991). As the city changes, socio-cultural values are brought into starker relief, highlighting questions of locality and global change, modernity and tradition, identity and indifference, cultural resources and the production of images.

GANPATTANA

Thailand's economic growth in the 1950s, largely based on its exports of primary goods (especially rice), was harnessed by the regime of Field Marshal Sarit Thanarit (who assumed power 1958) towards a pattern of national development which ultimately favoured the metropolis over the countryside, and resulted in conspicuous inequalities between city and rural provinces where the majority of the population lived and worked. The urban settlement pattern of Thailand had always been one dominated by the capital city, administratively and economically. Economic change and development planning compounded this level of primacy (Sternstein 1976, pp.74-94; London 1980). The first three national development plans (the first commencing 1961) followed World Bank advice in aiming to boost manufacturing and export capacity while establishing an energy and transport infrastructure to support an economy based on free market competition. With an impressive Gross National Product (GNP) growth rate of 8

per cent per annum in the years 1956-70, Thailand nevertheless saw many of the benefits of development flow to the expanding city of Bangkok (Figure 4.1): the major roads funded by US aid all centred on the metropolis, reinforcing its hold on the hinterland; a middle-class consumer market grew in the city, expressed conspicuously in the growth in numbers of motor car and urban service users (Chattip 1971; Pasuk 1980).

Ganpattana (development) was achieved at a significant price. While there had always been dissident voices in Thailand, official acknowledgment of the environmental, social and culturally disorientating costs of economic change did not occur until the Fourth National Social and Economic Development Plan was brought forward in 1977. The policy issues focussed on redirecting urban growth from Bangkok to major designated provincial centres, addressing the problem of the great disparities in living standards and income between urban and rural populations, responding to the rapid deterioration in natural resources and in addition recognising the importance of a measure of conservation and cultural policy in counteracting the more destructive effects of untrammelled economic-led change (NESDB 1976, ch.VII). Specifically, the conservation objectives of the Fourth Plan centred on the preservation of a number of ancient cities (including Sukhothai) and the preservation and rehabilitation of the old part of the city of Bangkok, known as Rattanakosin Island. Other measures of this period included the formation of the Office of the National Culture Commission (ONCC) in 1979, with its brief to formulate plans, promote and develop culture, draw on 'culture' in relation to educational economic and political development as well as participate in the enforcement of culture-related laws (ONCC 1989). The current Seventh Plan recognises the cumulative effects of the rapid economic growth and social change of the past years by stressing the need for balanced socio-economic development and income distribution, responsible environmental management, social stability and cultural identity (NESDB 1992).

Critics may claim that the stress on 'national' cultural development is merely a continuation of a long-term process initiated by the State on behalf of the dominant Central Thai to integrate a culturally

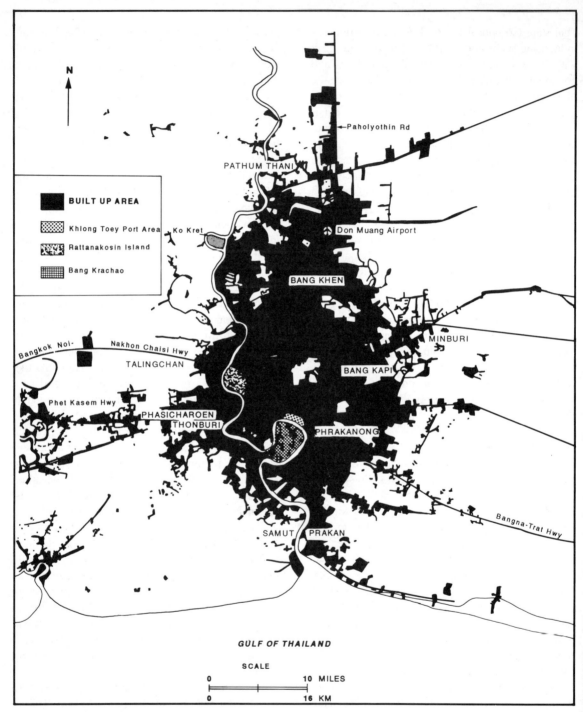

Figure 4.1   Bangkok: approximate extent of the built-up area, 1992

diverse population and ensure social order among Thais generally (see Reynolds 1991). Certainly it is noticeable that when cultural policy is advocated as a development instrument, it is almost always accompanied by reference to social order. At a less official level, responses among Thais to the effects of those changes of which 'development' and urbanisation are both a part, have taken a variety of forms, from the reassertion of Buddhist values of non-attachment and charity, to studies of folk arts and ethnic minority cultures, the restoration of artefacts, literary production and social criticism, architectural conservation or renovation and academic inquiry. The following discussion deals with a number of these interrelated responses with particular reference to Bangkok.

BANGKOK - CENTRE OF CHANGE AND TRADITION

It is clearly impossible to separate Bangkok from any discussion of development issues or modernisation in Thailand generally, since the city has been implicated in so many of the changes, whether as an agent or a recipient. Just as Krung Thep, since its inception as royal capital in 1782, has always acted as the principal interface between Siam (the former name of Thailand till 1939, and from 1945-49) and the world of the foreigner, a beachhead of Western cultural influence from outside the kingdom, it has also been the site where broader national trends and power struggles have been played out. The flow of the rural poor to Bangkok, which accelerated markedly after World War Two, changed the social, demographic and physical environment of the capital irrevocably. The city was transformed from a small and comparatively sedate settlement of Thai bureaucrats, elite families of noble birth, lesser civil servants and dependents with its busy trading community of Chinese merchants and entrepreneurs and a sprinkling of European officials and traders - all nestled in a rich network of gardens and paddyfields connected by canals - to a sprawling and bustling, concrete-and-asphalt automobile city whose crowded population represented people from all regions of the country, and whose unskilled workers were drawn disproportionately from its poorest provinces.

National inequities were expressed in urban form in the contrasts in living environments and standards of living: while the middle class moved into Western-style bungalows in the expanding suburbs, the poor crammed into the older congested quarters of the inner city or in the interstices found in the urban fabric. The vast slum of Khlong Toey, which developed adjacent to the new river port of that name and expressed one of the dominant features of modern Bangkok, fully symbolised - as much as the new regional headquarters of organisations such as the Food and Agriculture Organisation (FAO), Economic and Social Commission for Asia and the Pacific (ESCAP), South East Asian Treaty Organisation (SEATO), United Nations International Children's Emergency Fund (UNICEF) and United Nations Educational Scientific and Cultural Organisation (UNESCO) - the city's enhanced role as an international administrative centre in the Southeast Asian region. A burgeoning tourist trade from the mid-1970s boosted the urban service infrastructure established during the Vietnam War years for Rest and Recreation (R & R) visitors, prompting changes in the formal and informal, respectable and unrespectable occupational sectors of the workforce - from hotel waiters to vendors of imitation Swiss watches, from guesthouse proprietors to Pat Pong dancing girls.

What are the elements of Bangkok's urbanism? Some academics have insisted that urban life is a characteristic peculiar to the West, and that Southeast Asian civilisation had no urban traditions prior to the colonisation and urbanisation of the region by European powers. However, as others have pointed out (e.g. O'Connor 1983), the fact of the overwhelmingly agricultural nature of the Southeast Asian economies up until quite recently should not detract from the cultural, political and economic significance of urban centres in the region. Certainly with reference to Siam, an understanding of urbanism is indispensable to an appreciation of important elements of the cultural tradition. Two points should be emphasised in relation to Bangkok's function as the key economic and political site of the Siamese state, regardless of the specific details about urban form which will be outlined later. First, by virtue of the absolute authority of its rulers until the first third of this century and the circumstances of its foundation as the new royal capital from at least 1782, Bangkok was the principal site of significant change and in-novation in Siam. Second, by virtue of the nature of Siamese kingship and its Indic urban heritage de-rived from the eleventh century polity of Cambodia, Bangkok was heir to an idea which fixed the royal city as the symbolic centre of power (O'Connor 1991). Thus, two tendencies involving change and continu-ity respectively were to coexist in the history of Bang-kok's development.

To talk about 'Bangkok' in the context of the Indic urban traditions is in fact inappropriate; more suited is the term *Krung Thep Maha Nakorn*[4] (City of An-gels, Great City), the first superlatives of a long title endowing the site of the city with glory and sacred-ness, as fitting the seat of the monarch linked with the gods. The name *Bangkok* is a popular name of the place, derived from its natural setting (*Bang* means 'settlement on a waterway'; *Kok* is the name of a fruit tree), which predated royal settlement of the region by some 400 years. When King Taksin re-established the power base of Siam in the Thonburi-Bangkok area in 1768, he imposed on an old-estab-lished riverine and canal-based settlement of *bang* (population settlements on waterways) and *ban* (vil-lages) another structure and a new set of meanings. The sites of the twin settlements of Bangkok (on the East bank) and Thonburi (on the West) had once shared the same bulge of land formed by a wide loop in the Chao Phraya River until, in the seven-teenth century, a channel was cut to shorten the route to the capital city of Ayutthaya 74 kilometres north-wards. Henceforth this channel became the main path of the river and the principal channel of transport. The twin riverside settlements became the sites of important fortifications and trading activity prior to the fall of Ayutthaya in 1767.

The creation of the royal city, first on the Thonburi side in 1768 by King Taksin, and then, in 1782, at Bangkok, by Rama I of the new Chakri dynasty, over-laid the simple structure of the riverine agricultural communities with the hierarchy of aristocracy, bu-reaucracy and royal court. This hierarchy was de-fined first by the very name of the royal city, which bespoke its status as the seat of power of the Lord of Life. Physically, Rattanakosin Island was formed by the cutting of a moat around an elbow of land at the curve of the river. This had occurred before the Chakri

Figure 4.2   The floating city, Bangkok, circa 1900. View across the Chao Phraya River from near the mouth of Khlong Lod. (Source: Ernst von Hesse-Wartegg, Siam das Reich des Weissen Elefanten, 1899)

dynasty was established, although the palace re-mained on the Thonburi side until King Taksin was overthrown. Following the assumption to power of Rama I (Pra Puttayodfa), the newly named Rattanakosin Island became the site of the king's royal household and administration. Outside the walls of the palace compound-proper were settled many of the nobility and their retainers.

Prior to royal settlement at Bangkok, there had been a sizeable Chinese trading community (of the Tiochiu speech group) occupying that space. They were moved to a position outside the new city walls to a place near Wat Sampeng, which formed the ba-sis of today's Chinese business district of Sampeng (Skinner 1957). Within the fortified city (defined physically by two rings of moats which also func-tioned as canals, the inner moat surrounding the palace precinct) there were few structures established on the low-lying flood-prone estuarine land. Most commoners lived on dwellings known as *phae* which floated on the river or its tributary canals (Figures 4.2 and 4.2). This 'aquatic' or 'floating' city which so fascinated the foreigners who visited Bangkok, was marked by hierarchy.

The structures on land principally comprised the palace complex with its chapel royal, the *wat* (tem-ples), many of which in fact predated Krung Rattanakosin, and the palaces of the nobility. Many of these early *wat* near the palace, subsequently, were established as 'royal' *wat* and thus were absorbed

Figure 4.3   The core of European riverside settlement in late nineteenth-century Bangkok, since moved away from the river along Silom Road. Note the Thai timber houses with characteristic raked gables. (Source: J.T. Child, The Pearl of Asia, *1892)*

within a hierarchy which conferred the traditionally high status given to places of royal patronage. Such temples were favoured by renovation, the addition of new *chedi* (stupas), and sacred Buddha images. The temples which had formerly served the communities among the patchwork of gardens and rice fields thus became subject to a system of placement in an urban-centred status order. So today's royal temple, Wat Chana Songkram, literally 'Wat of the Victorious War', was so named by Rama I's brother as a sign of gratefulness because his troops rested near the temple on return from a victorious campaign against the Burmese. The original name 'Wat Glang Na' (The Wat at the Centre of the Rice Field) reflected its natural site and local identity in the pre-Rattanakosin settlement. Another temple, Wat Sangwet, was first known as 'Wat Sam Jin' (the Wat of the Three Chinese), no doubt because of the identity of its first patrons. It then became known as 'Wat Banglamphu' after the name of the khlong nearby, and later it was renamed because of royal patronage. Official renaming of such institutions thus lifted them out of their environmental context and located them within another hierarchy centring on the king and his family (O'Connor 1991).

The link between kingship and the Buddhist religion had been intermeshed since at least the Sukhothai period of the thirteenth century. Making merit for the future life by building new temples was a common ambition for monarchs, the nobility and

the well to do. So in the early years of the Bangkok period, old and revered images were brought from the ruined temples of Ayutthaya and other settlements (including Vientiane) to embellish the city. According to the traditional pattern, around the palace and the royal city were clustered the temples with the most revered relics. The first kings were active in promoting the building of new temples throughout the region of the capital. *Wat* building had been so active in the first three reigns, in fact, that Rama IV (1851-68) began to emphasise the repairing of temples rather than the building of new ones. Of a later period, one could remark: 'Every now and then we come to the enclosure of some temple, often deserted and falling into decay, for the Siamese think that they make much merit by contributing towards the building of a new temple, but money spent upon repairs is far less meritoriously employed...they serve a few generations of worshippers, and then they are allowed to moulder quietly away' (Thompson 1910, p.46).[5] In one sense, such a situation truly represented the realities of the transience of all things, as taught in the Dhamma ('the truth' or 'true principles' of the Buddhist doctrine) (Figure 4.4).

Although chronologically young, Bangkok was built to resemble the old capital and thus to perpetuate the idea of a traditional Siamese royal centre. This phase of urbanistic reconstitution also coincided with a time of economic and population change which was to affect the functions and appearance of the city. In the royal poem *Inow*, King Rama II described a fictional city which in almost all respects was a description of his own city of Krung Thep. It was an inventory of the major landmarks and features of Bangkok, including the *phae*, the *teuk* (brick and stucco buildings of the nobility), the gilded roofs of the temples and spires of the *chedi*, the great swing which identified an urban ritual space (in this instance a Brahmanic ritual), and the Moslem mosque, which identified the city as a place of ethnic diversity. This was essentially the view from the perspective of the palace and the ruler. He mentioned neither the *bang* nor the *ban,* nor the markets at the junctions of the canals (*khlong*), which demarcated the city of the common people. These absences from the inventory in themselves confirm the hierarchical

Figure 4.4   The transience of things.

(top)   Talingchan. An old wihan, bearing an emblem dating its construction from the reign of King Rama IV, decays outside the precinct of a recently-built successor. (Source: *M. Askew*)

(bottom)   Bangkokians from the inner city celebrate Kathin (the end of Lent) by contributing towards the building of a new temple building in Rachaburi Province. (Source: *M. Askew*)

ordering of places in Rama II's capital.[6]

How were the elements of Krung Thep, the reconstituted Siamese city of Krung Sri Ayutthaya, connected? Did they ever form a unity? From the perspective of hierarchy at least, the city was knit together by the rituals and occasions which marked the lives of the monarchs and the festivals of the Buddhist religion. So the great barge processions of the newly-invested kings marked out the royal temples, defining the city as a royal domain; the cremations of the kings and relatives at the Pramane Ground next to the palace complex (now *Sanam Luang,* or the royal grounds, used for popular recreation) focussed on the historic centre of Krung Rattanakosin; the seasonal festivals of *Thod Kathin* (the giving of robes to the monks after Buddhist lent) and *Songkran* (new year) highlighted the *wat* as the great centres of the city's religious identity. Religious occasions were almost always accompanied with popular games and events, such as boat races, which echoed the lifestyles of forebears of the Ayutthayan period. The canals which were dug between the two moats of the city during the first reign were used for such festive water events. In a recent discussion of the cultural meaning of Bangkok, Professor Tagashi Tomosugi (1991, p.130) suggests that Bangkok embodies collective memories somehow crystallised in its major urban icons; moreover, the rituals of the royal city and its images (palace and royal temple, for example) functioned to fashion a cultural identity for the king's subjects. Such may have been the case for an agrarian society under an absolute ruler; but how might such ritual function in contemporary Thai society?

CELEBRATING THE FOUNDATION OF A ROYAL CITY

There has been no better expression of the defining nature of ritual and ceremony for Indic (or official) Thai urbanism than the Rattanakosin Bicentennial celebrations of 1982. The events were staged not to mark the establishment of Bangkok, but to commemorate the establishment of a dynasty and its capital. King and city were thus merged in a demonstration of order and continuity. In cultural terms, the Bangkok-based Chakri dynasty was presented as the carrier of the Thai nation's 'Great Tradition' (the preserver of monarchical institutions, Buddhism, literature and art). The celebration, which took place between 4 and 21 April, focussed on the Royal Barge Procession, a spectacular sight involving a flotilla of fifty-one royal barges which were rowed downstream along the Chao Phraya River to the old palace, long since abandoned by the Thai monarchs for the more modern Chidralada in the northern suburb of Dusit. After landing at the Royal Palace (*Phra Borom Maha Rachawang*) boat landing, the Royal Family proceeded to the main palace gate to pay homage to their ancestral spirits. If the details of this ritual may have escaped most of the spectators, the ceremony of homage was familiar enough to the majority of ordinary Thais who customarily pay respects to the *Chaw Thi* (land spirit) of their home. Homage and respect, the key features of Thai social relations (both between people and the supernatural beings that inhabit the world, unseen but nonetheless real) were enacted in the royal ritual, tapping a common cultural source. The link between the personal (HRH King Bumiphol Adulyadej and the Royal Family) and the dynastic sources of legitimacy and identity were displayed and, presumably, widely accepted. As one source remarked: 'there is a mysticism about our loyalty to the Chakri dynasty which transcends the material and the worldly, it cannot be explained...' (*Bangkok Post*, 6 Apr. 1982). The celebrations coincided with two other important events: Chakri Day (6 April) and *Songkran*, the Water Festival, to mark the end of the dry season, customarily the beginning of the Thai New Year.

Chakri Day witnessed a range of activities which tapped other memories of the city. In the morning, a procession marched to the Pra Phutta Yodfa memorial bridge to pay respects to the statue of Rama I, founder of the dynasty. This statue, modelled by the Italian sculptor Corrado Feroci, who founded the national art school (now Silpakorn University), was cast in typical realist heroic style. The bridge, the first to link the twin towns of Thonburi and Bangkok, had been unveiled by the unfortunate King Prajadipok (Rama VII) to mark the 150th Rattanakosin year in 1932. Later in that year, a coup by an alliance of bureaucrats and military men demoted Rama VII to constitutional monarch and the real power base

of Thai society was to change irrevocably. In this bicentennial year, however, there was no ambivalence. After 2 years of relative stability under General Prem Tinsulanonda following the traumatic and unsettling years of the later 1970s, this celebration seemed to function as a cohesive event, a celebration of the longest reigning monarch of the dynasty, a transcendent figure above the transient world of party politics and factional rivalry.

But what did it have to do with the city? The Governor of Bangkok announced that '...in no other capital city are the ideals of a people so concentrated, and no other capital city determines the ideals of a people as does Bangkok' (Sternstein 1982, Preface). Clearly the events marked out special places in the city. Two key areas in particular centred attention on the old Bangkok - the river processions (there were two) evoked the period when Krung Thep was literally a floating city, echoing the images of the old river and canal-based polity of Ayutthaya. The first river procession was a spectacular exercise in orchestrated nostalgia, comprising more vessels than the procession of the ill-fated Rama VII 50 years earlier, even if a mere shadow of the great procession at Rama IV's coronation in 1850 which had boasted over 260 vessels (Flood 1965, p.39). On 12 April, the same day that the second barge event carried the King and the sacred Buddha image Phra Bhudda Singh to Sanam Luang to be part of the Songkran festival, over 200 Chinese associations gathered on Yawarat Road (the historic heart of the Chinese business district of Sampeng) to pay respect to the past kings of the Chakri dynasty (*Bangkok Post*, 12 Apr. 1982). To an extent, what really were at stake in the celebrations were respect for the dynasty of the reigning monarch, respect for guardian spirits and ancestors, and re-enactment of a water-based ceremony that evoked something of the exotic past of the city. One can also emphasise the public expression of the integration of the Chinese merchant capitalist class into the symbolic fabric of the city.

Several years of preparation by scholars had generated a range of publications which collectively advanced knowledge about the sites and built structures of Bangkok. In terms of publicity about the city's past, the bicentennial year marks a watershed. While in earlier decades, there had been a number of notable publications about the historical Bang-kok[7], much detailed documentation and analysis was lacking. In 1982, however, detailed accounts of the Royal Palace and temple architecture, arts and crafts and historical architecture in Bangkok turned atten-tion to an urban past seemingly lost over the past 30 years in the race for modernity. From the perspec-tive of the government, the celebrations were to serve an essentially conserving function: to present an ar-ray of images and narratives which would highlight royal traditions and hence stability through hierar-chy.[8] The government committee charged with re-viewing all publications dealing with the celebrations stressed themes dealing with unity and coherence in terms of culture and polity: nation, capital and dy-nasty were to be united in a celebration of arts, culture and religion.

But if General Prem's government was stressing the genius of the Chakri monarchs in preserving the independence of the Thai nation, some Thai schol-ars, although a minority, took the opportunity to pro-vide more detailed analysis of urban change (for example, Piyanat et al. 1982; Pussadee 1982). Larry Sternstein's collection of essays was one of the few publications which took the opportunity to lament the lost city and provide an account (admittedly through republishing some existing essays) of some of the great planning failures which marked the his-tory of postwar Bangkok (Sternstein 1982). The Thai-language art and culture journal *Sinlapa Wattanatam* ran a series of articles exploring the old areas of Bangkok and at the same time published articles dealing with the historical role of Bangkok in the economic transformation of Thailand as well as so-cial studies of Thailand during the Bangkok period. It was an opportunity for the journal to ask ques-tions about the modern history of Thailand while not transgressing into the territory of a radical cri-tique of received history (*Sinlapa Wattanatam*, vol.3, nos 4-7, 1982). One book, authored by one of Thai-land's leading archaeologists and Sujit Wonted, the editor of *Sinlapa Wattanatam*, succeeded in gently correcting the meaning of the celebrations by point-ing to the fact that the settlement of the Bangkok-Thonburi area took place many years before the establishment of the royal city of the Chakri mon-archs (Srisaka & Sujit 1982).

DEFINING BANGKOK - RATTANAKOSIN ISLAND AND THE GREAT TRADITION

Throughout the 1970s, a movement had been de-veloping among concerned architects and other pro-fessionals to protect the old areas of the city from further damage and destruction through commercial development which had transformed much of the outer areas of Bangkok. Among such people was Sumet Jumsai, a Cambridge-educated architect with wide knowledge of architectural and social history. An advocate of research into Thai urban cultural and architectural heritage, he was an early critic of the superficial architecture which characterised the mod-ern built landscape of Bangkok (Sumet 1968). An-other was Sirichai Narumit-Rekagarn, an architect and writer with broad interests ranging from urban plan-ning, public housing to cultural preservation. His work included a study of old bridges of the city (Sirichai 1977). With like-minded colleagues and as-sociates, they formed the basis of two groups, the Conservation Group of the Association of Siamese Architects (ASA), and the Arts and Environment Pro-tection Association. The former group was spurred to pressure the government when a large shop-house development threatened to obscure *Phukbao Thong*, the old golden *Chedi* (known in the tourist literature as the 'Golden Mount') erected on an artificial hill in the early Bangkok period. The two groups were able to influence the cabinet to such an extent that the Rattanakosin Island Conservation Project was in-cluded in the Fourth National Economic and Social Development Plan (Figure 4.5). A committee of ad-visers was appointed in the following year to develop and oversee projects. In addition the ASA inaugurated an annual award for architectural con-servation.

The imminent bicentennial celebrations of the founding of the royal city were decisive in spurring the conservation program. A design competition was mounted in order to receive conservation plans and suggestions for projects. One of the first of these drew some criticism: it involved the demolition of an old theatre, the Chalerm Thai, built in the 1930s and one of the most popular in the city. The Chalerm Thai had been the focus of a popular recreation dis-trict in the period between World War One and World War Two when Rajdamnern Avenue (see later) was

Figure 4.5 Improving the past. A symbolic urban vista created according to the plans of the Rattanakosin Conservation Committee. Phukhao Thong in centre, Rama II memorial pavilion at right. (Source: M. Askew)

developed as a shopping centre for the fashionable and well-to-do of the city. Even today, the district, minus its theatre, is referred to as 'Chalerm Thai'. Despite some protests, the demolition took place, justified on the grounds that the theatre detracted from the existing arrangement of historical icons (the Pan Fa Bridge, the Mahakan Fort, Phu Khao Thong, and Wat Rachanada). In its place, a memorial to King Rama II, a royal reception pavilion and allied buildings were erected. Other projects on the eve of the bicentennial included the renovation and reconstruction of fragments of the old city walls and the Pra Sumein Fort at the mouth of Khlong (canal) Banglamphu (Office of the National Environment Board 1987).

State authority was again harnessed with the proclamation in 1984 of the Interior Ministry on land-use controls in Rattanakosin. Notably, the preservation measures for Rattanakosin Island were achieved by ministerial declaration and cabinet approval, not by parliament. Had the latter procedure been adopted, the plan may well have languished as had the first Master Plan for Bangkok, which remained in legislative limbo after 15 years of discussion. But in the case of Inner Rattanakosin, where at least 80 per cent of the land was in the hands of government ministries or the Crown, there was little problem in assuring compliance. Outer Rattanakosin, the area between the inner canal of Khlong Lod and the second ring formed by Khlong Banglamphu and Khlong Ong Ang, presented a somewhat different picture,

with much more land in private hands (Figure 4.6).

In Inner Rattanakosin, so densely studded with important royal buildings and temples of various periods already registered by the Fine Arts Department under the existing Ancient Monuments Act, detailed legislation was largely unnecessary. Outer Rattanakosin, however, required different treatment, which came with the 1987 municipal decree of the Bangkok Metropolitan Administration (BMA) concerning land-use control, construction and the regulation of building heights (Vira 1987, pp.44-6). The regulations concerning Outer Rattanakosin were not concerned with enforcing reconstruction of this area so much as preventing such changes as would transform the nature of the district and, more important, obscure the profile of the palace precinct. So most manufacturing was prohibited from the area, new or reconstructed buildings of over four floors were prohibited, large department stores and office buildings were also barred. The size of signs was regulated. One significant clause concerned the shop-houses which are a dominant feature of the streetscapes: new construction of shop-houses was to be subject to BMA approval, and alteration was to follow original design. Buildings destroyed by fire or accident were to be rebuilt according to original design (Seameo Project in Archaeology and Fine Arts [SPAFA] 1987, App.4).

The overseeing of building activity in Rattanakosin Island has been shared by the Rattanakosin Committee and the BMA, with a division of labour between public and private buildings respectively. While broadly effective, certain developments have slipped through the legislative and administrative net, highlighting aspects of the nature of power and change in Bangkok. The regulations on Outer Rattanakosin did not prevent the completion of the thirteen-floor New World Department Store, which replaced the old Banglamphu market situated near the north-west corner of the old city. This store had a substantial effect on the activities of small local traders; physically, it dwarfs the old shop-houses which survive along the main streets. Fines (charged per day) for exceeding the building height limit had no effect on the owners of New World, who continue to enjoy substantial profits. Although the BMA instituted a successful court action against the owners of the store, negotiations regarding the procedures for reducing the height of the building drag on.

Professor Srisaka's reminder (1982) that Thonburi was part of the historic city and thus deserved attention in a conservation program was ignored until high-rise office and hotel development in Thonburi threatened to overshadow the Royal Palace on the eastern side of the river. The appropriately titled 'Rattanakosin View' multistorey hotel, built on the Thonburi shore, was the decisive spur to the committee to extend the designated conservation area westward across the river to Thonburi 2 years ago (Office of Environmental Policy and Planning [OEPP] 1993).

In one sense, one might suggest that the process set in train in the period of the Bangkok bicentennial celebrations has merely hastened a tendency towards specialisation of functional areas in the city which are characteristic of the classic modern form of the Western city. Inner Rattanakosin was once the site for the special community of the court, with its functionaries, bureaucrats, craftspeople, royal concubines and soldiers. It was a city within a city. The Pramane Ground was the ceremonial space used for the rituals of the royal family. The palaces of the nobles which ringed the royal palace were both administrative and domestic in function. When King Rama V modernised the bureaucracy, the administration was still in the hands of the nobility, but there was a growing separation between place of work and living quarters. The bulk of the substantial palaces, such as Saranrom (now the finance ministry building) were given over to special governmental uses. Other structures, such as the three-storey Ministry of Defence, were specially designed as administrative buildings by foreign architects. Many of these buildings survive and are in use, while others are hidden behind modern structures.

Within the palace walls, King Rama IV instituted changes to a domestic environment that was formerly dominated by traditional Thai and Chinese fittings and symbols. From 1859 this monarch moved his family to a suite of buildings of Western design in the palace compound. His son King Rama V (otherwise known as King Chulalongkorn the Great) continued the trend by erecting more Western-style structures, in particular the unusual Chakri Throne Hall

with its distinctive Siamese gabled roofs atop a nineteenth-century neo-classical palace design. A tour of the Royal Palace grounds today presents the viewer with a visual narrative of the adoption of Western architectural forms by the Thai elite. By the twentieth century, particularly after the fall of the absolute monarchy in 1932, more institutions began to cluster in the old spaces formerly used by royalty, including the National Library (now in Samsen), the National Theatre and Thammasat and Silpakorn Universities.

Despite the trend towards institutional concentration in Inner Rattanakosin, the area designated for conservation, protection and renovation still houses a number of communities and hosts a variety of urban activities. The *Tha* (boat landing places) were the original foci of trading, population movement and social activity. Along the Chao Phraya riverside behind the Royal Palace, the two remaining landing places of Ta Prachan and Ta Tiang are still the sites of lively business activity, with many small traders and vendors living in the locality. At Ta Wang along Maharaj Road opposite Siplakorn University, many of the vendors live in run-down slum housing. The riverside area here, which also includes flats, was occupied from the time of the establishment of the palace as the site for the quarters of palace attendants. Nearly half of the present residents were born in Ta Wang. Brick and stucco shop-houses (*teuk thaew*) aged from over 100 to 60 years old line the streets behind the Royal Palace and the adjacent temples of Wat Maha That and Wat Phra Chetupon. The Rattanakosin Committee and the BMA have plans to develop much of the area along the river into recreational space and create a less congested thoroughfare. A plan to incorporate the Ta Wang people into the rehabilitation program as an alternative to relocation has been proposed, but at present the future of the poor people who live and trade at Ta Prachan is uncertain (Suwattana & Premsiri 1991).

Another project involves the clearing of the congested business area along Khlong Ong Ang which runs through the old Indian business community of Pahurat and the Chinese area of Sampeng. Saphan Han, a unique bridge lined with shops, once bestrode the canal near where it joins the river at the southern corner of Rattanakosin. Today, as in so many parts of Bangkok, space is at a premium and traders have used the *khlong* banks as a market space crossed by covered pedestrian bridges for many years. The BMA will not be renewing the traders' licences when they expire and will reclaim the *khlong* banks and bridges in order to clear the small shops and stalls which crowd these khlong banks and bridges so as to create a scenic vista.

The conservation philosophy which equates open space with good renovation policy, however justified on the grounds of good amenity planning, is going to inevitably result in a much more sanitised physical and less varied social environment in Rattanakosin. Perhaps it all began in 1982 when Sanam Luang, used as a bustling weekend market for many years, was cleared for the bicentennial celebrations to create a more dignified space around the Royal Palace. The market was never reopened, but relocated in the north of the city at Chatuchuk. The effort to preserve Rattanakosin reflects much about the Thai sensibility of heritage. Consensus could be reached among groups both because the matter of Rattanakosin Island was about the monarchy and its centrality in the Thai sense of cultural continuity; also it was because the territory of the area was not strategic for business development: other parts of Bangkok were far more desirable for developers, thus opposition to building restrictions was relatively slight. Infractions have certainly occurred, with hard cash persuading some officials to look the other way, yet the great property interests that blocked the passing of Bangkok's master plans for so many years were not threatened by the Rattanakosin Island proposals. Cultural and economic factors underlie the persistence of an old urban area that must be the envy of most Southeast Asian countries in its relative intactness.

CHANGING URBAN SPACES

Statutory protection of a privileged royal area of the city has helped to preserve the surviving physical manifestations of the Indic urbanism which once lay at the basis of the Siamese state. What about the other areas of the city that have not the privilege of such protection and do not form part of the 'Great Tradition'? Among such legacies are the prominent reminders of the Chinese presence in Bangkok. They include not only the architectural and decorative influences manifested in buildings associated with royalty or Buddhist temples, which are conspicuous in structures dating from the period of King Rama III (who had a particular liking for Chinese ornamentation), but also business and residential buildings as well as shrines associated with the Chinese community. Such physical residues as built structures and religious sites are not restricted to Sampeng. They are spread throughout Bangkok and the adjoining provinces, since the Chinese who arrived in ever-increasing numbers (and were crucial to the development of nineteenth-century Bangkok) filled a range of roles, from labourers to gardeners and merchants. They were supremely adaptable as urban dwellers, and took to the water as well as any Thai in this floating city.

Most European observers during the last century indeed made a point of emphasising that the owners of the floating shops on the river seemed to all be Chinese. Despite their connection with the ubiquitous shop-house, the Chinese of Bangkok were as at home on water as on land. They were particularly adept at horticulture and quickly monopolised that business from Thonburi through to Rachaburi in the west, and to Chonburi in the east. While the Chinese did not form the majority of the population in Bangkok, they were its most conspicuous group and its most industrious. Sampeng remains the heart of the Chinese community in Bangkok, despite the decades of ethnic intermarriage which have produced something of a fusion of cultures among Bangkok urbanites, particularly the middle class. It is all the more interesting that the district centring on the old roads of Yawarat and Charern Krung preserves much of its earlier fabric, since it was the site of so much economic activity from the earliest period of Bangkok's official founding and even before (Jenjob 1991). This area lies outside the Rattanakosin preservation area, yet it has been the site of some interesting restoration projects, in particular by the Siam Commercial Bank (Courtine 1991, pp.97-8). Yet it would appear that much of the area persists in physical terms not so much because of a concerted effort at preservation by individual proprietors, but because the mode of trading and living among the inhabitants has not necessitated radical and swift change to the built environment.[9]

Lamenting physical destruction of old urban areas can bespeak a shallow antiquarianism with limited foundations, but what if one asks about the significance of urban change in terms of evolving spaces and meanings in the city? How does one characterise the spaces of Bangkok as lived environments and the dynamics which underlie changes in the city? The social and functional character of Bangkok had been shaped by the interaction of natural, economic and institutional factors. Physically, in the early years of its establishment, Bangkok's nodal points were the *wat*. They were the centres of population settlements, serving the needs of the people for religion, education and recreation. If not based on rice-growing or gardening, the *bang* and *ban* dispersed outside the moat of the palace precinct on both sides of the river functioned as communities with identifiable activities and trades. Thus *Ban Mo* (or village of pots) was a settlement of potters; *Ban Phan Thom* was a settlement of craftspeople making monks bowls.

These *Yarn* (city quarter or district) settlements were equivalent to the areas of the European medieval cities given over to particular trades. In addition to identification by function, the *Yarn* were characterised by the different ethnic groups which settled; for among other things, Bangkok was distinguished from the surrounding country as a place of differences. This applies not only to the distinctive large community of Chinese who were settled in Sampeng, but others such as the Mon, Indians, Vietnamese, Khmer, Lao and Thai Moslem groups, not to mention the small group of Europeans who were to gradually increase their presence from the mid-nineteenth century. The locations of these co-existing groups were defined by the places where the king chose to settle them in the first instance, since he was the owner of all land.

The old neighbourhoods of Bangkok (often distinguished by their wooden houses with distinctive gable detailing) are still discernible by their locations, near bridges on the canals, beside the *wat*, clustered around the old palaces of noble families, and behind the shop-houses which gradually encircled them as the road network expanded in the old walled city. The original configuration of clusters of settlements on waterways and minor canals gradu-

ally gave way to larger settlements linked by pathways, or *trok* (lanes). The movement of population from the river and canal onto land was already under way by the time that King Rama IV embarked on a program of road-building, partly to impress a menacing West and partly to encourage trade. The first major road, New Road, extending southwards parallel to the river, was built on an old elephant track to palliate the desires of Western diplomats and traders to exercise and take the air. The royal stratagem of building roads together with the shop-houses clearly paid off with the increasing settlement of traders both outside and within the city walls. By the turn of the century the monasteries, as the greatest landowners besides the king and nobility, were also participating in this transformation by building shops and roads to ensure revenue.

The coming of the shop-house to Krung Thep was to make a significant impact on the ecology of the city; yet until a period well beyond the turn of the new century, a dual city - water based and land based - coexisted. As well, it was a city notable for its greenery - a 'city in a garden' as a local English Language newspaper described it. Well into the 1930s, even within the area once marked by the wall (which ran inside Khlong Banglamphu and Ong Ang), there remained gardens and banana groves. The Thonburi side of the river served its historical functions as a garden area effectively without undergoing substantial change, and much of this part of the city is still dominated by the canals, although residential estates are now displacing many old gardens. The memory of the old 'city in a garden' is something that tourist authorities have tried very much to embellish. The 'floating markets' which were so central to the economic life of the old Bangkok-Thonburi survive largely because of the tourist appeal, at least those which operate close to Bangkok (Dhida 1989). But while rural life was maintained in Thonburi, the Eastern bank was a site of continual change.

King Rama IV was proud of his new thoroughfares and gave them grand names suggesting a new sense of commercial urbanism: *Bamruang Muang* (Nurture the City), *Fuang Nakon* (Prosperous City) and *Charoen Krung* (Advance the City). Unlike the areas marked out for royal use and enjoyment on the rural outskirts of the city, with their names evoking nature, such as *Ploenchit* and *Chidlom* (literally 'close to the breeze'), these new roads were for merchants and trade and so bore strongly secular names evoking material progress. But it was the son of King Rama IV, King Chulalongkorn, and his contemporaries, who were to begin the process of refashioning Bangkok's urban form and appearance in earnest. The great boulevard of Rajdamnoen Avenue (the royal way) was cut from Sanam Luang to a new area north of the city wall (called Dusit from the 1890s). The avenue terminated at a new Royal Plaza in front of the domed baroque Ananta Samakhom throne hall (Figure 4.6), and in the plaza was installed an imposing equestrian statue of King Rama V (made in Paris), the first European monument of its kind to appear in Bangkok (the statue was given the special title of *praboromaroopsongma*). Modelled on the Champs Elysée and Regent Street, Rajdamnoen Avenue imposed a European model of urbanism on the oriental city.

Whereas Rama IV had relied mainly on his nobles to build bridges across the city's waterways, King Rama V instituted his own program by having a bridge built every year to mark his birthday. Thus the monarch, enjoying virtually sole power to direct substantial physical change, impressed his own identity on the emerging cityscape, naming the bridges with terms of progress and advancement. These decorated iron and masonry bridges remain a conspicuous feature of the inner city. King Chulalongkorn's building of residences for his many children along the river frontage north of the old city and around the area of

Figure 4.6   The baroque-style Ananta-Samakhom Throne Hall facing the Royal Plaza at the termination of the grand Rajdamnoen Avenue. (Source: M. Askew)

Samsen and Dusit marked the first stage of a suburbanisation process that began to disperse the population of the city. However it was a controlled process, with an absolute monarch in charge of its planning.

The new palaces of the fifth-reign period, built in a variety of designs from the simple neo-classical to the florid baroque, were the vanguards of suburbanisation. It was essentially for their inhabitants' benefit that the new roads, such as Chakrapong Road leading across the Banglamphu canal, were built. In the post-World War Two period, private landowners were to play the principal role in transforming the city. In the 1890s Rama V's program of railway expansion (fuelled more by a desire to integrate the outlying provinces politically than to enhance trade) further added to the capital's European urban iconography with the building of the impressive Hualampong Railway Station, modelled on the great nineteenth century stations of Paris and London. Even before this time, the expanding commerce of the capital, made possible by the opening of Thailand to the West through Rama IV's treaty negotiations, had impacted on the landscape and the functioning of Bangkok.

The 'great bazaar' of Sampeng and Pahurat straddled the only road deserving of the name by the mid-nineteenth century. It served both the 'indigenous' city of the Thai and the hierarchy of commodity and food markets throughout the city, also serving to connect the kingdom, by virtue of its international trading, with the outside world. The area of Sampeng still hosts the largest concentration of Chinese-born people in Bangkok, and this highly compact commercial-residential precinct continues to boast the city's highest population density (McGee 1967, pp.110-11; BMA 1991, pp.6-7). The smaller Pahurat, a centre of the cloth trade, is still distinctive by the concentration of Indian-run businesses.

Further south along the extension of Charoen Krung for a distance of 6.4 kilometres were sited the European legations, trading and financial houses which multiplied rapidly following the trading treaties of mid-century, as well as the first (and still the most famous) hotel, the Oriental. The river remained the central focus of urban activity and the conduit of most of the significant traffic into the metropolis until the pre-World War Two period. The river-based European presence in Krung Thep was most conspicuous in the area close to the trading activity. Observers noted at the turn of the century that there were no distinct European 'quarters' of the city to which the foreigners were confined, such as other oriental cities - although in one case, an attempt by Westerners to position a trading post further up-river was officially disapproved. Nevertheless there was a tendency for the foreign settlements to cluster of their own accord. It was at the junction of the New Road with Silom, Suriwong and Sathorn Roads that the distinctively modern and Westernised business precinct of Bangkok would emerge.

The Silom-Suriwong precinct was still a mixed business-and-residential area at the close of World War Two, notable for its shaded and quiet environs beyond the river bank business area; but within a decade after the war, fuelled by the upsurge in economic activity and the return of European business houses, this area was transformed to become Bangkok's prime piece of real estate. The original fulcrum of this area, the river frontage, is the site of the international hotels which now dwarf the old wing of the Oriental Hotel and the neighbouring European church buildings. But for the main purpose of business, the river might as well not exist. The business thoroughfare of Silom Road (meaning 'windmill' in Thai) stretches from New Road to Rama IV road, which was once a major canal.

The canals along which Silom, Suriwong and Sathorn Roads were once built have long been enclosed by concrete embankments. The trees which lined the streets have also been removed. With the almost complete transformation to an automobile-based transportation system, road-building became the major priority during the 1960s. Moreover, Field Marshal Sarit was intent on bringing the city into line with more modern counterparts; as a result the manually pedalled *samlors* were banned from the city in 1960 to make way for the motorised *tuk-tuk*. So the placid tree-lined Bangkok which had charmed the well-heeled tourists of earlier years gave way to the concrete and air-conditioned business city of the modernist period. A few years ago, an illustrated book of old postcards of Bangkok showed the tinted views favoured by visitors to the old city. In 1993 the Thai Danu Bank published a photographic history of Silom Road. Nostalgia must now refashion what modernity has so effectively wiped out.

The firm of Litchfield, Bowne and Associates, contracted by USOM to prepare the first master plan for Bangkok in 1958, remarked on the lack of clearly defined functional areas in the city compared to Western metropolises of similar size and importance. In Bangkok, commercial, residential and industrial activity took place in multifunctional districts which replicated themselves across the face of the urban landscape, despite the existence of some areas of more specific uses, such as government administration (Outer Rajdamnoen and Inner Rattanakosin) and elite residential (Dusit). In addition, they characterised the city as a collection of 'intimate' neighbourhood settlements, both in the sense of the propinquity of community members and the long-standing local knowledge necessary for inhabitants to find their way around the *trok* of the city which linked these old *ban* to each other. At the time when the Litchfield report was released (1961), Bangkok was on the brink of changes which would begin to alter this pattern of settlement.

NEW DIFFERENTIATIONS

Suburban development, expressed in the transformation of the rice fields and gardens of outlying land into bungalow settlements for the middle class and elite, symbolised one pattern of change in post-war Bangkok. Before the war the easternmost limit of the Bangkok's urban area was marked by Wittayu Road (Wireless Road) and the British Embassy. In the 1930s the British government had taken the bold step of shifting its embassy's location from the riverside to the sparsely settled Ploenchit Road, the title given by King Rama IV to a rural district marked by a temple under his sponsorship (Wat Patumwan) and a palace where he spent the summer months. Nearby was the home of the Indian businessman A.E. Nana, a canny entrepreneur with extensive landholdings in the area (Figure 4.9). The wide and flat rice-growing district stretching away to the east towards Khlong Prakanong was known more for its famous ghost story of Phi Mak and Khun Naag than anything else; but by the 1960s Bangkapi and Prakanong had become a major suburban frontier. Nana had sold much

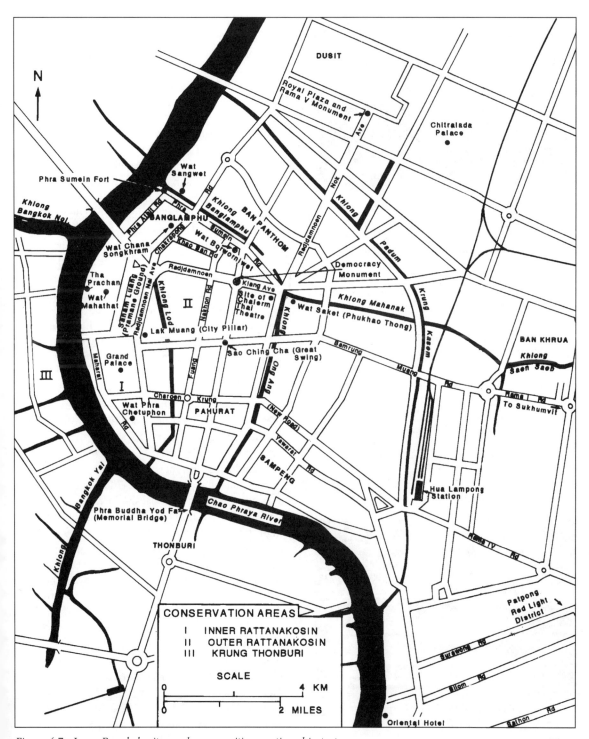

Figure 4.7   Inner Bangkok: sites and communities mentioned in text.

Figure 4.8   The trok and the city. Left, the congested neighbourhood of Trok Boworne-Rangsii; right and middle distance, Wat Boworniwet. The high-rise stores of Banglamphu in middle distance. (Source: *Thawedet Thong-on)*

of the land and carved out *soi* (subsidiary streets or lanes) to branch from the main thoroughfare of Sukhumvit Road.

Sukhumvit Road by the mid-1970s was lined with shop-houses and hotels, many built to house the American GI's on R & R from service in Vietnam. As well, the road boasted the Chokchai tower (erected 1968), with twenty-four storeys, the highest business building in the city at the time. The inner blocks hosted a scatter of suburban houses, businesses, and slums. The mouths of the soi often were the sites of local market places. This pattern of development was replicated for other parts of the expanding city, with the main roads attracting rapid commercial develop-

Figure 4.9   Old home of A.E. Nana, businessman and land developer, Sukhumvit Road. Rising behind is the modern head office of the Krung Thai Bank. (Source: M. *Askew)*

ment (represented by the shop-houses), suburban residences locating along the more accessible parts of the tributary *soi* (represented by bungalows), and poor communities subsisting on badly serviced land that was nevertheless profitable to the landowners in that state (represented by wooden houses of several stories linked by walkways raised above the waterlogged land or small huts on stilts). The *soi* began to replace the *trok* as the distinctive residential environment for many Bangkokians.

The process of suburban expansion had an effect on the inner areas, since many of the *ban* began to lose that mixed social character that had defined them in earlier years. The process in fact spanned a period of 20 years and should not be oversimplified, since the Sino-Thai (except the wealthiest) still inhabit the shop-houses of the inner city where they conduct their businesses. Pressures on housing and new priorities in the post-war period led to suburban settlement to the east and north of the inner areas. Many old neighbourhoods began to experience higher levels of population congestion as migrants from the countryside settled in search of work. The period can be characterised from the viewpoint of .old residents as: 'the coming of the strangers'. Wealthier residents of long-standing left the neighbourhoods and built more housing on their land (or, more commonly, converted rooms into small cubicle apartments) to rent.

Physically, the period saw a virtual invasion of the area by modern shop-houses. A lucrative investment for landowners, shop-house construction allowed for high density (three to four floors) and good rental on the least amount of land. North of the Banglamphu canal, old durian gardens, banana groves and compound houses of old families gave way to the *teuk thaew* for incoming Chinese or Sino-Thai business people. Over the last 30 years, these groups of newcomers have formed their own communities. While more affluent Thai residents moved to the suburbs of Pyathai, Bangapi and Bangkhen, or to the Thonburi side (*Fang Thon* as locals call it), the Thai of smaller means remained. Some of the ban declined into slums. The area of poor housing around the backpacker tourist precinct of Khaw San Road, near Wat Chana Songkhram, illustrates this process. Tucked behind shop-houses along Chakrapong Road and the back of a government ministry building on Rajdamnoen Avenue, the people of this neighbourhood sustain themselves by food vending.

But the process was never clear cut: urban succession was never complete in Bangkok. This is because much as modern Bangkok is at the mercy of private landowners, whose decisions reign supreme in matters of development, the distribution of landownership is wide enough for different types of activity to persist and coexist in the city. Not everybody sells their land to builders of high-rise condominiums or shopping complexes. Some old *bang* and *ban* were virtually enclosed by shop-house developments as they snaked along the main roads in the vanguard of residential development during the 1960s and 1970s. Along *soi* branching from the main roads which overtook the old *khlong*, in Pratunam, for example, communities of long-standing and mixed occupational character still exist.

The *soi* network which provided the basic spatial skeleton for an emerging sprawl of multi-use areas is now being overlaid by another more specialised pattern of functions which characterise urban development, as driven by an organised housing development industry, public housing agencies and financiers (the National Housing Authority and the Government Housing Bank), and highly-capitalised export-oriented industries. Housing estates are not new phenomena in Bangkok; yet the last 10 years or so have seen a marked development in the outlying areas towards more exclusive residential uses, particularly for the rich. The wealthy *mubanjatsan* residents enjoy seclusion and security in their mansions amidst landscaped environs, often abutting private golf courses and leisure facilities. The vendors and small entrepreneurs that are so much a part of other neighbourhoods are not to be seen, unless relegated to planned areas in the centre of the manicured estates.

However, basing this model of socio-spatial trends just on the wealthier estates would misrepresent the emerging patterns in Bangkok, because it is the variegated middle class which had provided the greatest impetus to suburbanisation in the period since the 1970s (Figure 4.10). But it is fair to say that the caricatured Roman-style mansions that represent the status aspirations of the very wealthy (named in the case of one development as 'Louis Style') are the

Figure 4.10   Two-storey condominium along a suburban soi. *Neo-classical facades are very popular.* (Source: M. Askew)

pinnacle of humbler, but nevertheless just-as-materialistic ambitions. The dominant paradigm is clear: the integrated shopping mall-business centre and housing estate are the current standards for the middle-ring suburban areas designed for convenient, centralised consumption of goods and leisure in the automobile-based city.

Complementing this horizontal sprawl is the vertical expansion of condominiums and 'tower' developments, which aim to provide greater convenience closer to the major business districts for local executives and foreigners. Aiming to provide everything for the modern bourgeois, these developments offer virtual self-sufficiency, with no relationship to the outside environment or neighbourhoods. Yet such is the reaction against a congested urban environment which is so numbingly debilitating on the senses and wasteful of time and energy, that the development

Figure 4.11 Havens for affluent urbanites. Condominium advertisement, Asoke Road. (Source: M. Askew)

of these exclusive zones seems to be the only possible trend. Not surprisingly, the images evoked by the publicity for condominiums and estates focus on the tedium of Bangkok and the freedom of a constructed paradise for the bourgeois family: father is linked to work by a new sleek expressway, and can easily communicate with the family via cellular telephone, assured that mother's Mercedes need not overheat in its trips to collect the children at the nearby school or to purchase necessities at the easily accessible branch of a department store chain that invitingly offers the convenience of one-stop shopping (Figures 4.11 and 4.12).

The other element in the emerging landscape of Bangkok's urban spaces is the specialised industrial estate. Promoted from the 1970s to attract overseas industry to well-serviced locations, the industrial estates of Samut Prakan, Minburi and Patum Thani form concentrated nodes in a sprawl of development that takes in provinces beyond the BMA. It has been a long-standing policy established by the NESDB that promoted industries be directed to locations beyond the middle-ring areas of the city. The recent investment boom has given further impetus to the trend of industrialisation in the outlying areas, creating a weird pattern of juxtaposed farmland, industrial plants and golf-courses. The populations inhabiting these areas comprise local people who have somehow adapted economically to such change, and workers of rural origin who are either housed by their employers near the plants or are transported from rented premises within the region. The separation of residence and workplace so characteristic of modern urbanisation

patterns is thus reflected not only at an intra-urban level, between office and housing estate, but at a regional and national level, between village and factory.

The existing pattern of environments represents the coexistence of different systems of activity and strategies of survival; so that, if longer term trends towards specialisation may be discernible, they remain just that, developing amidst older or alternative functioning socio-spatial patterns (Askew & Koanantakool 1992; TDRI 1991). Small-scale industry is still the dominant context of production, at the level of the family firm. Such small factories and firms are spread throughout the inner and middle districts of the city (TDRI 1990). While on the one hand this is a primary context of the sweated labour which is enabled by a state which constrains trade-unionism, and hence underlies the profitability of the export-led industrial economy, it is nevertheless symptomatic

Figure 4.12 A landscape of condos and hotels. A soi in Sukhumvit. (Source: M. Askew)

of enduring patterns of economic life which are based on small unit production geared around face-to-face interaction between employers and employees. The informal sector is evident across the city, with its residential correlate - the slum - a persistent element in Bangkok's community ecology. Slums, officially renamed 'crowded communities', provide something like 16 per cent of all housing stock for up to 23 per cent of the population in Bangkok. However the occupations of slum-dwellers are considerably varied, including people with a wide-range of work in both the formal and informal sectors (NESDB 1986, p.58; Angel & Sopon 1989).

STATE AND COMMUNITY IN THE PROCESS OF URBAN RESTRUCTURING

Both private interests and the state are bound together in the process which is transforming Bangkok, although in most cases the state has the capacity only to establish a broad framework while the private sector provides the major impetus towards changing urban areas. The newly adopted Bangkok Master Plan which was finally accepted in 1992 by the parliament after years of discussion and amendment cannot prevent manipulation by influential property interests, since land-use classifications are general enough for exceptions to be made by the Ministry of the Interior which has ultimate discretionary power (Property Market 1992). Even the 1982 proclamation of the so-called 'Green Belt' to the east and west of Bangkok has not prevented the expansion of residential development into those areas. State action has contributed both to the demise and the preservation of old landscapes and communities.

Bang Krachao, an agricultural area in Samut Prakan province bounded by a broad bend in the Chao Phraya River directly south of the city, is a region that is likely to persist, but not without protests from its inhabitants that they be preserved along with their environs. Like Thonburi, this area has served the city as a supplier of garden produce, functioning much as it has generations earlier, with most village settlements based on the old canals (Chulalongkorn University Social Research Institute [CUSRI] 1990). Many of Bang Krachao's inhabitants still pursue agricultural livelihoods like their forebears. It was nominated as early as 1961 in the Litchfield Plan for

preservation as a 'Green' area. Somehow Ban Krachao remained relatively little affected by the urban change occurring around it until relatively recently, when, in 1977, it was ear-marked as a green zone by the government fearing incursion by industry. This measure, preventing traditional owners from profitably selling land, effectively confined them to agricultural occupations, which in turn kept the area functioning in its traditional mode. In 1991, however, the Prime Minister's Office launched a plan to appropriate 9000 rai of the land for parkland. The irony of people being relocated from land which they had kept 'green' was not lost on the people of Bang Kra Chao, who mobilised to oppose this heavy-handed measure (The Nation 29 Sept. 1991).

But the communities that live here are not united: some are just as happy to sell their land at a profit and live on the proceeds, as have their counterparts in the new suburbs west of the river in Talingchan and Prasicharoen. Yet armed with the frightening knowledge that this was the only large expanse of greenery remaining on the fringe of the city, the government pushed ahead with its stipulation that Ban Krachao was to function as a 'Green Lung' of the polluted city. Industrial plants which had encroached on the area were to be progressively moved. A month after the first announcement, a settlement was reached which incorporated a community development program with the park project and the expropriation moves were postponed indefinitely (The Nation 19 Oct. 1991).

The community of Ban Khrua has not been so fortunate. This is an old settlement on the Saen Saeb canal lying east of the Padum Krung Kasem canal. Originally known as 'Asamak Cham', this village originated from a settlement of Cham Moslems taken prisoner during wars between Siam and Cambodia during the reign of Rama I and granted land near the old Mahanak canal. The community moved to its present site when the Saen Saeb canal was dug to link Bangkok with the eastern agricultural areas during the reign of Rama III (1824-51). The settlement, like so many traditional Ban neighbourhoods, focussed around a key noble (Praya Rachawangsan) as protector. The Chams were noted seafarers and had traditionally served in the Siamese navy since the Ayutthaya period. Some individuals were ennobled as rewards for service. A number of the wooden houses of these Lua*ng* (an honorific of bestowed rank) with characteristic fretwork on gables and windows, survive from the period of Rama V (1868-1912) (Jaruwan & Buffi 1992).

Comprising some 600 houses, with 705 families comprising a population of almost 3000, Ban Khrua is officially designated as a slum and became congested at the same time as other old inner areas of the city. Despite the presence of north-eastern migrants in its population, Ban Khrua's core of identity lies in its ethnic ancestry and religious unity. Traditional silk weaving is still carried on by the women in many households of this community. In 1989, the time of the decree appropriating the land of Ban Khrua North for use in the Expressway Authority's construction of a freeway link, one university study concluded that Ban Khrua was one of the only old yar*n* (city quarter or district) settlements remaining in the city which had preserved much of its old identity (Sowapa, Pontip & Duangpon 1989) (Figure 4.13). Since then, and as resistance in this unified community to resettlement has stiffened, Ban Khrua's predicament has attracted a great deal of attention from city residents. Emotional meetings have proclaimed the importance of preservation, and have gained greater force because it is clear that what is at stake is not just one community, but the memory of the character of the old city of *yarn* communities. Notwithstanding the interest of academics and others, however, this settlement may be destroyed to make

Figure 4.13   Ban Khrua, straddling Khlong Saen Saeb. An old neighbourhood in danger of demolition for an expressway by-pass. (Source: courtesy Sinlapa Wattanatam)

way for a freeway by-pass (*Bangkok Post*, 23 Jan., 2 Feb. 1992; *Nation*, 3 July 1992; Sowapa 1989)[10].

THE MEANING OF 'MORADOK'- HERITAGE AND IMAGES OF THE PAST

Press coverage, academic discussion, occasional public debate and an increasing number of journals devoted to topics involving culture and identity suggest that recent change has provoked greater reflection about the past, including the urban past, in Thailand. The term *Moradok*, once exclusively reserved as a term for treasure or personal inheritance, has now been appropriated by public authorities and private business alike in referring to national heritage. *Moradok* seems to be the Thai word closest in equivalence to the word 'heritage', popularised by international organisations such as UNESCO in their efforts at encouraging conservation and classification at a global level. A heightened consciousness of a 'national' heritage seems to have been stimulated by the issue of the famous 'Vishnu Lintel' taken by an American from Prasat Phanom Rung in Buriram Province (Subhadradis 1989; Keyes 1991). But it would be an overemphasis to interpret such expressions at an official level as a coordinated movement towards preservation and historical consciousness. The images and elements of the past in Thailand, as elsewhere, have continually been fashioned into icons for various purposes. There has always been an official face to Thai heritage, exemplified by the Fine Arts Department and boards and committees of the government charged with defining and promoting Thai culture. Much as governments have been prone to define culture by edict since the period of the Phibun Songkram regime of the 1930s, reverence for the past is probably most effective when it is promoted by members of the present Royal Family. Here, what has begun as philanthropy or the promotion of traditional crafts and arts by HRH Queen Sirikit and HRH Princess Maha Chakri Sirindorn has been transmuted into fashion by the Thai elite and middle class, reflected in the revival of Thai silk in women's modern fashionwear and the trend to teach children traditional Thai music.

By the same token, there have been efforts to promote nostalgia for the past in the private realm as well, represented perhaps most conspicuously by 'Muang Boran', meaning 'Ancient City'. Developed over the last decade by a millionaire businessman of Chinese extraction, the historical park of Muang Boran reacts to change by denying the present. In a sense, it is an 'anti city'. Located in Samut Prakan Province in an area that is part of Bangkok's urban sprawl, Muang Boran comprises replicas of notable Thai religious and royal buildings in addition to some which have been saved from demolition or decay. Khun Sai Lek, the owner of the project, sees the park as: 'a bulwark against the rising tides of socio-cultural change in present-day Thai society'. Moreover, it is designed in the belief that 'the East should and can never be like the West: our past glories are firmly rooted within an ancient culture and traditions dating back thousands of years' (Muang Boran 1990, p.20).

While the painstaking reconstructions of such buildings as King Taksin's audience hall (Thonburi period), the Dusit Maha Prasat (Bangkok period) and the Sanpet Prasat Palace (Ayutthaya period) are based on close research and exacting building standards with no expense spared, Muang Boran is intended to be more than an archaeologically precise museum piece. It aims to project an image of the historical past which emphasises harmony between the natural environment and the human landscape, and harmony between the rulers and the ruled of the Thai past. A number of parks have been established, peopled with statues representing mythical characters of the *Ramakien*, the Thai version of the *Ramayana*. A floating village and a land-based lowland village have been constructed to reflect the 'way of life' of Thai people in former days. A recent publication, Jittima's *The Old Market Town: The Heart of the Siamese Communities* (1992), reinforces this nostalgic image of the fully integrated Thai community. From any point in the park, the visitor - Thai or foreigner - can see in the distance the *chedis* and *prang* towers through the greenery.

The overall effect of these vistas, the managers hope, is to produce a composite image, much like the old Thai temple mural paintings, juxtaposing the dimensions of forest and human settlement, worldly life and that of the angels (*Muang Boran* 1990). Against this effort to fashion a coherent image of the

past in Bangkok is the more widespread phenomenon of the absorption of scattered historical and architectural images into the itineraries of private tour companies. 'Ancient city' is accorded a brief half-hour on the itinerary of most tour firms (with a superficial commentary to match) after which tourists are usually whisked away to visit the wonders of the Samut Prakan crocodile farm. Ancient City is more often than not the spectacle that its owner hoped it would not become: a 'Disneyland' version of the oriental city.

The Muang Boran historical park is one private entrepreneur's effort to provide what his government with limited means is unable to do, and much more effectively than the national museum can do with its limited funds and less-than-inspiring presentation of artefacts. Interestingly, the latter institution relies on a volunteer corps of *farangs* (foreigners) to provide interpretative lectures to tourists. Khun Sai also funds a publishing house under the same title, but which is independent in its management. Its publications include the journal *Muang Boran*, which is a major vehicle of information regarding historical and archaeological research. Not as popular in its orientation as *Sinlapa Wattanatam*, it produces work of a high quality by leading Thai academics and is not averse to publishing articles of opinion on matters of cultural policy and social change in urban areas. More recently the Siam Society, a scholarly organisation of long standing in the city, has expanded beyond the production of its academic English Language journal and launched a Thai magazine (*Siam Araya* [Siamese Civilisation]) dealing with matters of broader social interest, often with articles about the city.

Bangkok is host to a myriad of images and constructions which refer explicitly to its past, or inflect the national past in the city, as well as images which have nothing to do with its past. The 'Thai style' of life, encapsulated in aggregated icons of elegant women, elements of Thai architecture, ornaments and food, is the common currency of advertising in the tourist industry. Most of the larger hotels, no matter what design, now feature a Thai *sala* (shelter) somewhere in their grounds, regardless of how incongruous they may look. As an icon, there is probably nothing that seems to summarise the Thai past so effectively as the Thai-style roof (Figure 4.14). The

Figure 4.14   Ubiquitous image of Thai tradition, the Thai-style roof. Here a sala *(shelter) used by schoolchildren.* (Source: M. Askew)

practicality and elegance of its form is evident in such humble structures as the hundreds of roadside bus shelters throughout the country. Few symbols are so frequently used in logos and advertising as this simple but distinctive roof shape. Indeed it has been appropriated and projected almost as if it is a national signature.

In contemporary Bangkok, the elegant steeply raked gabled roofs of the old Thai-style houses tend to be used for restaurants much more than private houses. However there is a discernible trend among the wealthy to build Thai-style houses in their gardens, for formal entertainment or leisure. In the 1890s visitors to Bangkok lamented the numbers of these houses that were being demolished or removed from the city. In the 1950s, the antique collector and entrepreneur Jim Thompson had to search as far afield as Ayutthaya to find intact examples of traditional houses on stilts, which he re-erected in Bangkok. Now the Thai-style house is as much an item in the inventory of the cultivated Thai to accumulate as the antique chair, bookcase or betel-nut service. Few can pretend that the Thai house is fully adaptable to the modern lifestyle of the urban dweller. In addition, scarcity of timber and skilled craftspeople make the enterprise of building them an expensive one, available only to the well-heeled (*The Nation*, 26 Oct. 1990). The writer, politician and intellectual M.R. Kukrit Pramot, direct descendant of royalty and known for his deep knowledge of Thai history and the arts, is one of the very few urban dwellers who has attempted to recreate a traditional domestic en-

vironment in his house in Soi Suan Phlu, Bangkok (Van Beek 1983, pp.113-15). For others, the house is a leisure facility used in conjunction with the convenience of the modern townhouse (Tetoni & Warren 1988).

VISION AND DESPAIR

To what extent is the material transformation of Bangkok expressive of changing identity and culture? In architectural terms, the majority of buildings constructed during the last decade under boom conditions show that the architectural profession has done either of two things: largely reproduced variants of a now-freer international style of shapelier commercial towers and condominiums represented in most of the world's cities; or built business, commercial or residential structures in a highly monumental classical style. This is an oversimplified characterisation, but both cases are reflective of the client-driven nature of the architectural endeavour. There are exceptions to this portrait, and despite the dominance of crass monumentalism, there are good examples of sensitive and adaptive designs in institutional and domestic architecture in Bangkok (Suthit 1989).

Two responses to change in Bangkok can illustrate the options facing Thais concerned with the city and cultural change. Sumet Jumsai, still active as an architect, has produced a distinctive genre of building in his recently completed 'Robot Building' (the headquarters of the Bank of Asia), and the offices of *The Nation* newspaper. In the former building, Sumet has cleverly exploited the restrictions of setback regulations to produce a structure in the shape of a standing robot; in the latter he has devised one face of the structure to resemble the silhouette of a journalist seated at a desk. The finer points of the design should not concern this discussion so much as Sumet's approach to design practice in Bangkok itself. For in addition to producing buildings that are novel appearances in Bangkok's built environment, Sumet has played an active role as consultant and advisor to the Rattanakosin Conservation Committee in its reconstructions of buildings in the old city. In his modern architecture, Sumet does not obviously incorporate architectural elements of past Thai forms; indeed he has argued against this in terms of its shallow featurism, just as he has attacked post-modern classicism as the retreat of the untalented architect (Sumet 1987).

If, as it seems that, to Sumet the old and the new Bangkoks are totally separate entities, one to be restored and the other to be invented (in an interview with the author he described himself as 'schizophrenic' in his thinking about architecture), in his writing about culture he asserts clear continuities between past and present. Sumet's research on 'amphibious' architecture and symbolism in Southeast Asia is the basis of his view that in Thailand in particular, there are common cultural 'memories' among the people of a water-based lifestyle (Sumet 1988). Historically, Bangkok was a particular type of city, an aquatic, or floating city. At a conference some 5 years ago, he pointed out (Sumet 1989, pp.18-19):

> Bangkok, a city of more than 6 million, stripped of its canals and floating houses, now appears as an alien organism unrelated to its background and surroundings...it has become a great commercial pad on partially filled land which, despite all its land-based pretences, must succumb to the flood in the monsoon.

This has implications for his long-term proposals regarding Bangkok; for he advocates 'water-based' solutions for the ever-expanding and choking metropolis, including restoring aquatic waterfronts, digging additional canals, establishing floating parks and hotels as well as establishing floating communities on areas of the Gulf of Thailand (*The Nation*, 28 Apr. 1991).

But Sumet Jumsai is not the only one proposing a return to the water. One proposal suggests an upgrading of the riverside accessways and recreational areas and a rediscovery and renovation of Bangkok's network of canals to achieve a greater balance between land-based and water-based transport systems. This proposal, suggested in one of the Rattanakosin design proposals for 1982, envisaged the creation of a river-city which would restore the memory of Bangkok's aquatic past to a redeveloped strip stretching from Ko Kret in the north to Bang Krachao in the south. But it remains on the drawing board. Recent use of Khlong Saen Saep as a route for water-borne public transport has proven to be effective, and the

service has been extended to a number of the inner *khlong*, yet such pilot projects are a far cry from implementing a comprehensive alternative to road traffic or changing the ways people use the city (Kiat 1992; *The Nation*, 10 Aug. 1991; *Bangkok Post*, 9 Sept. 1992).

Sirichai Narumit-Rekagarn, also an architect, has taken a different course to Sumet Jumsai. With a common base in concern for the environment and social welfare, he has however abandoned practice as an architect in favour of teaching music appreciation at Chiang Mai University. His move to the northern provincial capital of Chiang Mai in 1984 was in fact a symbolic as well as practical desertion of Bangkok, the place where he was born and grew up.

Once an active campaigner in Bangkok for the preservation of historic buildings and culturally sensitive architecture, a president of the Association of Siamese Architects and vice-president of the Siam Society, he is now committed to cultural and environmental preservation activity in the northern region of Thailand, including attempts to control high-rise development in Chiang Mai. It is clear that to Sirichai, the transformation of Bangkok has rendered it, as Sumet claims, an alien presence in Thailand. But to Sirichai, Bangkok is beyond saving. The task is to insulate the rest of Thailand from the contamination of the materialist values of the metropolis. Like other intellectuals in Thailand, he emphasises the importance of local knowledge and local culture in the countryside as against metropolitan culture, the homogenising vehicle of accelerated modernisation (Emmons 1991; Sirichai 1988).

POWER AND SACRALISATION

Rather than casting an evaluation of Bangkok's changing spaces and surfaces in the exclusive terms of modernisation/ Westernisation versus indigenous cultural assertion, it may also be useful to think about the cultural meanings of the city as reflecting the 'great tradition' and 'the little tradition', a paradigm - arguably dated - of peasant socio-cultures advanced in the 1960s by the anthropologist Robert Redfield. These traditions (the great tradition of the urban-based hierarchy and cultural elite, the 'little tradition' of the villages and common people) intersect in the way that space assumes meaning in sacralisation. 'Little tradition' here does not refer to a specific object so much as a disposition expressed in a popular culture which has deep roots. This can be expressed in the gatherings of people at well-known shrines such as the Lak Muang (city pillar) or the Erawan Shrine. The latter is as well patronised as the first named, despite the fact that the Lak Muang was installed at the foundation of the city and the Erawan shrine was created in 1957. Things do not assume importance necessarily because of age alone, but by association, particularly with the powers of guardian spirits or forces of the other world. Nor do such spaces have to be large or imposing: in Banglamphu an old tree growing next to the gate of a palace once belonging to the brother of King Rama I is revered both by local people and visitors. It is said that the spirit of the original owner protected the area from damage during allied air attacks on Bangkok during World War Two. In Trok Boworne Rangsii, everybody respectfully stops to wai (bring the hands together in the manner of prayer to show respect) at least once during the day to a small spirit shrine which is so old that nobody remembers who first erected it. Cultural practices or perceptions at a popular level in the city are independent of official sponsorship. Witness the garlands and sashes spontaneously draped on the trees of Rajdamnoen Avenue following the violent suppression of democracy protesters in May 1992 (Figure 4.15).

Patterns of usage and popular interpretation can develop which counter the original purposes of places

Figure 4.15   Transforming spaces, Rajdamnoen Avenue, May 1992. Protesters gathering around the Democracy Monument. (Source: *courtesy* Matichon Magazine)

or objects. Thus very recently, the equestrian statue of Rama V at the Royal Plaza began to be worshipped by a number of people who believe that his spirit returns to earth twice a week. On the appointed days of Tuesday and Thursday, more and more people of all walks of life attend the gatherings, where individuals request personal favours or simply pay their respects with garlands and candles (*Bangkok Post*, 14 Jan. & 2 Feb. 1993). Civic statues on the European model (which were first introduced in 1907 with the Rama V statue) assume a far more powerful significance in the Bangkok cityscape than they do in Western cities; this is less to do with artistic or sculptural criteria than the importance of the personality represented and the power of his or her spirit, which is popularly believed to be inherent in the physical image.

Long association and age can render particular spaces sacred even (as in the following example) where a building is so poorly designed as a functional teaching space. The students who study at the old *Khana Aksornsat* Faculty of Arts building at Chulalongkorn University respectfully call this building *Thevalai*, or residence of the deities, and perform a *wai* every time they enter the hall. Built in a style reminiscent of a traditional *wihan* structure with gable, lintel and staircase embellishments of Khmer patterns, the building, constructed in 1929, has become of particular significance to the staff and students, who perform a special ceremony each year to pay respect to the building (*Bangkok Post*, 29 Jul. 1991)[11].

Such cultural patterns are not exclusive to urban areas of course, but the persistence and spatial concentration of these dispositions in the city ensure that not all spaces are of equal value; nor can they be evaluated in purely material terms. In the end, it is power and the force of respect that determine meanings and persistence in the city's fabric. The most recent example of this, and directly related to the fate of an urban space, is the case of the proposed new army Supreme Command Headquarters building near the royal plaza. The project, involving construction of a 32.5 metre-high building complex, had been approved by the first Anand government (appointed by the military following the February 1991 coup), but was opposed strongly in parliament in late 1992 because of its effect of overshadowing the Anata Samakhom throne hall and King Rama V equestrian statue. The BMA has no authority to prevent construction of buildings by government agencies, but even so, the military had not even informed the BMA about its project as formally required. The decisive case against the construction, even at the stage when millions of baht had already been expended on the foundations, was that the building would detract from a revered space associated with the monarchy in the city (*Thai Radt*, 18 Dec. 1992; *Bangkok Post*, 18 & 19 Dec., 1992).

It is hardly a coincidence that so many initiatives relating to improving the city are undertaken on the birthdays of members of the Royal Family, ranging from the cleaning of polluted canals to the renovation of royal *wat*, and tend to reconfirm the fact that much of the city is still seen to belong to the monarchy by association, even if not in fact. The centrality of respect and reverence for the institution of monarchy in the Thai socio-cultural complex is part of a broader system of reverence for figures in positions of authority, both in this world and that of the spirits. The strength of this disposition lies in its very persistence and conservatism, and should not be underestimated as a force for protecting at least some of the legacies of the past against change. It has less to do with a popular vision of the past which is centred on monumentalism as such (although of course national institutions promote this reification) than the broadly based cultural disposition to sacralise space by virtue of respect for revered power.[12]

On the other hand, collective action can transform the meanings of certain spaces through sacralisation, which in the case of the May 1992 events was brought about by popular political martyrdom. The area along Rajdamnoen Avenue, particularly the Democracy Monument, has now assumed a popular significance that it never had before. Designed to commemorate a coup in which only a small minority participated in 1932, and whose symbolism very few understood, the Democracy Monument is now associated with the popular democracy movement which did so much to morally empower elements of the middle classes and capture the attention of the world. Of course in this case, the meaning of the democracy monument lies less in its exact symbolism than its visual association with events.

Sulak's 'second-rate Western city' is continuing to grow. The inner area of old Rattanakosin has been effectively preserved to express in material form the Indic urbanism which once was a key element in the spatial arrangement of power in Thai society. Beyond this space the city continues to spread and change, and as the city continues to grow, the remnants of the old city, human and material, are swept aside or transmuted. Bangkok is not likely to become less important as the central economic and administrative engine of the Thai economy, or the key conduit of new cultural forms and images. Localism is gaining ground among a wide range of movements in Thailand, but it has yet to become a creative force in the city, except in some notable cases where groups have been mobilised against eviction or redevelopment. Local areas may be the wrong place to look for a surviving sense of place in a continually transforming city such as Bangkok; nevertheless common memories and associations, forged by patterns and relations between people and locales, are discernible on a number of levels. One can only hope that the capacities of urban dwellers will be strong enough to create a meaning in their environment that will withstand some of the destructive and fragmenting forces of current change.

ENDNOTES

1 Increasing urban settlement along the waterways of the old capital 150 years ago was giving rise to environmental and health problems. King Rama IV himself in the early 1850s was driven to proclaim an edict against the casting of animal carcasses into the Chao Phraya River.

2 Interestingly, the very implementation of foreign-backed projects reflects this problem, with overlapping schemes backed by various instrumentalities, all with responsibilities for urban infrastructure, including the Expressway and Rapid Transit Authority (ETA) and the BMA. At the time of writing, a team of specialists from Massachusetts Institute of Technology and Harvard University had been invited to Bangkok to help prioritise all the infrastructure and transport plans for the metropolis. They were, ironically, installed in a brand new high-rise hotel, the very location of which mocked their

mission: a narrow suburban soi (lane), which, through unregulated development of commercial and hotel properties, has increased traffic congestion and air pollution in the local area dramatically.

3 The recent announcement by General Chavalit Yongchaiyudh, Minister of the Interior, that a new city outside Bangkok is to be planned as a solution to the prevailing congestion, not only comes too late (after a much earlier identical suggestion in 1977), but lacks definition in terms of function (*Bangkok Post*, 25 Jan. 1993). The chosen site in Chao Choeng Sao Province, to the east, will reinforce development trends already begun with work on the new airport in that province.

4 The full title of the capital, given by Rama I, on the day deemed auspicious by the astrologers in 1782 (and later changed to accommodate the name of a famous Buddha image) is: *Krung Thep Maha Nakon Amorn Ratanakosindra Mahindra Yudhya Maha Dilokpop Naparatana Radhani Burirom Udom Rajnivet Mahastan Amorn Pimarn Avatarn Satit Sakkatuttiya Vishnukarm Prasit*, meaning: 'The City of Angels, Great City, the Residence of the Emerald Buddha, Capital of the World Endowed with Nine Precious Gems, the Happy City Abounding in Enormous Royal Palaces Which Resemble the Heavenly Abode Wherein Dwell the Reincarnated Gods, A City Given by Indra and Built by Vishnukarn'.

5 To an extent this observation remains true to this day, in that the construction of new temples in new suburbs or estates of Bangkok by the laity tend to be favoured above patronising older temples in less convenient locations -along the old *khlong*, for example. Abbots and monks are far less concerned than experts of the Fine Arts Department in restoring older structures in the *wat* compounds according to historically exact models, or in spending money to preserve the fragile mural paintings in the *bot* and *wihan*. The royal *wat* of the first class, which receive special attention, are the exceptions to this case. For comments on problems of preservation concerning *wat* in Bangkok see *Bangkok Post*, 'Outlook', 20 Jul. 1992.

6 A different view of the elements of Bangkok is presented in the eminent poet Sunthorn Phu's *Nirat Phukao Thong*, composed at around the same period as *Inow*. Here the poet describes his journey out of the city along Khlong Bangkok Noi, where he stops at the various markets (*talat*) and *ban*, all characterised by their particular goods or merchandise for sale.

7 In particular the popular descriptive work *Low Ruang Bangkok* (Stories of Bangkok) by S. Polainoij, first published 1960 with frequent reprints.

8 So the Prime Minister's prefatory remark on the official series of books went: 'It is because of their untiring efforts, profound capabilities and considerable wisdom that the nation and the new capital have been able not only to prosper, but also to remain independent to this day, becoming well known all over the world for its arts, customs, culture and religion' (Committee for the Rattanakosin Bicentennial Celebrations [CRBC] 1982, Preface).

9 Courtine (1991, pp.86-9) notes that among the surviving structures in the Sampeng/Pahurat area there are up to 200 dwellings modelled on original southern Chinese styles of brick-built habitations dating in construction from 1782 to 1910. In addition, there are the shop-houses, with some groups representing the original units built under the direction of King Chulalongkorn during the period 1875-80.

10 In mid-1994, public meetings were still being held to resolve the dispute.

11 Curiously this building was designed by an English architect. It is sad that such a vital place will soon be turned into a museum and the Faculty of Arts students and staff shifted to a modern multistorey building.

12 There are many studies of popular Thai Buddhism, spirit beliefs and the orientation of people to space, although these are overwhelmingly set in the rural and village framework. See for example Formoso (1990), Gesick (1985), Keyes (1975) and Tambia (1984).

REFERENCES

Angel, S. & Sopon Pornchokchai 1989, 'Bangkok slum lands: policy implications of recent findings', *Cities*, vol.6, no.2, pp.136-46.

Anuchat, Poungsomlee & Ross, H. 1992, *Impacts of Modernisation and Urbanisation in Bangkok: An Integrative Ecological and Biosocial Study*, Institute for Population and Social Research, Mahidol University, Nakhon Pathom, Thailand.

Askew, M. & Ko-Anantakool, P. 1992, 'Bangkok: The Evolving Urban Landscape' in Pongsapich, A. et al. (eds.) 1992, *Regional Development and Change in Southeast Asia in the 1990s*. Chulalongkorn University Social Research Institute, Bangkok, pp. 163-72.

Bangkok Post 6 & 1 Apr. 1982; 29 Jul. & 19 Oct. 1991; 23

Jan., 2 & 20 Feb., 20 Jul., 9 Sept., 18 & 19 Dec. 1992; 14 & 25 Jan., 2 Feb. 1993.

Bangkok Metropolitan Administration (BMA) 1991, *Statistical Profile of BMA. Bangkok: Metropolitan Administration*, Department of Policy and Planning, Bangkok.

Chattip Nartsupha 1971, *Foreign Trade, Foreign Finance and the Economic Development of Thailand*, Prae Pittaya Ltd, Bangkok.

Courtine, P. 1991, 'L'Habitat du quartier sino-indien de Bangkok: un héritage résidentiel conservé', *Inter-Mondes*, vol.2, no.1, pp.84-99.

Committee for the Rattanakosin Bicentennial Celebrations (CRBC) 1982, *Rattanakosin Painting*, CRBC, Bangkok.

Chulalongkorn University Social Research Institute (CUSRI) 1990, *An Environmental Development Plan for Bang Kra Chao*, (in Thai), CUSRI, Bangkok.

Dhida Saraya 1989, 'Damnoen Saduak Floating Market and its Changes', *Muang Boran*, vol.15, no.4, Oct.-Dec., pp.123-31.

Emmons, R. 1991, 'For Chiang Mai and the World', *Thailand Tatler*, Nov., p.53.

Flood, C.K. 1965, *The Dynastic Chronicles. Bangkok Era. The Fourth Reign (AD 1851-1868)*, vol.1. Centre for East Asian Cultural Studies, Tokyo.

Formoso 1990, 'From the human body to the humanised space. The system of reference and representation of space in two villages of Northeast Thailand', *Journal of the Siam Society*, vol.78, no.1, pp.66-79.

Gesick, L. 1985, '"Reading the Landscape": Reflections on a Sacred Site in South Thailand', *Journal of the Siam Society*, vol.73, no.1, pp. 157-61.

Jaruwan Lowira & Buffi, J. 1992, 'Ban Khrua: a rich past but an empty future?' (in Thai), *Sinlapa Wattanatam*, Oct., pp.176-86.

Jenjob Yingsumon 1991, 'Chinatown' (in Thai), *Sarakadi*, vol.7, no.79, pp.80-97.

Jittima Sutthasin 1992, *The Old Market Town: The Heart of Siamese Communities*, Muang Boran Publishing House, Bangkok.

Keyes, C. 1975, 'Buddhist Pilgrimage Centers and the Twelve-Year Cycle: Northern Thai Moral Orders in Space and Time', *History of Religions*, XV, pp.71-89.

Keyes, C. 1991, 'The Case of the Purloined Lintel: the politics of a Khmer shrine as a Thai national treasure', in Reynolds, C. (ed.) 1991, pp. 261-92.

Kiat Chivakul 1992, *Rethinking Planning Concepts for Bangkok: Between Land-based and Water-based Development*, Paper presented to the International Workshop on Research and Planning Methodologies for Metropolitan/Regional Development, 29 June - 3 July, Department of Urban and Regional Planning, Chulalongkorn University Bangkok.

Kwansuong Atipho 1991, *Unfolding Bangkok*. Special issue of *Thai Culture* (in Thai), vol.30. Office of the National Culture Commission, Bangkok.

London, B. 1980, *Metropolis and Nation in Thailand: The Political Economy of Uneven Development*, Westview Press, Boulder Colorado.

McGee, T.G. 1967, *The Southeast Asian City*, Bell and Sons, London.

Muang Boran 1990, *Muang Boran: A Nostalgic Look*, Muang Boran Publishing House, Bangkok.

The Nation, 26 Oct. 1990; 28 Apr., 10 Aug., 29 Sept., 19 Oct. 1991; 3 Jul. 1992, Bangkok.

National Economic and Social Development Board (NESDB) 1976, *Fourth National Economic and Social Development Plan (1977-1981)*, Office of the Prime Minister, Bangkok.

—— 1986, *Bangkok Metropolitan Regional Development Proposals: Recommended Development Strategies and Investment Programmes for the Sixth Plan (1987-1991)*, NESDB/ IBRD/USAID/ADAB, Bangkok.

—— 1992, *Summary. The Seventh National and Social Development Plan (1992-1996)*, NESDB, Office of the Prime Minister, Bangkok.

Nid Shiranan 1989, 'The Contemporary Thai City as an Environmental Adaption' in *Culture and Environment in Thailand*, The Siam Society, pp.371-92, Bangkok.

National Statistical Office (NSO) 1991, *Population and Housing Census of Thailand. Preliminary Report*, Office of the Prime Minister, Bangkok.

O'Connor, R. 1983 *A Theory of Indigenous Southeast Asian Urbanism*, Institute of Southeast Asian Studies, Singapore.

O'Connor, R. 1991, 'Place, Power and Discourse in the Thai Image of Bangkok', *Journal of the Siam Society*, vol.78, no.2, pp.61-73.

Office of Environmental Policy and Planning (OEPP) 1993, Interviews with Mr Usar Kianchaipiphat and Ms M. Siriwan relating to the plans and policies of the Rattanakosin Conservation Committee, Jan. 1993.

Office of the National Environment Board 1987, *Plan for Rattanakosin* (in Thai), Ministry of the interior, Bangkok.

Office of the National Culture Commission (ONCC) 1989, *Towards New Dimensions of Culture and Development*, ONCC, Bangkok.

Pasuk Phongpaichit 1980, 'The Open Economy and its Friends: The 'Development' of Thailand', *Pacific Affairs*, vol.53, no.3, pp.441-60.

Piyanat Bunnag et al. 1982, *Canals in Bangkok: History, Changes and their Impact (1782-1982)* (in Thai), Chulalongkorn University, Bangkok.

Property Market 1992, 'There is no Comprehensive Plan for Bangkok' (in Thai), no.2, pp.43-50.

Pussadee Tiptus 1982, *Houses in Bangkok: Character and Changes during the last 200 Years (1782-1982)* (in Thai), Chulalongkorn University, Bangkok.

Reynolds, C. (ed.) 1991, *National Identity and its Defenders: Thailand 1939-1989*, Monash Papers on Southeast Asia no.25, Monash University, Clayton, Victoria.

Rigg, J. 1991, *Southeast Asia. A Region in Transition*, Unwin Hyman, London.

Sinlapa Wattanatam, vol.3, nos 4-7, 1982.

Sirichai Narumit-Rekagarn 1977, *Old Bridges of Bangkok*, Siam Society, Bangkok.

Sirichai Narumit-Rekagarn 1988, 'From the Country Looking Back to the City' in *Lectures for the Munlanitigomonkimthong Foundation* (in Thai), Bangkok, pp.17-36.

Skinner, G.W. 1957, *Chinese Society in Thailand: An Analytical History*, Cornell University Press, Ithaca.

Sowapa Prasiripong, Pontip Usuparat & Duangpon Kumnunawet 1989, *Preliminary Research on Ban Khrua North: A Case Study of Economy, Society and Culture* (in Thai), Centre for the Study of Culture and Language, Mahidol University, Bangkok.

Seamo Project in Archaeology and Fine Arts (SPAFA) 1987, Final Report. *Workshop on Community-Based Conservation and Maintenance of Historic Buildings/Living Monuments, August 23-30*, SPAFA, Bangkok.

Srisaka Vallibhotama & Sujit Wongted 1982, *Where did Khrung Thep Come From?* (in Thai), Chao Phraya Publishers, Bangkok.

Sternstein, L. 1976, *Thailand: The Environment of Modernisation*, McGraw Hill, Sydney.

Sternstein, L. 1982, *Portrait of Bangkok*, Bangkok Metropolitan Administration, Bangkok.

Sternstein, L. 1984, 'The Growth of the Population of the World's Pre-eminent "Primate City": Bangkok at its Bicentenary', *Journal of Southeast Asian Studies*, vol.15, no.1, pp.43-68.

Subhadradis Diskul, M.C. 1989, 'Stolen Art Objects Returned to Thailand', *SPAFA Digest*, vol.10, no.2), pp.8-12.

Sulak Sivaraksa 1990, *Siam in Crisis*. 2nd ed. Thai Interreligious Commission for Development, Bankok.

Sumet Jumsai 1968, 'Architecture Thailand '68. Crisis and Outlook', *Thailand Economic and Industrial Review*, Bangkok Post Publications, Bangkok.

Sumet Jumsai 1987, 'Why the Robot?' in *Robot Bank. A Statement in Post High-Tech*. Asia Property Co., Bangkok.

Sumet Jumsai 1988, *Naga. Cultural Origins in Siam and the West Pacific*, Oxford University Press, Singapore.

Sumet Jumsai 1989, 'Oceanic Origins of Thai Culture' in *Culture and Environment in Thailand*, The Siam Society, Bangkok, pp.11-19.

Suthit Wangroongaroona 1989, *Thailand. Two Decades of Building Design 1968-1989*, Sang-Aroon Arts and Culture Centre, Bangkok.

Suwattana Thadaniti & M.R. Premsiri Kasemsunta 1991, *The Study of Ta Prachan Area, inner Bangkok. Paper presented to the Third International Training Workshop on Strategic Areal Development Approaches for Implementing Metropolitan Development and Conservation, 11-16 Sept.*, UNCRED/ Municipal Council of Penang, Penang, Malaysia

Tambia 1984, *The Buddhist Saints of the Forest and the Cult of Amulets*, Cambridge University Press, Cambridge.

Thailand Development Research Institute (TDRI) 1990, *Urbanisation and Environment: Managing the Conflict. Research Report no.6*, TDRI, Bangkok.

—— 1991, *National Urban Development Policy Framework. Draft Final Report*, TDRI, Bangkok.

Tetoni, L.I. & Warren, W. 1988, *Thai Style*. Asia Books, Bangkok.

Thai Radt 18 Dec. 1992.

Thompson, P.A. 1910 (1987), *Siam. An Account of the Country and the People*, White Orchid Press, Bangkok.

Tomosugi, T. 1991, *Rethinking the Substantive Economy in Southeast Asia*, Institute of Oriental Culture, University of Tokyo, Tokyo.

Van Beek, S. (ed.) 1983, *Kukrit Pramoj: His Wit and Wisdom. Writings, Speeches and Interviews*, Editions Duang Kamol, Bangkok.

Vira. Rojpojchanarat 1987, 'The Conservation of Monuments in Thailand' in SPAFA 1987, pp.39-49.

ACKNOWLEDGEMENTS

The author wishes to thank Victoria University of Technology (Melbourne, Australia) for providing the study leave and funding necessary to pursue the research on this chapter, to the National Research Council of Thailand for permission to undertake research in Thailand, and to the Department of Urban and Regional Planning, Chulalongkorn University and the Chulalongkorn University Social Research Institute, Bangkok, for providing facilities. Association with the work of the Thailand Development Research Institute was also of great importance. Valuable assistance was provided by the staffs of the Thai Information Centre of Chulalongkorn University Library, the Library of the Siam Society, Bangkok, and the National Archives of Thailand. Thanks must also go to the many people who offered advice, material and suggestions, including Prince Subhadradis Diskul, Dr M.R. Akin Rabibhadana, Professor Srisaka Vallibhotama, Associate Professor Kamthorn Kulachon, Associate Professor Suwattana Thadiniti, Dr Dhidar Saraya, Dr Suneit Chanintaranond, and Dr Paritta Ko-anatakool. Thanks to Pranee Monthongdaeng, whose perseverance and help were invaluable. To the people of Banglamphu, Ban Panthom, Ban Denk Din, Trok Boworne-Rangsi and Trok Kieniwat who gave their time and opinions, thanks are also extended. All errors of fact and interpretation, however, are the author's.

5 Traditional and recent aspects of the urban development of Chiang Mai, Thailand[1]

Guy Lubeigt

Chiang Mai city, capital of northern Thailand and of the province of the same name, is situated in the high valley basin of the Ping River, at an altitude of 305 metres (1000 feet). The city is bordered to the north, east and south by the Ping swamps (Figure 5.1). From the base of Doi Pui (1635 metres; 5365 feet) - on the slopes of which is located the Summer Palace of the Thai sovereigns[2] - and the base of Doi Suthep (1053 metres; 3455 feet) which is crowned by the celebrated pagoda of Wat Phra Boromathat, the capital stretches as far as the River Ping. The Royal Palace and the Wat of Mount Suthep thus dominate the ancient city which is still known by the name 'Rose of the North'.

With a population of 200 000 inhabitants (out of the provincial total of 1.4 million), Chiang Mai is in fact the second city of the kingdom of Thailand.

Its ancient city, pagodas, markets and restaurants, its many artisans and their products, its freshness in summer, the charm of its sites and inhabitants, all make Chiang Mai a particularly popular destination for travellers.

Between 1987 and 1988 the number of foreign tourists staying in Chiang Mai city rose from 490 000 to 570 000 (a 17 per cent increase in one year). In 1989 the increase reached 13 per cent. Thai tourists increased from 1.4 million in 1987 to 1.6 million in

Table 5.1 Population growth in Chiang Mai municipality 1959-89

Year	Number	Percentage of the province	Percentage of the Northern region
1959	64 773	8.46	1.19
1962	70 813	8.55	1.21
1967	81 579	8.58	1.15
1972	93 353	8.89	1.15
1977	105 230	9.41	1.14
1983	150 499*	12.21	1.48
1989	159 497	12.23	1.52

* In 1982-83, a number of districts in the urban area were incorporated within the municipal boundaries.

(Source: *Chiang Mai municipal administration, March 1990*)

1988. With nearly 2.5 million visitors per year, the 'Rose of the North' therefore receives twelve times more visitors than it has inhabitants, and the province of Chiang Mai two times more. It is clear that

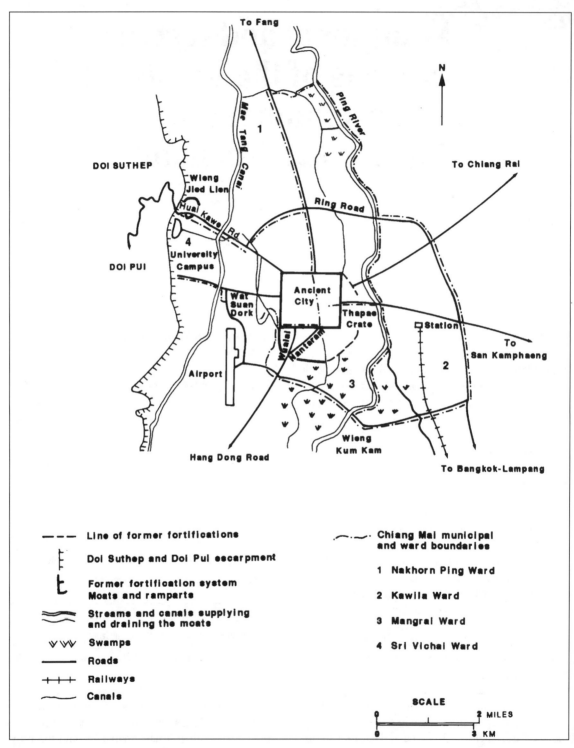

Figure 5.1   Chiang Mai: site and situation

such a sharp and massive escalation in the number of tourists cannot be without consequences for Chiang Mai's development, its lifestyle, traditions and the activities of its inhabitants.

A CITY ENDOWED WITH A RICH CULTURAL HERITAGE

A city of legends

Chiang Mai was the capital of the kingdom of Lanna (the country of the 'Million Rice Fields') until 1892, the date of its annexation by King Chulalongkorn of Siam (1868-1910) who had married the princess and heiress of Chiang Mai, Dara Rasmi. However the capital remained a nominally independent principality until 1939. For the Siamese in the south, Chiang Mai was for a long time an inaccessible, quasi-legendary city about which little was known except that it was home to innumerable temples, delicious fruit, very beautiful women and cold winters.

At the end of the nineteenth century, Chiang Mai engaged in sustained commercial relations, by means of caravans, with all the kingdoms of the region. Seven thousand mules enabled commerce with the Shan states of Burma; a thousand other mules enabled commerce with Yunnan; 5000 porters maintained the link with lower Burma and 4000 others travelled to the Shan states. Three thousand cattle equipped with pack-saddles transported merchandise between Chiang Mai and Lampang and more than 8000 elephants were used for transport across the entire north of the country. The northern ethnic groups were already rubbing shoulders in the city's markets: Khon Muang (northern Tai), Shans, Siamese, Tai and Haw from Yunnan, Burmese, Karens, Lawas and various mountain tribes.

Chiang Mai could only be reached from the south by a long and difficult voyage along the valleys of the Chao Phraya River, by steamer as far as Nakhorn Sawan and then along the Ping River, which was only accessible by canoe. The journey lasted 66 days in the dry and 50 days in the rainy season. It was also possible to reach Chiang Mai on elephant-back from Nakhorn Sawan. Whatever the method, it took several weeks - veritable expeditions - to cover the 700 kilometres (435 miles) separating Bangkok from the northern capital.

This isolation was broken by the arrival of the railway (1927), then the highway and, later still, air links. However, until the end of the 1960s, Chiang Mai was little more than a small sleepy town huddled around the walls of the old city - a market town where transactions took place between the people of the plains and those from the mountains, and where the traditional products from the orchards (longans, lychees, rambutans, mandarins) and tobacco fields of the alluvial lands of the Ping valley were sold. Chiang Mai was also famous for its eighty-five buddhist temples (of which thirty-six were within the ancient city walls), and its artisans (goldsmiths, lacquerware makers, basket weavers, textile weavers, potters and carvers) who attracted Siamese pilgrims and visitors in large numbers. The inhabitants lived in those days by the rhythm of the monasteries whose drums beat out the ritual hours of the day, and to that of the *samlor* (taxi-tricycles) which travelled slowly up and down the streets of the urban area.

A Tai creation[3]

Before the thirteenth century, the Chiang Mai region was occupied by people about whom little is known. The Lawa, Mon and Tai doubtlessly already intermingled here. The first Tai chieftain known historically was Mengrai who, in 1286, succeeded in uniting some Tai *muang* from the north to form the Lanna, the land of the 'Million Rice Fields'. He established a solid alliance with the neighbouring Tai kingdoms of Sukhothai and Phayao, which, according to northern Tai records, allowed him to consolidate his kingdom by creating at least six new cities in it. The most beautiful was Ping-ka Nakhorn ('City on the Ping'). In fact this city was only a continuation of a much more ancient human settlement whose inhabitants already practised irrigation[4]. In 1296, King Mengrai decided to install himself there and to make it his capital, the forerunner of the modern-day *Chiang* (city) *Mai* (new). Mengrai's eighteen successors reigned directly over Chiang Mai until 1551, the year in which the city was conquered and the kingdom of Lanna became a vassal state, subject sometimes to the kings of Burma and sometimes to the Thai of Ayutthaya. From 1292 to 1939, forty-five kings ruled over the city before it became the administrative centre of one of Thailand's seventy-three provinces. But throughout its history, Chiang Mai, being situated at the centre of Tai country, never lost its particular character (Wongtangsawad, 1985).

A royal capital

According to historical records, the construction works at Chiang Mai, King Mengrai's 'new town', were carried out between 1292 and 1296 using 90 000 labourers. At that time, the city formed a quadrilateral measuring 1000 x 800 *wah*[5], covering 320 hectares (790 acres) and surrounded by a 20-*wah* ditch. The city walls rose 2 *wah* and reached a thickness of 1.5 *wah* in places. Each side was pierced by a 4-*wah*-wide gate: Hua-Wieng (literally 'in front of the town') in the north; Tai-Wieng ('behind the town') in the south; Tae-Pae ('Gate of the Raft') the eastern gate, since the Ping River flowed at the foot of the eastern wall; and Suan-Dork ('Flower Garden') the western gate, which faced the mountain.

Later two other gates were made in the walls: Chang Moi in the north, and Suan Proong in the south. According to tradition, the first was put through by King Sam Fang Gan (1411-42) who wanted to make it easier for his aged mother, who lived outside the town, to enter and check the progress of the work on the various temples she was having constructed. The second is due to King Tilokaraja (1447-87) who wanted to create a direct link to a residence located outside the city walls. Beyond these anecdotes, it appears that Chiang Mai's development in the fifteenth century was in full swing and that important suburbs had already been created around the ancient city. No permanent bridges existed at that time to cross the ditches. People simply placed across them temporary gangways made of bamboo which could be dismantled rapidly. The city gates were closed between six in the evening and six in the morning. In times of war, all the gangways were lifted and the gates blocked from the inside by wooden beams. Conquered several times, but never completely destroyed - as was Ayutthaya in 1767 - the town has kept part of its military architecture.

While a royal city, Chiang Mai was also a market town. It has been possible to calculate that each reign corresponded on average with the time it took to construct 2 *wat* inside the town. But the nobles and merchants constructed 923 other *wat* outside the city

walls and in the rest of the province. The town of Chiang Mai consequently possesses a religious and artistic architectural heritage of outstanding importance.

An artisans' town

Isolated for a long time within its province, surrounded by its rice fields and rich alluvial lands, Chiang Mai has kept the most ancient traditions of northern Siam. These traditions are found particularly in the various forms of production using timber, clay, stone, lacquer, bone, ivory, cotton, silk and copper as primary materials. No other town in Thailand brings together such a complete range of craftspeople specialised in the use of traditional techniques. Seeking to serve the needs arising from the development of the royal town and its pagodas, the artisans set themselves up outside the ramparts to the south of the royal city, between Chiang Mai Gate and Wat Nantaram. The Wualai Road and Nantaram Road districts are famed for their various goldsmiths and silversmiths, weavers, lacquer workers and carvers carrying out their crafts and trades in traditional timber houses characteristic of the Lanna Tai architecture of the nineteenth century.[6]

These artisan neighbourhoods were established in a zone which was urbanised following the creation of the royal capital. An examination of the map of Chiang Mai shows that the eastern part of the old city, whose ramparts bordered the natural swamps of the Ping River valley, were regularly threatened by floods resulting from the monsoon rains. To protect the town the kings had constructed a long earthen levee bank running from the north-east corner of the old city to serve as a dyke to hold the Ping's waters to the east. This dyke was lengthened to encompass all of the southern part of the urban area, which was reclaimed from the swamps and also threatened by floods. It is not known exactly when this earthen levee was constructed but it is clear that it also had a military function since the conserved parts, to the south-west, still reveal a wide corner tower and show that the upper part of this levee, pierced with narrow doorways, was surmounted by a small brick wall.[7] In addition to this dyke-wall, a stream-canal allowed the water to be drained towards the south and served at the same time as a protective ditch for the neighbourhoods where the artisans lived. Over the centuries these neighbourhoods, nestled between the southern dyke-rampart and the moats of the royal city, have been protected by the fact that the urban area - which was blocked in the north and south by swamps and in the east by royal, religious and administrative lands and wealthy residences - has extended principally towards the east, beyond the Ping River.

Throughout its history, Chiang Mai has been able to maintain part of its ramparts and moats, its religion and its pagodas, as well as its inhabitants and artisans with their customs and techniques. This important cultural heritage, specifically Tai, constitutes a richness unequalled in Thailand.[8]

THE DEVELOPMENT OF CHIANG MAI

Development factors

Part of Chiang Mai's heritage is a remarkable series of trump cards which has provided the bases of the town's growth. But, above all, this growth has been made possible by two concomitant factors: the development of road and air transportation and the massive influx of Thai and foreign tourists.

An extensive transportation network

Thailand is criss-crossed by an extraordinary complex of river, road, rail, maritime and air transport routes, the diversity, convenience, and even the comfort of which are probably without equal in a newly industrialised country. The traveller can move around easily and everywhere by coach or by luxury vehicle thanks to an extensive road network, tarred and metalled on major highways and finished off by a multitude of very good secondary roads with a surface of crushed laterite. As for the railways, if they are still not very rapid, at least they enable regular links between all the main towns. In addition, since 1979, the date when the Chiang Mai airport runway was lengthened to take heavy carriers, the air transportation service provided by Thai International Airways and Bangkok Airways[9] has allowed several daily connections between Chiang Mai and Bangkok. The establishment of direct links with China (Kunming) and the other Southeast Asian capitals is under way. The construction of new buildings (hangars, warehouses to supply spare parts, kitchens) to sustain the development of the airport's international role is planned for the near future.

From Bangkok it is now possible to reach Chiang Mai in 12 hours by express train, in less than 10 hours by coach or in 90 minutes by plane. Visitors and traders can easily move between these two cities. The simple tourist now has a problem of too much choice: everything has been done to guarantee total freedom of movement under the best conditions and at the lowest cost. In these conditions, travel agents across the world have no trouble in encouraging tourists to visit the sites of Thailand.

The massive influx of tourists

International tourism brought Thailand 196 million baht in 1960. In 1990 it provided 100 000 million baht ($A6000 million [$US4000 million]). The increase is even more breathtaking when one considers the number of arrivals: in 1986 Thailand welcomed 2.4 million tourists[10]. In 1990 it received 5 million.[11] The visitors to Chiang Mai city and its surrounding area are principally Thai tourists. At the end of the 1960s, numerous trips were organised by train and coach to enable the Thais to visit the north of Thailand. At the start of the 1970s foreign tourists, benefiting from the excellent infrastructure which had been put in place, also began to flow towards Chiang Mai. In 1990, the average length of stay in Chiang Mai city varied from 4.06 days for Thais to 4.65 days for foreigners.

The modernisation of Chiang Mai - concrete and pollution

The influx of tourists, which has caused an abrupt awakening for the 'Rose of the North' until then lazily sleeping at the foot of Mount Suthep, has been accompanied by the extraordinary in-flow of capital in search of quick returning investments.

In 1982-83, the government launched the first 5-year tourism development plan in Chiang Mai. It included among other developments the construction of a cable car to the summit of Doi Suthep at a cost of 100 million baht. This project was abandoned following a lively attack from the town's ecologists grouped together in the 'For Chiang Mai' Association. But in October 1989, a new group of

Figure 5.2   A poster advertising a new suburban estate on the outskirts of Chiang Mai: 'A Place in the Stars'. (Source: Kwansuong Athipo)

businesspeople relaunched the project with the cost readjusted to 300 million baht. Despite considerable pressure and numerous threats[12], the ecologists continue to oppose the project which they say will destroy the natural beauty of the site and its monastery.

A second 5-year plan was entered into in 1987-88 to encourage the craftspeople and factory owners to produce essentially for export. In Chiang Mai, this plan has led to a stronger development of the San Kamphaeng – Bo Sang zone and its specialisation in handicrafts. The general result is that land and property development is now offering some particularly profitable prospects to investors.

Real estate promotion: the era of speculators

At the start, we did not know whether or not we were going to launch our project for a high-rise tower on the banks of the Ping River, but as there was no law forbidding its construction, we launched a condominium project of twenty-one storeys with 117 apartments, car-parking provision and a treatment system for polluted water. Public opposition to this type of project could affect our sales promotion.[13]

From the start of the 1980s, land and property development in Chiang Mai city experienced an unprecedented growth. At the time of writing (1990), a score of large hotels[14] and thirty-two condominiums[15] were being constructed in the urban area. To this must be added twenty or so large settlements created around the outskirts and along the highways

leading out of town. With so many buildings being erected, the city of Chiang Mai is taking on the appearance of a vast construction site.

The erection of joint-ownership high-rise build-

Table 5.2   Change in the number of houses* in Chiang Mai municipality, 1982-89

Year	Number
1982	26 289
1983	26 368
1984	26 877
1985	28 680
1986	30 226
1987	31 498
1988	31 796
1989†	35 591

* The statistical source refers to 'houses' without differentiating the individual residential units within multiple occupancy buildings.

† The year 1989 corresponds to the arrival on the market of numerous condominium units under construction since 1987.

(Source: *Chiang Mai municipal administration, March 1990*)

ings is proving to be a good investment: it is not necessary to acquire vast plots of land in order to

Figure 5.3   New condominiums built on the banks of the Ping River, causing soil subsidence and water pollution. (Source: Kwansuong Athipo)

construct high-rise buildings. Three or four thousand square metres (32 000-43 000 square feet) are quite sufficient for the construction of a twenty-storey tower. In these circumstances, the building site situated near the city centre, even when it costs more to buy, is made quite profitable by the construction of a condominium. This aspect has not escaped the notice of the Chinese-Thai developers from Bangkok who, following in the tourists' wake, have in a very few years bought almost all of the zone where fallow land was common (see Figure 5.2). Faced with this rash of high-rise towers, Chiang Mai municipality has decided to prohibit this type of construction within the limits of the ancient city. Future condominium projects will be pushed out from the city centre, which could make them less attractive to buyers coming from elsewhere. But the launch of new estate settlements continues on the city's periphery.

The strengthening of the hotel infrastructure, made possible by the finance companies of national and international groups, continues on the city's outskirts with the construction of a number of large new hotels, designed to accommodate even more tourists. In the next few years, the Tourism Authority of Thailand (TAT) is expecting an 8 per cent annual growth in the demand for rooms (Figures 5.4, 5.5). In 1990 fourteen hotels, benefiting from the privileges granted to investors by the Investment Board, were either under construction or on the drawing board. Planned to come into operation between 1991 and 1993, they will add a total of 4117 new rooms to the 9474 counted in 1989.

In 1990, the city of Chiang Mai had only two luxury hotels, which is why the projects supported by the Board of Investment are essentially devoted to first-class hotels. The investment needed to construct each additional hotel room lies between $A31 000 ($US21 000) and $A150 000 ($US102 000). The average cost of building a high-quality construction room is valued at $A81 600 ($US54 500). But for first-class hotels the investment will be at the top end of the range. The sums at stake are therefore colossal. Thus, in order to maintain its image among the VIPs who visit Thailand's north, the Royal Orchid (278 rooms, 470 employees) has begun a series of renovation works at a total cost of $A2.1 million ($US1.4 million) to be spread over 1990 and 1991.[16]

Changes in the city's population

The apartments located in the high-rise towers are not destined for the inhabitants of Chiang Mai. The market targeted by the speculators is that of Bangkokians or Chinese and Japanese foreigners. The first group makes use of the dwellings as secondary residences or waits for prices to rise before reselling them with a comfortable profit to other non-occupying speculators. The second group makes use of Thai figureheads[17] in order to acquire the dwellings as a base for their business stays in Chiang Mai or for speculation. In both cases, the Thai residents of Chiang Mai reap no benefit from these operations; indeed they are being gradually pushed out of the city. Those who sell their central city land make use of the profits from the sale to purchase another plot of land or a cottage in a quiet estate on the urban periphery. But the developers of these estates are themselves also Sino-Thais from Bangkok; they have bought vast areas of land at low prices, often in the swamps, in order to service and subdivide them.

As a result, the Chinese from Bangkok are becoming more and more established in the urban area, tending to manipulate the city's growth, while the Tai of Lanna are taking refuge on the outskirts. The cost of these changes is catastrophic: in just a few months a traditional way of life maintained for centuries can be annihilated. The traditional urban fabric, with its little timber cottages, in which the inhabitants used to reside, is little by little disappearing in favour of speculative constructions for non-residents.

In order to discourage the property developers, a pharmacy professor from Chiang Mai University Hospital Centre, Mr Sakchai Asyakhun, has put forward an original idea printed in leaflets which are circulating around the city together with petitions aimed at preventing any further high-rise construction. Mr Asyakhun proposes the construction around the condominiums of a steel pipe scaffolding to a height of 30 metres (100 feet) 'in the style of the Louvre scaffold structures'. These 'cages', constructed by the owners of adjacent sites, would be adorned with immense panels carrying the following inscription: 'Maximum Security for the City'. These structures would have the effect of blocking the occupants' view

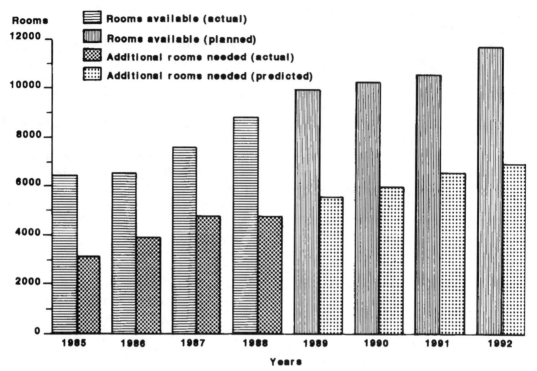

*Figure 5.4   Tourist growth as measured by increases in rooms, 1985-92. (*Source: *Baring Securities Thailand Research, October 1990)*

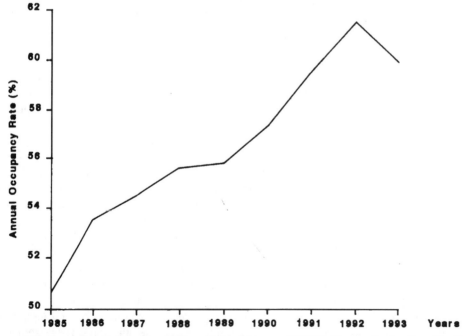

*Figure 5.5   Annual occupancy rate of Chiang Mai hotel rooms, 1985-93. (*Source: *Baring Securities Thailand Research, October 1990)*

of the scenery and surrounding private properties. They would discourage the purchase of apartments in these high-rise blocks and, consequently, also the property developers.

This project by the Chiang Mai inhabitants is, among many others, aimed at maintaining a minimum level of quality of life in their city.

Environmental degradation

The outbreak of apartment blocks in a townscape traditionally composed of timber cottages and a few two-storey or three-storey houses in brick and cement, has profoundly upset the traditional functioning of the city. In particular, the stacking up of apartments in condominium towers has led to a considerable increase in new vehicles in the built-up area and their concentration near the high-rise buildings in neighbourhoods where the width of the roads is inadequate for such traffic. City dwellers themselves are succumbing to the necessities of modern life: motorbikes, with all their associated pollution, have invaded the streets of the city centre steadily pushing out the traditional *samlor*. Ecologists, gathered in the 'For Chiang Mai' Association, describe the situation in the following terms:

> The development is such that, in peak hours, the city now has to deal with a terrible confusion of traffic in which motorised *samlor* and motorbikes discharge waves of nauseating fumes. As for the mountain ways of life, these have been sold out in the same old way to trekking enthusiasts and hordes of Westerners who pass through only to fill their bags with exotic souvenirs. If nothing is done to check this tide and its consequences, the pollution of Chiang Mai and its provinces will be worse in a few decades than that of Bangkok. Normal tourists will no longer come to see the 'Bangkok of the North', where the temples will be hidden by high rise towers and apartment blocks and where the temple bells will no longer be heard above the din of traffic... ('For Chiang Mai' Association pamphlet, 1990).

Engulfed in shrill noises, exhaust fumes, building site dust, the 'Rose of the North' will very quickly lose the calm and serenity which made up the charm of its living environment. As for the treatment of household refuse and liquid wastes, this simply con-

Figure 5.6   Apartment block rises above the traditional streetscape, featuring temple and wooden residences, Tae Pae district, Chiang Mai. (Source: Kwansuong Athipo)

sists of emptying them into the Ping River, all to be transported downstream.

Transformation of the townscape

In April 1990, under pressure from residents and the 'For Chiang Mai' Association, the Chiang Mai municipal council undertook a series of measures aimed at ending the activities of investors who were using any means possible in their effort to obtain building permits, slowing the anarchic development of new constructions, preserving Chiang Mai's tourist sites and features, and protecting the composition of the various neighbourhoods of the city.

In Chiang Mai municipality, the construction of buildings of more than sixteen storeys is now prohibited within 100 metres (328 feet) of the agglom-

Figure 5.7   A wall painting in Chiang Mai protesting against high-rise building developments spurred by domestic and overseas tourism. 'Tourism in the city will destroy this city'. (Source: Kwansuong Athipo)

eration's eighty-five monasteries. On the banks of the Ping River, buildings of more than twelve storeys are prohibited. Municipalities will no longer issue permits for the construction of condominiums within the built-up area:

> ...for high rise towers are not necessary in Chiang Mai. The single aim of most of the investors who construct them is to sell what is in fashion.[18]

The city centre within the ancient city walls are reserved for religious sites and administrative and service activities, and new construction of condominiums and large hotels is prohibited.[19] The neighbourhoods located between the moats and the Ping River are dedicated to tourist activities: small-scale hotels, restaurants, small souvenir shops and the like. The neighbourhoods located to the west between the city centre and the foot of Mount Suthep, where the zoo and the university campus are situated, are classed as residential. But the construction of apartment blocks is continuing there, despite the more and more spirited protestations of the residents.

On the other hand, craft activities, closely linked to the demands of tourism, have been encouraged by the Board of Investment to concentrate to the east of the city, on one or other side of the road from Chiang Mai to San Kamphaeng. Only craft enterprises and commercial outlets linked to tourism have been authorised to set up on this axis since 1985. All noxious industrial activities have been encouraged to transfer to the Lamphun industrial zone. Chiang Mai's land use pattern is shown in Figure 5.8.

The renewal of artisan activities

The reconstruction of traditional dwellings

Preserved by a very simple way of life, the traditional artisans of Chiang Mai have been able to maintain across the centuries the integrity of their manufacturing techniques. But the demand, resulting from the massive influx of tourists in the 1970s, has made them realise that the purchases by the visitors could bring them comfortable profits. They have therefore gradually developed their output in response to growing demand. The stalls, set up on the ground floors of the old timber huts, sometimes give way to ultra-modern, air-conditioned shops. But the workshops have remained in the backyards, where the artisans often work under difficult conditions.

Craftspeople and shopkeepers have noticed that tourists' attention is regularly attracted to the old traditional timber houses in the Lanna style, replete with gilt and carved wood decorations. The most enterprising have salvaged old houses, often in ruins, purchasing them at low prices from owners delighted to off-load them. These traditional houses were dismantled and then rebuilt in the old neighbourhoods. They open directly on to the footpath and serve as stalls for the artisans and small shopkeepers.

Another type of traditional residence, made popular by the houses of Jim Thompson and Khamtien in Bangkok, and much admired by tourists, is the large imposing residence mounted on piles, with a terrace reached by a staircase. At the start of the 1970s, this type of house was extremely rare in Chiang Mai. It has been made popular again by Ban Sai Thong, an artisan enterprise specialising in wood carvings, which was one of the first enterprises to be established outside Chiang Mai on the road to San Kamphaeng. Tourists were flocking to visit the residence/shop of Sai Thong and to make their purchases there. This success prompted a number of other artisan/traders to restore or to reconstruct similar residences as places to display their goods. These large timber dwellings transformed into museums and shops give witness to the serenity of an ancient lifestyle but necessitate constant and very costly maintenance; previously they had been abandoned by their occupants in favour of what seemed to them to be modern.[20]

Among these new Lanna-style residences, the houses of Mrs Banyen Aksornsiri are noteworthy. The first (no.77 Wualai Road), to the north of the neighbourhood known for its lacquerware craftspeople, had been transformed into a museum for wood carvings and traditional everyday objects. This house was destroyed by a fire in March 1990. However Mrs Banyen had already had several other houses built, which operate both as shops and museums for popular arts and traditions, on Hang Dong Road, the prolongation of Wualai Road to the southeast of Chiang Mai and near the crossing of the airport and ring roads. Because of their location, tourists cannot fail to see them.

The career of Mrs Banyen is illuminating. As the

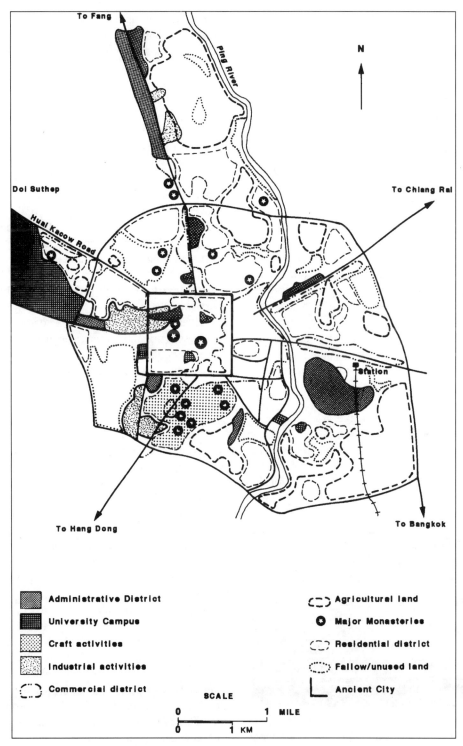

Figure 5.8   Land use in the Municipality of Chiang Mai, 1987

Figure 5.9   Wat Phra Singh, Chiang Mai, a 14th century temple renowned for its scripture library and decorative woodwork. (Source: Kwansuong Athipo)

owner of a stall on Wualai Road, she very quickly noted that the passing tourists were looking for antiquities and she decided to move into second-hand goods. This investment proving to be very worthwhile, she specialised further and became an antique dealer in the 1970s. Very soon it became impossible to find genuine antiques in the region. Mrs Banyen kept her collection and took up making reproductions. Her success was immediate and has served as a model for all the artisans in her neighbourhood. The lacquerware-maker Vichaikul, who used to live in the same area, has followed the same path. He has also established a second salesroom on Hang Dong Road, next door to Mrs Banyen.

About a score of residences of this style, for the most part souvenir and decoration shops, have been reconstructed in Chiang Mai. But to attract customers, certain shopkeepers are looking for more novel ideas. In 1989, one of them had a copy of a traditional Lanna-style monastery, with a triple-tiered series of roofs, constructed near the airport on Hang Dong Road. A wide range of antique reproductions are sold there without the Buddhist devotees raising the slightest protest at this commercial use of a traditional religious building design.[21]

The interest which tourists show in these old dwellings has allowed Chiang Mai's inhabitants to better understand the richness of their architectural heritage. The sales made by the visitors are enabling the development of traditional wood trade (carpentry, furniture-making, carving) and the maintenance of ancient techniques by opening up the prospect of jobs to young people coming into the workforce.

From textiles to craft industries: the birth of Artisans Road

Several traditional weaving trades have survived in the Chiang Mai artisans' neighbourhood, but the main production takes place in the small village of San Kamphaeng, situated 13 kilometres (8 miles) east of the city (Figures 5.11 and 5.12). This village has been known since the 1930s for its traditional silk weaving. It was apparently the Shinawatra family, original residents of the village, who introduced silk weaving here. From that time the family has owned two large workshops (400 employees) in San Kamphaeng, a factory (500 employees) in San Kamphaeng printing 1800 metres (1970 yards) of silk per day for export around the world, and a factory in Bangkok (600 employees). The Shinawatra family appears to have begun the cluster of craft activities on this stretch of highway which can now be referred to as 'Artisans Road', an extension towards the east of the Chiang Mai built-up area. Silk, cotton fabric and painted umbrella factories have clustered in one part or another along the Chiang Mai-San Kamphaeng Road and on the branch road leading to the village of Bo Sang. These establishments have been joined by numerous other craft enterprises (basket, lacquerware and bronzeware makers, wood carvers, silversmiths and goldsmiths, potters) and form the hub of the most recent extension of the city of Chiang Mai. San Kamphaeng-Bo Sang represents an urban network in the process of formation. This zone,

Figure 5.10   View of the reconstructed Tae Pae Gate, part of the old town wall, Chiang Mai. (Source: Doosadee Thaitakoo)

recognised since 1985 by the Board of Investment is exclusively reserved for traditional craft production - to which now are being added new activities and trades (lapidaries) attracted by the regular flow of tourist coaches which guarantee a continuous clientele.

The factories producing craft objects, being large consumers of labour, offer numerous jobs to the young women of the region. In textiles, the female workers receive 1000 to 3000 baht per month according to their qualifications, in a region where the minimum salary would be less than 65 baht per day.[22] At the goldsmiths and silversmiths, workers are paid by the piece or by the weight of engraved silver. They earn 120-150 baht a day. The women who decorate the celadon pottery receive 40-50 baht a day while the men make the pots. The women who draw designs on umbrella silk are paid by the piece and earn about 5000 baht per month. In sum, thousands of workers live and work in the enterprises along 'Artisans Road'. Since the end of the 1970s, the built-up area of Chiang Mai has developed very rapidly along this highway. Consequently intense land speculation has resulted and now that the large craft enterprises of Chiang Mai and especially Bangkok, enticed by the advantages which the Board of Investment grants them to invest in this zone, are trying to establish there, the price of plots fronting on to the road (rice fields flooded during the monsoon, or swamps) has escalated from a few dollars per square metre in 1970 to $A50 1987, then $A150 in 1990. These enterprises make very large investments in order to sell their goods to the tourists without, in many cases, even making the products in Chiang Mai.

Ban Tha Wai: an example of successful redeployment

A new artisan centre is developing about 10 kilometres (6 miles) to the south of the built-up area in the little village of Ban Tha Wai, located in the district of Hang Dong where several industrial and commercial craft activity zones are found. Ban Tha Wai, like all the villages of the region, formerly used to make a living from rice cultivation, orchards and basket-weaving based on traditional techniques. Deprived of future prospects, the young used to leave to find work in Chiang Mai and Bangkok. Since 1984, Ban Tha Wai has been totally redeployed. The peasant cottages have been brought closer to the dirt road which crosses the village, shops and warehouses have been built, and the most affluent of the villagers have had constructed a number of very beautiful traditional houses in carved wood. Bamboo and rattan are still used there, but what has suddenly made the village's fortune is woodcarving, another set of techniques handed down from their ancestors. Ban Tha Wai has become the village of wood carvers specialised in the reproduction of old sculptures and statuettes with their lacquers, glass mosaics and gilt.

The copyists of Ban Tha Wai began by producing animals (pigs, ducks and hens), then threw themselves into a very diverse range of carvings: swans, dragons, carved mirrors, various decorative pieces. The humble peasants, who drew a supplementary income from crafts skills have now become full-time artisans who supply not only the tourist shops with Burmese, Tai, Chinese and Indian 'antiques' but also the art and decorative markets around the world. Each day, trucks and containers filled to the brim leave the village. The most sought-after pieces are reproductions of nineteenth-century Burmese genies and Buddhas (Mandalay style), and also horses and elephants. The village now includes about sixty woodcarving enterprises compared with ten or so basket-weavers at the end of the 1970s.

The speculators have not yet had time to acquire plots of land in Ban Tha Wai. Being more distant from Chiang Mai, speculation is less profitable here than within the built-up area. Furthermore the inhabitants no longer want to leave the village. They even refuse to take themselves into Chiang Mai or Lamphun to work on the teak timbers of the most important enterprises. The big merchants must therefore bring the primary materials to Ban Tha Wai, put in their orders and take away the finished products. As a result, three large 'antique dealers' from Chiang Mai have made a fortune from this trade: Rattaporn Antiques (which, in 1987, was already exporting carvings worth $A250 000 ($US167 000) to the United States, Europe, Singapore and even Bali); Tussanaporn Antiques and Banyen Folk Art. All three owned shops in the city and extensions on the San Kamphaeng or Hang Dong Roads. The development

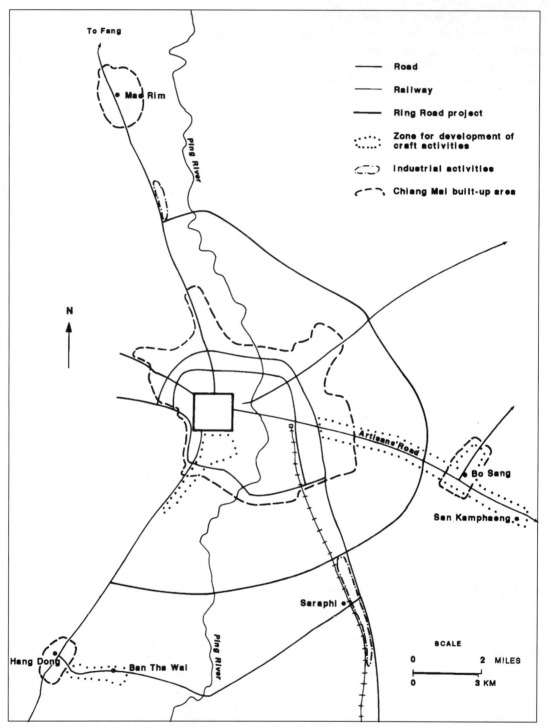

Figure 5.11 Development of craft activities in Chiang Mai region. (Source: *Department of Geography, Chiang Mai University*)

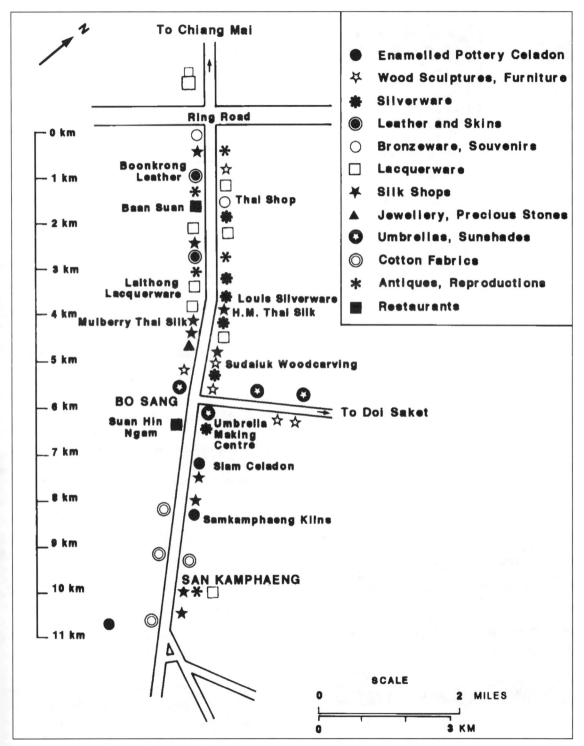

Figure 5.12   Artisans' Road, Bo Sang and San Kamphaeng, 1990

*Figure 5.13   A Westerner, oblivious to his offensive appearance in a Chiang Mai temple precinct. (*Source: *Kwansuong Athipo)*

of tourism, supported by the survival of old craft techniques in the city of Chiang Mai and its surrounding areas, has thus made possible a notable improvement in the incomes of craft workers in the region. The successful redeployment of Ban Tha Wai village, which is directly profiting its inhabitants, is a characteristic example. Most of the villagers have recreated for themselves a traditional, specifically Tai living environment, an environment that was threatened with complete disappearance in the Chiang Mai region not long ago. One might ask, however, whether these reconstructed dwellings really correspond to the taste of inhabitants anxious to maintain their traditions or whether their primary function is to attract tourists.

*Figure 5.14   Tourists crowd the doorway of a wat building at the Doi Suthep Monastery on the mountain overlooking Chiang Mai. (*Source: *Kwansuong Athipo)*

CONCLUSION

The development of the Chiang Mai urban area under the influence of the massive influx of tourists and property developers has caused an abrupt transformation of the city's morphology. The appearance of a large number of high-rise towers and apartment blocks which are totally foreign to the urban landscape has drastically altered the living environment of the city's inhabitants. The inhabitants of the working-class neighbourhoods, with their quiet little streets lined with monasteries and stalls, have suddenly been confronted by new motorised forms of transport on an enormous scale. Such areas are not designed at all for this kind of traffic. Suddenly, too, there has been a considerable increase in the need for drinking water and electricity. Along with these have come various forms of pollution not previously encountered (noise, exhaust fumes, an increase in the amount of household refuse left in the channels running behind the dwellings, a lack of sewers to clear liquid waste, etc.).

Property speculation in the centre of the city has led to a displacement of its owner-occupying inhabitants by absentee owners. The 'Khon Muang' Tai have a tendency to leave the city centre in order to establish themselves in the residential zones located at the foot of Doi Suthep or in the large estates located on the still green periphery of the built-up area. They have been replaced by Sino-Thai speculators from Bangkok as well as Chinese (from Taiwan, Singapore, Hong Kong) and Japanese. The structure of artisan neighbourhoods is going through the same evolution and is also tending to break down. Craftspeople and traders now no longer patiently wait for the client to come to their shop: instead, they try to move their shop and locate it on the routes frequented by the clients. Shops are regrouping in the specialised production and sale zones now constituted by the linear extensions of the built-up area. The renewal of craft activities seems to have engendered a return, although perhaps only superficially, to ancestral traditions and techniques but, at the same time, it has forced the inhabitants of the 'Rose of the North' to enter suddenly into a way of life for which they were little prepared and which they perhaps did not want.

ENDNOTES

1 This paper first was first published in Pierre Bernard Lafont (ed.) 1991, Pén*insule indochinoise. Etudes urbaines*, L'Harmattan, Paris. It appears here with the kind permission of the original publishers and has been translated from the French by W.S. Logan.

2 The Royal Palace of Doi Pui was constructed towards the end of the 1960s with funds provided by the province's inhabitants who, for prestige reasons, wished to see the royal family stay there.

3 *Tai* refers to the Tai-speaking ethno-linguistic groups, including the Shan of Burma, the Khon Muang of northern Thailand, the Lao of Laos and north-eastern Thailand, and the Thai or 'Siamese' of central Thailand.

4 Chiang Mai historians mention four ancient, proto-historic towns: Wieng Jied Lin, whose circular ramparts are still clearly visible in aerial photos; a still unknown city of which the traces (a system of dykes and canals) have been discovered in the grounds of the university; Wieng Suan Dork, on the site of the present-day Wat Suan Dork, which also possessed ramparts and moats; and Wieng Kum Kam which was probably built in a former bed of the Ping River by King Mengrai. The annual floods would have led the king to rebuild his capital a little further from the river on the present site. For further discussion of this point, see Wongtangsawad (1985).

5 One wah is equal to about 2 metres (6.5 feet). A measure of area traditionally and still used in Siam.

6 The most ancient structures have been destroyed by fires which, each year, ravage the neighbourhoods of the old cities of Southeast Asia, where the major part of the houses are still made of timber.

7 Tettoni (1989) reports that this wall would have been built towards the end of the eighteenth century at the end of the Siamese-Burmese wars.

8 Sukhothai, which has lost its inhabitants, now only possesses ruined city walls and pagodas. Ayutthaya, conquered by the Burmese in 1767, saw its artists, scholars and artisans taken into slavery in Burma. The majority of the population having fled during the razing of the town; the court, the nobles and the merchants abandoned the site in their turn. Most of the monuments were destroyed by the Tai themselves because of their need for an enormous amount of materials to construct their new capitals at Thonburi and then at Bangkok (1782). But the latter became a town of which

the bulk of inhabitants are ethnically Chinese, or the result of Chinese-Tai intermarriage. It was their legendary flair for commerce and business which made Bangkok's prosperity.

9 Bangkok Airways was created in January 1986.

10 Among these were 600 000 Malaysians attracted by the facilities (casinos, night life) allowed in the towns close to the Malaysian border.

11 Including 900 000 Malaysians, 530 000 Japanese and more than a million Chinese from Hong Kong, Singapore and Taiwan. The Chinese are coming as much for tourism as to study the possibilities for commercial exchanges and for setting up in Thailand after Hong Kong returns to China in 1997.

12 Mr Nit Chaivanna, Ban Huay Kaeow School principal and an active member of an ecological association which was campaigning for the protection of Chiang Mai's environment, was assassinated on 28 December 1989. The assassin has not been found.

13 Statement made by Mr Montri Juesrikul, Sales Director for the Mae Ping Condominium, 18 April 1990.

14 Hotel guest capacity will be tripled between 1990 and 1994. But, in 1989-90, the occupancy rate of the big hotels was only 60 per cent. A hotel of 800 rooms is being built next to the Chiang Mai Orchid.

15 Jointly owned apartment blocks generally located in towers of ten to thirty storeys. This type of individual accommodation has been particularly sought after in Bangkok since 1985.

16 The occupancy rates in this hotel were only 60 per cent in 1990 (60 per cent foreigners and 40 per cent Thais), less than half the average registered for the city.

17 Thai legislation prohibits foreigners from acquiring real estate in their own right.

18 Mr Pairat Decharin, Governor of Chiang Mai.

19 These measures are coming too late to preserve the character of the city. The Minister for the Interior, who presented the bill to ratify them, has made it clear that the measures will only take effect after his official signature and their publication in the Royal Gazette. But the law will not be retrospective for projects which have already received a building permit.

20 Another factor had contributed to their disappearance: these dwellings were particularly vulnerable to fires.

21 This fact is revolutionary in a Buddhist context. It would be considered sacrilegious in neighbouring Burma. It can therefore be asked whether there has not been a

decline in Buddhist religious consciousness resulting from the development of commercial activities in the Chiang Mai region.

22 At the time of writing (1990), the rate of exchange was $A1 = 16 baht and $US1 = 24 baht.

REFERENCES

Tettoni, Luca Invernizzi 1989, *A Guide to Chiang Mai and Northern Thailand*, Asia Books, Bangkok.

Nuansiri Wongtangsawad 1985, *The Former Human Settlements in Lanna*, University of Chiang Mai, Chiang Mai.

ACKNOWLEDGMENTS

The author would like to thank Professor Asadang, Director of the Department of Geography in the University of Chiang Mai, and also Professors Manas and Wongtangswad who helped in the course of the author's investigations in April 1990.

6

Phuket: urban conservation versus tourism

Doosadee Thaitakoo

Phuket, an island province in southern Thailand, is widely known to Thai and foreign tourists as the 'Pearl of the Andaman', so called because of its renowned scenery and natural environment of beach and ocean. Phuket is the largest island in Thailand with a total area of 550 square kilometres (Figure 6.1). With another thirty small surrounding islands, the province of the same name comprises a total area of 600 square kilometres (DTCP, I978, p.11; JICA I989, vol.1, p.47). The name 'Phuket' is derived from the local dialect word *bhukit*, which means mountain, a natural term of reference given the island's mountainous land form. Highly favoured by large-scale foreign and local investment in resort development over the past decade, Phuket is one of Southeast Asia's pre-eminent attractions for European and other foreign tourists. Recent upgrading of its airport to international status and the advent of direct flights to Phuket from overseas (avoiding the delays of the stop at Bangkok) have made the island resort even more accessible and as a consequence have increased the tourist flow. Current journalistic assessments regard the future of the island's tourist economy with optimism, despite recent misgivings about the environmental consequences of untrammelled beachside and town developments (Van Zuylen 1993, pp.14-17). This essay deals with the issue of tourist devel-

opment versus local identity, particularly as reflected in Phuket town's architectural and urban heritage (Figure 6.2).

ORIGINS AND DEVELOPMENT

Following contact with Europeans and their discovery of a local tin industry during the sixteenth century, Phuket became valued by outsiders more for its industrial resources than its natural beauty. Phuket was firstly called 'Insalam' by the two Portuguese explorers, Duarte Fernandes and Mendez Pinto, although the ethnic Malay inhabitants had long called it 'Chalang' or 'Salang'. Later adapted to 'Thalang', the actual meaning of this name remains obscure (Siam Society 1986, pp.16-21).

In 1592 Linschotten of Holland called the island 'Gunsalan' and remarked that there were numerous deposits of tin there, with tin mines already operating. Following treaties with the King of Siam, the Dutch East India Company proclaimed in 1664 that 'the Honourable Company shall henceforward enjoy perfect freedom to carry on trade in Siam, Ligor, Octgang, Salang, and all other places and countries belonging to the King's dominions' (Ministry of Foreign Affairs 1968, p.3). In 1685, the French, enjoying a brief period of influence in Siam, were granted a monopoly over the tin trade on the island (ibid. p.8).

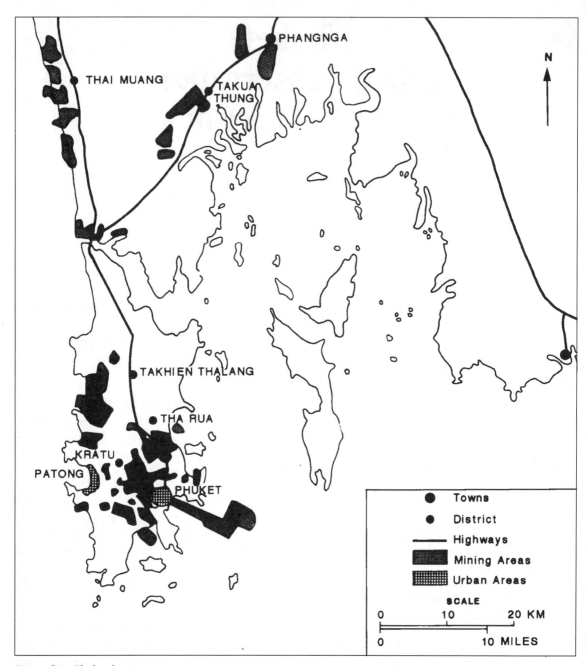

Figure 6.1   Phuket: location

By the seventeenth century, Phuket had thus become an important focus of activity and a prize for
which rival European powers eagerly competed. In
1686 Constantine Faulkon - the talented European
adventurer who worked his way to the position of
Barcelon, chief minister of Siam - remarked that the
island was full of jungles and that there was no town
centre at all. Its population then numbered around
6000 inhabitants. The villagers of the island worked
as wood-cutters, farmers, and tin-sifters. The tin-sifters

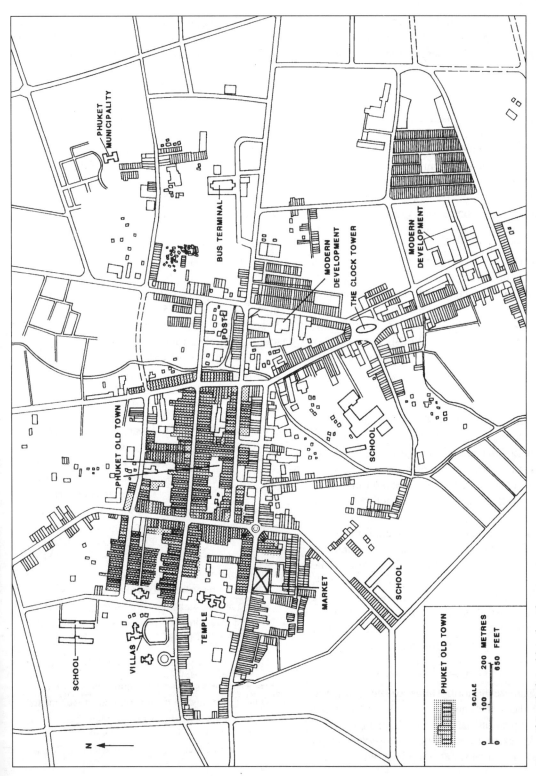

Figure 6.2 Phuket: old and modern towns

were actively engaged in the barter system of trade (Kachorn 1963, pp.181-6). The island was known for its powerful elite of Chinese entrepreneurs, whose arrival had predated European contact (Somboon 1978, pp.6-8; Thailand Development Research Institute [TDRI] 1987, p.127).

Known officially as 'Thalang' in British circles, the island was more popularly named 'Junkceylon'. The French trade in Phuket had fallen off by 1700, due partly to their expulsion from Siam in 1688 and the reorientation of French trading interests towards India. In addition, the trade of the island became depleted owing to depredation by Chinese and Malay pirates and to bad management by its Chinese governors (Cushman 1991, pp.5, 8). Tin was mined by the locals and smelted on the island, but few Europeans called in to trade until the British, in the guise of Captain Francis Light (who was stationed at Thalang from 1772 to 1781 before he moved to Penang), established closer trading ties, particularly between the island and the British possession of Penang (Nanta 1974, pp.5-42). However the British stopped short of annexing Phuket, preferring Penang as an administrative base and a more defendable settlement.

Pirate raids and especially Burmese attacks on the island in the period 1785-1812 reduced the population from 15 000 - 20 000 to an estimated 6000 inhabitants (Siam Society 1986, pp.66, 98). But even in such hard times of wars, which resulted in serious food shortages, tin still was being mined to purchase weapons (Cushman 1991, p.8).

The Burmese invasions caused painful loss. As a result, the location of the administrative centre of the island was changed. Among the names of the towns and villages on the island recorded in 1784 were Ban Takhien, Ban Don and Tha Rua (Fell 1988, p.64; Siam Society 1986, pp.56-64). The small settlement of Tha Rua, situated on the southern part of the island, was a port of considerable importance. It was ruled separately from Chalang by the successive governors Luang Phuket and Phra Phuket. The customary Siamese honorific titles *Luang*, *Phra* and *Phraya* indicate that the town at Ta Rua was, at that time, of a lower official rank than Thalang town. In Ta Rua there was a large Portuguese settlement, as well as a fine market street composed of large brick

buildings, among which rose the spacious houses belonging to the Europeans who resided here while their ships lay at anchor in the harbour (ibid. p.57).

After the Burmese attacks of 1809, the whole island was placed under the immediate jurisdiction of Chalang. This change, however, probably took place only after Tha Rua town, the capital of the district, together with Thalang town, were completely destroyed by the Burmese in that year (Siam Society 1986, p.86). From the last quarter of the eighteenth century, a Macao Chinese was appointed as the chief collector of royalty-in-kind on tin-mines for Junkceylon island. This appointment evidently included not only the tin-smelting monopoly, but also the collection of crown dues on the net produce (ibid. pp.96-7).

The location of the town centre of the island changed many times during the period of the Burmese invasions in 1785-1812. Finally it was relocated in an existing settlement, where tin was abundantly found, at Phuket[1] (Sunai 1975, p.20).

Dr Bradley's record of his visit to 'Poket' (Phuket)[2] in 1870 also gives a lively picture of the town. He began his account noting that (Siam Society 1986, p.169):

> the island was, some few years ago, divided into two provinces, and called Salang and Poket. Before this division the island consisted of only one province called Salang, the principle inhabitants of which were Malays, with only a few Siamese, and they cultivated rice and caught fish sufficient for their own consumption. Exports were unknown. The present governor of the island was then Phra Palat. He was sent to Poket when it was only a fishing village, and being an enterprising sort of a man, he determined to see what treasures were concealed beneath the soil, and was so far successful as to find something which he thought would in a few years amply repay the outlay which he might make.

He then continued (Siam Society 1986, pp.169-71):

> The Chinese soon flocked in numbers to Poket, and Phra Palat furnished them with funds to commence work, and the place prospered and grew apace, when he was appointed governor; and now (1870), what was then a paddy field, is covered with brick houses

Figure 6.3   The traditional townscape of Phuket's Old Town. (Source: D. Thaitakoo)

and a numerous population. The immigration continued to increase, and now there are about 25 000 Chinese in Poket. And most of them are employed at the tin mines. The population is sufficient for working the tin mines and also for the cultivation and for the land, consisting of Chinese 25 000, Malay 200, Siamese 300, Siamo-Malay 200, Total 25 700. Tong Ka Bay is the port of Poket. A good road leads to the town, which is 1 1/2 miles distant from the Harbour Master's Office, and that is about 2 miles from the junk anchorage. There are about 6000 piculs (approximately 4000 tons) of tin exports yearly. I can safely say that this is one of the richest islands Siam possesses.

In sum, the island and its tin industry, fuelled by Chinese entrepreneurship and labour, began to show renewed vigour in the second half of the nineteenth century and Phuket was the principal town on the island (Cushman 1991, p.8; Siam Society 1986, p.169).

TIN MINING AND PROSPERITY

Phuket's Chinese miners were said to number close to 50 000 by 1884. Tin production was reckoned at 5000 tons, and the Chinese smelters continued to process much of this output. A major impetus to the growth of the industry arose from the new alignment of forces manifested in the tax-farming concession won in the years 1872-3 by Khaw Soo Cheang, the governor of Thalang, and the neighbouring governors of Takuapa and Phangnga. Later, as Phraya Wichitsongkhram and his descendants lost power and the members of the Tan clan became the dominant

economic force on the island, mining factions came to predominate in both the political and economic spheres. An active foreign trade in tin made Phuket town the most favourable place to work and live, and, as a result, the town was more developed than any other centre, even Thalang (Damrongrajanuparp 1961, p.194).

Phuket was first characterised in the royal records when King Rama V visited the town in May 1890. It was stated that the streetscapes were formed by two-storeyed shop-houses along both sides of the streets. Observers noted that 318 of these shops were built in bricks and mortar and another 367 were of wooden construction; all of them, old and new, were in good condition. There were 2767 people living along the principal street (National Archive of Thailand [NAT] R.5 M.53/14 v.2). This district was further highlighted during the visit of the Crown Prince (later to become King Rama VI) in 1909. It was then observed that, apart from Bangkok, there were no other places more highly developed in Siam than Phuket. Evidence of such status could be easily recognised by visitors in the forms of the Chinese theatre, the ice-factory, the brewery, many rickshaws and horse-carriages, and the four motor-cars. The market-streets were full of the Chinese people in and along the edges of two-storeyed shop-houses, and beyond this lively marketplace there were some attractive villas (NAT R.6 M25/1).

The rising price of tin on the world markets from the late 1890s was the most important incentive for both the Siamese government and the local miners to upgrade the administration and technology of the industry at the turn of the century.[3] As a result the production and export of tin was significantly increased (Cushman 1991, pp.77, 99). During the prosperous years of the 1890s, the tin mined in Phuket was smelted according to traditional methods in small Chinese blast furnaces made of clay known as *Relau Tongka*; following this process it was exported. But after the introduction of a modern smelter in Penang by 1902, a large amount of tin ore produced in Phuket was exported to Penang. This was facilitated by the Straits Steamship Company which introduced a service to Phuket in 1906. After this the proportion of tin ore gradually increased and reached its peak in the years 1913-14. The other factor causing the increased production of tin from 1910-14 was that the applications from the Western companies seeking concessions in tin mining were looked on more favourably from 1910 after the Department of Mines was placed under the Ministry of Agriculture in 1909 (ibid. pp.75, 100).

Through kin and business connections, the Chinese elite of Phuket town and island were closely linked to the British-controlled island of Penang, which they considered more progressive and modern than any other place they had ever seen, even Bangkok.[4] Penang was the model of modern development for Phuket town from the early twentieth century up to the years of World War Two. The prosperity which followed the introduction of the bucket-dredge allowed such aspirations to be realised in the landscape of the township.

As a consequence of the Penang connection, the design and appearance of many shop-houses and houses in Phuket reflect the inspiration of that island's colonial architecture, though the oldest twin shop-houses in the town were built in 1887 by a member of the Tan clan of local Chinese, showing a facade distinctively Chinese in inspiration[5] Soon after this development, many shop-houses in Phuket town were laid out in small blocks within walking distance of each other. Some of them were designed or supervised by architects from Penang.

Investment in the tin industry was stimulated from the years of World War One to 1930 by rises in the price of tin (which peaked in 1918 and again in 1927). As a result many more foreign companies came to operate tin dredges on Phuket Island (Cushman 1991, p.101). At the height of the tin boom in 1927, there must have been be a considerable number of visitors to Phuket since the first hotel was put up in the town, in the same year, by the family of Thansiriroj. Named the 'On On Hotel', the building was designed and supervised by a Penang architect. The frontage comprises four shop-houses of two stories, and forty-nine bedrooms at the rear built to the same height. For the time, it was quite an imposing building and even today the On On Hotel remains attractive to foreign visitors (Cultural Centre of Phuket Province [CCPP] 1990, vol.2, p.47).

The outbreak of World War Two in Europe, and the occupation of the region by the Japanese soon after, cut off the Thai tin trade from the world market, but production recovered after 1946 (TDRI 1987, p.128) when the United States of America became the largest buyer of tin-ore from Thailand (Department of Mineral Resources [DMR] 1992, pp.22-3, 232-9). From the late 1950s the Thai government promoted the establishment of locally based tin-smelting (leading to the establishment of Thaisarco, a smelting factory, in Phuket in 1965) which had the effect of bringing more profits to the country as well as the local miners. Phuket became the leading centre of the tin mining industry, enjoying its prosperity and development through the increasing World Tin Metal Price until 1980, although it had to accept the negative environmental impacts in the form of damage to local beaches and the coral reefs. Then the price of tin declined sharply to reach its lowest in 1985, an event which signalled the collapse of the world market, resulting in the marked decline of tin production among major tin producers in the Economic and Social Commission for Asian and the Pacific (ESCAP) region (that is, Thailand, Malaysia, Indonesia and Australia) during the years 1981-87 (DMR 1992, pp.69, 71). The impact of this collapse on the Thai economy has been substantial: the tin royalties collectable by the government were cut by two-thirds; and the number of workers directly employed in the industry was also cut by more than half (TDRI 1987, p.132). Due to this collapse and a strict tin conservation policy, Phuket has been economically pushed away from tin-mining to the option of tourism, based on the attractions of its natural setting and attractive summer climate.

LOCAL IDENTITY

Phuket expresses its local culture through custom and tradition (most notably the tradition of vegetarianism). In addition the town's architecture gives its urban environment a special identity. Many significant examples demonstrate the typical character of the shop-house architecture that was built during the period 1877-1927. All of them were two-storey shop-houses covered with the gable roofs which run parallel to the frontage. The main elements of facades are the openings in the form of arches that were placed in between the orders of pilasters and decorated beams which combined to produce delicate facades. Some of these structures, for example, the Chartered Bank and the Aekwanich Company (built in 1907), have been made much more distinctive by their verandahs or arcades. This design was apparently recommended by Khaw Sim Bee (1856-1913), otherwise known as Phraya Rassadanupradit, a Superintendent Commissioner of Monthon Phuket (Phuket Region). His reason for proposing these extensions was to protect the pedestrians from the monsoonal rains that fall in Phuket eight months a year. This style of shop-house architecture has been characterised as the 'Sino-Portuguese' style.[6] There is however no surviving evidence of original Portuguese architecture since the buildings housing the Portuguese community were burnt down by the Burmese in 1809.

Although Penang was the model for developing the town of Phuket and as a consequence influenced the appearance of its shop-houses, the shop-houses in Phuket express a distinctiveness through their verandahs which create safety, comfort and convenience for the pedestrians. In short, the Phuket shop-houses stand out on the basis of Baroque-inspired architecture with verandahs and arcades. This could be called 'Phuket style', architecture not to be found in any other town or city in Thailand. Khaw Sim Bee was a central figure in modernising Phuket and the tin region with the participation of the local miners. During his time as the Superintendent Commissioner of Monthon Phuket, many public buildings were built as infrastructure, including the Phuket City Hall, built in the years 1907-13 under the supervision of an Italian architect; the Chartered Bank and Police Station, built in the years 1907-10; a Chinese temple, built in 1908; and a second Chinese Language School, established in 1911 (the old one was built in 1887 and is now used by the Association of the Phuket Hokkien Solidarity) (CCPP, vol.1, 1990, pp.6, 49; vol.2, p.62). The Phuket people have created a local architectural identity through employing the vocabulary of Chinese and European architecture, an achievement which contributes strongly to the physical expression of the local history and culture of the community.

THE TOURIST INDUSTRY

The crucial turning point for Phuket was the ad-vent of the tourist industry. Since the South Thailand Regional Planning Study was conducted in 1974, Phuket has been selected as both the centre of tourism development and the growth-pole of southern Thailand (Hunting Technical Services Ltd 1973-4; National Economic and Social Development Board [NESDB] 1976, pp.48-9, 250, 256). However, tourism expanded only slowly in the first years. A more concerted effort to study the potentiality and feasibility of tourism development in Phuket as well as the programs for mass tourism promotion were seriously carried out in 1978 (Pacific Consultants International 1978). As a result, Phuket's share in the Thai tourism market increased dramatically year by year; expressed in terms of the percentage of all international tourists to Thailand, its share rose from 4 per cent in 1983, to 6.2 per cent in 1984, 6.4 per cent in 1985, and 9 per cent in 1986 (JICA I989, vol.2). Hotel construction has been another striking indicator of transformation in Phuket Island and town. The first hotel was built in Phuket in 1927; 65 years later, in 1992, there were 248 hotels providing 16 087 rooms on Phuket Island (TAT 1992). Of this figure, the largest number of eighty hotels (32.26 per cent) and 5133 rooms (31.91 per cent) were at Patong Beach, and the second largest group of fifty-three hotels (21.37 per cent) and 3677 rooms (22.86 per cent) were concentrated in Phuket. The rest are distributed on other beaches and small islands.

Table 6.1   Population of Phuket Island in 1990 and 1991

Year	Provincial population	Tourist population	PP/TP
1990	168 481	1 254 215	7.44
1991	177 090	1 300 000	7.34

(Source: *'Phuket Province' data in Pradchamas Lanchanon 1993, p.95; Tourism Authority of Thailand (TAT) 1991*)

In 1990, as Table 6.1 shows, 1.25 million tourists visited Phuket and, with its provincial population of 168 481, there were thus seven tourists for every islander, and this proportion remained the same in 1991. These figures represent considerable profit for the tourist industry on the island. With this temptation many of the local people left their own careers in tin-industry and agriculture for tourist businesses of various types and scales. In addition, the tin crisis during the years 1980-85 had pushed most of the people in this sector away to the tourism sector. Up to now the tin price remains low and there is little stability in the international tin market (TDRI 1987, pp.129-30). So there was clearly little choice among local people as to the options for making a living in Phuket.

With seven tourists for each islander, and well-documented changes to the economy and natural environment of the island (in line with beachside settlements and islands in the region which have experienced similar impacts), one can quite reasonably hypothesise that the process is likely to result in the gradual eclipse of the local culture and environment in the face of international influences, unless the local culture and environment are particularly resilient, or supported in some way. Is this hypothesis acceptable? - For Patong beach, many people who visited there twice within the last 15 years acknowledged that the natural beauty of Patong beach has been totally replaced by the agglomeration of buildings including high-rise hotels, shop-houses, department stores, restaurants, bars, hospitals and housing areas, all characterised by an architecture driven by the requirements of investors, the tastes of Western tourists, and the design preferences of commercial architects. Thus, Patong, once a naturally calm fine beach settled with fisherpeople's huts, featuring local vegetation of coconut and rubber trees, has been transformed to look like the other Thai tourist nodes of Pattaya, Hua Hin, and Ko Samui. Patong beach has been transmuted into an urban consumer area where, somehow, one cannot distinguish whether one is in Pattaya, Hua Hin, Samui or Patong. In other words, Patong reaches the state of being an international resort but loses its sense of locality (Figures 6.4, 6.5 and 6.6). Such is the logic of the contemporary pattern of international resort development.

For Phuket town, however, the identity of the old centre can still be perceived through the visual appearance of the unique style of architecture built during the peak period of the tin industry in the 1890-

Figure 6.4   Phuket shop-house facades express the local identity through their verandahs and balconies. (Source: D. Thaitakoo)

1930 period. However many new shop-houses have replaced the old ones that could not serve the new requirements of commercial activities. Most of them make little effort to embellish the existing historical elements of the townscape, impacting purely by virtue of their height and mass. Aesthetically the impact has been negative. These developments have broken the continuity of the fine edges of this special district. Moreover, there are some huge buildings, including a hotel/apartment block and a shopping arcade that threaten the integrity of the townscape through their sharp juxtaposition with nearby old shop-houses. Not so far from the old district may be seen the varieties of buildings, that is, the drab shop-houses that line the featureless streets, and the drive-in shop-houses around the markets or bus terminals that form the low lying districts developed in recent years; contrasting with these areas

Figure 6.5 . The townscape of modern Phuket. (Source: D. Thaitakoo)

Figure 6.6   Traditional versus modern at Patong beach.
(Source: *D. Thaitakoo*)

are then the modern design of luxury high-rise hotels and shopping centres patronised by well-heeled
tourists or locals. These scenes of new urban environments show neither an awareness of cultural heritage in architecture and site-planning nor any sense
of place.

PERCEPTIONS OF CHANGE

The new settlements at Patong beach and in Phuket
have brought us to a critical point: why do modern
values overshadow cultural identity? Is it because
there is no longer any need for cultural identity in a
modern society?

In Phuket many local people and long-term residents feel acutely a sense of loss of their local identity. This is noticed in terms of the decline in the
speaking of the local dialect, the rarely worn local
costume, and the demolition of old familiar buildings in the townscape. Many people date such
changes from the decline of tin-mining and the rise
of a tourist-generated service economy. Some people specify that the modernisation (fashion, manners,
consumer tastes, behaviour) which the tourists bring
to Phuket is the major cause of changes in the character of the town's cultural identity. This external
pressure of tourist development has made Phuket
an attractive place for outsiders to invest in, giving
rise to the transferral of land-ownership and usage
from local people to outsiders. Many modern resorts/
hotels, golf courses, shopping centres and housing
estates have been established by outside capital,
bringing further changes with the influxes of both
the tourists and migrants from other parts of Thai-

land. To local people, such impacts include water
shortages, sewerage and garbage problems, a high
cost of living, an increase in crime and social segregation. Investors, outsiders and tourists are the greatest beneficiaries of the recent changes to Phuket,
according to local people.[7]

One aspect of local cultural heritage stands out as
being able to be preserved and enhanced. It is the
celebration of vegetarianism which has been held
by tradition every October at the Chinese temples of
the island. During 9 days of ceremonies, most of the
Phuket people dress in white (the symbolic colour
of purity) and they make and eat special tasty dishes
made from vegetables only. The reason for having
no meat for their meals is to give life to lives - a way
to make merit. Another ceremony involves the pierc-
ing of Chinese monks' cheeks by knives or swords
without pain. This ritual is the pride of the Phuket
people. This traditional festival has been promoted
as a tourist magnet by the TAT, particularly since
1987 - 'Visit Thailand' Year.

Among the tourists who are accused of being the
major cause of the changes in the cultural identity of
Phuket, there are also some who share the opinion
that it is insensitive tourists and profit-oriented investors who should be blamed. The tourists perceive
the cultural identity of Phuket in many forms: the
ways of life of the islanders and the townsfolk as
well as their friendliness, the tradition of vegetarianism, and the unique townscape of the old shop-
houses and structures in the town centre. Others
observe that the locality of Phuket has been invaded
by urbanisation. Some feel that the vegetarian ritual
is artificially enhanced purely for the sake of tourist
promotion, and that it is not in the real way of life of
all local people. Tourists notice that the old architecture in the town has been ignored and replaced by
the new meaningless buildings, giving rise to the
great danger of a characterless town centre being
developed. Even Thai newcomers to the town are
alert to the impacts of change through tourism and
the demise of local identity. There is strong support
from many people (locals, newcomers and tourists
alike) for the view that the maintenance of an authentic cultural identity is needed for the Phuket
people's way of life and for the appreciation of it by
visitors.

THE URBAN ESSENCE

Of all expressions of cultural identity, the townscape is the only concrete one that really belongs to the place and time which constitutes Phuket. The local dialect and the tradition of vegetarianism are possibly found in some other towns in southern Thailand, but such an urban environment can be found only in the old centre of Phuket. Even in Songkhla, where the Hokkienese people have also been settled for a long time period, there is a different style to the built environment.

It is not only the special style of shop-house architecture that attracts attention, but also the meaning beyond those facades. The built environment of this district is the outcome of a process of historical development expressing the ways that the Hokkienese have met a variety of needs - physical, economic and cultural. Theoretically, if one accepts that the symbolic aesthetics of the environment is important for the fulfilment of people's identity needs (Lang 1987, p.179), it should lead to the demand for urban conservation for this old town centre. Many local property owners have clearly embraced this idea as is seen by their actions of conserving the shop-houses and houses which they have purchased or inherited. They say they have done so for 20 years or more, not only because the buildings hold individual family memories, but also because in combination the buildings constitute the character of their hometown. If this old centre is replaced by modern buildings, Phuket will lose the identity that their ancestors successfully established over a period of more than a hundred years.

Many studies have recommended that urban conservation is needed for the old town centre of Phuket. The South Thailand Regional Planning Study assigned the function of this town centre to be the service centre for both the townspeople and visitors. The expansion of a new centre should be planned while the old town centre should be conserved for tourist attraction (Hunting Technical Services Ltd vol.2, 1973-4, pp.1145-49). This old town centre, consisting of the distinctive shop-house architecture, would perform a useful role in shaping tourists' perceptions. However, this unique district was filled in by modern buildings before any decision about implementation was reached.

Then, in 1976, the Tourist Organisation of Thailand started a survey for the first Tourism Master Plan for Phuket. This development policy gave the highest priority to the conservation of the local identity of Phuket, followed by the preservation of the natural environment, the development of Phuket as an international recreation area, and the conservation of the town character (Tourist Organisation of Thailand [TOT] 1979, p.2). A structure plan for the town of Phuket was drafted soon afterwards which proposed a commercial land-use for the old town centre (*Government Gazette* 1976, sec.115). At this time the Thai Department of Fine Arts responded to this development by attempting to register individual buildings for protection under the Preservation Act, although by law, the owners could reject such an effort. Academic institutions were also involved in this effort to find a solution to the problem of development threats to Phuket town. One study aimed to create a policy for conserving and maintaining the old town of Phuket (Doosadee 1979), while another aimed at establishing and implementing a policy of conservation with development (Kammeier & Sirirattana 1984).

The most recent master plan was the Study on Potential Tourism Development for the Southern Region which assessed Phuket tourism as having a very high potential for further development. In particular, the historical architecture and streets in Phuket's old town were considered as an important cultural resource for tourism development strategies (JICA vol.1, 1989, p.11). The actual phenomena have indicated, on one hand, a high degree of achievement of those plans in terms of economic growth; on the other hand they reveal a low degree of achievement in terms of environmental conservation and community development. Evidence of this poor state of affairs includes: firstly, the rapid economic growth in Phuket through tourism sector expansion; secondly, the haphazard growth of the international ocean resorts at Patong, Kata, and Karon beaches; and thirdly, the threats to the traditional townscape and to local cultural identity posed by building speculation and development and tourist promotion.

How do such plans bring about tragedy? The first remark must be that those plans and policies were carried out at every stage without any participation of the local people in the decision-making. So the people were not recognised as necessary, useful, or important to the planning process which would in many ways influence their quality of living. Neither individuals nor the community ever had an opportunity to set the direction that they might have wanted for developing their homeland. This 'top-down' planning policy gave rise to the results found in a recent survey: that Phuket has had high economic growth rate during 1987-89 but without community development (JICA 1989).

What are the peoples' opinions on the concept of urban conservation in Phuket? Many local people, working residents, tourists, and scholars share the view that urban conservation depends mostly upon the local people themselves: they must have strong awareness of the necessity and the advantages of establishing an urban conservation program. It is the local people's mission to teach their children to recognise the merit and benefit of having this cultural identity together with an improved quality of life. It is hoped that with the support of the governmental agencies dealing with education and the labour force, the local children will have the proper learning and training as well as working opportunities for them to earn a living 'in Phuket' with the pride and will to conserve their cultural heritage. Other support from the government in the form of zoning regulations and technical assistance will help; cooperation from considerate tourists and responsible investors will help much more to achieve the goal of keeping the cultural identity of Phuket safe from loss.

In addition, some tourists have suggested that the economic growth fuelled by tourism should be slowed down in favour of eco-cultural tourism. Folk arts and handicrafts should also be promoted for both conservation of the arts, craftsmanship and income generation. The tourism growth model of Pattaya should be immediately and absolutely stopped.

The working residents have stressed the continuity of this cultural heritage which they believe can be safeguarded by the cooperation of all communities. The scholars have urged that development and conservation are compatible. Such views support each other. But sustainable development is impossible unless the conservation of resources is implemented through some workable program of co-ordination.

In turn, the vital actions of conservation will lead to sustainable development. Ideally, such urban conservation will support and enhance everyday lives, ensuring that this cultural identity will not be assimilated completely by a 'placeless' modernism, or the uncommitted pluralities of post-modernity.

Urban conservation in this sense is an agreement among communities of people that they will protect their town centre from any changes by using it as it is, keeping it in good condition, and enhancing it to be both a community's pride as well as a generator for employment and income, arts and culture, and creativity. Those ideas have to be coordinated in order to perform urban conservation functions, and the Municipality of Phuket is the appropriate agent for carrying out this task. In turn, the private investors and other beneficiaries from tourism development in Phuket have a good opportunity to contribute their assistance, either financial or technical. The Department of Fine Arts is another important agency that can provide the technical assistance for maintenance and restoration of structures. The DTCP can participate in this project through its mechanisms. It would be a great contribution if the DTCP can designate the areas for urban conservation and for urban development. And for its successful promotion activities, the Tourism Authority of Thailand is capable of promoting a combination of natural preservation and urban conservation in order to reach ecocultural tourism goals.

There are few objections to the principle of conserving cultural identity in the author's survey findings, suggesting that there is a high potential in Phuket for urban conservation. Existing efforts in the community have already been recognised by the award given to the people of Phuket in 1993 by the Association of the Siamese Architects for their many private initiatives in urban conservation. The Municipality of Phuket and its representatives are the key starting points for initiating policy and encouraging acceptance of the conservation objectives. It is hoped that the spirit and power of the community will accomplish such an important goal.

The questions then emerge: Why was there no cooperation concerning development sooner than now? - Is it because of differences of opinion among the townspeople about development? What has prevented cooperation between agencies in the past?

Local people, academics, some private landowners, the Department of Fine Arts, the Office of National Environment Board and the Tourism Authority of Thailand are in agreement on the principle that the conservation area of the old town of Phuket must be officially designated. There are, however, private owners who prefer to have this area left open to land development. Officials of the Municipality of Phuket admit that they are so busy with routine work that they do not have much time to concern themselves about it, although if there is the law for urban conservation they, as the implementing agency, will enforce it. Surprisingly, the Department of Town and Country Planning has ignored the urban conservation policy for Phuket by designating the old central area for commercial land use. Moreover it is planning to widen Thalang road, the oldest road in Phuket, which will accelerate the demolition of the historic architecture. The DTCP is to be blamed for making no effort to protect such a special district though it has the legal power to do so, and some of its officers are willing to implement such measures. It will be more effective if the DTCP can revise the meaningless existing Master Plan for Phuket because its participation is needed for the effective urban conservation of the town.

The project of urban conservation offers a potential social tie bringing people to think, work, and live together in revitalising the old town centre and achieving better qualities of life and environment for all people. That is to say, urban conservation can generate many activities, social, economic and political, which will lead to community and urban development in the real sense. In short, the proper urban conservation policy of action will lead to the sustainable development that many people are searching for in Phuket.

ENDNOTES

1 This is made clear by several French, English, and Portuguese maps consulted at the Bibliothèque Nationale, Paris. It was only after the last Burmese attack and invasion in the early part of the nineteenth century that the administration and the government of the island was transferred to Phuket city, and advantage taken of the harbour facilities available there.

2 Hereafter 'Phuket' will refer to the town, as distinct from Phuket Island.

3 The first development was the establishment of the Department of Mines under the Ministry of the Interior in 1896. A branch office was set up in Phuket in 1898 to supervise concession licences. The second one was that many coolies had been brought from China by a shipping company in Penang to supply workers to the west coast mines. Lastly, a more modern extraction method called 'bucket dredging' was introduced in 1906.

4 It was also noted that, largely due to the convenience of closer proximity, the people in Phuket town preferred to go to Penang, rather than to Bangkok, for matters as various as medical treatment, the purchase of equipment and luxuries (NAT, King Rama V).

5 Interview with owner S. Tantawanich in 1992.

6 Colonial Portuguese architecture is not by itself a distinctive style, but rather a blend of influences derived earliest from Moorish, and later from Italian renaissance and baroque styles (see Guillen-Nunez 1984, pp.50-53; Wong 1970, p.10).

7 In an effort to arrive at some conclusions about perceptions of change and identity in Phuket, the author conducted a survey there in 1992. Four target groups were chosen for the survey: one, the local people who live/work in the old houses or shop-houses in the old town (including both the owners and the renters); two, the people who have worked in governmental agencies in Phuket for some time so that they know Phuket well (including both locally born people and outsiders); three, academics who deal with 'Phuket' in Bangkok; and four, the tourists.

REFERENCES

Cultural Centre of Phuket Province (CCPP) 1990, *Data on the Cultural Environment*, Office of the National Environment Board, Bangkok.

Cushman, J.W. 1991, *Family and State: The Formation of a Sino-Thai Tin-Mining Dynasty 1797-1932*, Oxford University Press, Singapore.

Damrongrajanuparp, HRH. 1961, *Sarn Somdej* (in Thai), vol.6, Kurusapha, Bangkok.

Department of Mineral Resources (DMR) 1992, *A Hundred Years of the Department of Mineral Resources* (in Thai), Department of Mineral Resources, Bangkok.

Department of Town and Country Planning (DTCP) 1978, *A Study Report of Phuket* (in Thai), Ministry of the Interior, Bangkok.

Doosadee Thaitakoo 1979, *Phuket: A Study in Architectural Conservation through Planning Measures*, Master of Urban and Regional Planning Thesis, Chulalongkorn University, Bangkok.

Fell, R.T. 1988, *Images of Asia: Early Maps of South East Asia*, Oxford University Press, Singapore.

Government Gazette, Government of Thailand, Bangkok.

Guillen-Nunez, C. 1984, *Images of Asia: Macao*, Oxford University Press, Hong Kong.

Hunting Technical Services Ltd. 1973-4, *South Thailand Regional Planning Study*, vols 2, 3 & 9, Hunting Technical Services Ltd., London.

Japan International Cooperation Agency (JICA) 1989, *The Study on Potential Tourism Development for the Southern Region of Thailand. Final Report*, 3 vols. Tourism Authority of Thailand, Bangkok.

Kachorn Sookpanich 1963, *Constance Faulkon and Foreign Affairs in the Reign of King Narai the Great* (in Thai), Kawna, Bangkok.

Kammeier, H.D. & Pornjai Sirirattana 1984, *Towards a Conservation and Development Plan for Phuket* (in Thai), Asian Institute of Technology, Bangkok.

Lang, Jon 1987, *Creating Architectural Theory*, Van Nostrand Reinhold, New York.

Ministry of Foreign Affairs, Treaty and Legal Department 1968, *Treaty Series*, vol.1:1617-1869, 'Bilateral Treaties and Agreements Between Thailand and Foreign Countries and International Organisations', (in Thai, English & French), Ministry of Foreign Affairs, Bangkok.

Nanta Voranetivong 1974, *Sir Francis Light: The Governor-General of the Prince of Wales Island* (in Thai), Department of Fine Arts, Bangkok.

National Archive of Thailand (NAT), *The Official Reports of the Phuket Region in the Reign of King Rama V and VI* (in Thai), R.5 M.53/14 v.2; R.6 M25/1, Bangkok.

National Economic and Social Development Board (NESDB) 1976, *Regional Development Guidelines for Southern Thailand in the 4th National Plan*, NESDB, Bangkok.

Pacific Consultants International (PCI) 1978, *Master Plan and Feasibility Study, Tourism Development of Phuket (Interim Report)*, Report to Tourist Organisation of Thailand, PCI, Tokyo.

Pradchamas Lanchanon 1993, *A Study on Problems of Drainage System and Water Treatment for Urban Development: A Case Study of Phuket Municipality* (in Thai), Master of Urban and Regional Planning Thesis, Chulalongkorn University, Bangkok.

Siam Society 1986, *Old Phuket: Historical Retrospect of Junkceylon Island*, 2nd edn., Siam Society, Bangkok.

Somboon Kaentakien 1978, *The History of Phuket* (in Thai), Petchaburi Teachers' College, Petchaburi, Thailand.

Sunai Rajapantarak 1975, *Phuket* (in Thai), Barnakij, Bangkok.

Thailand Development Research Institute (TDRI) 1987, *Thailand Natural Resources Profile*, TDRI, Bangkok.

Tourism Authority of Thailand (TAT), Statistical Office 1991, *Annual Report of Phuket 1990* (in Thai), TAT, Bangkok.

Tourism Authority of Thailand (TAT), Statistical Office (1992). *New Hotels and Hotels Under Construction. Monthly Report.* Bangkok: TAT (in Thai).

Tourist Organisation of Thailand (TOT) 1979, *The Master Plan for Tourist Development in Phuket: Physical Planning* (in Thai), TOT, Bangkok.

Van Zuylen, G. 1993, 'Phuket: Better than Average', *Business Review*, Thailand, vol.22, no.270, July, pp.14-17.

Wong, Shiu Kwan 1970, *Macao Architecture: An Integration of Chinese and Portuguese Influences*, Imprensa Nacional, Macao.

ACKNOWLEDGMENTS

The author wishes to express appreciation and thanks to the local people in Phuket and to the scholars and tourists in Bangkok for their valuable contribution of ideas and attitudes to this work. Thanks also is extended to the author's students for their assistance in the survey of Phuket town.

7

Dizzy development in Hua Hin: the effects of tourism on a Thai seaside town

Annette Hamilton

Hua Hin is famous in Thailand as the first seaside resort. Located around 230 kilometres (143 miles) south of Bangkok, it is the largest town in Prachuab Khiri Khan province, and has been the focus of urban development in the region for around 70 years. Much of its renown derives not merely from its natural resources, such as the long stretch of white sandy beach, the once-abundant local fish, prawns and squid, the cooling summer breezes and attractive hillscapes, but from the way in which members of the Thai royal family and aristocratic elites made the town a favoured area for summer palaces and bungalows, particularly in the 1920s and 1930s. The presence of a Royal residence in a place has always conveyed a particular symbolic value in Thailand, which goes beyond merely the desire to be near to seats of power. Royalty partakes of a sacred quality, and the places inhabited by Royal family members take on something of the transcendental significance attached to the monarchy itself. Hence Royal patronage of Hua Hin, which continues to this day, has made it something more than just a seaside town.

The beginning of interest in the seaside as a pleasure resort in Thailand intersects with the assumption of modernist values and Western practices among the elites. Hua Hin is located close to the present-day provincial border with Petchaburi province,

where King Rama IV (King Mongkut) had his hilltop palace, known as Phra Nakhon Khiri, at Khao Wang, recently restored by the Fine Arts Department and now a major tourist site complete with hillside cable-car. In 1868, this King travelled south from his palace along the seaside cart-tracks which passed through what is now Hua Hin to Wa-Ko, 15 kilometres (9 miles) south of Prachuab Khiri Khan town. Here, accompanied by the Governor of Singapore and a contingent of French scientists, as well as other foreign guests, he viewed the eclipse of the sun which he had predicted in advance with complete accuracy (see Cook 1992). His son, King Chulalongkorn, Rama V, hailed by Thai people today as the Father of Modernity, also visited the area. He left his royal mark on Phraya Nakhon Cave in Khao Sam Roi Yot, 63 kilometres (39 miles) south of Hua Hin, and had a beautiful pavilion built which is illuminated by shafts of sunlight at midday in the far depths of the cave. This too is an important tourist attraction in the region, one which has long been especially significant to Thai visitors.

Without doubt, it was the building of the railway to the south, joining Bangkok and the Malayan border, thence to Singapore, which opened up this coastal region to its first phase of tourist development. The railway construction began in 1912, and

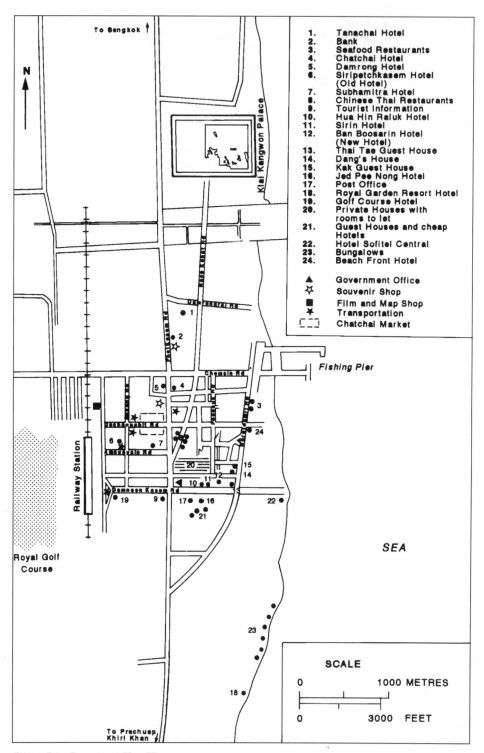

1. Tanachai Hotel
2. Bank
3. Seafood Restaurants
4. Chatchai Hotel
5. Damrong Hotel
6. Siripetchkasem Hotel (Old Hotel)
7. Subhamitra Hotel
8. Chinese Thai Restaurants
9. Tourist Information
10. Hua Hin Raluk Hotel
11. Sirin Hotel
12. Ban Boosarin Hotel (New Hotel)
13. Thai Tae Guest House
14. Dang's House
15. Kak Guest House
16. Jed Pee Nong Hotel
17. Post Office
18. Royal Garden Resort Hotel
19. Golf Course Hotel
20. Private Houses with rooms to let
21. Guest Houses and cheap Hotels
22. Hotel Sofitel Central
23. Bungalows
24. Beach Front Hotel

▲   Government Office
☆   Souvenir Shop
■   Film and Map Shop
★   Transportation
[⸬] Chatchai Market

Figure 7.1   Downtown Hua Hin

by the 1920s the seaside area of Hua Hin was well-known to various members of the Thai royal family. Elite accounts attribute the 'discovery' of Hua Hin to Krom Pra Nares Vorarit, minister responsible for supervising the railway construction. He and his party camped there and liked the area. Subsequently he bought land and built not only his own house but also nineteen other lodging houses known by melodious names which, in English, meant 'happy heart', 'without worries', 'enjoy eating' and 'sound sleep' (Ranaa 1988). Many of these residences had a particular symbolic significance, in that much of the teak used to build them came from the extensive cremation buildings used during the rites for the death of King Rama V (Chulalongkorn). After the ceremonies were over, the timber was dismantled and auctioned among buyers of Royal rank. This association of the timbers of the buildings with the most famous and important King of Thailand provided an even more

Figure 7.2   Royal Waiting Room, Hua Hin Railway Station

singular significance to the town's development. In addition to Prince Nare's bungalows and palace, the Prince of Chantaburi had a sizeable compound just a little further down the shore, while Prince Chakrabongse built a complex of bungalows and a Victorian-style gazebo on a scenic group of rocks near Hua Hin village. It was from these rocks that the town took its name, *Hua Hin* meaning 'Heads of Stone'.

Access from the railway station, with its beautifully detailed Royal Waiting Room (still in use; see Figure 7.2), was provided by a road which Her Majesty Queen Prasripatcharintara Prapanpeeluang had constructed for the purpose. Horses and carts, or bullock-carts, were available to collect visitors from the railway and convey them to their destination near the seafront. (As motor cars became common in Bangkok, the aristocracy moved its horses and carriages to various up-country properties). As well, there were travelling carts, imported from Cambodia, with a roof under which ladies could sit, while the gentlemen accompanied them on horseback.

With the growing popularity of Hua Hin, King Rama VI (Vajiravudh) offered part of the beachfront land to the Royal Railways Department, for development under the control of the Director General of the State Railways, Prince Purachatra. Combined with another block acquired from, Nai Arbus, an Indian, a hotel began to be constructed and was finished in 1922. The hotel was built in elaborate European style with the latest in facilities, at a cost of 128 366.78 baht ($A7550 or $US5134, a huge sum at that time) and included fancy fretwork decoration and a formal garden containing topiary. The hotel came to be known as the Railway Hotel before its incarnation as the Hotel Sofitel Central Hua Hin in 1986. Famous people from all over the world were invited to visit and stay. Foreigners mostly lived in the hotel, while Thais, including important visitors, either stayed in their own bungalows or in the Railway Hotel bungalows, of which Bungalow D was the most luxurious and reserved for the most important VIPs (Ranaa 1988). At the same time as the Railway Hotel was being built, King Rama VI also commissioned the construction of a golf course, under the supervision of Mr A.O. Robins, an engineer from Petchaburi. Both the hotel and golf course were officially opened by

the King who broadcast live from the hotel on 1
January 1923; he played golf for the first time on 28
June 1924. The golf course was subsequently ex-
tended, and the new course was opened by King
Rama VII in 1928.

In 1926 a brand-new covered market, Chatichai
Market, was constructed on the main street of Hua
Hin. The most modern in Thailand, it marked a new
beginning in consumption practices, operating 7 days
a week and replacing the old weekly market which
had previously existed to the north of the town.

In 1927 construction began on a new Royal Palace
for King Rama VII right on the beachfront to the
north of the town, designed by Momchao Ittitepsawan
Kritdakorn, Director of the Fine Arts Department, and
given the name 'Klai Kangwol', or 'Far from Care'.
The King was in residence here in 1932 when the
revolutionaries in Bangkok declared the end of the
absolute monarchy, an event which still lives in the
minds of many of the older townsfolk as if it happened yesterday.

Thus, by the early 1930s, Hua Hin town had undergone a radical development process, largely propelled by the new Westernised fashion of summer
seaside resorts which was taken up enthusiastically
by members of the Bangkok elites. The popularity
of the seaside was an entirely new thing in the country at the time. Previously, royal summer palaces had
always been sited on top of mountains: in Thai thinking, the seaside is lower (and therefore less honourable), while exposure to the sun (which darkens the
skin) is to be avoided. The transformation in the social evaluation of the seaside probably affected Hua
Hin more than any other seacoast area; it was already a site of royal interest and approbation, it was
relatively close to Bangkok, and the railway made
travelling comfortable and convenient. These developments had a profound impact on the region, since
each bungalow and palace required numerous servants and gardeners thus providing local people with
royal employment, while the demand for fish, fresh
vegetables and so on stimulated the agricultural sector. In addition, the demand for builders and building materials meant that the town experienced a huge
influx in population. The elite interest in the Hua
Hin area, and the influx of population, resulted also
in further stimulation of the fishing industry which

*Figure 7.3   Until the late 1980s fishing provided an
important part of the local economy. Small fishing boats
on shore near the fishing pier, 1986*

in any case was expanding to meet new demand in
metropolitan Bangkok (Figure 7.3). Apart from fishermen, women were employed to sort and clean
squid. There were abundant local catches of prawns
to be dried and processed, and a market in sea-prod-
ucts for decoration, and tourist sales grew up with
carved and pasted sea-shell hangings and trinkets.

While most accounts of Hua Hin commence with
its royal and elite aspects, the local stories are just as
interesting, although very much less well known.
Mythological narratives accounting for landscape,
islands and sacred trees are quite common, at least
in this southern part of the country. Foundation stories, explaining the origins of particular villages and
local shrines, are also well known and frequently
told, forming part of a regional oral history, only
fragments of which seem to have been recorded
anywhere. Many shrines exist to invoke the protection of named founding ancestors in particular places,
and Hua Hin is no exception. In the account following, the author has relied both on interviews with
old people in the town, and on the published account of Hua Hin's history found in the Memorial
Book for Mr Arun Krasaesin (Krasaesin 1984).

The founding ancestors of Hua Hin are said to
have been Nai Tong and Nang Yuu Krasaesin of Baan
Bangcharm, and Nai Wat and Nang Kaew of
Bangkaew, both villages in present-day Petchaburi
province. Around 1834, due to increasing pressure
on arable land and fishing sites in Petchaburi, the
two families, together with other relatives, were per-

suaded to travel south through Cha-Am, Bang-Kwai, Bor Fai, Nong Sakae and Khao Takiab. They found these places already occupied. However, between Bor Fai and Nong Sakae was an uncleared area, where land seemed fertile and there were many creeks (or *khlong*). At first they farmed only temporarily, returning home after their harvests, but they found travelling with carts and buffaloes too exhausting and hence decided to settle there. The Hua Hin area at that time was known as 'Baan Samorieng', after the name of the creek which ran inland just north of the present-day fishing pier. The family of Nai Wat and Nang Kaew settled at what is now known as Don Klang village. The most important person at Samorieng (Hua Hin) was Nai Tad, descendent of Nai Tong and Nang Yuu. A fisherman by trade, he was also known as Khun Daan or Nai Daan, and took responsibility for all who lived in Samorieng village and gave permission to people to settle there. The details of family relations and subsequent settlements in Hua Hin and Khao Takiab are too complicated to mention here: suffice to say that local people have a much older narrative of settlement of the region, and a seven-generation genealogy going back to the original families.

Sacred sites of various kinds exist in and around Hua Hin town, again not recognised in the 'official' literature and tourist-oriented materials. A shrine to Khun Daan commemorated him near Chatichai Market. This, like a number of other shrines, was built for travellers who would invoke the protection of the founders on their journeys into the jungle behind the town, where they sought various raw mate-

rials and traded with the Karen (a 'hill-tribe' people) from the hinterland, who provided honey and other jungle products in exchange for dried fish and town resources. A similar shrine was built for villagers who went to Chongtahong Forest. Today, an important shrine lies at the top of the road leading west from Hua Hin, and those travelling from the hinterland stop here to make offerings of boiled chicken, rice whisky and other items dear to the heart of the founding ancestor, to ensure a safe journey and speedy return.

This part of the coast seems to have long been important for Chinese trade, and possesses a large number of Chinese shrines of various kinds. Chinese merchants sailed their junks south from Bangkok and stopped at Samorieng village, paying respects at an important shrine on the seafront. The merchants brought an image of Chao Mae Kwan Im (the Goddess of Mercy), and of other Chinese Gods. Several Chinese shrines are popular today, the most elaborate being on the high point looking north above the rocky headland, while an important shrine to Kwan Im is located near the fishing pier. The town thus contains multiple sites and narratives of significance which create a cultural and symbolic meaning to the spaces of the town quite unrelated to its long history of association with Bangkok aristocracy and elites.

By the end of the nineteenth century, it seems that most available land in the coastal district had been taken up. Behind the coastal strip lay the uplands, and then the mountains of the Tenasserim Range, forming the border with Burma. Coastal land was in very short supply, since there is only a short strip which runs into the mountains along the border with Burma to the south. Behind Hua Hin extends a substantial zone of cultivable land, but without any reliable water source until the uplands behind Faa Prataan are reached, where the Pranburi River has its source. Karen people lived by cultivation of dry rice and by trading with coastal people throughout this upland area, and they also crossed into Burma on the other side. There are a number of ancient foot-tracks linking the two coasts across steep mountain paths, with indication of ruined settlements here and there. This land was not occupied to any extent by lowland Thai farmers until perhaps the 1950s and 1960s, although a number of old villages in the hills

Figure 7.4 'Founding Couple', statues erected at Khao Takiab, with Hua Hin beach in the background

immediately behind Hua Hin provided bamboo, timber, rice, vegetables and other materials for the town's early development.

The importance of the 'first settler' families increased with the town's rapid growth. Members of a few families came to play increasingly prominent administrative roles, and formed the nucleus of a local elite which dominated town affairs until recent times. In 1937 Hua Hin became the first regional area in Thailand to have a Municipal Council, and members of several 'old' families, the Hua Hin 'natives', provided Municipal Officers, Lord Mayors and office-bearers of numerous local associations. The Krasaesin family was particularly prominent, as were members of several other intermarried families, in particular Sathukarn, Karnchanomai, Dechapanya, Sanwiriya, Chootrakul, Mangcharoen. Mr Arun Saraesin, for example, was Member and then President of the Prachuab Khiri Khan Provincial Assembly, President of the Hua Hin Fishermen's Association, first Landing Controller at Hua Hin Fishing Harbour, permanent Vice-President of the Fishery Association of Thailand, a member of the Library's Board of Directors and of the District Scout's Committee. Members of these families continue to occupy local positions, particularly at the Municipal Council, the number of which has of course vastly expanded of recent times. Increasingly they have been called upon to represent the interests of 'local people' against the pressures created by outside investment and its social consequences.

It was also members of these families who, as they became more affluent, began to build the substantial and elegant teak and timber houses in the narrow streets and lanes behind the beachfront, replacing the humble bamboo-and-thatch huts which most local people occupied. This was the nucleus of the old town of Hua Hin, with some houses on stilts out over the water, and various shrines located in and around it. The fishing catch came in here, merchants and fishermen haggled, women cleaned and dried squid, ceremonies were held and people lived in close sight of each other in their houses open to the street. Spatially, this was the centre of town, with the sea on one side, the main road and then forested mountains on the other, and the palaces and bungalows of royalty and the aristocrats spread out to the

north and south.

Chinese merchant families provided another important presence in the town. Chinese workers and vendors seem to have lived in the town for many years. There are around ten particularly prominent Chinese (now Sino-Thai) families in Hua Hin; although they started as merchants of mixed goods, or as restaurateurs, many obtained extensive real estate holdings in parts of the town which are now the focus of tourist development and have become extremely wealthy by local standards. Much of the development of second-level tourist facilities has been in the hands of members of these families, who have constructed smaller hotels and bungalows for rent, and invested in new housing developments further out of town.

More recent events in the town and region must be understood against this particular historical background. Hua Hin has now become an 'international' tourist resort, a site of massive condominium development, and a prime area of investment by the newly affluent Bangkok bourgeoisie. It is one of the chain of sites for the young European backpacker brigade in search of 'cheap' and 'authentic' local experiences. The spatial and historical past of the town differentiates it from other popular Thai seaside resorts (for example Pattaya and Phuket) which were never anything more than impoverished fishing villages or areas of small-scale agriculture. The present social order of the town still bears the marks of this historical past, but is now infinitely more complicated by the surge of new arrivals, and of new money, destabilising the old pattern of family-based elites and local power. The cultural foundations of this town, once proudly described as the 'Queen of Tranquillity', have been greatly transformed over the past 5 years, and there are now clear signs of decline in the area's popularity among international visitors, who seek something other than luxury hotels and a condominiumised landscape. This latest development phase has occurred as part of the boom of the late 1980s, and has brought into play significant conflicts between old and new residents, as well as older groups of powerholders, some of whom have been able to benefit disproportionately from the opportunities offered. Local small-scale businesspeople too have responded in different ways: some have gone over to international-tourist-orientated businesses, while others have given up and retreated to more rural areas and other regional towns. Some have made substantial profits from previously valueless land and retired to live in comparative luxury. Many poorer women have married foreigners and gone to live abroad.

Although there were of course changes in the town, and continued growth, until around 1984-85 Hua Hin remained much the same. The old Railway Hotel, its 1920s elegance now somewhat dimmed, continued to provide quite adequate services to the many tourists who frequented the town. There were several other old-style Thai and Chinese hotels in the town area, nearer to the railway and main road than to the beachfront, and a few old guesthouses such as the Hua Hin Ralug, providing plenty of overnight and holiday accommodation, except perhaps at festival periods when the town was awash with visitors and many slept on the beach. The King visited every April; aristocrats and other elite members continued to use the beachfront bungalows for holidays and weekends, or made them available to their personal associates. One of the largest beachfront bungalows served as a recreation station for Protestant missionaries in Asia, and a Christian presence was also strong in the town.

Hua Hin was very popular too with young people and families, large groups chartering buses from far afield to come and enjoy New Year's Day or other festival days. They came to sit on chairs under umbrellas on the beach, eat fresh-cooked seafood, drink, sing and generally amuse themselves. Beach vendors provided their needs; souvenir sellers lined the beachfront and the access road; the Railway Hotel provided toilets, showers and water for foot-washing outside its premises, and the simple wooden bungalows on the other side of the access road were popular with holiday groups. Up until 1986, very few *farang* (foreign) tourists came to Hua Hin, and if they did so it was usually because they knew a Bangkok resident who recommended it as an excellent place to get away from other tourists, or because they read a brief description of it in some travel guide which said it was sleepy, undeveloped, inexpensive and 'quaint'. In fact in 1986 foreign guests accounted for only around 6 per cent of all visitors to Petchaburi-Prachuab Khiri Khan provinces over-

Table 7.1   Foreign tourists: arrivals, length of stay, revenue

Year	Number of tourist arrivals	Average length of stay (days)	Revenue (million baht)
1977	1 220 670	4.51	4607
1978	1 453 839	4.84	8894
1979	1 591 455	5.09	11 232
1980	1 858 801	4.90	17 765
1981	2 015 615	4.96	21 455
1982	2 218 429	4.79	23 879
1983	2 191 003	4.91	25 050
1984	2 346 709	5.47	27 317
1985	2 438 270	5.58	31 768
1986	2 818 092	5.93	37 321
1987	3 482 958	6.06	50 024
1988	4 230 737	7.36	78 859
1989	4 809 508	7.63	96 386
1990	5 298 860	7.06	110 572

(Source: *TAT 1990*)

all; most went to Hua Hin, but even so accounted for only around 20 000 as against around 150 000 Thais (Tourist Authority of Thailand (TAT) 1987, pp.3-42, and Table 3.15).

However, all this was about to change, and to do so with an extraordinary rapidity. Since the Fourth National Development Plan (1977-81), the Thai Government began to place increasing importance on tourism as a major means of increasing foreign earnings. Tourism superseded rice as the kingdom's top revenue raiser in 1982; by 1986 tourism produced 37 321 million baht ($US1382 m; $A2073 m) of revenue, as against textile products (31 268 million baht; $US1158 m; $A1738 m) and rice (20 315 million baht; $US752 m; $A1128 m). By 1990 revenue from tourism rose to 110 572 million baht ($US4423 m; $A6635 m). During this development plan, massive infrastructure improvements, such as extensions to Bangkok's

Don Muang Airport, provision of duty-free shops, an airport-city limousine service, extension of immigration facilities and expansion of police forces specially to protect tourists were put into place (reported in *The Nation*, 1 Dec. 1986 p.6). The state thus geared itself up to do everything possible to foster international tourism. The strategy was extraordinarily successful: not only did arrivals increase quite consistently, but so did average length of stay and consequently the revenue generated!

By 1990, a total of 37 408 013 'tourist nights' were spent in Thailand by international visitors, around 47 per cent of whom came from East Asia and the Pacific (including Australia). This represented a 1.98 per cent increase over the previous year (TAT 1990).

While Thai tourists (estimated at 26.05 million in 1986, TAT 1987, pp.2-13) vastly outnumber foreign tourists, their journeys tend to be much shorter and they spend much less money. The National Institute of Development Administration estimated that travel by seventy-three Thais was necessary to provide one additional job in the kingdom. Each Thai tourist on average spends 742 baht when visiting the provinces, while each foreigner spends around 5400 baht, and while each type of tourist produces a flow-on effect estimated at 1.7 (that is, 1281 baht for a Thai and 9249 baht for a foreigner), the much greater average expenditure of a foreigner makes his/her overall impact on the economy far greater (TAT 1987, pp.1-2, 3-24). The sectors most affected were transportation, food, drink and tobacco, the service sector and the agricultural sector. In Prachuab Khiri Khan and Petchaburi provinces, the amount spent by tourists is much higher than in the kingdom as a whole, and thus it is estimated that every thirty-five Thais and every five foreign tourists generate one job for local people (ibid). Thus, foreign tourism generates around 4000 jobs, and Thai tourism a further 4300.

While most Westerners think of tourism in Thailand as predominantly Western, in fact there are far more non-Western foreign visitors, particularly taking into account the huge numbers of Malaysians who cross the southern border to Hat Yai and other southern towns. While the number of Westerners has without doubt increased in recent years, so too has the number of other Asian tourists. The 1986 figures are shown in Table 7.2:

Table 7.2   Countries of residence of tourists visiting Thailand in 1986

Country of residence	Number
Malaysia	652 887
Japan	261 549
Singapore	220 725
USA	172 575
Hong Kong	164 677
West Germany	114 478
Australia	103 317
UK	99 489
France	97 540

(Source: *adapted from TAT 1987, pp.2-6*)

In the light of problems with tourist provision, a number of Government Master Plans for tourist development were prepared in the 1980s for a variety of regions, including the two provinces of Petchaburi and Prachuab Khiri Khan. Unfortunately the boom took place with little regard for reports or planning documents of any kind, and nowhere was this more obvious than in Hua Hin (Figure 7.5).

The transformation of Hua Hin provides a good example of the complexity of the 'development process' in Thailand; dramatic growth-rates and all the classic markers of an economy in expansion have led to the kingdom being identified as one of the new 'Asian tigers', and debate in Thailand over whether or not it should be, or is already, a NIC (Newly Industrialised Country) has been constant over the past few years. Models of development which see the process as basically the effect of external factors, particularly transnational investment by European/US/Japanese-based companies, tend to interpret the local-global relation as one of passivity-activity. Local areas, environments, cultures and social patterns are depicted as being at the mercy of expansionist investment which enters from outside and has no regard for the existing ways of life. Residents of local areas are caught up helplessly in the

Figure 7.5   Beginnings of the development boom in Hua Hin. Old houses are dismantled, new hotels built. Jed Pee Nong Hotel under construction, 1986

process and, unable to resist, either move away or become incorporated as wage-labourers for the rapacious capitalist sector. While there is some reality to this view, it is far from fully explanatory.

In Thailand, at least, local groups, sectors and individuals participate actively in the restructuring consequent on developments of various kinds; the 'local' is not homogeneous and passive but contains differing interest groups often in social and/or economic competition, and the opportunities offered may be seized by some in unexpected ways with unpredictable consequences. The discussion of Hua Hin town presented here is just one aspect of a broader and more detailed analysis of the effects of the expansionist development of the late 1980s for Hua Hin and adjacent districts in Prachuab Khiri Khan and Petchaburi provinces. The study as a whole reveals that 'development' takes place at multiple levels, depends on local structures of influence and power,

and can be harnessed to quite varying local aims and sensibilities. Finally, it is impossible to disentangle external from local influences. The global economic provides the conditions through which development can take place, but the local and regional responses and initiatives are what make everything 'happen'.

In 1986 there were 31 889 people registered as resident in Hua Hin Municipality (TAT 1987). Increasing tourist demand had already expanded the available visitor accommodation: there were at that time thirteen hotels with 635 rooms, and fifteen bungalows with 196 rooms, with an average occupancy rate of around 50 per cent. In addition there were many private houses, town houses and bungalows which Bangkokians used for their own holidays and rented out at other times of the year. By 1988 the available accommodation had expanded dramatically: there were now three first-class hotels with 466 rooms, room prices ranging from 7000 baht ($US280) at the Royal Garden, down to 660 baht ($US26.40) at the Sailom, with most in between. As well there were thirty-one bungalows at the Sofitel and fifty-one other bungalows in and around town, and a further 364 rooms in second-class hotels and guesthouses (Prachuabkhirikhan 1988). The volume of foreign tourists had increased sufficiently to warrant the employment of a full-time Tourist Information Officer by the Municipal Council by 1986; a second was added in 1988. Tourism to Hua Hin was actively promoted, with an Official Guide Book and promotional video and other literature being made available in other popular tourist areas.

A TAT survey in 1986 found most residents of Hua Hin enthusiastic enough about the further expansion of tourism in the area; most people believed their lives and living conditions, including public utilities, would be better. Sixty-eight per cent said it would produce more jobs, while 32 per cent considered it would produce no benefit at all. Most approved of having new accommodation, restaurants with bands, bars and nightclubs (TAT 1987, pp.3-24). However the transformation of the old Railway Hotel into the Hotel Sofitel Central Hua Hin precipitated the beginning of a series of conflicts with local people which have not been resolved to the present day.

The old Railway Hotel became the spearhead of the new development of Hua Hin, much as it had done in the early phases of the town's development. In a consortium arrangement with the French Accor Group, which operate a series of resort chains under the name 'Sofitel', and Bangkok-based financial interests associated with the Chirativat family companies which includes the Central Department Store chain, the old premises were closed and then totally refurbished with luxury fittings to the highest European standard under the supervision of French interior designers. The group obtained a 30-year lease from the Railways Department which still owns the land. A huge advertising campaign in the Bangkok papers began, featuring this as the last word in luxury holidays at the seaside, while stressing the long-standing association of Hua Hin with the royalty and aristocracy. While some wealthy Bangkokians might visit the Sofitel, its main attraction has been for farang (foreigners), whether from Bangkok or, more importantly, from Europe.

The run-down bungalows were pulled down, and replaced with luxury air-conditioned versions with hot water, television, refrigerators and so on. The prices of rooms and bungalows went through the roof: where one could get a room at the Railway Hotel for 120 baht in 1985, and a whole bungalow for around 450 baht per night, the new tariffs, with room rates of 1815-4356 baht for rooms and 1815-2904 baht for bungalows, ensured that only the most affluent, whether Thai or foreign, would dream of staying there. The concept of a high-class luxury hotel did not sit comfortably with the use made of the hotel area by local people. The road which provided the only means of public access to the sea-front swarmed with people on foot, on motor-bikes and push-bikes. Until around 1985, souvenir vendors had lined the access road with their mobile stalls selling all manner of trinkets, hats, shell-ornaments and other items. The Municipal Council had been prevailed upon by the Railways Department to remove a number of these vendors to a special 'plaza' constructed around 300 metres from the beachfront, and many were forced to transfer their businesses there. They complained that visitors could not find them unless they were right at the front of the plaza, and indeed one business after another folded there, many

creeping back onto the main road. This time on mobile vans and trolleys.

A second problem arose from the local custom of horse-rides along the beach. The local horse-owners kept their horses near the access road (obviously waiting for custom), which meant that there was a constant pile of horse manure to manoeuvre past to get to the waterfront. Guests of the Sofitel could of course access the beachfront elsewhere, but they were still subject to the thunder of out-of-control horses (many of them retired race-horses) not to mention all the other rubbish along the beach, and indeed in the water itself.

A third cause of tension arose from the ceaseless insistence of mobile vendors and masseurs that every tourist, most especially every foreign tourist, required their services. Some sold sweets and fruit, others hot dried squid, while several Indians carried trays of peanuts and pulses on their heads on ceaseless rounds up and down the beach, selling small bags for 10 baht. The thirty or so 'masseuses' were probably among the most insistent. Each carried a small book in which the tourist wrote comments on the expertise of the massage (and often other, much less flattering, remarks). Very few masseuses had any formal training, although Thai therapeutic massage is an important aspect of the Thai medical system and is taught particularly in famous temples, and some village women do develop an expertise. Most of the masseuses came from Petchaburi 67 kilometres (42 miles) away to the north, while the food vendors were almost all local people who had lived in the town for two or three generations at least, many of them inheriting the beach-restaurant from their parents.

Since the 1920s, local people had made a living on the beach. In earlier times they had permanent restaurants set up, and provided visitors with sun-umbrellas, reclining beach-chairs and small tables, for a charge. At the urging of the Sofitel's new management, the local council insisted that the permanent restaurants leave the beach in 1985. They were replaced at once by 'mobile' restaurants, from which the vendors continued to supply a ceaseless variety of cool drinks (alcoholic and otherwise), and delicious fresh-cooked meals produced from portable charcoal-burning stoves.

Obviously the beach-stalls cut into food and drink profits at the hotel, and foreign tourists were quite happy to sit on the beach all day, ceaselessly eating and drinking. As local people point out, tourists spend in one day what most Thai families earn in a month. Hence these became extremely valuable businesses, and provided the means whereby many otherwise poor local families were able to sponsor their children's education and upward mobility. The hotel management complained repeatedly to the Municipal Council, and heated meetings were held; the beach-stalls were for a time declared illegal, and the police came and arrested the vendors more than once. However the sentiment of local people, and of other Thai visitors, was on the side of the vendors, and various compromises were reached, including a demand that the vendors become responsible for the mess on the beach. While the total number of stalls was reduced, many of the same vendors remain on the beachfront to the present day, although the number in 1992 was less than half it had been in 1988.

The Sofitel, however, did find ways of making its immediate surroundings less attractive to Thai visitors, particularly by removing access to external toilets and showers which people had used after bathing. Entrepreneurial locals immediately responded by providing large vats of fresh water which, for a small cost, could be splashed over the body and used for washing the feet. However the only public toilets available were well back from the beach in the 'plaza' area; these were totally inadequate and inconvenient. The hotel management wished to create an exclusive beach-front environment for its well-heeled guests, but had been unable to extinguish patterns of local use and enjoyment. Efforts by successive hotel managers to get rid of both vendors and Thai beach-users from the immediate vicinity of the hotel failed largely due to the determination of local businesspeople and the influence of the 'first families' who continue to occupy prominent and influential positions in the town, especially on the Municipal Council. However at the end of 1993 the vendors had been removed from the hotel beachfront area. The beachfront north of the access road was packed with umbrellas and tables, and vendors were cooking away from the beach area and bringing the food ordered in by motorbikes with plates balanced on trays.

Further down the beach the Royal Garden Resort Hotel presents an image much closer to the idealised European holiday resort. Another consortium arrangement, this time with the participation of Scandinavian Air Services, the Royal Garden is a main centre for package tours, particularly from Germany. Very few Thai visitors came to the Royal Garden, and it developed into a centre for water-sports, including jet-skis, parasailing and yachting. Usage along the beachfront has become quite markedly stratified, with Europeans and Thais occupying separate areas and doing quite different things in them.

The influx of European visitors from 1987 on led to a second wave of development, this time in the area back from the beachfront. Not everybody wished to pay enormous prices in luxury hotels; many who came once on package tours realised they could have a much cheaper and more interesting holiday next time by doing it themselves, and soon the entire area behind the main beachfront was being given over to new facilities to satisfy these new requirements. A number of the old and splendid teak houses were demolished, to be replaced by small-scale hotels, with much more modest tariffs than those at the luxury hotels. Restaurants which had supplied the needs of Thai tourists found themselves with European customers in search of Vienna schnitzel and fish and chips. Those who adapted quickly, particularly by providing menus in English, German and French, began to make substantial profits. Europeans with the concept of the three-course meal, washed down with plenty of beer, ordered soups, fish, prawns, steak, chips and ice-cream, where the Thai customer would have rice and one or two dishes. Restaurateurs who learnt to speak minimal amounts of English and/or German had a captive market, and several families could be seen nightly studying from grammars and dictionaries as they struggled to increase their facility with language.

Local people who could speak English or German suddenly had access to new forms of livelihood: as taxi-drivers, guides, hotel porters and receptionists, waiters, and so on, on the legitimate side, and of course as crooners and nightclub singers and 'girlfriends' and 'boyfriends' of the tourists on the less respectable side. All along the narrow *soi* and laneways people opened their houses up, renting rooms to tourists, providing food and drink services, opening 'bars' which stylistically duplicated the exotic tropical resort mode and/or provided huge video screens with popular foreign movies to attract tourists. Houses at the southern edges of the fishing village began to be converted into the 'Happiness Bar', the 'Dew-Drop Inn' and the 'Swiss Family Cottage' and the peace and charm of Hua Hin began to give way to the ceaseless thrum and throb of hand-propelled concrete mixers, delivery trucks full of cement and gravel, building, renovating, demolishing and rebuilding facilities for the foreign tourists who were flooding in between October and February of each year. A great many strange encounters between Thais and tourists took place at this time which exemplified the cultural confusions consequent upon development.

Many of these arose from the very different understandings between Thais and foreign tourists about money, responsibilities, and appropriate behaviour. Issues around prices were important. In Thailand, all prices are set by bargaining between provider and client. While most hotels and guesthouses advertised standard prices, these too could be negotiated, and a 'discount' may be offered depending on circumstances. This uncertainty as to 'correct' prices unsettles the Western tourist while the refusal to haggle properly perturbs the Thai service-provider. *Samlor*, the three-wheel vehicles propelled by a person pushing a bicycle, common all over up-country Thailand, provided the main form of local transport in the town (Figure 7.6). Westerners, huge and heavy by contrast with most Thais, and burdened down with heavy luggage, needed a *samlor* to travel from the railway station or bus terminal to their hotels. The *samlor* drivers quickly learnt that they could charge anything they liked, as against the standard 5 or 10 baht charged to locals, depending on how much was to be carried and how far was travelled. When tourists learned they were paying two, three or five times the normal local price they complained vehemently, firstly to their hotels, then to the local council, finally to the police. The council held a meeting with the *samlor* drivers, and issued a decree setting out the right prices for different lengths of journey in

Figure 7.6   Tourists negotiate a ride in a samlor *in the main street of Hua Hin, 1988*

the town area and signs advertising this were placed prominently around the town.

Local guesthouses and small hotels soon realised that many tourists arrived without knowing where they were going to stay, and began to give a commission to the *samlor* drivers who took tourists to their hotels. Those who did not want to pay to have clients brought to them went in turn to complain to the local council. More meetings were held, and the practice was declared illegal, but still continues and causes much ill-feeling among those providing tourist services. The existence of a 'double-pricing' (or 'quadruple-pricing') system provides constant sources of tension between tourists and locals: 5 baht for a bowl of noodles to a local, 20 baht to a tourist is not considered unreasonable. Tourists, on the other hand, have come to Thailand because it is cheap, and expect to pay no more than locals. When they discover the disparity, they become filled with righteous indignation, and cause 'scenes' in restaurants and markets which embarrass locals who believe it is essential to be dignified about public interactions.

More serious problems stem from the misunderstandings by tourists as to what is going to be provided for them. Most Westerners imagine when they are obtaining a service, for example, hiring a motorbike, that they will be covered by some kind of insurance, or at least will be asked about it. However, many local people simply set up a small business outside their houses, and the provision of insurance would not be thought of as part of the service. Many tourists have had accidents, and found themselves paying out thousands of baht in compensation. Other local transport provision includes 'taxis' - generally small trucks with an enclosed rear and two parallel seats, known elsewhere in Thailand as *siilor*. However, these do not operate like normal taxis, instead charging a fixed price for journeys to particular tourist destinations. The prices charged are quite high - around 500 baht is an average - with petrol extra. On one occasion, a taxi was hired in nearby Pranburi to take a lone female tourist to Khao Sam Roi Yot national park. On arrival, she proffered a pair of sunglasses to the driver in payment, declaring they were worth much more than 500 baht. He spoke virtually no English, but insisted he wanted payment, and seized her light backpack. She argued back furiously, saying she would take him to the police. Fortuitously, a local Park Ranger passed by and stopped. Nonplussed by the dispute, he paid the 500 baht to stop the argument.

Another example concerned a man and his son, who hired a local boat to take them to an island not far from Hua Hin. This island is known for its good fishing and is mentioned as a scenic place in a number of tourist guides. The boat had no cover or protection: the island had no facilities, neither food nor water; the tourist brought nothing with him, expecting that a place mentioned in a tourist guide would have appropriate facilities. They returned from the island badly sunburnt and dehydrated. The man refused to pay the boatman for the journey. He in turn was indignant, saying that he had done what he agreed to do, namely he had taken them to the island. The tourist went to the local police to charge the boatman with failing to provide an appropriate service. The local police, never having heard of such a charge, did not know what to do and went to the Municipal Council. The tourist information officer was obliged to intervene; she suggested that he make out his complaint in writing in triplicate, but in fact nobody knew to whom such a complaint should be addressed. Finally the Lord Mayor was asked to solve the dispute. He took money out of his own pocket and gave half to the boatman and half to the tourist, and both went away mollified.

On another occasion, a German tourist paid for 4 days stay at a new, well-advertised, second-class tourist hotel. He found the air conditioning in the room did not work. He went and demanded his money back. The proprietor refused, saying she had charged him only the rate for a fan-cooled room. He said he had booked an air-conditioned room. She refused to refund his money, and in his anger he threw a lamp from the hotel desk onto the floor. The proprietress, a member of a prominent Sino-Thai family, went at once to the police and demanded that the tourist be arrested. The police came and arrested both him and his wife. They spent the day in the local lock-up with an assortment of local criminals and drunks. Again, the local tourist information office was called in to mediate, and a compromise was reached whereby the tourist was charged for the broken lamp, and the remaining part of his room-rent was refunded. He went away swearing he would take the entire local council to the tourist police in Bangkok.

Tourists, and other foreigners, frequently fail to understand the importance of local sensibilities. In a particularly famous local incident, several tourists were drinking at a local bar, and the European bar-owner was foolish enough to pass disparaging comments about one of the royal princesses. A local townsman overhead the remark, went to the police, and had the bar-owner arrested for *lèse-majesté*. He was forced to surrender his passport, then paid a large amount of money to retrieve it and left the country on the next train south.

Without doubt some of the strangest local manifestations of global tourism appear in the realm of interpersonal relations. Relationships spring up quickly in the context of an exotic tropical holiday, and all too often these involve locals and tourists. In one case, the son of a local restauranteur was courted by a married German woman. She left her husband and child and moved into the restaurant with the young man and his mother, where she chopped vegetables and served at tables. Finally they both went back to Germany, and married. The unfortunate young man spent a year living, unemployed and unpopular, with her and her mother's family in Germany, until she finally paid his fare back to Thailand. Not long afterwards, back serving in the restaurant, he met another German woman, who also fell in love with him, and he returned to Germany with her, still not sure about whether he was divorced from his first wife. This relationship too collapsed, and he returned once again, to resume waiting on tourist tables. In another case, a Scandinavian woman took a shine to a local *samlor* driver, moved him in with her to her luxury hotel, and gave him a great deal of money. He was married, with two young children. His wife was angry at first, but when he offered her half of the money, she accepted the situation. The same woman returns every year to the area, and continues her relationship with the man. He and his wife have been able to use the money to buy a new townhouse on the outskirts of town. Similar events take place ever year in the town, causing no end of puzzlement to the respectable local townsfolk, who simply cannot understand why foreign people would want to engage in relationships with those who, by local standards, are unimportant or 'low-class'.

As the influx of foreign tourists continued into the 1990s, property development and speculation became the hobby of the newly affluent Bangkokians, and many were attracted to Hua Hin because of its association with the aristocracy and elites. Many invested in holiday houses in and around the town. Locals were summarily evicted from houses they had lived in for years. A considerable number of 'new' foreign residents arrived to start tourist-oriented businesses, or to retire with their Thai wives, adding considerably to the complexity of the town. Locals found the value of their properties doubling and trebling within months, provided it was anywhere near the beachfront. Those who sold then wanted to buy something else in the town, and new housing developments sprang up, with large and elaborate houses as well as townhouses and smaller bungalows. These in turn became attractive to less affluent outsiders, and possession of a house in Hua Hin became a sign of social status even among the lesser bourgeoisie from Bangkok.

Along the waterfront itself, where the old bungalows had been located to the south of the town, as well as along the waterfront towards the north, between Hua Hin and Cha-Am, condominiums arose, and became the key to the new landscape. Many of them were developed in association with their original owners, some of whom are members of the royal family. Competing interests began to cause great difficulties: water supplies were inadequate, and the Municipal Council was obliged to find solutions to

all kinds of development dilemmas. Great dissatisfaction was expressed by some local people, especially the residents of the old fishing village of Khao Takiab at the southern end of Hua Hin, who were left without water and electricity on more than one occasion. However by 1990 development had begun in that area also, and by 1992 two huge condominium developments overshadowed the village altogether (Figure 7.7). Also at Khao Takiab are two Buddhist temples, one a 'traditional' one and the other a 'spiritual centre' appealing to all kinds of syncretic Buddhist elements. The latter has become increasingly significant to the Bangkok bourgeoisie who have houses in Hua Hin, and who have flooded the *wat* and its charismatic monk-leader with donations until the precincts, studded with garish examples of contemporary Buddhist iconography, are beginning to resemble a Buddhist Disneyland.

At this *wat*, located spectacularly on the top of the hill at Khao Takiab, carloads and busloads of visitors arrive every weekend. The Abbot, wearing tailored robes and Ray-Ban sunglasses, greets his supporters from the terrace of his grand house overlooking the sea. Respects are paid to a variety of images and shrines, including an image of the *rusii*, or wandering monk, who is associated with the Buddha's enlightenment (Figure 7.8), and to the huge brand-new image of Chao Mae Kwan Im (the Goddess of Mercy), located high on the Western side looking out over the ocean, donated by a wealth Bangkok woman in satisfaction of a vow. Wealthy devotees have begun to endow funds for the building of *kuti* (meditation huts), many of quite a luxurious standard on marble

Figure 7.7   Condominiums on the beachfront at Khao Takiab village, 1992

Figure 7.8   Image of the rusii *(wandering monk), associated with the Buddha's enlightenment, in the grounds of Khao Takiab temple, 1988*

bases with astonishing ocean views. Many nuns are in residence at the *wat*, ministering to the needs of the monks, selling blessed images and amulets, while donations of sacred images are made to the huge collection inside the lounge-room of the Abbot, replete with a large TV set and excellent sound system. On the adjacent hillside, the much older and more conservative *wat* at Khao Krailat also receives many visitors, mostly tourists seeking to take photographs and videos of the surrounding countryside. The two *wat* exemplify, in the religious domain, the contrast between syncretic modern Buddhism, oriented towards images and magical powers, and the more traditional system, with its repetitive provision of ritual comfort to local people, and simple dependence on a local community.

The effects of development of Hua Hin thus spread very widely. Apart from the area discussed above, the impact of the town's development is also felt in the hundreds of small villages and hamlets in the hills behind (Figure 7.9). In the villages which used to provide building materials such as timber and bamboo for Hua Hin, virtually everybody from those villages now works in town on construction sites, so that the villages are becoming totally dependent on income from the town and are beginning to function like suburbs. The pressure on development along the coastal strip has led many to seek new land to build holiday houses and resorts in the hinterland, with several new Country Clubs, a golf course, and other 'Mountain Resorts' underway. Even in the most remote hinterland village, where the author has spent

successive periods of time in 1989, 1990 and 1991, a place where there is no electricity and people eke a bare living from agriculture, the livelihoods and opportunities of people are found to have changed: now the village headman spent his days catching butterflies in the mountains, to be mounted on plaques and sold to the tourists, while the president of the Housewives' Association was raising turkeys for tourists' Christmas dinners.

The case of Hua Hin exemplifies the complicated consequences of a development process which lies at the intersection between foreign tourist demand, and both metropolitan and local Thai sensibilities. While Hua Hin's historical and cultural base is quite unique, the pattern of development of the past few years has begun to spread rapidly in both directions up and down the coastline. As land prices skyrocket, and investors who wants to participate but cannot afford the prices in Hua Hin itself seek nearby areas

Figure 7.9   Advertisement for new townhouse development near Hua Hin, 1992

for development, the new landscape of beachside condominiums, townhouses, hotels, restaurants and nightclubs is cloned virtually overnight. This process demonstrates dramatically the way in which local interests almost at once restructure their activities to meet new opportunities, and is typical of the risk-entrepreneurship which has been one of the most significant factors in the Thai development boom.

The importance of the newly affluent, Bangkok-based largely Sino-Thai bourgeoisie in this process cannot be overemphasised. However, there are powerful local factors at work as well; traditional local elites are still deeply engaged in struggles over development. In Hua Hin, the old families, the 'Hua Hin natives', still play an important part in the structure of local power and influence. Local Sino-Thai families are at the forefront in the redevelopment process. The social structure of the town - once neatly apportioned to non-resident aristocracy, Hua Hin 'native' families, Sino-Thai business families, and poor townspeople and villagers - has been complicated by comparatively wealthy foreigners, European expatriates and retirees who have married Thais and built substantial houses, Europeans of much lesser means who run bars and businesses which appeal to other Europeans and to tourists seeking an alternative to the local chilli-hot dishes, Bangkokians interested both in profit and social status who have moved to the town and constructed an affluent bourgeois lifestyle there, and Bangkok-based entrepreneurs interested in developing even more housing estates, resorts and condominiums. As well, of course, the inevitable arrival of Pattaya-style clubs and venues has begun, the latest being a transvestite beer-bar playing non-stop Madonna tapes. In this process, it is hard to avoid the conclusion that everything which made Hua Hin what it was, historically, architecturally and culturally, is being rapidly obliterated.

While local people had few qualms about the tourist developments in 1986, the situation changed rapidly and by 1988 reservations about the final effects of all this on Hua Hin were expressed to the author by a number of older influential town residents. By 1992 it was clear that their doubts were more than justified. One of the most beautiful of the old bunga-

Figure 7.10   The Melia Hotel on the Hua Hin beachfront, with older fishing village houses on the left, 1992

lows, on the waterfront where the town meets the fishing village, which had been recommended for cultural conservation by the TAT, had been pulled down and replaced by an enormous multistorey hotel, now dominating the whole beachfrontage of the town, constructed by Spanish interests in conjunction with one of the princes (Figure 7.10). In greater and greater numbers, local people are unable to afford accommodation in the town, and rows and rows of new townhouses now stretch along the coast and even on the other side of the hills behind Hua Hin.

As the coastal strip between Cha-Am and Khao Takiab takes on the ambience of Florida or Waikiki, and the qualities which made Hua Hin attractive in the first place disappear forever, the fate of Hua Hin, like that of many other coastal parts of Thailand which have been given over to tourism, remains, in the face of political uncertainty and international economic downturn, extremely unpredictable. Perhaps in Hua Hin's case the level of internal demand from Thai people will be enough to sustain its popularity; and perhaps the demand from international tourism will continue to escalate in spite of everything. Meanwhile, a strange social mosaic emerges in the town mirroring the disjunctions in the built environment: Thai *haute bourgeoisie* and aristocracy, Chinese shopowners, Italian, French, German and Swiss exiles seeking their fortune in the bar-trade, elderly Western exiles with their young Thai brides, displaced villagers from far in the mountains seeking their fortunes and an endless stream of sunburnt foreigners.

REFERENCES

Cook, Nerida 1992, 'A tale of two city pillars: Thai astrology on the eve of modernisation' n Gehan Wijeyewardene & E.C. Chapman (eds), *Patterns and Illusions: Thai History and thought*, Australian National University, Research School of Pacific Studies, Canberra & Institute of Southeast Asian Studies, Singapore.

Krasaesin Sampan 1977, *Memorial Book for Khun Somboon Krasaesin: Family Genealogy* (in Thai), privately published on the occasion of his funeral.

—— 1984, *Memorial Book for Khun Arun Krasaesin* (in Thai), privately published on the occasion of his funeral.

The Nation, 1 Dec. 1986.

Prachuabkhirikhan 1988, *Hua Hin the Queen of Tranquillity*, Official Guide Book, Hua Hin Municipal Council, Hua Hin, Thailand.

Tourist Authority of Thailand (TAT) 1987, *Master Plan for Tourism Development of Petchaburi Province and Prachuab Khiri Khan Province*, vols 1 & 2, Thailand Institute of Scientific and Technological Research, Bangkok.

—— 1990, *Thailand Tourism Statistics Report*, TAT, Bangkok.

Ranaa (pseudonym) 1988, 'Conversations: Hua Hin in the Past' (in Thai), *Dichan Magazine*, Bangkok, 1-15 June, pp.105-25.

ACKNOWLEDGEMENTS

This paper forms part of a larger study on media, communication and globalisation in Thailand. Research was carried out in Hua Hin town and hinterland villages in Prachuab Khiri Khan Province at various times from 1986-90. Grateful acknowledgement is made to Khun Boonchuey Srisarakam, Governor of the Province until 1989, and to the Lord Mayor of Hua Hin, Khn Jira Phongphaiboon. Particular thanks to Tippawan Thampusana, Tourist Information Officer, friend and adviser, and the numerous people in Hua Hin town who provided their stories, memories and histories. A longer study of the town's development is in preparation under the title *Local Memories, Local Histories: Communication and Transformation in a Thai Coastal Province*. Research was generously funded by Macquarie University Research Grants and by the Australian Research Council.

8

Bugis Street in Singapore: development, conservation and the reinvention of cultural landscape

Kuah Khun Eng

DEVELOPMENT AND CONSERVATION: SOME THEORETICAL CONSIDERATIONS

This paper explores the role of the state in directing the transformation of the urban landscape in Singapore and its attempts to reinvent the cultural landscape when this was considered to be beneficial to both its population and economy. The paper argues that development and cultural conservation are not mutually exclusive but can coexist in a symbiotic relationship. In this context, the re-creation of Bugis Street is seen as an important step in the direction of development, conservation and reinvention.

Since the end of World War Two, there has been an increased awareness of the need for the preservation of historical monuments and cultural landscapes throughout the world. Erder (1986) argues that there has been a conscious evolution of the concept of conservation. This is attributed to the fact that monuments are now accepted as symbols rather than merely physical relics of the past. Similarly, cultural landscapes provide clues to the way of life, the cultural norms and social behaviour of a group of people. The symbolic meanings behind these cultural artefacts allow for the reconstruction of the past upon which the essential continuity of a society can be established (Erder 1986).

The understanding of cultural preservation has,

therefore, to be seen in its totality where a monument is no longer considered only within its immediate surroundings, but as part of a complex of buildings, a settlement or a region. And the act of preservation is seen to transcend the single building and to embrace the conservation and rehabilitation of the whole environment in which the society maintains an interest. The issue of interest to us here is the social production of historically significant built environment and the impact of such cultural reinvention on the people.

However, the desire to preserve is often perceived as being at odds with the objectives of development and rapid modernisation. This is most vividly seen in developing and industrialising countries where the pressure on land for commercial and industrial activities often coincides with landscapes of cultural significance. In the early phases of development, it is often economic rationalism that wins the day.

In recent years, there have been a number of significant studies of the impact of world economic forces on cities, exploring factors influencing the decision-making processes behind the patterns of urbanisation and the spatial forms of the built environment (for example, Harvey 1985, King 1990a, King 1990b). Scholars have increasingly argued that the development of city forms and the preservation of heritage are subjected to the forces of capital accumulation and that this process has its roots in Marx's historical materialism. Castells (1976) conceived space in its dialectical relation to social structure. He argued (p.78) that:

> the transformation of space must be analysed as specification of transformation in the social structure. In other words, one must see how the fundamental processes constitutive of social structure are articulated and specified spatially. We shall use the terms of spatial structure to describe the particular way in which the basic elements of social structure are spatially articulated.

What this approach advocates, according to Mateju & Vecernik (1981 p.74), is that:

> the socio-spatial structure reflects the dialectics of nature and forms of organisation of society. In the course of development, space acquires specific meanings and contents and 'reflects' constituent features of the social structure.

To them, 'conflicts between old and new spatial forms are thus transformed and modified expressions of the conflict between an old and an emerging social structure'. The following discussion reveals how conflict is being generated and played out when the Old Bugis Street was demolished and a new one created.

Another point to be noted is that in a planned city where development is controlled by the central authority, socialised consumption becomes more important: it places increasing pressure on the relationship between the allocation of goods and services on the basis of needs rather than the ability to pay. Correspondingly, there is a redrawing of the boundary between housing provision via the market and housing provision via need-oriented criteria (Harloe & Lebas 1981, p.25). The state becomes the key player here. This view was first expounded by Ebenezer Howard in the late nineteenth century when he argued that the internal colonisation of a country, in terms of city development, should be deliberate. Howard saw the need to create a Garden City, attainable through systematic development and controlled growth and argued that, to achieve this end, land should not be held by private landlords but,

instead, by a common authority, namely the State (Mumford 1938, pp.394-401).

There are also concerns about the development of large urban centres in developing countries, especially those formerly held as colonies. One approach argues for a global perspective, placing the development of cities and the urban built environment in a world system paradigm such as that expounded by Wallerstein (King 1990a, p.8). In this world-system theory, the cities in the peripheral zones take on the characteristic features of those found in the core regions. The question facing these scholars is whether, in developing countries, the emergence of major cities and urban environments came after the formation of independent nation-states (see, for example, Anderson 1986) or whether their historical origins lie in colonialism. King (1990a, p.9) takes the latter position, arguing that the historic role of colonialism is responsible for accelerating 'the internationalisation of capital and being instrumental in creating the present international city system'.

DEVELOPMENT AND CONSERVATION: COLONIAL AND POST-COLONIAL SINGAPORE

In Singapore, the various forces that shaped the city's structure included not only the colonial influences but, significantly, also those of the indigenous and immigrant communities. During the early years of immigration, the various waves of immigrants that arrived in the colony had carved out for themselves sections of the city in which they worked and lived. A natural division occurred among the population where the Chinese could be seen congregating in and around the present Chinatown district, the Indians in the Serangoon district and the Malays in Kampong Glam.

Under British colonial rule, the appropriation of territory by the different ethnic groups was reinforced by the official land-use policy which recognised these ethnic enclaves. Members of the Town Committee saw (Buckley 1902, p.81):

> the extent of the native population which has accumulated at Singapore and the rapidity with which it daily increases renders it expedient that in providing for its accommodation a timely attention should be

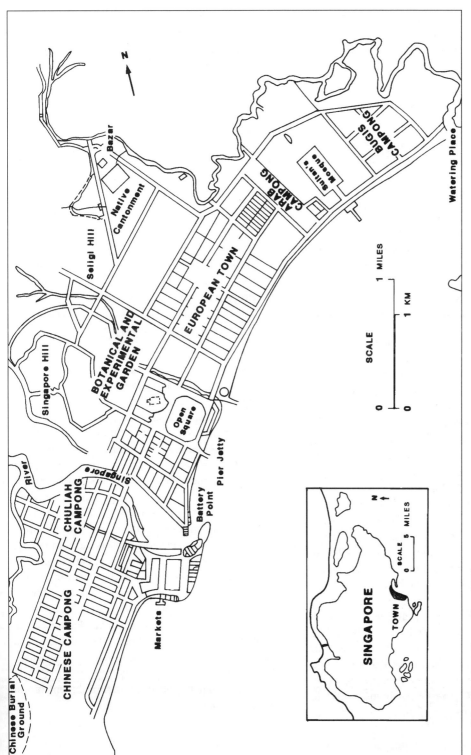

Figure 8.1   Singapore Town Plan, 1823

paid to its further regulation, with reference to the circumstances of the place and the peculiar character and institutions of several class of inhabitants of which the society will be composed.

As early as 1822, the land-use pattern was conceived as a hierarchy of occupational and ethnic zones, such that:

in allocating lands, first preference should be given to merchants, second to artisans and third to farmers... the separate nationalities and provincial groups should inhabit distinct areas of the town... (Master Plan, Report of Survey 1955, cited in Wong & Ooi 1989, p.791).

In 1823, a Town Plan was drawn which formalised the land-use pattern and the allocation of land for the ethnic groups at that time (Figure 8.1). After independence from the British in 1963 and up to the present, the Master Plan continues to provide the blueprint for the overall land-use pattern in Singapore. The desire of the government to forge ahead with the development of Singapore has meant a deliberate policy of redesigning and redefining Singapore's physical, urban and cultural landscapes.

From the 1950s to the 1970s, the rapid transformation of Singapore's landscapes has been closely linked to economic development. The separation of Singapore from Malaysia in 1965 was a watershed in the rapid economic growth of the country. With a small land size of 582 square kilometres (225 square miles) and without a national hinterland, the very survival of Singapore is dependent on its ability to industrialise, trade and provide services and hence to generate sufficient employment opportunities for its population. Foreign investments were encouraged through tax incentives, labour stability was achieved through the control of trades unions, preventing unnecessary industrial strikes, and a stable wage policy was enforced. Concurrently, sectors of the land were carved out for various economic uses. Much of the central district was given to business and government with the residents relocated to the newly created 'New Towns'. The Jurong Industrial Estate, situated at the western part of the island was designated as an industrial zone for factories, both international and local. The overall strategy was to provide sufficient land for economic activities.

The late 1980s witnessed an acute awareness of the need for the conservation of the environment and cultural landscapes. In one sense, an increased standard of living had fostered a more intense historical imagination and a deeper appreciation of the aesthetics of heritage landscapes, monuments and artefacts. These cultural heritage features have become important symbols in helping Singaporeans to recapture a sense of the past, and have fulfilled a crucial function in the current search for the nation's identity. As Hewison (in Bagguley, Mark-Lawson & Urry 1990, p.109) said,

We are all aware of problems and troubles, of changes within the structure of society, of the dissolution of old values and standards... The heritage represents some kind of security, a point of reference, a refuge perhaps, something visible and tangible which...seems stable and unchanged. Our environmental heritage...is a deeply stabilising and unifying element within our society.

This greater awareness on the part of both the Singaporean public and government has made conservation into a realisable goal. Particularly for the latter, conservation is also seen to have a vital economic dimension. The conservation of historical sites, buildings and artefacts is seen as a key to the tourism industry's future prosperity. Consequently, as Hewison claimed, heritage has become a socially organised construction and the past and the nation's and city's heritage has undergone an inevitable commodification. Here, in the eyes of the Singapore state, the tension between conservation and development is resolved in the new attention given to establishing a profitable cultural tourism industry.

In Singapore, apart from restoring and redeveloping the existing cultural landscape, wholesale 'invention' is also another way of reviving elements of the heritage lost as the result of rapid development. That is, as defined by Hobsbawn (Hobsbawn & Ranger 1983), invention has meant the reproduction of the built environment and the re-establishment of cultural traditions.[1]

PHYSICAL LANDSCAPE, URBAN LAND-USE AND THE MASTER PLAN

The small land size of Singapore island is both an asset and a liability.[2] In terms of physical landscape, the low terrain, small slow streams and a generally sheltered shore allowed for the physical landscape to be modified at relative ease. Singapore is also blessed by having no extreme climatic hazards such as severe storms and earthquakes which means that work can be carried out with minimum cost (Wong 1989, p.772). Politically, a strong government has allowed for strategic planning in terms of land-use patterns. Rapid modernisation and industrialisation meant the building of factory complexes and public housing. Competition for land-use became intense. Many of the older districts in the central region were targeted for redevelopment. At the same time, outlying areas were developed for high-density living and for factory complexes. Land was also reclaimed from the sea to extend the physical size of the island. Various government and statutory boards were involved in this process of physical and social transformation. For example, the Economic Development Board, later the Jurong Town Corporation, was responsible for transforming Jurong into the largest industrial estate in Singapore from an area previously occupied by ridges, swamps and coral-fringed coasts.[3] Similarly, the Housing and Development Board (HDB) was responsible for the development of public housing estates and New Towns, changing not only the physical landscape but also the demographic distribution with currently over 80 per cent of its population living in HDB flats (Pugh, C. 1989, pp.833-59).

Development of land-use comes under the Ministry of National Development and its Department of Planning. On the other hand, the redevelopment of urban areas is the responsibility of the Urban Renewal Authority (URA). Development and land-use patterns are governed by the Planning Act and the Master Plan serves as the main co-ordinating mechanism for both private and public developments. The People's Action Party (PAP) Government continues to fashion its planning policies according to the Master Plan which has undergone several revisions to meet changing needs. The fifth revision was in 1985 with provision for development of land up to 1990. Under the Master Plan, the island is divided into three main planning areas: the Central, Urban and Island Planning Areas. These planning areas are further subdivided into planning districts in order to facilitate the estimation of future population and community and other requirements (Ministry of National Development 1985b, pp.3-5). The Master Plan also indicates the predominant or intended uses of land. One of the Plan's goals is to preserve or promote the character of the various areas.

The main objective of the Master Plan is to ensure the provision of adequate and appropriate sites for urban and non-urban uses, for the different commercial, industrial, residential and social needs of the community as well as the co-ordination of physical development. The revised fifth Master Plan allocated land provision for various needs for a projected population of 2.75 million by 1990. The Plan regulates land development through land-use zoning, density and plot ratio control and reserving lands for schools, open spaces, infrastructure and other essential community uses (Ministry of National Development 1985a, p.3). Its strategy is to curb urban sprawl through the development of a green belt and give appropriate inducements to reduce population and overcrowding in the central districts. A policy of decentralisation was introduced and New Towns were created to cater for the rising population and future development. These New Towns would be connected to the central by arterial roads. In addition, selected key villages and settlements would be developed and expanded to serve as centres for the agricultural and rural communities. The Master Plan takes into consideration the Concept Plan which is a long-term strategy aimed at developing Singapore into a well-planned city state.[4]

THE ROLE OF THE URBAN RENEWAL AUTHORITY (URA)

During the 1950s and 1960s, the PAP Government inherited an island where the main concentration of activities was found within the central district. Land within the central district was taken up by factories, warehouses and port facilities catering for Singapore's primary economic function as an entrepot. A large proportion of the land was privately owned. It was therefore not an easy task to redevelop the area unless the government could solicit full co-operation from the landowners.

In 1974, the URA was established and empowered to redevelop the Central District. The Land Act of 1974 empowers the URA to acquire land from private landowners (with compensation) for redevelopment purposes. The result was a sizeable increase in floor space for commercial, shopping and hotel purposes. Property tax and tax concession also encourage factories to relocate in outlying districts. Likewise, the completion of the early phase of HDB flats redistribute the population from the central to the new housing estates. Although the URA has successfully transformed the physical environment of the Central District into skyscrapers, catering mainly for commercial, financial and hotel sectors, there is also an increasing awareness of the centre becoming a ghost town at nightfall. Consequently, there has been a significant redevelopment of residential buildings in recent years in and around the central district. The URA has also succeeded in increasing the provision of open space from 0.16 to 0.28 hectare per 1000 population (Wong & Ooi 1989, pp.788-812).

CONSERVATION AS AN IDEOLOGY

Singapore is a multi-ethnic society comprising a Chinese majority (78 per cent); a sizeable Malay population (14 per cent); a smaller Indian population (7 per cent) and other ethnic groups (2 per cent) (Census of Population Office 1992, p.5). Since attaining independence as a nation-state, the government has invested much efforts into creating a national identity where Singaporeans of different ethnicities would view themselves as belonging to a single citizenry. This moulding of a single identity as citizens is an on-going process and is based on a recognition of unity with diversity.

In 1986, the former senior minister, S. Rajaratnam, commented that:

a nation must have a memory to give it a sense of cohesion, continuity and identity. The longer the past, the greater the awareness of a nation's identity...a sense of a common history is what provides the links to hold together a people who came from the four corners of the earth.[5]

This comment was made coincidentally with the move by the government to build a strong Singa-

pore national identity. A strong multicultural Singapore identity can only be achieved if its population has a historical cultural past to look to. Similarly, a common set of moral values can be derived from the various cultures that form the fabric of Singapore society.[6]

On a pragmatic note, the preservation of historical and cultural landscapes is important for the tourist industry. A 1986 report commissioned by the Singapore Tourist Promotion Board (Singapore Tourist Promotion Board [STPB] 1986, p.II-2) argued for:

a new recognition that conservation can be a contributing facet of product development. (Conservation has been described as the management of existing resources to prevent decay or destruction by neglect or thoughtlessness.)

It also noted that visitors to Singapore are of the opinion that Singapore should 'preserve old buildings, stay Asian' (STPB 1986, p.II-8). In short, it makes good rational economic sense to preserve the existing cultural landscapes as tourism contributes substantially to the national economy, providing, in fact, 6.2 per cent of Singapore's Gross Domestic Product (GDP) in 1990.

In the Planning Act, *conservation* is defined as:

the preservation, enhancement or restoration of (a) the character or appearance of a conservation; or (b) the trades, crafts, customs and other traditional activities carried on in a conservation area (URA 1991c, p.27).

Conservation thus includes the preservation of as much as possible of each area's architecture and ambience; the improvement of the physical environment by providing pedestrian walkways, plazas, landscaping and control of signage; the enhancement of the character of each area by introducing new activities while sustaining the old traditional activities of tourist value; and the provision of guidelines for the private sector to be heavily involved in the conservation effort (URA, not dated).

The URA which doubled as the Conservation Authority is responsible for establishing areas for conservation purposes, together with advice and suggestions from other relevant authorities with related interests. It has conceived a Conservation Master Plan for the island. The Conservation Master Plan aims to create a balanced mix of new and old buildings in order to preserve 'the distinctive Asian identity in Singapore' (URA, not dated, p.2). These include buildings with significant architectural heritage, ranging from the colonial styles to those with a mix of Chinese and Straits influence. In this role, the Conservation Authority identifies five categories of buildings and areas worthy of preservation: historic districts and significant areas; bungalows in good class areas and their fringes; additional monuments for preservation in the central area; secondary development areas; buildings of outstanding architectural and historical value in pockets in the rest of the island; and state-owned properties worthy of conservation.

Examples of these historic districts include Chinatown, Kampong Glam, Little India, Cairnhill and the Emerald Hill Areas, Singapore River and the so-called 'Heritage Link' (Figure 8.2). The total area for conservation constitutes about 4 per cent of the land area in the Central Area, totalling 2600 hectares (6425 acres), including the Marina Bay. Chinatown is the area south of the Singapore River allocated to the Chinese under Sir Stamford Raffles' 1828 Town Plan. Kampong Glam was originally a large tract of land granted to Sultan Hussain Shah by Raffles after the signing of a treaty which permitted the establishment of a factory for the East India Company (URA 1988, 1991a). Subsequently with the establishment of the palace and mosque, the district attracted a substantial number of Muslim immigrants. Central to this district is the Sultan's Palace compound and the magnificent Sultan Mosque. Little India developed more spontaneously, not being foreseen in Raffles' Town Plan. It started off as an area for cattle but gradually became the focus of Indian traders and shops, especially noted for their spices.[7] Today, the area is also dotted with Hindu temples. The Heritage Link is bounded by the Singapore River, Clemenceau Avenue, Orchard Road, Bras Basah Road and the Esplanade and is dotted with historical monuments, including the Supreme Court, City Hall, Victoria Memorial Hall, National Museum as well as schools and churches, all of neo-classical style.

The secondary conservation and development areas involve salvaging the remains of prewar historic buildings (circa 1900-40), mainly around the fringe of the Central Area and on the eastern side of the island. Most of these are well-established neighbourhood communities with a mixture of residential homes and shop-houses. They include Jalan Besar, Beach Road, Blair Plain, River Valley, Joo Chiat and East Coast Residential Corridor and Geylang Old Town.

Of all the conservation projects, Kampong Bugis represents one of the most interesting. It involves not only the development and extension of the area, together with the Kallang Basin, but also the re-creation of Bugis Street, taking it back to the physical layout and social ambience it had before the decision to replace it by a Mass Rapid Transit (MRT) station and to relocate it in an adjacent site. The Kampong Bugis Development Plan comprises two distinct districts within it: Kampong Bugis and Bugis Street. Although Kampong Bugis is yet to be fully developed, Bugis Street has been reinvented and has started functioning once again (Figure 8.3).

THE OLD KAMPONG BUGIS AND BUGIS STREET

By the time the British took over Singapore, the Bugis were already well-established traders and constituted a sizeable group, apart from the Chinese, Malays and Indians. Raffles noted the existence of (URA, not dated, pp.84-5):

> Bugis Campong [sic]...where they...occupy the whole extent from Campong Glam to the mouth of Rochore River, but it is conceived that they may be more advantageously concentrated on the spot beyond the residence of the Sultan. In this case a part of Campong Glam, immediately adjoining the Sultan's residence...In the allocation of the Bugis town it will be equally necessary to attend to economy in the distriction [sic] of ground by laying out regular streets inland towards the river and obliging the inhabitants to conform thereto.

Through time, the area surrounding Bugis Street developed its own activities and unique characteristics and evolved its own identity. It also became separated from Kampong Glam and acquired its present name Kampong Bugis.

The original site of the Bugis Kampong where most Bugis resided lay between Rochor River and Kelang

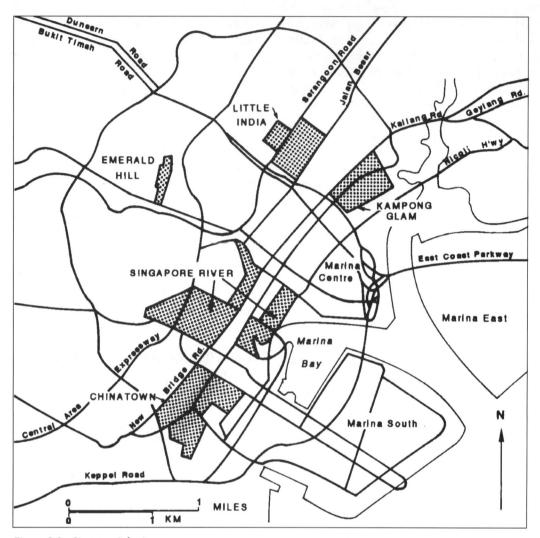

Figure 8.2   Singapore's heritage areas

(Kallang) River. Today, the area is bounded by Nicoll Highway, Crawford Street, Kallang Road, Sims Avenue and the proposed Kallang Expressway, located at the fringe of the Central Area. Along the northern boundary of Kampong Bugis are the Lavender and Kallang MRT stations and to the south, the National Stadium and Kallang sports and recreational areas. It is now being rehabilitated as part of the planning sub-zone within the Kallang Development Guide Plan which adjoins the Central Area.

Within Kampong Bugis is found the famous Bugis Street. The street first appeared on the map titled *A General Plan of the Town and Environs of Singapore*

in 1857.[8] Originally called Charles Street, it was re-named Bugis Street between the years 1857 and 1878.[9] The change in name can probably be attributed to the sizeable Bugis population living in and around the area and was in tune with the colonial policy of allocating residential districts according to ethnic composition. The 1824 census showed that there were 1925 Bugis out of the total Singapore population of 10683, forming the third largest group (Comber 1959, p.50), while the 1847 census showed a doubling of the Bugis population to 2269 out of a total of 59 043 (Chan 1964, p.9 footnote 1). Although named Bugis Street, it was not monopolised solely by the Bugis

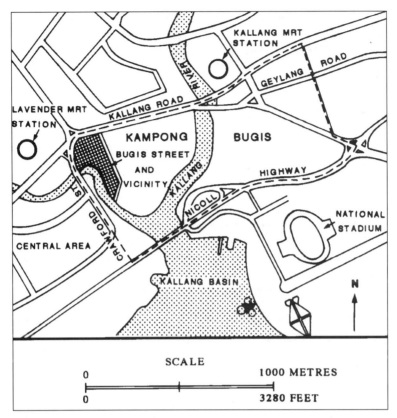

*Figure 8.3   Site plan of Kampong Bugis (*Source: *Urban Renewal Authority (1990),* Kampong Bugis Development Guide Plan, *p.2)*

people, and there were then and are today other ethnic groups, mainly the Chinese but also Indians and Malays, living and working in the street.

Among the Chinese, Bugis Street is most commonly known as *peh-sua-pu,* literally 'the floating of white sand'. It probably acquired such a name because of the abundance of fine white sands in the area. Occasionally, it is also known as the *hak-kai* (the dark street) by the Cantonese-speaking Chinese recalling the old shadowy Singapore Street lit by oil lamps (Chan 1964, pp.13-14). But the name brings to mind another set of activities which made the street a notorious place in Singapore. From the 1920s onwards, the region surrounding Bugis Street had acquired a name for itself as a 'red light' district. Bugis Street and adjacent streets were streets where brothels operated legally during the colonial years. Bugis Street was an entertainment avenue where sex and food went hand in hand. There were outdoor food stalls

catering for the people while the prostitutes paraded the streets, soliciting potential clients (Chan 1964, p.16). During the post-war years, the street became a favourite night spot for single Singaporean and European men who patronised the area from midnight onwards, seeking alcohol and sex. But, rather than the female prostitutes, it was the transvestites who created the biggest name for themselves and whose existence became known internationally.

Although Bugis Street acquired notoriety, this reputation was only confined to the hours after midnight. To the majority of the local population, Bugis Street during the day was one of the streets established in the early settlement period, with a variety of prewar and postwar shop-houses of one to four storeys, where the old buildings were interspersed with new ones. These shop-houses were traditionally divided into two main parts. The ground floor functioned as a shop whereas the upper floors were usually residential dwellings. For single-storey buildings, the residence was located in the back portion of the building.

A myriad of activities flourished in the Bugis street but, unlike most streets, Bugis street functioned on a 24-hour basis, divided into three main time periods. Each time period catered to a different set of people plying their trade. The first period encompassed two sessions from dawn till six or seven in the evening. From about 5 or 6 o'clock in the morning, there would be itinerant hawkers selling early meals for breakfast. The shops opened till six or seven in the evening. In the evening period, from 6 or 7 o'clock till about midnight, the place transformed into a bazaar where itinerant hawkers peddled food and their wares and curios to the people. The midnight till early morning hours period catered for the *feng-liu han*, those who led a wild and exciting life and who came in search of drinks and fun.

These three time periods represented three separate types of lifestyles in contemporary Singapore. The first two periods catered for the ordinary families which formed the bulk of the clientele. The midnight period was representative of the carefree type of lifestyle for individuals, there being considerable number of westerners and single men patronising the place. Many came to enjoy and some patronised the female prostitutes and the transvestites.

There was also the residential aspects to be considered. Many of the shop-owners lived in the shop-houses with their family and their employees. Not unlike the other Chinese, they constituted a close-knit neighbourhood community. Most knew one another and participated in neighbourhood activities including gossiping and attending the funerals and weddings of the neighbours.

Thus the street and its back and side lanes bustled with life during day and night. It was full of 'heat and noise' (*re naun*). There was plenty of activity, movement, talk and noise throughout the 24 hours. The spontaneous organic growth of the activities and social interaction of its local population, the people who patronised and the passers-by who simply enjoyed a walk through the street, all contributed to the life and the chaos of the street. It was a kind of familiar chaos that people appreciated and enjoyed.

KAMPONG BUGIS DEVELOPMENT PLAN

The Kampong Bugis Development Plan was conceived under the new revised Master Plan (Singapore Institute of Architects 1990; URA 1990). It became part of the Kallang Development Guide Plan, adjoining the Central Area. Kampong Bugis was proposed to be a transitional area between the high-density housing and commercial areas to its north, and the sports and recreational areas to its south. A major commercial fringe centre is also being proposed around the Lavender MRT station which will provide commercial facilities as well as high-density housing at the periphery of the Central Area. Neighbourhood centres such as the Bugis sub-zone are strategically located within Kallang area. Bugis Street, which was located in the area earmarked for the development of Lavender MRT (subway, opened 1992) station, was relocated. This is a case where development goals came first and the conservation of a cultural area fell into a second position.

This development involves substantial redevelopment of the entire Kallang Basin. At the same time, it also aims to conserve and 'retain buildings of historical, cultural and architectural interests' (URA 1990, p.15). These include the Indian Temple, Geylang shop-houses, Gay World (theatre and stadium) and the People's Association Building. It also proposes to phase out the existing incompatible and hazardous industries and the gasworks. In terms of residential development, high-intensity and medium-high-intensity residential buildings have been proposed for Kampong Bugis, with a gross plot ratio of between 2.6 and 3.3. The heights of the building will be four storeys for the land near the waterfront while those behind will have seven to ten storeys. There will also be a commercial centre near the Lavender MRT Station and a neighbourhood centre near the Kallang MRT Station which will provide office and shopping together with residential space for Kampong Bugis. It also proposes a building to house the arts and recreational activities.

To integrate the region with the rest of the island, an efficient network of expressways, arterials, primary and local access roads will be constructed. The Kallang Expressway is proposed to link up further north with the proposed Paya Lebar Expressway. At

Figure 8.4   A newly-restored shop-house building in the Bugis Street district (Source: *K. K. Eng*).

the same time, Crawford Street is proposed to be connected with Nicoll Highway, and Mountbatten Road will be realigned to join up with Stadium Link to allow for improved traffic flow.

The whole idea is to integrate the new with the old, particularly revitalising the traditional activities and communal spirit that existed in the area. For

example, the Gay World, which was started in 1936 with the name 'Happy World' provided a range of entertainment from cinemas to concerts and *ronggeng* (a Malay musical dance) for not only those living locally, but also in other parts of Singapore. In the early days, the nightly and seasonal expo activities provided the glitter and chaotic atmosphere of

Figure 8.5   Blending old and new architectural forms: spiral staircases of a shop-house building (Source: *K.K. Eng*).

enjoyment, eating, trading, shopping and leisurely walks for families, groups of friends and isolated individuals. The atmosphere was one of happiness and gaiety, hence the name Gay World.

THE REINVENTION OF BUGIS STREET

Bugis Street is a famous street, both by local and international standards. The street became regarded as worthy of preservation. There was a major push by the conservationists who saw the street as one of the few remaining areas which offered a cultural landscape infused with a sense of the traditional that is fast disappearing in Singapore's race towards modernity. To the pragmatic bureaucrats, the place could be appropriated for tourism. The attraction of Bugis Street therefore lies very much in its ability to generate the kind of social ambience that served to lure people to the place, again and again. When it was decided in 1986 to demolish the street to make way for the MRT station, there was a very strong outcry in favour of its preservation, especially when the STPB came out in support.

Constantly searching for new tourist spots, the STPB judged Bugis Street with its unique social characteristics to be a major tourist attraction and, under the Tourism Product Development Plan of 1986, argued the need to re-create the Street. The STPB put the following case:

Bugis Street became world renowned because it has a special ambience which came about from the unique mix of spontaneous activities and rustic streetscape. The tourist could mingle with the local crowd anonymously and enjoy the site, sound, smell and colourful tradition of street activities developed around the outdoor hawker stalls.

STPB hopes to re-create Bugis Street by recapturing the colour and ambience of the original outdoor activities on the site identified. The proposed site has the scale and mature charm of Europe and the random character necessary to stage this project. To successfully re-create Bugis Street, Government must allow for spontaneous street activities. Visitors like to participate in impromptu, harmless fun and non-flagrant activities. Organised activities are contrived and do not have the same appeal.

The government will provide for services infrastructure to ensure that basic health and hygiene standards are not compromised. The private sector will be invited to operate the facility. To be implemented in stages, the target date for full completion is 1989/90. Hawker-type food displayed, prepared, served and eaten in the open-air will be one of the principal attractions of new Bugis Street. Food preparation and eating areas will be properly demarcated. Proper sanitary measures will be observed both to ensure a pleas-

Figure 8.6   Bugis Street fruit stalls attract crowds of local shoppers and tourists (Source: K. K. Eng).

Figure 8.7   Shopping for local specialties (Source: K. K. Eng).

ant environment as well as to safeguard the whole-someness of the food[10]

The result was a compromise where an alternative site was found to house Bugis Street, and, in November 1988, the STPB awarded the task of redeveloping and managing the resited Bugis Street to a private company. Construction work began in mid-1990 on the various blocks to be built on the site which is bounded by Victoria Street, Rochore Road, Queen Street and Cheng Yan Place, just across the street where the original Bugis Street had been situated (STPB, not dated). The policy was to deliberately re-create Bugis Street in the same style and form as had originally existed (Figure 8.4, although cf. Figure 8.5). Much effort went into making the new place look old. To this end, not only were the shop-houses replicated in shape and style, but they were also made to appear aged. For example, old roof tiles and paints were used to create a weathered impression.

To create the kind of social ambience that existed then, the shop-houses will accommodate food stalls with the original Bugis Street itinerant vendors (hawkers) as well as restaurants, retail shops, a beer garden which will serve beer to the small hours of the morning, a cabaret and dance-hall, a pub and a theatrette for glittering show performances. There

will also be a night market (pasar melam) which will offer a wide range of products and services from over a hundred *pasar-malam* push-carts. Jacks-of-all-trades, such as the fortune-teller, roving photographer, cobbler, calligrapher, street barber and so forth, will ply the street, thereby adding, according to the planners, colour and activity to the scene (Figures 8.6 and 8.7).

Unlike in the past when spontaneous chaos was the hallmark of the street, the activities found in the re-created Bugis street are all planned and well co-ordinated. Although the street has all the previous street vendors, serving the same kinds of food and beer as before, as well as additional programs, it has failed to reawaken the kind of social atmosphere of yesteryear. What the planners failed to realise is that, while the physical infrastructure could be re-created, it is not possible to re-establish the kind of social relationships and social interaction, the familiar and friendly neighbourliness that existed among the residents, shop-owners, workers, customers, hawkers and passers-by. Old Bugis street was not just a street, it was a neighbourhood housing an intimate community in the traditional sense. Hence, there existed a strong bond and a sense of solidarity among the people of the street. This is something which no amount of planning and re-invention could achieve.

In the words of some planners, the new Bugis street will have to be allowed a measure of freedom to develop its own new identity. It is hoped that less restriction and more freedom will allow a new character to evolve that is comparable to the earlier one.

Old Bugis street represented a phase of individualism where those who operated the shops and those who were hawkers were their own boss. There was freedom in their actions and interaction with others - a freedom to do what they wanted. While earning a living was important, there were other non-monetary considerations. Customers were also regarded as friends to a large degree. These people did not confine themselves to buying and selling of things. The social intercourse included assisting each other in odd pieces of work as well as gossiping. Shopkeepers and hawkers had established among themselves and with the customers this sort of social intimacy, and it was this familiarity, not only of the environment but also of the social interaction, that provided Bugis Street with a distinct identity of its own. This also explained why the shopkeepers and hawkers were reluctant to move to a new area, and why the consumers themselves were so sceptical about the re-creation of the street.

The new Bugis street is a corporate institution, managed by a team of professional operators, whose ultimate aim is profit-making. In the reinvented Bugis Street, the hawkers rent space from the corporate body and pay premium prices for the use of the space. The self-ownership of the place is now replaced by a patron-client relationship where the hawkers are now the clients of a powerful corporate patron. But the corporation, in turn, is ultimately answerable to the state which has issued the business licence for the management of Bugis Street. In this sense, the introduction of a bureaucratic management represents a hierarchy of dominance and power among the participants. The hawkers and itinerant traders who were once their own boss are now at the bottom of the hierarchy, giving them practically no voice in the running of their own affairs, let alone that of the street. There are also all kinds of restrictions inhibiting not only business activities but also social interaction and expression.

The leisurely lifestyle is now replaced by fierce competition. To survive, one has to operate within the modern rational economic paradigm. The previous mode of business operation is now fully commodified. Profit-making becomes an important criterion as one struggles to earn enough not only to maintain the household but also to pay the high rent demanded by the management. There is now a new set of rules and regulations that governs the operation of the business, the conduct and the behaviour of the vendors. There are also new rules governing cleanliness and hygiene, not only of the place but also of personal appearance. In a certain way, the bureaucratic set-up transformed the social structure of the street. The informality has now given way to a structured formality, which serves to place a psychological restraint on both the vendors and the customers, inhabiting the spontaneous development that we have seen in the bygone era. The organic components and growth is now replaced by a mechanistic one. Gone is the chaos; in its place is a pristine clean environment. It is precisely because of this systemic approach to development that Singapore is known to be a well-planned city.

Previously Bugis Street housed an established alternative culture, representing the antithesis of the accepted popular culture. It was the alternative fringe culture that attracted both the locals and the foreign visitors to patronise the place. This culture now is fast becoming marginalised. The fact that the transvestites were, sociologically speaking, a group of social deviants popular among some groups, contributed significantly to the street's cultural uniqueness. Old Bugis Street represented an alternative culture, a venue where the participants could engage, albeit fleetingly, in deviant behaviour in a highly structured and disciplined society. The reinvented street does away with this, closing up an important outlet for those who wanted and needed to be diverted from their daily routine.

Physically, the old site was like any other prewar street, with its fair share of old houses and dilapidation. Yet it differed from others in many aspects. The physical organisation gave it its sense of social existence - a place of spontaneous growth that was reflected in its flexible spatial arrangements and chaos of activities. Every bit of space was utilised. The shophouses doubled both as shops and residences. Similarly, the 5-foot (1.5 metre) pathways served as extra space for parading their goods during the day and as communal space for social intercourse in the early evening; by nightfall, they again reverted back to commercial activities of a different sort. It was this sense of chaos, excitement, the elements of activities, of lust, of mystery that surrounded it that provided Bugis Street with its identity as probably the most exciting street in Singapore.

The reinvented street has an entirely different socio-ecological structure. The long-time residents have been relocated to the HDB flats. Established social networks have been disrupted as a result of people moving out of the area. In return, the place is now inhabited by businesses of various kinds. Instead of a worn-down live-in residential-and-working area, the place now exudes an air of commercialism. The age-old intimate social relationships among groups of people who had inhabited the old Bugis Street for decades could not be reproduced in the new street. Without the residents, the neighbourhood no longer exists. In a way, the new street is sterile for this lack of residential intimacy. For those old residents of Bugis street who have re-established businesses in the new street, the feeling of uprootedness cannot be underestimated. Many no longer feel they belong nor do they feel a sense of historical continuity with the new street. They continued to speak, with nostalgia, of the old street.

The new Bugis street, in the eyes of the local population, is reinvented for the tourists. Places and events invented for the tourists involve a sense of artificiality. Like so many socially constructed places, it represents, to the locals, an unauthentic manufactured heritage, no matter how good the reproduction is. And this manufactured heritage does not belong to them. To many of the locals, the old represents the totality of life itself where the good and the bad came as a package deal. But the reinvented one lacks this sentiment and is an empty shell. It also serves to highlight the great divide between perceptions of what is Singaporean and what is not. In short, Bugis Street no longer belongs to the people; it has been appropriated by the STPB for the tourists. The major promotion campaigns launched by the STPB to lure tourists into visiting Bugis Street serve especially to further alienate the local people from the street.

Since the re-created street began operating, the number of people visiting it has been significantly low. In a bid to attract old and new local clientele and to encourage tourists, the new management of Bugis Street, a private operator, decided to reinstate what the street was both famous and, on the part of the morally upright, loathed for - the transvestites. Together with the STPB, it staged a transvestite show as part of the 41st annual conference of the Pacific Asia Travel Association in Hong Kong, in which four female impersonators performed several song-and-dance acts at a lunch hosted by the STPB (*Straits Times*, 18 Apr. 1992). The STPB was looking into the possibility of reinstating such shows as a means of re-establishing the original social ambience and increasing visitor numbers. However, a public outcry put a stop to this. The STPB, together with the Ministry of Trade and Industry, has now decided against this strategy. Commenting on the issues, the STPB stated that (*Straits Times*, 18 Apr. 1992):

> the old Bugis Street has been associated with the presence of transvestites in the minds of tourists. In planning the redevelopment project, STPB did not consider introducing shows by female impersonators as a way to capture this aspect of Bugis Street.

It now acknowledged that:

> it had to balance the need of attracting tourists and maintaining a wholesome atmosphere that will appeal to Singaporeans.

Thus the issue now is between economic rationalism on the one hand and moral and social values on the other. The desire to attract more tourists seems a sufficient reason to reinstate the transvestite shows. Transvestites and their shows are a drawcard in the intense competition among the various social places. Bugis Street not only has to compete with the existing hawker centres, but also with pubs, nightclubs and the recent karaoke clubs, not forgetting other entertainment places like cinemas and theatres. It wants to be able to compete for the attention of different categories of people. The hawkers want family and social groupings to patronise them. At the same time, they also want a slice of the nightlife market. Transvestites used to throng the old Bugis Street after midnight and to those who are in favour of reinstating them, the question of morality hardly surfaces. They argue that the family and other social groups would have already retired into their comfortable homes by midnight and therefore the transvestites would not affect them. As one said (*Straits Times*, 18 Apr. 1992):

> Bugis Street isn't Bugis street without the *aquas*[11]; there's nothing wrong with these shows. Anyway, how much harm can the transvestites do?

Despite this good economic rationalism, in a nation-state which also prides itself of a high level of morality and social responsibility to its citizenry, the public outcry has certainly had an impact on the issue. The urge then is to 'keep transvestite skeletons firmly locked in the closet' (*Business Times*, 30-31 May 1992) and to make morality absolute with no pandering to commercialism. The fear is that an extension of this liberalism would result in moral anarchy in the nation-state. Hence, there is no negotiation when it comes to moral values and Bugis Street critics would claim that this is one case where democracy is working for the people.

While transvestites are outlawed, it does not spell the end of them. The Bugis Street operation management circumvents this restriction by employing transvestites as their customer relations officers. It argues that the objective of employing the transsexuals as public relations officers is to explain the history of the old Bugis Street to the visitors (*Straits Times*, 20 Apr. 1992). But these trans-sexual public relations officers are subject to strict regulations, including a prohibition on soliciting customers. The transvestites resent these restrictions. One said recently (*Straits Times*, 20 Apr. 1992):

> in the old Bugis Street, we were very free. The minute we got off our taxis at 10 p.m., we would fly like birds to our customers. Here we can only sit down at a table if someone calls us.

The types of operation permitted in the reinvented Bugis Street also reveal another kind of dominance: that of the state. Left on its own, the market forces would lead to the reinstatement of the transvestites and their shows. However, the power of the state invested in the bureaucracy ensures that this move is permanently forestalled. Hence, the frustration of the private operating management team. This also reflects the interventionist role of the government in both the economic and social arenas, the state here acting not only as an economist, but also as moral guardian for its citizenry.

This reinvention of Bugis Street serves as a kind of microcosm for wider societal processes. Much of the development in Singapore is rational, government-led and subject to intense bureaucratic intervention. The people have little say in the direction as well as the actual operation of the developmental projects, although the private sector is now incorporated in the decision-making process. Public participation is minimal. Because of the very Confucian attitude of the people towards the paternalistic government, the chances of any overt protests would be slight. The people have therefore developed a different set of mechanisms to cope with this dissatisfaction and to resolve the mounting tension - passive resistance, subtle boycott and the adoption of a non-positive attitude - all assisting to send a message to the decision-makers. In a way, the state also encourages this form of resistance as a way of checking the power of the Planning Department, URA and the STPB.

THE FUTURE OF THE REINVENTED BUGIS STREET

The success of the new Bugis Street is dependent on the extent to which it can develop a new identity, irrespective of whether this identity is similar or not to the old one. In order to generate a sense of belonging to the place, it needs to develop a sense of intimacy in the social relationships among the various groups of people who patronise it. This can only be achieved in the long run. The success also depends, in part, on the balance between tourism and local patronage. It is the latter that will give character and depth to the street and help to establish the street as an authentic social and cultural landscape, to transform its manufactured image into a naturalised and established one. Its future is also dependent on the extent to which the street is allowed a free hand to develop its own spontaneous chaos, noise and flamboyance. Too many rules and regulations as well as restrictions will inhibit the natural growth of the region.

The success of the new Bugis Street can also be seen in its integration within Kampong Bugis as well as the wider Kallang Development scheme. There is no doubt that when Kampong Bugis and the Kallang Basin become fully developed, the reinvented Bugis Street will benefit from the residential population and commercial activities of the area. In a sense, Bugis Street has to become part of the wider neighbourhood. It therefore has to cater for the wants of the local people. In the long run, it is they who will allow the street to continue flourishing and to evolve its very own identity, albeit one that would most likely be vastly different from the previous one.

CONCLUSION

The relationship between the development of space and land-use patterns in Singapore city and the conservation efforts are subject to the forces of capitalism, especially through the agency of government intervention, even though there are some considerations given to non-economic factors such as cultural identity and moral values. In many ways, the changing use (and abuse) of space in Singapore is also seen to be closely linked to a shift in the dominant social ideology, that is, the popular consciousness, and hence to Singapore's changing social structure. At present, the city's land-use policy is a reflection of the need to accommodate the demands both of the people and of economic development; in other words, a reflection of a social structure that is primarily based on capitalistic forces but with an increasing emphasis on the people's values.

The Bugis Street case study illustrates that while it is possible to reinvent a desired physical landscape, the cultural mosaic of the area is, in the final analysis, dependent on the people who patronise and interact with the area. The old and new Bugis Streets show us that the human factor is crucial in providing the streets with an identity. Take them away and, no matter how beautifully structured the physical landscape, the area will become sterile and devoid of excitement.

Despite this, it is an important step by the government in the areas of conservation. Much efforts is needed to preserve the few heritage environments left in Singapore for it is only through them that the Singaporean is reminded of his or her history. In short, conservation and even reinvention are important in informing us of the changes and continuities

that have taken place in our social history. At the same time, any form of cultural reinvention should take into consideration the social and cultural continuity of groups of people that make the place what it is. The human dimension should therefore be given a high profile in the planning of land-use patterns and conservation of any historical and cultural landscape.

POSTSCRIPT

Only very recently, the mood in Bugis Street has turned for the better, with small groups of local people beginning to patronise the place once again. This can be attributed to the more relaxed rules of the authorities in allowing a more open approach to entertainment. Gone are the transvestites, to be replaced by a variety of cabaret and karaoke bars which are luring back a section of the young population. One of these bars, the 'Boom Boom Room' recently put on a cabaret show that was 'part drag, part Las Vegas and part smut' (*South China Morning Post*, 24 Feb. 1993). However, the success of this new approach is dependent not only on patronage by the people but also on the co-operation of the authorities. As the co-owner of the bar observed:

> the cabaret is closely scrutinised by the authorities, and has so far been spared the thumbs-down fate of old-style Bugis Street shows.

To a large degree, the place will benefit from less bureaucratic intervention, allowing the operators and entertainers to use their artistic talents and imagination to the fullest.

ENDNOTES

1 Hobsbawn sees *invented traditions* as 'traditions actually invented, constructed and formally instituted and those emerging in a less traceable manner within a brief and dateable period - a matter of a few years perhaps - and establishing themselves with great rapidity'. For a detailed discussion on this issues, see Hobsbawn & Ranger (1983).

2 When Singapore left the Federation of Malaysia, there was much worry about the island state's inability to survive economically and politically because of its small land size. However, after three decades of rapid economic development and political stability, Singapore has attained the 'mini-dragon' status of a successful

newly industrialised country (NIC). Many commentators have been forced to revise their analysis and to conclude that the island's smallness has contributed to the political stability and economic growth.

3   For a detailed discussion on the reshaping of Singapore's physical environment, see P.P. Wong , 'The transformation of the physical environment' in K.S. Sandhu & P. Wheatley (eds) (1989, pp.771-87).

4   For a discussion of the Concept Plan, see URA (1991b).

5   For this quotation, see URA (not dated).

6   For a discussion of the social engineering and the moral value systems in Singapore, see Kuah 1990.

7   The STPB plans to re-establish Little India's historical past and to promote it as a centre for the spice trade, emphasising to the tourists not only the sights but also the smells and tastes of the spices, thereby shifting tourism away from the conventional approach of sightseeing.

8   The map entitled *A General Plan of the Town and Environs of Singapore, 1857* is held by the National Museum, Singapore.

9   A second map of the *Town and Environs of Singapore*, by J.A. McNair, Major R.A.A.I.C.E., Colonial Engineer and Surveyor General of the Straits Settlement, drawn in 1878, showed the name 'Buggis Street'. This map is also held in the Singapore National Museum.

10 For further discussion of the 're-creation of Bugis Street' see STPB (October 1986).

11 The general Singaporean population commonly refer to transvestites by the Chinese term *aqua*.

REFERENCES

Anderson, B. 1986, *Imagined Communities: Reflections on the Origin and Spread of Nationalism*, (3rd edition), Verso, London.

Bagguley, P., Mark-Lawson, J., Urry, J., et al. 1990, *Restructuring: Place, Class and Gender*, Sage Publications, London.

Buckley, B.C. 1902, *An Anecdotal History of Old Times in Singapore*, Frazer and Neave, Singapore.

Business Times 30-31 May 1992.

Castells, M. 1976, 'Theory and ideology in urban sociology' in C.G. Pickvance (ed.), *Urban Sociology: Critical Essays*, Tavistock, London.

Census of Population Office 1992, *Singapore Census of Population 1990*, Singapore National Printers, Singapore.

Chan, S.K. 1964, *A Study of A Street (Bugis Street): A Street of No Night*, University of Singapore, Dip.Soc.Sci. Research Paper, Singapore.

Comber, L.F. 1959, *Chinese Secret Societies in Malaya*, J.J. Augustin Pub., New York.

Erder, C. 1986, *Our Architectural Heritage: From Consciousness to Conservation*, UNESCO, Paris.

Gamer, R.E. 1972, *The Politics of Urban Development in Singapore*, Cornell University Press, Ithaca.

Harloe, M. & Lebas, E. (eds.) 1981, *City, Class and Capital: New Developments in the Political Economy of Cities and Regions*, Edward Arnold, London.

Harvey, D. 1985, *Consciousness and the Urban Experience*, Basil Blackwell, Oxford.

Hobsbawn, E. & Ranger, T. 1983, *The Invention of Tradition*, Cambridge University Press, Cambridge.

King, A.D. 1990a, *Urbanism, Colonialism and the World-Economy: Cultural and Spatial Foundations of the World Urban System*, Routledge, London and New York.

— 1990b, *Global Cultures: Post-Imperialism and the Internationalisation of London*, Routledge, London and New York.

Kuah, K.E. 1990, 'Confucian Ideology and Social Engineering in Singapore', in *Journal of Contemporary Asia*, vol.20, no.3, pp.371-83.

Lewis, M. 1993, 'The Return of Bugis Street' in *Sawasdee*, Feb. 1993.

Lim, W.S.W. 1990, *Cities for People*, Select Books, Singapore.

Mateju, P. & Vecernik, J. 1981, 'Social Structure, spatial structure and problems of ecological analysis: the example of Prague' in Harloe, M. & Lebas, E. (eds.), *City, class and capital*, Edward Arnold, London.

Ministry of National Development, Planning Department 1985a, *Report of Survey: Revised Master Plan 1985*, Ministry of National Development, Singapore.

— 1985b, Written Statement *1985*, Ministry of National Development, Singapore.

Mumford, L. 1938, *The Culture of Cities*, Harcourt, Brace and Company, New York.

Pugh, C. 1989, 'The Political Economy of Public Housing' in Sandhu, K.S. & Wheatley, P. (eds.), *Management of Success: The Moulding of Modern Singapore*, Institute of Southeast Asian Studies, Singapore.

Sandhu, K.S. & Wheatley, P., (eds.) 1989, *Management of Success: The Moulding of Modern Singapore*, Institute of Southeast Asian Studies, Singapore.

Singapore Institute of Architects 1990, *Kampong Bugis Development Guide Plan*, Singapore Institute of Architects, Singapore.

Singapore Tourist Promotion Board (STPB) 1986 , *Tourism Product Development Plan*, Oct. 1986, STPB, Singapore.

—— 1991, *Singapore Annual Report on Tourism Statistics 1991*, STPB, Singapore.

—— (n.d.), Update on Tourism *developments/projects*, STPB, Singapore .

South China Morning Post, 'Singaporeans roll up for Kumar's smutty cabaret', 24 Feb. 1993.

Straits Times, 'No transvestite shows for Bugis Street', 18 Apr. 1992.

—— , 'Bugis Street gets trans-sexuals to be customer relations officers', 20 Apr. 1992.

Urban Renewal Authority 1988, *Historic Districts in the Central Area: A Manual for Kampong Glam Conservation Area*, Urban Renewal Authority, Singapore.

—— 1990, *Kampong Bugis Development Guide Plan (draft)* Urban Renewal Authority, Singapore.

—— 1991a, *Historic Districts: Conservation Guidelines for Kampong Glam Conservation Area*, Urban Renewal Authority, Singapore.

—— 1991b, *Living the Next Lap*, Urban Renewal Authority, Singapore.

—— 1991c, *Development Control Handbook Series: Conservation*, July, Urban Renewal Authority, Singapore.

—— (n.d.), *A Future with a Past: Saving our Heritage*, Urban Renewal Authority, Singapore.

Wong, P.P. 1989, 'The Transformation of the Physical Landscape' in Sandhu, K.S. & Wheatley, P. (eds.), *Management of Success: The Moulding of Modern Singapore*, Institute of Southeast Asian Studies, Singapore.

Wong, A. K. & Ooi, G.L. 1989, 'Spatial Reorganisation' in Sandhu, K.S. & Wheatley, P. (eds.), *Management of Success: The Moulding of Modern Singapore*, Institute of Southeast Asian Studies, Singapore

ACKNOWLEDGMENTS

The author thanks the following sources for their help in preparing this paper: those people interviewed in Bugis Street for sharing their feelings; the STPB officials who provided information; the URA for the use of its library; Professor Wong Siu-lin of the University of Hong Kong for his support; and Eric Tsang of the HKU Sociology Department for assistance in preparing the maps.

9

Post-independence Kuala Lumpur: heritage and the new city image

Jimmy Cheok-Siang Lim

THE FORMATION AND GROWTH OF PRE-INDEPENDENCE KUALA LUMPUR

Historical background

To begin to understand Kuala Lumpur one must look at its historical context with particular reference to other urban areas in the Malay archipelago, namely Melaka (Malacca), Penang and Singapore. In comparison, the history of Kuala Lumpur is relatively short and recent. Kuala Lumpur became prominent only with the establishment of a seat for the British Resident who, until 1879, was located at Klang, the old capital of Selangor.

The Portuguese set up Melaka in 1511 as a medieval fortification during the reign of King Manuel II of Spain. At the time of conquest, Melaka was already a flourishing city of commerce (Hall 1985)[1].

In 1641 the Dutch, relying on support and reconnaissance from Batavia, defeated the Portuguese to start the next era of colonial conquest which lasted until their eventual displacement by the British in 1795 or 1818. In 1786 the British had seized Penang under a treaty from the Sultanate of Kedah. They were to acquire Singapore in 1819 as their trade thrust further eastwards through the activities of the East India Company. Under the British, Penang, Melaka and Singapore, which were known then as the Straits

Settlements, became important ports and the seat of British colonial power. Within the British colonial framework, Penang (including Province Wellesley) and Melaka were administered by British Resident Commissioners, while Singapore was administered by a Governor[2].

The Straits Settlements flourished and became important centres for commerce, education, trade, urbanisation and rapid development. While they became very wealthy, Kuala Lumpur remained a backwash of Klang, an 'outpost' for tin mining.

The founding of Kuala Lumpur

When Kuala Lumpur was being established, the Malay Peninsula was divided into three economic zones of influence: Kedah and Perak were under Penang; Selangor and Negri Sembilan under Melaka; while Johore and the entire eastern part of the Malay Peninsula comprising Kelantan, Trengganu and Pahang were dependent upon Singapore. However, Melaka's importance as the leading port had by then been overtaken by Penang and Singapore.

Besides trading in spices, the main growth activities in the Federated Malay States were rubber plantations and mining in and around Kuala Lumpur, namely in Sungai Ujong, Lukut and the Klang Valley. It was the movement of mining workers into these areas at the end of the nineteenth century which led to the establishment of Kuala Lumpur.

Kuala Lumpur as a settlement

Kuala Lumpur translated means 'muddy estuary' of two rivers - the Klang and Gombak rivers. At the junction of the estuary is the settlement's oldest mosque, Masjid Jamie Jamek. By 1857 there was already a settlement of Sumatran Malays in the vicinity of Jalan Silang. Rivalry between the Sumatran Malays and the Bugis (seafarers from Makassar, Sulewesi) led to the Selangor Civil War of 1866 in which the settlement of Kuala Lumpur was badly damaged and almost abandoned.

Chinese prospectors from Negri Sembilan joined in the conflict by supporting Raja Mahadi to attack Kuala Lumpur in 1870. In 1872 Kuala Lumpur came under siege by Raja Mahadi and Captain China Yap Ah Loy. Yap Ah Loy, whose predecessors had sided with the Sultan and Raja Abdullah in the earlier dispute, was assisted by Gengku Kudin who was then in control of Ulu Yam, Rawang, Kuala Kubu and Serendah (districts to the North of Kuala Lumpur). Tengku Kudin, with the help of Bendahara Wan Ahmad of Pahang and some Englishmen, succeeded in defeating Raja Mahadi in March 1873. This was the start of British influence in Selangor.

After the defeat of the Sumatrans, Yap Ah Loy began rebuilding the town of Kuala Lumpur. From 1874-1885 he controlled the economy of Kuala Lumpur and maintained law and order. However, the town grew with no proper planning.

The British Residency

Until 1880 when the British Resident moved to Kuala Lumpur, all administrative, judiciary, public works and land survey matters were part of the combined duties of the magistrate periodically sent there to maintain some semblance of civic order. The relocation of the Residency to Kuala Lumpur saw the consolidation of law and order and the start of proper town administration. It also stimulated the growth of Kuala Lumpur and led to an influx of British Colonials eager to exploit the resources available in the Malay States. Roads, railways, postal services, telegraphs, telephone, electricity, piped water, health care and other services spread out from Kuala Lumpur to link

Penang to the north and Singapore to the south. To a large extent the growth and importance of Kuala Lumpur, being inland, was only made possible by road linkages[3]. Consequently, it became a regional centre.

Apart from the activities of the British, Kuala Lumpur's further rise in importance was due to the formation of the Federated Malay States in 1895, when it was selected to be the headquarters of the federation. This was to pave the way for Kuala Lumpur's emergence as the capital of Malaya and, subsequently, of Malaysia.

The growth of Kuala Lumpur was accelerated due to the profitable mining activities around it. This made development of the new town relatively easy. Increased economic activity attracted both Europeans and Asians to the growing community. By 1887 there were 518 brick houses in Kuala Lumpur. Some semblance of planning was introduced and the survey plan of 'Kuala Lumpur and Environs' produced by the Selangor Survey Department in 1889 showed the basic structure for the growth plans of modern Kuala Lumpur.

Kuala Lumpur assumed a cosmopolitan character, becoming the centre for recreation, entertainment, sports, education and religion as well as being the administrative centre of the Resident-General. Planters flocked to popular establishments in Kuala Lumpur to get away from the plantations and to savour the comforts provided.

Establishment of the local authorities

After the rebuilding of the whole town by the British, the Sanitary Board was formed in 1890 to regulate and maintain streets and drains and to control growth. In 1921 town planning was formally introduced to Kuala Lumpur. A town plan was prepared in 1939 and gazetted to control urban growth for a town of an area of 11 square miles (28.5 square kilometres) and a population of approximately 50 000 (PAM 1976, p.13). By 1947, the population had grown to 176 000.

The functions of the Sanitary Board were taken over by the Municipality of Kuala Lumpur in 1948. After an amendment to the *Municipality for Kuala Lumpur Act (1948)*, the first election of representatives to the new Municipal Council took place in 1952.

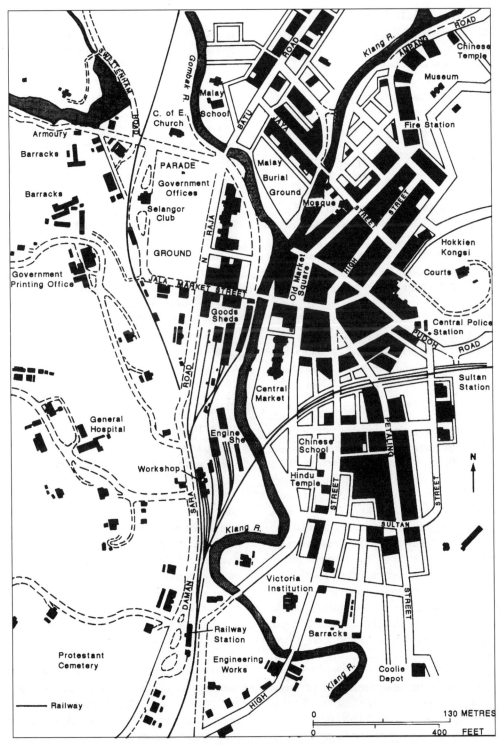

Figure 9.1   Kuala Lumpur in 1895. (Source: *after Federal Town Planning Department 1950, p.83)*

KUALA LUMPUR THE FEDERAL CAPITAL

Post-independence Kuala Lumpur

With independence in 1957, the Constitution of the Federation of Malaya provided for the Municipality of Kuala Lumpur to become the Federal Capital and this was achieved under the *Federal Capital Act (1960)*. The status of City of Kuala Lumpur was bestowed on 1 February 1972. An agreement concluded between the State of Selangor and the Federal Government established Kuala Lumpur as the Federal Territory of Kuala Lumpur on 1 February 1974. The Lord Mayor was the Chief Administrator for Kuala Lumpur, a city which had grown from 93 square kilometres (36 square miles) in 1970 to 243 square kilometres (94 square miles) in February 1974. The 1994 population of Kuala Lumpur of 1.5 million is expected to reach 2 million by the year 2000.

The choice of Kuala Lumpur to be the Federal Capital was a logical geographical decision, given its central location on the Peninsula and its connections with Penang, Malacca and Singapore by road and rail linkages and with the coastal Port Klang (formerly Port Swettenham).

Since the settlement of Kuala Lumpur in 1857, and after the British intervention in 1870s, some grand administrative buildings were constructed such as the General Post Office and the State Secretariat. Other impressive buildings constructed during the colonial period include Loke Chow Kit's department store (now the Industrial Court), Hong Kong Shanghai Bank Building, the Selangor Club, St. Mary's Church and Loke Chow Kit's Residence (now the Malaysian Institute of Architects Building). These buildings provided premises for new government offices. All Government departments and Ministries were centralised in Kuala Lumpur (or 'K.L.' as it is commonly called).

The development of Petaling Jaya, a satellite township to the south-west of Kuala Lumpur, as a residential and industrial centre contributed very much to the growth of Kuala Lumpur as a federal territory. It started a trend - the de-urbanisation of Kuala Lumpur and its subsequent sprawling growth pattern. Prior to this period most inhabitants lived in the urban centre and periphery of Kuala Lumpur, above shop-houses or, in the case of the more afflu-

ent, in bungalows or semi-detached dwellings while government employees lived in government quarters laid out as spacious compounds. The residential areas of Kuala Lumpur were restricted to Jalan Ampang, Jalan Pekeliling (Circular Road), Jalan Sultan Ismail (Parry Road), Jalan P. Ramlee (Treacher Road), Jalan Raja Chulan (Weld Road), Jalan Imbi, lower Jalan Bukit Bintang, Jalan Kia Peng and Jalan Selatan enclaves. Senior government servants were housed at the Bukit Petaling and Lake Gardens enclaves. Other government workers attached to the public utilities and public transport were housed nearer their place of employment; for instance, at Brickfields and Sentul in the case of the Malayan Railways employees.

Following the success of Petaling Jaya, private developers began providing private housing to cope with the growth and demand. Many new housing schemes were developed near Kuala Lumpur. The 1960s and the 1970s saw major growth in Kuala Lumpur. A new dual carriage highway linking the newly founded satellite city of Petaling Jaya, built in the early 1960s, was completely obsolete by the early 1970s and was upgraded and expanded to become an eight-lane highway by the late 1980s.

Post-1969 Kuala Lumpur

In tracing Kuala Lumpur's growth, 1969 must be noted as an important turning point for intervention which has given further impetus to Kuala Lumpur's rapid expansion, both economical and physical. As the Selangor Civil War of 1866 had badly damaged the settlement of Kuala Lumpur but indirectly provided the excuse for British intervention, so the racial riots of 1969 between the Malays and Chinese saw the introduction of numerous laws which effectively paved the way for many of the developments in present-day Kuala Lumpur.

After independence in 1957, the newly independent Federation of Malaya, together with North Borneo, Sarawak and Singapore, united in 1963 to form Malaysia. As an entity it survived until Singapore withdrew by mutual agreement in 1965. During the early years of nationhood of a society consisting of people from different cultural background and religious beliefs, much adjustment was needed to create a comfortable balance.

Political aspirations and euphoria accompanying the recent independence overflowed into local politics. With everyone trying to secure political niches for themselves, usually along racial lines, the result was the formation of numerous opposition parties to challenge the Government formed by the Alliance Party, a composite of the three major racial groupings, namely the UMNO (United Malay National Organisation), MCA (Malaysian Chinese Association) and the MIC (Malaysian Indian Congress).

In the 1969 elections the predominantly Chinese-dominated political party DAP (Democratic Action Party), an affiliated associate of the PAP (People's Action Party) of Singapore, won the majority of seats in the Malaysian Parliament and in the State Assembly of Selangor. This sudden polarisation of racial groups caused a short-lived civil commotion to flare up in Kuala Lumpur. Due to swift action by the Government and the unbiased stance of the police force, the crisis was brought under control with minimal loss of life. Realising the disparity of wealth existing between the Chinese and the Malays (the *bumiputra* or, literally translated, 'princes of the soil'), the Government introduced the First Outline Progressive Plan (OPPI) and the New Economic Policy (NEP) for implementation 1971-1990. Under this program, the Urban Development Authority (UDA) was established in 1971 to complement other government or semi-government agencies charged with the implementation of the New Economic Policy. The UDA was to play a major role in restructuring the urban identity and growth of Kuala Lumpur.[4]

The Urban Development Authority

The UDA's main role was to implement government policy and to ensure that it filtered down to the grass-roots level. Its main objectives were two-fold: to increase *bumiputra* property ownership in terms of stock and value; and to provide commercial premises for *bumiputra* in strategic urban areas.

As spelt out in the Act[5], the UDA was to:

a) promote and carry out projects in urban development areas for:

  i) development, redevelopment, settlement, re-settlement and public housing; and

  ii) improvement in environment, services, amenities, traffic circulation, vehicle parking, recreational and community facilities and other public improvements for the promotion of National Unity, health, safety, convenience and welfare;

b) promote and carry out projects in urban development areas with a view to achieve the distribution of opportunities among the various races in the fields of commerce and industry, housing and other activities; and

c) translate into action-programs the government's policy to 'restructure society through urban development'.

It was a massive order and task. The success and level of achievement of UDA depended on the leadership of the authority and the degree of dedication, responsibility and competence of the executives within it. The UDA was the major player in many projects in Kuala Lumpur. By virtue of its structure and power it could often 'over-rule' and 'over-ride' the authority of the DBKL (*Dewan Bandaraya Kuala Lumpur* - City Hall of Kuala Lumpur) in planning and development matters. By using 'national unity' and the 'distribution of opportunities' as the rationale for their actions, the UDA was able to carry out urban restructuring exercises which would not have been possible under normal circumstances. The participation of the UDA in almost any project in Kuala Lumpur was compulsory during this period. Plans affecting Kuala Lumpur's urban growth had to be submitted to the UDA for evaluation, comments and approval prior to application to the DBKL for further vetting and approval. Many of Kuala Lumpur's notable developments and buildings in the 1970s and early 1980s had the UDA's involvement and participation.

New Economic Policy (1971-1990)

The New Economic Policy (NEP) was a 'socio-economic engineering' plan unlike anything tried elsewhere in the world. Its objectives were:

i) to restructure Malaysian society so as to reduce and eventually eliminate the identification of race with economic function. In this respect,

the Plan incorporates a two-pronged New Economic Policy for development. The first prong is to reduce and eventually eradicate poverty, by raising income levels and increasing employment opportunities for all Malaysians, irrespective of race.

The second prong aims at accelerating the process of restructuring Malaysian society to correct economic imbalance, so as to reduce and eventually eliminate the identification of race with economic function. This process involves the modernisation of rural life, a rapid and balanced growth of urban activities and the creation of a Malay commercial and industrial community in all categories and at all levels of operation, so that Malays and other indigenous people will become full partners in all aspects of the economic life of the nation...

These policies and programs will be implemented in such a manner that no one will be deprived of his rights, privileges, income, job or opportunity. Accordingly, to afford the necessary opportunities for more education, better jobs and higher incomes to the disadvantaged, the sum total of such opportunities open to all Malaysian must be expanded rapidly. This expansion is an essential element in the New Economic Policy. (*Second Malaysia Plan 1971-1975*, 1971, p.1)

ii) the eradication of poverty, irrespective of race, was laid down as one of its other main aims.

KUALA LUMPUR'S PHYSICAL DEVELOPMENT

Dewan Bandaraya Kuala Lumpur (DBKL) - City Hall of Kuala Lumpur

During the NEP period the City and later the Federal Territory of Kuala Lumpur were under the charge of three Lord Mayors (*Datuk Bandar*): Datuk Bandar Tan Sri Lokman Yusoff from February to May 1972; Datuk Bandar Tan Sri Yaacob Latiff from July 1972 to February 1983; and Datuk Bandar Tan Sri Dato Elyas Omar from February 1983 to September 1992. A sizeable list of 'Notable Buildings' was constructed during the tenure of each *Datuk Bandar* (see Appendix A).

The first Lord Mayor, Tan Sri Lokman Yusoff, was appointed Commissioner of the Federal Capital in 1967 and in 1972 became Commissioner of the City of Kuala Lumpur. He held his post for only three months before his death. His successor, Tan Sri Yaacob Latiff, served as Lord Mayor for over ten years. Much of the building activity under his tenure was the result of the UDA's input.

By comparison with his predecessors, Tan Sri Dato Elyas Omar was young when he took office. He proved to be an indefatigable worker and a man of vision. During his period of tenure, the Kuala Lumpur skyline was transformed dramatically, riding on the crest of economic 'boom' and into the trough of a recession. The economic downturn did not halt the progress towards making Kuala Lumpur into a garden city or towards its proclamation as a 'City of Lights'.

The growth of Kuala Lumpur and its physical surrounds since independence has been the result of a combined effort between the Government and local business entrepreneurs. Government effort and concentration was focussed on the City Centre, while the extension of the suburban sprawl was very much in the hands of private developers. Immediately after the setting up of the new satellite town of Petaling Jaya, a major housing development scheme for bungalow lots was launched at the Bukit Tunku (formerly Kenny Hills). It was to be the forerunner of many such housing developments in years to come. By the early 1960s the Socfin Estate set aside a large tract of its oil palms at Damansara for a new housing estate, following similar lines to those of Bukit Tunku.

This was to become a township in its own right, called Damansara, consisting of housing, both low density and high density, recreational facilities, commercial centre, schools and other institutional buildings. Other notable growth areas were the Taman Seputeh or 3rd mile Old Klang Road area (1967-71), Bangsar (1973), Taman Desa (1975) and Cheras Area (1975). Some were better laid out and constructed than others, and had more facilities.

With the major growth areas pushing at Kuala Lumpur's seams, the careful planning needed by the local authority was not forthcoming. A lack of planning coordination became evident everywhere. Approvals were given haphazardly, without due consideration to the structural plan let alone to the local plan. Often streets were left disjointed and unconnected or they were even discontinued as they crossed into adjoining developments due to topographic constraints. These shortcomings are now being painstakingly rectified at tremendous cost to the ratepayers and with extreme inconvenience for local residents.

Other evidence of ill-conceived schemes was the regular flooding of the main arterial roads of Kuala Lumpur due to torrential tropical rainfall. Owing to the lack of engineering understanding and concern, many natural watercourses and run-offs were deviated or obliterated by massive earthworks; or water from a development site was channelled into a single outlet, far too small to sustain the volume of water. Extensive programs by the Department of Irrigation and Drainage were carried out to improve water discharge and flow from all major estuaries and streams linking into the Gombak and Klang rivers network.

Major improvements to the existing ring-road system around K.L. were carried out in the 1980s. Further improvements to major highways linking the city to surrounding towns, the airport, Port Klang, the new capital of Selangor, Shah Alam, and new residential growth centres have contributed to the increase in car ownership in K.L. The proposed north-south highway which will ultimately link the northernmost state of Perlis to the southernmost state of Johore will further increase the current traffic load on K.L.'s roads. Residents of K.L. are already bemoaning the fact that the traffic congestion appears to be as bad as in some other Asian countries (Lim 1991 (b)).

Changing attitudes and trends

The growth of Kuala Lumpur from the 1970s to the 1990s is largely due to sustained economic growth and to the continued migration from the rural areas. The capital is a magnet for those seeking to improve their financial situation speedily. The city's physical form is also a direct result of changing attitudes towards traditional social values and particularly the diminishing importance of the traditional extended family by comparison with the Western concept of the nuclear family unit.

The physical transformation of Kuala Lumpur may be characterised by studying three distinctive housing developments and growth areas which may be classified under the following periods:
a) Immediate post-independence period, 1950s-1963
b) Transitional period, 1966-1973
c) Boom period, 1976-1984
d) Condominium period, 1988-1993.

Immediate post-independence period, 1950s-1963: the Kenny Hills development

A section of the north-western corner of Kuala Lumpur was developed by the Anglo-Thai Cooperation during the early period of post-independence. The site comprised approximately 100 acres of mainly hilly terrain. The very small amount of flat land within the site was located at the foothills and formed part of the Harrisons and Crosfield Estates or belonged to other owners such as the Russel family, owners of the Boh plantations, and the Shell Company. The proposed development was on the upper hill terrain and involved a subdivision into large housing lots averaging between 40 000 and 60 000 square feet (approx. 3700-15 500 square metres). According to an original resident[6], the land price was 7.5 sen per square foot in early 1950s but, by 1956, had risen to 35 sen per square foot, with the condition imposed that a house of the value of at least $30 000 had to be built within six months of purchase. The development is not more than a mile from the G.P.O. on the Selangor Club padang which was then the central square of K.L.

Kenny Hills is today Kuala Lumpur's elite residential area. Land prices range between RM 60-80 per square foot. Many of the properties are sought after because of the quality of the environment and its closeness to nature. The fact that natural features such as the terrain and vegetation were not disturbed or destroyed during Kenny Hills' development makes this suburb most salubrious and environmentally attractive. The timelessness of its natural beauty, with people living in harmony with nature, is exemplary for other development projects in Malaysia. However, much to the regret of those advocating the preservation of natural elements and their blending into development projects, this example has not been repeated in later developments.

That Kenny Hills, now renamed Bukit Tunku (Tunku Hills), was able to preserve much of its pristine forests, natural reserves and natural features was probably more a matter of chance and circumstances rather than through intent or planning. As a young nation, the economy and technology of that period were unable to sustain the use of expensive, heavy earthmoving equipment. This would probably have

Figure 9.2   Kenny Hills. A bungalow on a one-acre lot nestled into the natural landscape. The driveway on the left leads to another house. (Source: J.C.S. Lim)

been one of the main constraints determining the manner in which the estate was designed - with roads hugging the contours and building plots surveyed to take advantage of the natural surface run-off. Existing ravines and water courses were not altered. Minimal clearing of the natural flora was carried out and plots were sold off complete with vegetation. Only when the house owners commenced building did terrain reshaping and the removal of trees occur to facilitate construction. Most of the construction of the infrastructure was carried out by human labour with support from light earthmoving equipment.

The philosophy of not going against nature but building to harmonise with nature was way ahead of its time. The minimal impact on the environment fits the current trend of 'back to nature' and emphasis on

Figure 9.3   A typical bungalow from the Harrisons and Crosfield Estates acquired by the government. Currently rented out to the private sector, such buildings are under threat of demolition. (Source: J.C.S. Lim)

the preservation of nature. The depletion of earth's precious resources, such as oxygen, and the thinning of the ozone layer has led to the questioning of the manner in which development is currently being carried out. It is for this very reason that Bukit Tunku is an important example, pointing as it does to a new direction for future Malaysian urban developments.

Transitional period, 1960-1973: Socfin Estate, Damansara Heights development

Following the success of the Bukit Tunku (Kenny Hills) development, another large tract of agricultural land further west was earmarked for housing development. The Socfin estate, consisting predominantly of rubber and palm oil plantations, was subdivided for housing development. In comparison with Bukit Tunku, Damansara Heights had larger amounts of relatively flat land. The terrain for palm oil estates is generally rolling with gentle grades. Rubber, by contrast, can be planted on the steepest of slopes.

When Bukit Tunku was planned and developed in the early 1950s, economic growth in Malaysia was relatively slow. By the early 1960s, however, when Damansara Heights was developed, the economy was gaining impetus. Damansara also had the use of more 'early-model' heavy earthmoving equipment during construction. The result was that more of the natural features were removed. The hills were cut and valleys filled in, slopes stepped and terraced to accommodate buildings. All trees, shrubs and top-soil were removed or mixed in with the earth for back fillings. Nevertheless, pockets of natural terrain were preserved due to the difficulty of access and the inappropriateness of equipment for the job.

As this earthmoving equipment was fairly basic, the hills, although terraced, still bore some resemblance to their original silhouette. However all the trees from the housing plots were removed. The plots were smaller, at 7000-15 000 square foot, than those of Bukit Tunku and the building density was higher. There were more roads, and retaining walls became a significant element in the suburban streetscape. The lack of trees and natural floral is a predominant and conspicuous feature of Damansara Heights. It is regrettable that, unlike Bukit Tunku, this development was to become the model for other housing schemes in Malaysia.

Under this development, not only was the estate subdivided into smaller plots, but individual bungalows based on standard designs were constructed and sold. The Xanadu model in 1970, with a land area of approximately 7000-8000 square feet (650-740 square metres), was sold for approximately R.M. 47 000 per house. The prices of properties in this residential suburb being offered for sale in 1994 range from RM 1.3-1.8 million. Damansara has matured and some of its former greenery has been restored. With time we can look towards the replanting and regeneration of a more lush tropical landscape.

Boom period, 1976-1984: Bangsar Hills neighbourhood

As the development of Damansara was coming towards its final stages, a major development was being planned adjacent to it. This was the Bangsar Estate, a total development of 60 hectares (150 acres). It was situated approximately three kilometres to the south-west of Kuala Lumpur towards the Pantai valley and was separated from Damansara to its north by a rocky ridge traversing in an east-west direction and bound on its southern boundaries by the Klang River.

By now most of the housing schemes contributing to the growth of modern Kuala Lumpur were by private developers who were former owners of large rubber holdings. Many large tracts of land near the town area were owned by Chinese traders who had acquired their properties from the local Malays. These Chinese entrepreneurs were the pioneer developers following in the footsteps of the British.

Mr Ng Eng Lian, the developer of Bangsar Hills, was one such entrepreneur. Before embarking on this scheme he had tried at a modest-sized development at a hillside suburb called Taman Seputeh, along the southern bank of the Klang river and off Jalan Syed Putra (formerly known as Lornie Road). This small development consisting predominantly of linked, two-storeyed terrace houses sprawled in a delightful manner across the landscape and proved to be most popular with the younger professionals during the 1970s. The initial selling price for these terrace houses in early 1971, with a land area measuring approximately 22 by 80 feet (6.7 by 24.4 metres), was RM 28 000. By 1973 the price had risen to RM 32 000, and the 1994 market price is RM 200 000-250 000. This suburb has, incidentally, the largest residential concentration of architects per square kilometre in Malaysia.

The Bangsar development on the other hand was much larger in scale. Not only was housing planned but there were other types of development proposed. Its ultimate intent was to create a township to serve the needs of the surrounding dormitory suburbs, including Pantai Hills, Damansara, Brickfields and parts of Petaling Jaya. At the time of writing Mr Ng's vision has been realised.

The most sophisticated earthmoving equipment was used in the development of Bangsar in the 1970s-1980s. The extensive earthworks for this project were carried out in the shortest of time. During its construction and after the initial phases were completed, the major link road between Bangsar and Kuala Lumpur, Jalan Travers and Jalan Maarof were always flooded after an afternoon's torrential rain. This would bring the peak hour traffic out of Kuala Lumpur to a standstill, a problem solved only recently with the implementation of the overall improvement scheme to the waterways around Kuala Lumpur.

All the natural features of the site were removed; all vegetation, outcrops and natural water run-offs were levelled. Bangsar today bears testimony to human ingenuity and success in taming nature. This will be the success story to be retold many times over in the history of the development and growth of Kuala Lumpur. Developers now approach every site as a challenge: all that Nature has provided must be taken off, all natural features eliminated, valleys filled in, hills levelled, and on the exposed red earth, now devoid of any topsoil cover, the roads, drains, houses and playgrounds are built. Before the house buyers take possession of their keys, some token landscaping will be provided to comply with a mandatory requirement needed to obtain a Certificate of Occupancy. It is to the Local Government's credit that such a statutory requirement was introduced to instil in the developers a sense of responsibility towards creating a friendly environment conducive for pleasant living.

Condominium period, 1989-1992

Following the boom of the late 1970s until the mid 1980s, the Malaysian economy took a dip into recession. Many housing projects were left incomplete or were abandoned by the developers, many of whom absconded with the purchasers' monies. The surrounding landscape was littered with the remnants of the broken dreams of house owners who lost their life's savings. The Government, together with financial institutions, had to intervene to salvage and resuscitate some of these projects in the hope that the innocent house owners might recover at least part of their deposits. Many culprits were prosecuted while many others made off with the ill-gotten gains to foreign countries which do not have extradition treaties with Malaysia.

It was with this at the back of their minds that most Malaysian developers entered the next phase of the development in Kuala Lumpur. Having barely survived the recession of the 1980s, many were glad to be given another opportunity. There were a number of new players too, often foreigners with funding from Hong Kong, Taiwan or even Singapore who helped fuel the next upswing in Kuala Lumpur's building industry. These developers concentrated on building high-rise or up-market condominiums, this being an area of development with which they were familiar in their homeland. The building industry's sudden take-off took everyone by surprise; no-one ever thought it possible considering that memories of the industry's recent debacle were still fresh and evidence everywhere bore silent testimony to the fact.

Selected locations in prime residential suburbs of Kuala Lumpur were targeted for the development of these condominiums. Most popular were the Bangsar Hills, Damansara, Sri Hartamas, Taman Desa, Kampong Kerinchi, Jalan Ampang Hilir/Jalan Ritchie and Jalan U-Thant enclaves. Even the foot hills of lush Bukit Tunku were not spared. In 1991 the author commented on this process in the editorial of the journal *Berita Akitek*:

> They say that mushrooms grow very fast, but in the tropics, especially in Malaysia, 'Condominiums' grow even faster. Now 'condo developments' no longer belong exclusively within the grasp and dominance

of some developers. It is common property. The purist concept of what condominium developments should consist of has been 'watered' down to a level that is nothing more than a glorified larger-scaled, low-cost apartments with 'frills and thrills'. This cycle has brought with it developments of shapes and sizes. All under the name of 'Condominium'...

> Kuala Lumpur has probably the most number of high-rise condominium developments in Malaysia... We are told that 'densities' have gone through the roof and that the old mandatory '60 persons maximum per acre for a minimum of 2 acres development for condominium' is now an 'appendix' to the New Testament, and is no longer applicable. Currently '200 units/acre' is closer to the norm. And why not if the city can sustain and support such densities?; if quality of life of residents and users of the city can be maintained? Ultimately the test is whether the smooth functioning and activities of the city can be maintained. (Lim 1991 (a))

Many of the ills associated with condominium living were not understood by local developers or the city officials and approving authorities. There was no effort made to monitor or evaluate what the resultant impact of high density, high-cost and high-rise development on the environment and quality of life would be. Studies ought to have been made to ascertain the best possible answer to new problems created by these huge projects and to formulate new guidelines to manage their development.

It would appear that was no in-depth consideration of whether existing services and facilities in that location were adequate to handle the extra loadings. Other problems previously experienced in Kuala Lumpur - such as whether the drains were adequate to take the additional overflows and discharge; whether there was sufficient water and water pressure to service these elevated sites; whether the road networks were adequate to handle the increased traffic volume generated - were not carefully scrutinised at the planning application stage for these condominium projects. The planning guidelines and development policies of the local authority were inadequate and ill-equipped to handle such developments. The impact of these developments is now affecting the surrounding residential neighbourhoods.

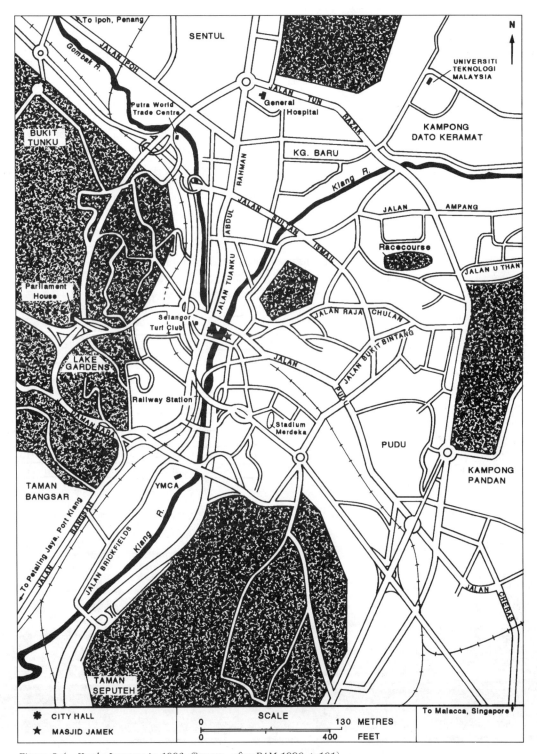

Figure 9.4   Kuala Lumpur in 1993. (Source: *after PAM 1990, p.101*)

The Jalan Ampang arterial road, the Federal highway, the Sungai Besi feeder and the inner and outer ring roads have become the bane of commuters working in Kuala Lumpur. Traffic is bumper to bumper at most times, with massive bank-ups a daily occurrence.

Kuala Lumpur, the leading metropolis of Malaysia, ought to have set an example by planning and encouraging the development of a concentrated enclave of high density residential dwellings or condominiums within one suburb, with a concentrated commercial development nearby to complement it. This would have presented Malaysian planners, architects, researchers and those associated with the design and planning of the environment a valuable model in which to study the advantages and pressures not previously considered or understood. With the scattered, sporadic, haphazard and uncoordinated development, which is the current norm, a 'laboratory-like' opportunity for experiment has been missed.

Kuala Lumpur - city centre development

To balance the discussion of growth in outer Kuala Lumpur the focus will now shift to the city area, especially the Central Business District (CBD). Its recent development can be discussed using similar periods to those defined earlier; that is:
a) Transitional and Boom Periods, 1966-1984;

b) Post-boom period, 1984 onwards.

Transitional and boom periods

During this crucial period in the development of the capital, the DBKL was under Mayor Tan Sri Yaacob Latiff (1972-83). He had assumed the post barely two years after the civil unrest in Kuala Lumpur in 1969, which was described earlier as a major interruption in the development of Kuala Lumpur. The years after 1969 saw many new agencies working on behalf of the government to implement the New Economic Policy (NEO). In an effort to restructure society so that wealth was distributed more equitably, the ownership of many new developments in the CBD obtained new equity participation by the *bumiputras* who had until then been mainly landowners in the rural areas. This was carried out under the charge of the Urban Development Authority (UDA).

The thinking of the planners during this period was to encourage the entrenched residents to leave their traditional enclaves within the city. Most of these were Chinese who had been settled there ever since the Kuala Lumpur was founded in 1857. They generally lived above shop-houses. With rezoning these former mixed residential/commercial properties in the CBD were not permitted to be redeveloped with residential use. The result was that all new developments in central Kuala Lumpur had no residential provisions, leading to the rapid de-urbanisation of

Figure 9.5   Panoramic view of Kuala Lumpur from the peak of Bukit Tunku. The greenery in the foreground shows the

the city and indirectly contributing to the growth of the major peripheral housing projects described earlier in the chapter. Former city dwellers had now to seek alternative housing in the suburbs.

The new suburban housing schemes tried to replace for the residents the benefits that had been lost when they moved from the inner city. Schools, town centres, markets, community halls and other facilities commonly found in the Malaysian towns were provided. But it was more difficult to replace the texture, tradition, fabric and mosaic of urban living. The proximity to urban facilities, with which the former inner city residents were familiar, were no longer available. Many of the older people found adjustment to the new lifestyle difficult, but for the young it was a pleasant change.

As demand for alternative housing outside Kuala Lumpur increased, more of the former rubber estates or large compounded villas were converted for housing purposes. This period saw Kuala Lumpur losing most of its heritage buildings. The need to replace the traditional with what was thought to be new, or the need to obliterate traces of colonial history, caused many fine old buildings to be torn down, all in the name of progress. Many streets lost their landmarks. Jalan Leboh Ampang and Medan Pasar lost two fine buildings, the old Hong Kong Bank building and the old Citibank building. Bukit Mahkamah lost the former courthouse complex to make way for the new Malayan Bank Building.

Streets of shop-houses built with finely sculptured facades were torn down to make way for faceless 'modern-style' shopping complexes with little architectural merit. The street facades of the rows of shop-houses were often classical in spirit, formalised by a centrally placed pediment with two symmetrically designed ends to finish off the elevational treatment of the street block. Under the UDA's policies, no individual lot in the CBD was allowed to be developed unless amalgamated with other adjoining properties. The resulting massive developments were to have a profound impact on the traffic, pedestrian and urban-scape of Kuala Lumpur. Many street facades along Jalan Ipoh, Jalan Tunku Abdul Rahman (Batu Road), Jalan Bandar (High Street), Jalan Cheng Lok (Foch Avenue), Jalan Tun Perak (Mountbatten Road), were randomly destroyed by infill developments, thereby disrupting the strong and continuous rhythm and a sense of unity of the street.

Kuala Lumpur was going through an exciting time. All and sundry were getting into the act as developers. Previously humble shopkeepers who owned properties in Kuala Lumpur suddenly found that their family home or shop-house was worth a goldmine and opted to cash in their new found wealth. Tempering this joy was apprehension at having to set aside 30 per cent of their equity for 'new partners', as provided for under the NEP. This was initially

extent of the Kenny Hills development. The city centre is in the right-hand half of the picture. (Source: *J.C.S. Lim*)

Figure 9.6   Jalan Cecil: hawker stalls and a prewar shop-house. (Source: *J.C.S. Lim*)

unfamiliar for the traditional Chinese families who had always worked within the family unit. However, as time went on this formula was understood and accepted by all investors and developers. The city centre in the meantime, with most of the inhabitants moved to the suburbs, had lost its original character. Kuala Lumpur lost its Asian-ness. It was a dead city at night, devoid of life and other activities which existed before. It stayed that way for many years.

Post-boom period

When Tan Sri Yaacob Latiff was replaced by Tan Sri Elyas Omar as the new Mayor of Kuala Lumpur in 1983, growth of the CBD was still proceeding at a rapid pace. But after 1984 the economy of Malaysia started slowing down and the CBD was almost devoid of any construction activity. The only activity was on projects which were in the midst of construction. The decline in economic wealth accentuated the dreariness and lifelessness of the inner city area.

Towards the end of the recession, the DBKL embarked on a program of arresting the decay, bringing life back into the city and stimulating growth. Compulsory acquisition of equity into developments by UDA was no longer permitted. The UDA had by then suffered from some unwise investments. Individual development proposals were permitted without being required to amalgamate with adjoining properties or to be referred to the UDA, a reversal of the policies set when Tan Sri Yaacob Latiff was the Mayor.

Mixed developments in downtown areas were encouraged. Liberal approvals were given for proposals introducing more residential development. This deliberate policy resuscitated the city centre of K.L. The DBKL provided locations for hawkers and petty traders to ply their trades. Some streets were closed off to cars at selected days and times so that shopping and trading could be enjoyed in a city otherwise dominated by cars. On Saturdays the site of the former low-cost apartment at Jalan Suleiman off Jalan Tunku Abdul Rahman was set aside for a day-long open market where agricultural produce was sold. It was a way of introducing the countryside to the inhabitants in the city. The carnival atmosphere softened and warmed the impersonal lifestyle of the modern city.

A new crop of apartment buildings began to appear in the city. Jalan Hicks and the Ceylon Hill enclave previously earmarked for commercial use has become a new residential district surrounded by commercial developments. High-rise apartments were now popular with the expatriate community work-

Figure 9.7   Jalan Petaling: cacophony of architectural styles. (Source: *J.C.S. Lim*)

ing in Kuala Lumpur, the days of expatriates occupying huge and luxurious villas with well manicured gardens being long gone. The varied needs of the expatriate community encouraged more variety in the design of high-rise apartments.

The destruction and demolition of heritage buildings in inner Kuala Lumpur went on unabated until 1984. Objections from numerous citizen groups to the continued destruction of the old city centre led to the formation of a conservation movement to preserve and save the vanishing heritage, known as *Badan Warisan Malaysia* (Heritage of Malaysia Trust). Through a combination of careful planning and being seen to be a responsible, non-confrontational organisation, the Trust was able to earn the confidence of the Government and therefore made

Figure 9.9   Jalan Silang: the Cahaya Suria building, an example of the UDA's commercial development in central Kuala Lumpur. In the background is the headquarters of the Malayan Bank (Maybank). (Source: J.C.S. Lim)

Figure 9.8   Jalan Sultan: the four-storey building was an invention which marred the streetscape of Kuala Lumpur throughout the 1970s. They replaced the individual prewar shop-house tenement. (Source: J.C.S. Lim)

tremendous headway towards achieving its goals. The *Badan* (as it is popularly know in Malaysia) will be discussed in greater detail later in the chapter.

Kampong Baru - a village within a city

As a modern city Kuala Lumpur is unique. No other city can boast of having two rivers joining at its centre, a hilltop nature reserve covered with primary jungle, and, not far away, a traditional Malay village which appears to have stood still as the rest of the city surrounded it.

Known as *Kampong Baru* (new village), this traditional village is now a Malay reserve. No land transfer out of the hands of Malays is permitted. Development within this enclave need not be referred to DBKL, although it is within the federal boundaries, but is referred to the settlement's Council of Elders. This restriction is meant to protect the rights of the Malay owners to maintain their land holdings, and to prevent or discourage any unwelcome redevelopment or investment opportunities.

All the elements of a traditional village are still found here. Houses are of timber, some grouped around open spaces while others are lined along narrow streets without destroying the rural ambience. In the middle is a village centre where shops and the traditional wet market is located. This scene of a salubrious oasis in the heart of a city is completed by fowls and ducks running around the compounds taking refuge under shady fruit trees.

Unlike their Chinese counterparts in other parts of K.L., who discovered that they were sitting on goldmines during the 'boom', the Malay owners found no takers for their land and thereby missed out on the profit-making of the period. The Government, realising this anomaly in development opportunity among the Malaysian landowners, proposed a redevelopment program for Kampong Baru in 1991. This was intended to encourage more commercially viable projects yielding higher financial returns and bringing the settlement into the twenty-first century. The need for improvement is essential, but there are always other options which may present a more creative and innovative solution while still catering for everyone's aspirations. To lose a rare, culturally-rich traditional reserve in this typological category would be regrettable. Other options for stimulating revenue and additional income for the reserve inhabitants without having to destroy the kampong environment must be considered and can be found. Its protection and conservation through an adaptive re-use program can generate income otherwise thought to be impossible. To date there has been no indication of what the future holds for Kampong Baru.

THE CONSERVATION MOVEMENT

The destruction of major parts of Kuala Lumpur's heritage in the late 1970s and early 1980s prompted many of the nation's concerned citizens to group together for a common cause. Losing the common battle to save Court Hill brought together all the splintered groups. Under the coordination and guidance of a former British public servant, now a well respected member of the 'Establishment', Tan Sri Mubin Sheppard[7], the first conservation association in Malaysia named the *Badan Warisan Malaysia* (Heritage of Malaysia Trust) was constituted in 1982. It was founded to promote the permanent preservation of Malaysia's architectural heritage for the benefit and education of the nation. Its formation paved the way for others in different parts of Malaysia including Penang, Melaka, Sarawak and Perak.

Badan Warisan Malaysia

Although founded in 1982, the *Badan* was incorporated in August 1983 under the provisions of Section 24 of the *Companies Act (1965)*[8]. The original subscribers of the Company were:

Dato Harun M. Hashim   (Judge)
Jimmy Cheok-Siang Lim   (Architect)
Chen Voon Fee   (Architect)
Tan Sri Mubin Sheppard   (Writer)

The reason for incorporating the *Badan* as a Company was to provide the necessary mechanism for it to acquire and dispose of heritage properties[9]. At the time of its incorporation there were numerous buildings under threat, namely the Peninsular Hotel (formerly Loke Hall), the Majestic Hotel and the Central Market. As the *Badan* aimed at being non-confrontational and at maintaining a respectable and responsible image of dedication towards conservation, it could not be seen to openly and vocally campaign against the destruction of these buildings. Therefore another group consisting of younger members formed another society called *Persatuan Sahabat-Sahabat Warisan Malaysia*, with the objective of complementing the activities of the *Badan*.

Persatuan Sahabat-Sahabat Malaysia

The *Sahabat,* as it was popularly known, was formed in January 1984 and is officially registered with the Registrar of Societies as the 'Friends of the Heritage of Malaysia Society'. The original office bearers were:

Zehan Albakri   (President)
Yang Chong   (Vice President)
Rosedina Shamsuddin   (Vice President)
Lam Seng Fatt   (Hon. Secretary)
Faridah Abdul Kahar   (Hon. Treasurer)

They were supported by an enthusiastic Council

and a group of young members. Their first campaign was to save the Majestic Hotel. A series of fund-raising functions were organised. A film premiere, a 'Save the Majestic' Ball, and numerous media appearances designed to win public support were organised. The campaign was a success; the Majestic was not demolished but converted into an art gallery. This inspired the young members to further their pro-conservation activities. Other activities included providing building information to the *Badan* and public promotion[10].

Impact of the conservation movement

The main concerns of the newly formed conservation associations were to convince the Government that Malaysia had the good fortune to possess a wealth of architectural treasures reflecting its rich cultural history. Further, as many of these buildings were Government owned, it was important that these heritage assets should be properly maintained. In this context, attempts at preservation, conservation and restoration of such buildings should have their strategy and implementation properly directed to ensure that historic authenticity was not lost.

Since the Government had shown a willingness to put funds into this important area, it was important that these large sums of money were not misspent. The Government also had to be convinced that conservation need not be expensive and that careful and sensitive planning was far more critical than the mere expenditure of funds. Finally, it was important that the Government appreciate that the *Baden Warisan Malaysia's* approach to conservation practice was following worldwide guidelines and was governed by the following dictum: 'Sensitivity, Simplicity, Sincerity'.

The *Badan* embarked on numerous projects without seeking Government funding or aid. Indeed very few organisations or Government bodies would provide aid for ventures of a conservation nature and the funds for the *Badan*'s projects were all raised by its members. Some of the buildings saved in the early days of the conservation movement were the former Peninsula Hotel, now occupied by the Malaysian Institute of Architects (as their secretariat, with the *Badan* as a tenant) and restored almost to its former glory without losing its essential character; the Hotel

Majestic which has been restored, repaired and converted for use as the National Art Gallery; and the Central Market, formerly the wet produce market of Kuala Lumpur, designated for demolition to make way for a five-star hotel, but now restored, refurbished and converted into Kuala Lumpur's cultural market. This centre has operated for almost seven years and is enjoyed by both locals and tourists. It is hard to imagine Kuala Lumpur existing without the Central Market[11]. After these and several major projects outside the capital, the *Badan*'s credibility was entrenched in the minds of the public and the Government.

There were other programs aimed at educating and winning the public and Government: seminars were organised regularly, public lectures given on conservation, documents and handbooks about Malaysian heritage published, foreign experts invited to exchange experiences, and public fund-raising activities held. During the tenure of Tan Sri Elyas Omar, Kuala Lumpur became a very heritage conscious city. Elyas played a difficult role balancing the opposing pressures. That a large portion of Kuala Lumpur still has many heritage buildings may be attributed to his efforts. The DBKL has produced a handbook of guidelines showing how conservation may be done and explaining what development may be permitted in conservation areas. The city heritage buildings were classified and zoned according to their importance in the context of conservation and preservation.

The Ministry of Local Government and Housing is currently working with the *Badan* to draught legislation to protect Malaysia's heritage. Until the formation of the *Badan* the nation's heritage and monuments were under the purview of the Museum as provided for under the *Antiquities Act (1976)*. The provisions of the Act are inadequate to protect the ancient and heritage structures for prosperity. It is hoped that the new legislation will be more beneficial for conservation.

CONCLUSION

Like all emerging nations, Malaysia went through a transitional period of soul searching - getting to grips with its new identity and stepping into the world, unsure of itself, seeking recognition, winning friends and trying to find its own feet. A study of Kuala Lumpur's development and growth provides a telescoped review of what the nation went through. The description of the different development periods of Kuala Lumpur is commensurate with Malaysia's economic growth and growing confidence.

Pessimists had predicted the disintegration of the multi-racial society, especially so immediately after the civil unrest of May 1969. Like the civil war of 1866 when Kuala Lumpur was completely destroyed and then rebuilt, 1969 heralded a new birth and great impetus for the growth of the nation in general and Kuala Lumpur in particular. The unrest may in hindsight now appear to be a symbolic 'cleansing' of that which had anything to do with the legacy left behind by the colonial period. The resulting rivalry between the Chinese and the Malays in 1969 may be seen as the final chapter of the British policy of 'divide and rule' or a fore-runner of the 'apartheid policy' in South Africa.

Prior to independence neither the Chinese nor the Malays were ever considered as a cohesive racial grouping. The Chinese were categorised according to their various dialect groups (Cantonese, Hokkien, Hainanese, Hakka, etc.), while the Malays were classified into regional groupings (Bugis, Javanese, Kelantanese, Pantanis, etc.). With such a distinctive set of divisions, the complete integration and co-operation between the ethnic groups was never a realistic goal. Independence forged all these different ethnic groups to think and work towards a single nation and a single national identity.

Being made up of divergent ethnic sub-groups, the two main racial groups had difficulty thinking and acting collectively, much less as a single nation. The racial conflict of 1969 shocked everyone in the country. It brought a sense of realisation and realism as well as a resolve that there was to be no repetition of what had happened. The identity crisis of the Malays and the Chinese was real and some urgent solutions had to be found to allay the mutual fears and apprehensions. The Malays' fears were epitomised and expressed in the book *The Malay Dilemma*, written by Malaysia's current Prime Minister, Dato Seri Dr Mahathir Mohamad, when he was a relatively junior member of the United Malay National Organisation (UMNO). It was banned for a

while for fear of fanning racial sentiments. That this publication is today freely available only serves to demonstrate the maturity of the population and the establishment of tolerance, understanding, sensitivity and mutual respect for each others' rights. It also partly explains why Malaysia is today economically vibrant, dynamic and progressive. The harmony and success of Malaysia's plural society is viewed with envy by many of the former industrialised nations. It was towards this end that the various NEPs were introduced, that is, as a formula towards correcting the prevailing imbalance in the distribution of wealth. The experimentation is now a proven success.

Kuala Lumpur is today a bustling city of modern high-rise buildings and new construction activity, new condominiums, streets full of cars and tree-lined streets. Green is the predominant colour. The new city image and the increase in wealth has not affected the people who, by and large, have not lost their friendliness and warmth. As a result some of the ills besetting other modern cities do not apply to Kuala Lumpur. It is still a city safe to walk at night. Law and order is the pride of Malaysia; muggings, so commonplace in some cities, is not the norm in Kuala Lumpur. Cleanliness is foremost in the mind of the local authorities. But unlike some other Asian cities which have lost their identity, Kuala Lumpur is still very much intact, due to the efforts of citizens' movements and caring authorities. Notwithstanding the transformation it went through in the 1970s and 1980s Kuala Lumpur is still a very livable and an environmentally friendly city. We are hopeful that with time it will become an even more comfortable and easy to live in city.

ENDNOTES

1 Tome Pires, a 16th century Portuguese visitor, described Melaka as 'a city that was made for merchandise, fitter than any other in the world... Malacca is surrounded and lies in the middle, and the trade and commerce between the different nations for a thousand leagues on every hand must come to Malacca'.

2 The Colony of Singapore included the Christmas Isles and the Cocos-Keeling group of islands in the South Indian Ocean. Melaka included the island of Labuan off the coast of North Borneo, later to be incorporated within the Colony of North Borneo (still later Sabah).

It became another Federal Territory of Malaysia in 1987, Kuala Lumpur being the other Federal Territory.

3 In 1889 there were almost 52 miles (83 kilometres) of good roads from Kuala Lumpur; by 1901 there were over 600 miles (950 kilometres).

4 Other major agencies entrusted with the OPPI included MARA (Majli Amanah Rakyat) and PERNAS (Perbadanan Nasional Berhad).

5 *Urban Development Authority Act (1971)*, Part II, Clause 3 (1).

6 Dr C. C. Too was one of the original residents who bought a property at Kenny Hills. At that time both he and his wife Lum Swee Lan had only recently returned from their studies in Hong Kong. They are both living in Kenny Hills, now renamed Tunku Hills.

7 Tan Sri Mubin Sheppard was the 'Establishment' on matters of Malay culture, art and handicraft.

8 *Memorandum and Articles of Badan Warisan Malaysia.*

9 The *Badan* had eight principal aims and objectives. These were:

a) to promote the permanent preservation for the benefit and education of the people of Malaysia of all buildings which because of their historical associations of architectural features or for other reasons are considered by the Council of the *Badan* to form part of the Heritage of Malaysia;

b) to buy take or otherwise acquire buildings or land or any estate or interest therein;

c) to repair, renovate, restore, rebuild and generally to maintain, and develop any designated buildings or land;

d) with the provision of suitable safeguards to sell, let on lease or tendency, exchange, mortgage or otherwise dispose of buildings or land or any estate or interest therein;

e) to provide furnish and fit out with all necessary furniture, equipment and other fittings and to maintain manage such buildings and other premises as may from time to time be required for the purposes of carrying out the objects of the *Badan*;

f) to make such arrangements to enable the public to view and enjoy any buildings;

g) to obtain publicity and to advertise in order to make its objects and activities known;

h) by publishing books or pamphlets or in any other appropriate manner to make known to the public

the existence of buildings of particular beauty or historical, architectural or constructional interest.

10 The *Sahabat* had six main aims and objectives:

a) to encourage, support and assist the Heritage of Malaysia Trust;

b) to increase public interest in the Heritage of Malaysia;

c) to encourage and to provide facilities for organised visits of young people to old buildings which have been designated as part of the Heritage of Malaysia;

d) to receive donations and subscriptions from persons desiring to support this Society;

e) to assist the Council of the Heritage of Malaysia Trust in raising funds, such as printing, publishing and circulating pamphlets, leaflets or pictures, or selling membership badges;

f) to assemble information about buildings which may form part of the Heritage of Malaysia, and to transmit this information to the Council of the Trust.

Constitution of Persatuan Sahabat-Sahabat Warisan Malaysia, 27 February 1991.

11 Outside the capital, the *Badan* also had some notable early successes such as the *Gedung Raja Abdullah*, the storehouse and residence of the first Malay tin-mining pioneer, in Klang. This building had been occupied by the police since 1903 but was on the verge of demolition to make way for two badminton courts before being saved and converted into Malaysia's first tin mining museum. It is now a Klang landmark. The *Istana Tengku Long*, in Kampong Raja, Besut, Trengganu, was also saved from destruction through a major *Badan* project with funding raised from Malaysia's petroleum company, Petronas. A long abandoned Malay palace built entirely of timber, the entire building was dismantled and re-erected in the compound of the Trengganu State Museum.

APPENDIX A: PERIODS OF MAJOR GROWTH OF KUALA LUMPUR

Immediate post-independence: 1957-1971

Person influencing the growth: YTM Tunku Abdul Rahman (Prime Minister)

	Public and institutional buildings	Year
1	Merdeka Stadium	1957
2	Government Office, Petaling Jaya	1958
3	University of Malaya (Campus)	1959
4	Maternity Hospital	1960
5	EPU Office	1960
6	Stadium Negara	1962
7	Parliament House	1963
8	National Museum	1963
9	Subang Jaya Master plan	1963
10	AIA Building	1964
11	Chartered Bank	1964
12	Subang International Airport	1965
13	National Mosque	1965
14	Colgate Palmolive	1965
15	General Hospital	1966
16	Setapak Church	1967
17	Prime Minister's Office	1967
18	University Teaching Hospital	
19	UMNO Building	
20	Geology Building of Malaysia	1968
21	National Blood Centre, Kuala Lumpur	1970
22	Bank Negara	1970
23	Wisma Demansara	1970
24	New Faculty of Arts Building	1971

	Residential buidings	Year
1	Sulaiman Court Housing	1958
2	Kington Loo's House	1959
3	Brunei House	1960
4	Award Winning House (BEP)	1961
5	Dr A.F.H. Acria's House (Penang)	1963
6	Subang Jaya Master Plan	1963
7	Syed Nahas Sahabuddin's (K.L.)	1964

	Residential buidings	Year
8	Link House in Taman Seputeh	1968
9	Lim Kean Siew (Penang)	1968
10	Drs Yu & Chin (K.L.)	1968
11	The Hexagons (K.L.)	1971

Transitional and boom period: 1972-83

Person influencing the growth: Tan Sri Yaacob Latiff (Second Lord Mayor of K.L.)

	Public and institutional buildings	Year
1	Dewan Tunku Counselor (UM)	1972
2	K.L. Hilton Hotel	1972
3	Ampang Park	1973
4	Ming Building	1974
5	Hong Leong Building	1975
6	Madrasah Islamiah	1976
7	Australian Chancery (K.L.)	1978
8	Bangunan Dato Zainal (K.L.)	1978
9	Wisma Lee Rubber	1980
10	Bumiputra Bank Building	1980
11	Wilayah Complex	1982
12	Bangsar Mosque	1982
13	Public Bank	1978
14	Wisma Central	1973
15	Equatorial Hotel	1973

	Residential buildings	Year
1	Doshi's House (K.L.)	1973
2	Madam Lim Tet Kin (K.L.)	1975
3	Cheras Low Cost Link Housing	1976
4	Timber House	1977
5	House for T.Y. Chiew	1980
6	Ibrahim Hussain's House	1982
7	Desa Kudalari Condominium	1983
8	Link House at Damansara Heights (K.L.)	1983

Between boom and condminium perid: 1983-92

Person influencing the growth: Tan Sri Datuk Elyas Omar (Third Lord Mayor of K.L.)

Public and institutional buildings	Year
1 General Post Office	1984
2 Dayabumi	1984
3 Restoration of Bangunan Sultan Abdul Samad	1984
4 United Asian Bank	1985
5 Plaza Atrium (K.L.)	1985
6 UBN Tower	1985
7 Apera ULG	1985
8 Kompleks Pusat Islam (K.L.)	1985
9 Bangunan LTAT	1985
10 PWTC	1985
11 MAS Headquarters	1986
12 LUTH Complex	1986
13 Railway Extension	1986
14 Komplex Nagaria	1986
15 Off-Course Betting Complex	1986
16 Wisma Genting	1986
17 Maybank Towers	1987
18 MCB Plaza	1987
19 Central Market	1987
20 Lot 10	1990
21 Merdeka Square	1990
22 New Telecom Building	1990

Residential buildings	Year
1 Desa Kudalari	1983
2 Roof-Roof House	1984
3 Madam Quek's House	1984
4 Ng Lu Pat's House	1984
5 Walian House	1984
6 Jalan Perumanan Gurney	1984
7 M. House (P.J.)	1985
8 Downtown Condo	1985
9 Z House	1986
10 Pangsa Murni Housing (Wangsa Maju)	1986
11 TTDI Bungalows	1986
12 Desa Damansara	1987

REFERENCES

Federal Town Planning Department 1950, Kuala Lumpur in 1895, FTDP, Kuala Lumpur.

Hall, Kenneth R. 1985, 'The opening of the Malay world to European trade in the sixteenth century', *Journal of the Malaysian Branch of the Royal Asiatic Society*, Vol. 58, pp. 85-106.

Mahathir bin Mohamad 1970, The Malay Dilemma, D. Moore for Asia Pacific Press, Singapore.

PAM (Malaysian Institute of Architects) 1976, A Guide to Kuala Lumpur Notable Buildings, PAM, Kuala Lumpur.

PAM (Malaysian Institute of Architects) 1990, *1890-1990: 100 Years of Kuala Lumpur Architecture*, PAM, Kuala Lumpur.

Second Malaysia Plan, 1971-1975 1971, Government Printers, Kuala Lumpur.

Lim, Jimmy C.S. 1991(a), 'Of condominiums and mushrooms', *Berita Akitek*, No. 1, January 1991, p. 1.

Lim, Jimmy C.S. 1991(b), 'When snails travel faster than cars in K.L.', *Berita Akitek*, No. 2, February 1991, pp. 1 and 3.

10 Conservation of cultural settings: the case of Yogyakarta's inner city *kampung*

◆

Haryadi

Yogyakarta is a small city located in the middle of the island of Java. Historically, it was situated at the heart of an ancient region known as Mataram, the site of the first central Javanese empires (UNCRD 1989), and later it became the centre of the Yogyakarta Sultanate, founded by the Sultan of Mangkubumi in 1755. The centre of this city is the Kraton, the residence of the Sultan and his close relatives and from which he governed the kingdom (Figure 10.1). It is surrounded by a thick wall with several gates in it. This wall acted as a defensive mechanism to protect the Sultan from enemy attack. After independence from the Dutch in 1945, the city became the capital of Yogyakarta Province, which is co-terminous with the old Yogyakarta Sultanate. This province is now one of the twenty-seven provinces in the Republic of Indonesia.

During the eighth and ninth centuries, Indian-influenced rulers governed this kingdom. At that time, Hinduism and Buddhism dominated the religious activities and lifestyles of the people, and temples such as Borobudur, Prambanan, Kalasan and thousands of others were the foci of religious ceremonies. In the ninth century, the capital of the kingdom moved to east Java. There were no major activities in the Mataram area until the end of the sixteenth century when Islamic power began to emerge. The activities of the followers of Islam were based at Kotagede, an old city situated to the south-east of present day Yogyakarta. This second Mataram revival was initiated by Panembahan Senopati in 1584.

Mataram achieved its greatest territorial extent under Senopati's grandson, Sultan Agung. In 1765, increasing social, cultural and economic activities resulted in rapid physical development within and outside the Kraton compound. A north-south axis was laid out, named *Kraton-Palputih* (the Kraton to White Statue axis). This axis, known today as Malioboro and Mangkubumi Streets, was designed to integrate the Kraton with its surroundings, especially the northern part of the city.

In 1790, the Vredeburg Fort was built next to this axis, in front of the Kraton. The construction of this fort indicates the beginning of Dutch military domination in this area. It marks also the beginning of Western influence. The Governor's residence, bank, post office, church and meeting hall were built along the axis not far from the fort. These facilities served the Dutch people who lived in this area. The cultural diversity in this area was enriched by the multiplication of Chinese shop-houses, also along the axis. The Chinese served as intermediaries between the Dutch and the indigenous Javanese, especially in trading activities.

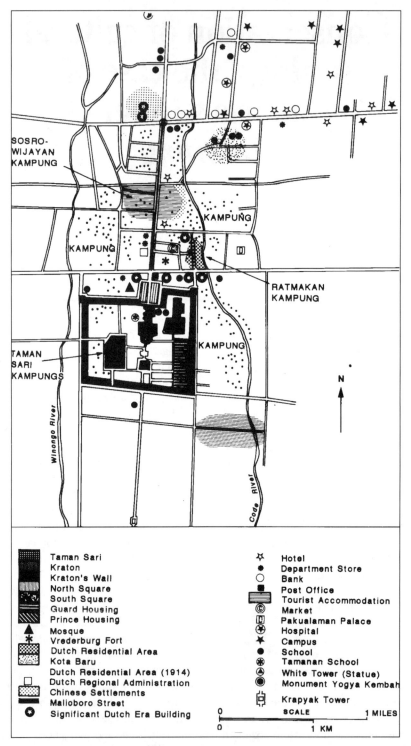

Figure 10.1   Yogyakarta's inner city and its images

The Javanese lived behind the Dutch and Chinese buildings and in the area surrounding the Kraton. Usually, their residences consisted of temporary structures made from bamboo and arranged haphazardly into a compound. Similar structures could be found in the rural villages. Such was the embryo of the *kampung*. For their daily necessities, the Sultan built a large market for them, named Beringharjo. Traditional markets such as this can be found in every Javanese city and provide one of their strongest townscape images.

During the last years of the Dutch colonial period, Yogyakarta played a key role as the capital of self-proclaimed Republic of Indonesia and, under the first president, Sukarno, the Indonesian people's struggle for independence from the Dutch was organised from this city. At that time, Suharto (the second and present president) was a deputy to the Commander-in-Chief of the Indonesian military forces. During the fight against the Dutch, he and his troops engaged in the guerrilla warfare around Yogyakarta.

MODERNISATION PRESSURES IN YOGYAKARTA

Nowadays, as the result of economic development programs, rapid physical development is occurring in Yogyakarta. Many new physical structures are being constructed which are huge in scale and, taking place in its inner city, are resulting in the destruction of the old city fabric. This old fabric makes up the

Figure 10.3   Major mosque in front of the Kraton. A group of Kraton employees bring traditional symbols to the mosque precinct during the gunungan *ceremony. A syncretic process between traditional and Islamic influences still appears to occur in this area. (Source: Haryadi).*

cultural settings of Yogyakarta, having existed there for centuries and providing the most significant visual images of the city (Figure 10.1). Examples of these images are the Kraton with its traditional timber architecture (Figure 10.2), Alun-alun (the Square), Masjid Agung or Grand Mosque (Figure 10.3), the Dutch buildings, Vredeburg (the Dutch fort), Gereja Ngupasan (the Old Church), the Malioboro shopping street, the Chinese shop-houses, Pasar Beringharjo (the bazaar or Beringharjo Market) and the *kampung* (traditional settlements) at the back of and surrounding these buildings.

Of these images, the *kampung* seems to be the most vulnerable in the struggle to cope with the pressures of modern development in Yogyakarta and, for this reason, is the focus of this chapter. Many *kampung* are being destroyed directly or indirectly following the process of physical development. Since land is scarce in Yogyakarta's inner city, physical development must take place in the already built-up areas. Many of the houses in the *kampung* are still temporary structures with most of the residents being low-income people. Hence, compared to other townscape images, this is the easiest to remove. Even where *kampung* are not actually removed, they remain in poor physical condition.

The activities of the *kampung* residents are connected to the outside settings such as Pasar

Figure 10.2   Traditional Javanese ceiling found around Yogyakarta. Architects nationally and internationally have been inspired to design buildings with this type of ceiling (e.g. Jakarta International Airport). (Source: Haryadi).

Beringharjo, the sidewalks along shopping streets, and other working places (Haryadi 1989). These places are now undergoing improvement programs. However, it is shown that these programs are planned for the middle class rather than *kampung* people. Eventually, these programs will cut the link between residents' activities in the *kampung* and their traditional working-place activities. As a result, the *kampung* will become isolated from the rest of the inner city which is now being transformed into environments for higher income people.

APPROACHES TO *KAMPUNG* CONSERVATION

There are two common approaches to conservation: socio-cultural and physical. Some observers argue that these are two distinct approaches that cannot be combined, while others say that they are, in fact, closely interrelated. From the latter point of view, the conservation of the socio-cultural aspects of an environment will be reflected automatically in the conservation of its associated physical settings. The discussion in this chapter will be based on this second interpretation. An effort will be made to identify the social and cultural components of Yogyakarta's inner city *kampung* settings that directly relate to the physical or spatial components. Rapoport's (1977) theoretical framework on culture will be used to explain this relationship.

Reading Rapoport's diagram (Figure 10.4) from left to right, it is seen that cultural background determines people's activity systems. In addition, the system of activities directly relates to the system of settings, that is, the physical and spatial components of

culture. By knowing the *kampung* residents' systems of activities, the corresponding systems of settings can be identified. Systems of settings include not only settings in the *kampung* but also those outside settings commonly used by the *kampung* residents when conducting their activities. Based on the Rapoport framework, it can be argued that, since the system of physical settings directly relates to the system of social and economic activities, the conservation of systems of settings must be based on the conservation of *kampung* residents' systems of activities.

SOME CHARACTERISTICS OF THE *KAMPUNG*

In his examination of the common patterns of Southeast Asian cities, McGee (1967) pictures the city in Southeast Asia as a mosaic of ethnic quarters, each with its own specific characteristics. These ethnic quarters were the very dense Chinese shop-house areas (usually in a city's centre), the spacious low-density compound of the Europeans, and the rural-like settlements of the indigenous population scattered around the periphery of the city. McGee argues that rapid population growth and the emergence of a middle class contributed to the rapid growth of cities in Southeast Asia. The rapid growth of population caused by migration from the villages resulted in the proliferation of squatter settlements in the city, while the emergence of the middle class has led to the growth of Western-style suburbs.

The growth of cities encroaches upon the rural-like settlement on the city periphery and subsumes these areas into the city system. In the case of Indonesia, these areas become *kampung* settlement within

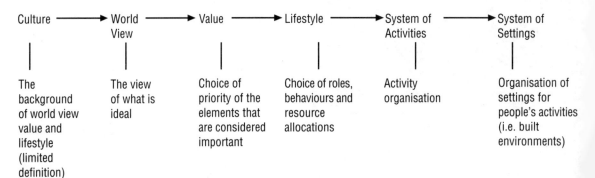

Figure 10.4 Relations between culture, behaviour, system of activities and system of settings (Based on Rapoport 1977).

Figure 10.5   Location, types and development stages of a kampung *(Source: Atman 1975, Williams 1975, Haryadi 1989)*

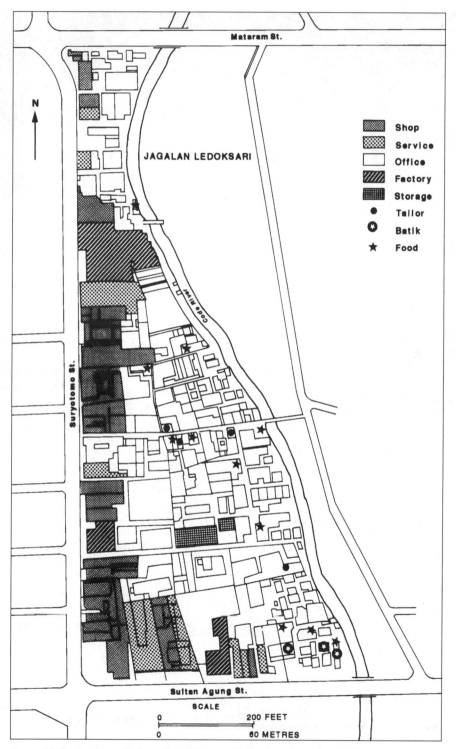

Figure 10.6   The form of a kampung (Kampung Ratmakan, Yogyakarta) (Source: Haryadi 1989)

the city boundaries, still maintaining their rural-like settlement patterns characterised by a low density of houses, homogeneity of the residents, and different types of vegetation. However, over time, the *kampung* undergo changes in the density of houses and the heterogeneity of their residents (Geertz 1965). The highest density of houses with the most heterogeneous residents are usually found in the urban *kampung* close to the inner city. These can be characterised as less organically integrated into the city system than other urban residential areas. Geertz mentions that many of the houses still existing in most urban *kampung* today are small bamboo or combination brick-and-bamboo structures placed haphazardly in crowded profusion, with very little space between them except around a few of the more solid stone houses.

Atman (1975) identifies four types of *kampung* according to the development processes transforming them. These are:

1 the rural *kampung* or rural settlement on the city's periphery where the rural way of life prevails over the influences of city culture;

2 the semi-rural *kampung*, which is a rural *kampung* that is progressively incorporating many urban elements within it;

3 the semi-urban *kampung*, which is a non-urban environment that has suffered the destruction of its former rural characteristics because of urban infiltration; and

4 the urban *kampung*, which is a fully urbanised area, incorporating some city services and features characteristic of the city.

The transformation from rural-like settlement into urban *kampung* also involves a process of transformation from village dwellers into urban *kampung* dwellers. Geertz (1965) indicates that this transformation is followed by a change in the occupational structure from agricultural to non-agricultural work, usually creating a bazaar-type economy based on *pasar* or peddling activities.

Figure 10.5 shows these four types and the development stages of *kampung* according to Atman (1975) as modified by Williams (1975) and Haryadi (1989). Sullivan (1980), on the other hand, distinguishes three types of urban residential areas in Indonesian cities. The first type is the well-planned, well-serviced and

Figure 10.7 Shady paths in the kampung *attract a variety of activities. Motorcyclists must stop their engines before entering this* kampung *from the busy external streets. This avoids noise and air pollution in the* kampung, *a condition rarely found in today's public housing. (Source: Haryadi).*

equipped, upper-income district in which every house along a road can be reached by car. About 10 per cent of Indonesian city families live in houses of this type. The second type is an old form found throughout urban Indonesia and contains a majority of urban residents. Kampung Ratmakan in Yogyakarta, shown in Figure 10.6, is a good example of this type. Sullivan (1980, pp.2-3) describes its form as follows:

lines of permanent houses and commercial buildings arrayed along main thoroughfares, behind which, in

Figure 10.8 Children in the kampung *interact easily as there is no physical and social boundary between houses and families in the* kampung. *Paths, house fronts, public baths and open spaces are settings for this interaction. (Source: Haryadi).*

spaces defined by the main building lines, are mazes of alleyways and closely-packed dwellings whose quality varies from 'permanent', through 'semi-permanent' to decidedly 'temporary'.

A contrast with the first type, the houses inside this area cannot be reached by car or any other means of transport wider than the average human being. Even riding a bicycle is prohibited, except for the postal workers who have to deliver hundreds of letters as quickly as possible (Figure 10.7 and 10.8).

Finally, the third type comprises squatter settlements without any general planning and located on the most marginal, unattractive and usually government-owned land. Usually this third type is referred to as illegal *kampung* (*kampung liar*) whereas the second type is legal.

CULTURAL ECONOMIC ACTIVITIES IN THE *KAMPUNG*

McGee (1967) characterises the economic structure of Southeast Asian cities as a mixture of Western capitalism, represented by banks and trading firms, and semi-capitalistic and preindustrial forms of economic organisation such as the Chinese loan associations and the indigenous populations' mobile street markets. Geertz (1965 as cited by McGee 1967) labels the latter a bazaar economy and defines it as a type of economic activity in which the total flow of commerce is fragmented into a great number of unrelated person-to-person transactions. The bazaar economy provides employment opportunities for vast numbers of people at a marginal or near marginal level of living. The central institution of this economy is the *pasar* (market), described by Geertz (p.30) as follows:

> the market place is the climax of this pattern (i.e. pattern of small scale processing and peddling activities), its focus and centre, but it is not the whole region, thinning out somewhat only in the most rural of villages.

Geertz (p.46) argues that the *pasar* is the place where commercial ties are carefully insulated from general social ties. Friendship, neighbourliness and even kinship are one thing; trade is another. The market is an institutional structure in the Javanese society where the formalism, status consciousness, and introversion so characteristic of the culture are relatively weak. Bargaining, credit balance and trade coalitions all respond quite directly and explicitly to the narrow concerns of material advantage.

However this does not mean that the bazaar economy is not related to culture at all. The bazaar economy includes economic activities that are based on the people's cultural background, that is, the lifestyles of a certain group of people. These activities persist for a long time and changes very slowly. From the villages, farmers bring vegetables, chickens, eggs, fruits and other rural products to the city and sell this merchandise in the *pasar* where the interpersonal communication is not markedly different from that which they find in the village. This can happen because many sellers and workers are also coming from the village. There are no lifestyle differences between them. In other words, the *pasar* is a cultural defence mechanism in the city for those who have rural backgrounds. On the one hand, this place becomes a buffer for them to cope with the pressure of city life while, on the other hand, it can help them to learn the city life.

Many *kampung* residents, most of whom are migrants and circulators (mobile rural people who travel back and forth between their villages and the city), are involved in this type of bazaar economy, whether they operate inside or outside the *pasar*. Baross (1984) argues that, although a kampung is usually considered primarily as a human settlement, more importantly it is a human workplace or economic system. For many residents in the *kampung*, the first priority in the use of this place is for work activities and only then for dwelling. Examples of these activities are:

1 food and domestic activities, which include trading food, cooking, raising chickens and fish, washing and ironing;
2 housing activities, such as room renting and house repairing;
3 home industry, with *batik* painting, knitting, and sewing as examples;
4 caring activities, such as caring for and feeding of babies;
5 inside and outside *kampung* activities, such as scavenging and hawking;
6 working in people's houses as helpers or gardeners;

7 informal manufacturing, such as the making of chips, soft drinks, cookware, *sate*-sticks and sandals; and

8 other activities that include borrowing money and *arisan* (collection of money from the members of a group, usually every month, and each member has a chance to receive the money).

These activities are now standardly categorised as 'informal economic activities'.

DEVELOPMENT: A SOURCE OF DISTURBANCE FOR *KAMPUNG* ACTIVITY AND SETTING

Kampung residents' activities consist of daily, weekly, monthly, yearly and intermittent activities that are interrelated into a system of activities. These activities occur in different settings and at different times, involving a number of people, objects, rules and norms associated with these activities and settings. Like the activities, these settings are considered to be organised into a system, since one cannot understand what happens in any particular setting unless one also knows what happens in others (Rapoport 1986). This means that what happens in one setting will influence what will happen in others.

The investigation of activities and settings should be within the context of the system. In other words, the investigation must look at the linkages between activity systems and the linkages of settings in which these activities occur. As an example, the need for preparing breakfast for customers in the *warung* (food stall: a setting) forces the *warung* owner to buy materials at night in the retail area of a *pasar* (market: a setting) and cook food in the kitchen (a setting) at home early in the morning. These settings are parts of places of different scales. The linkages between settings reflect the house-settlement systems of *kampung* residents that accommodate their activities. As is shown, the systems incorporate settings outside the *kampung's* boundary such as the *pasar* and *warung* along the main street.

The disturbance to these activities and settings occurs when development disrupts the systems of activities and their corresponding systems of settings. A hypothetical example is the renovation of the *pasar* in the inner city. As noted, a *pasar* is a traditional setting where activities of many *kampung* residents take place. People work and find inexpensive goods there. It is a setting where people from the villages surrounding Yogyakarta and the *kampung* residents surrounding the inner city engage in small retail activities. Because of its lucrative location, many investors are competing for opportunities in this place.

In this example, an investor manages to win a commission from the local government to develop the *pasar*. The objective is to improve the *pasar's* physical condition so that a better and healthier environment can be created. However, many criticisms are raised with regard to the way the investment has been arranged. A large amount of money is needed for the renovation of this *pasar*. The local government has to repay the money plus interest to the investor. According to the plan, the repayment funds will come from the rent of space in the *pasar*. It is predicted that the rent for retail space will be so high that the traditional *pasar* users, consisting mainly of low-income retailers including *kampung* residents, will not be able to afford it. Sooner or later, they will be replaced by higher income retailers.

If this happens, a critical part of the *kampung* residents' system of settings and an important place for their particular activities will have been removed from the system. As this is typical of other development activities in this area in their neglect of the *kampung's* system of settings, it can be predicted that eventually the whole system will be destroyed. The destruction of the system will eventually lead to major disruption of the *kampung* which will find itself isolated from the inner-city system, its roots pulled out. As a result, it will be easily removed from the inner city and replaced by the big enterprises, as, indeed, has been occurring in the Kuningan 'Golden Triangle' in Jakarta. Tall buildings in the international style will replace the local settlements.

Since the *kampung* provides one of the key cultural images in the Yogyakarta inner city, the loss of this type of environment will be extremely serious from the point of view of the cultural heritage. This raises the issue of how to effectively conserve the heritage of the *kampung* area, how to respond to the rapid urban development that is threatening the ambience of this unique environment.

CONSERVATION: A DEVELOPMENT APPROACH USING THE CONCEPT OF 'CONTINUITY OF CHANGE'

Development can be defined as the process of change towards modernisation. However, many people argue that the process will bring severe problems if rapid and uncontrolled development occurs. For many city residents, the rapid pace of development is a stressful experience rather than an improvement in their quality of life. Rapoport (1983) argues that many development programs in the developing nations are of this kind. Modernisation is occurring so fast that people find it difficult to comprehend the meaning of development. Worse than this, their traditional social structures are disturbed badly, resulting in the emergence of deviant forms of behaviour. To avoid such negative impacts, Rapoport also argues that development is a culture change and that its pace should be moderated to accommodate the gradual change of people's social structures. To achieve this goal, striking a balance between development (change) and conservation (continuity) should be considered as a sensible approach in urban policy-making. Hence, there is an urgent need to identify which cultural components persist (or change very slowly) and which others are changing rapidly. This leads to the notions of the 'core' and 'periphery' of a culture. The core persists or changes very slowly, while the periphery changes fast.

Conservation of the core is seen as the key to achieving a continuity of culture and to avoiding social and cultural breakdown, whereas processes of change of the culture's peripheral components may be allowed. The critical identification of these two components should be based on methods of historic observation. Several *kampung* consisting of old ones at one end of the scale and the new ones at the other should be selected purposefully. The next step is to identify the characteristics of each *kampung* and to arrange these characteristics in an order based on their age. From this, one should be able to identify which characteristics persist or change slowly and which others change rapidly.

CONSERVATION OF CULTURAL ACTIVITIES

Usually conservation has a physical connotation.

Conservation of buildings, old artefacts, traditional villages and old cities are typical foci of attention. While such work is unquestionably important, consideration should also be given to the conservation of non-physical components because, whether the concern is the environment or culture, physical components (objects, space, boundaries) and non-physical components (people, activities, time) always co-exist. Dealing with one component without including the other is incomplete. As discussed in the preceding text, one then could argue that conserving a system of activities will lead to the conservation of a system of settings. In terms of *kampung* residents, conservation of their activity systems must go hand in hand with the identification and conservation of settings in order to allow those activities to continue.

Systems of activities are culturally determined. Rapoport (1986) mentions that people with different cultural backgrounds have different systems of activities. For example, a farmer's system of activities will be different from that of a city dweller. Systems of activities, being part of the cultural characteristics of people, have a direct bearing on the spatial aspects, that is, the systems of settings. In the inner city, planners tend to make adjustments to the land-use patterns for economic reasons and often the presence of *kampung* becomes an obstacle for them. Conventional planning approaches generally propose *kampung* improvement, clearance, population resettlement or other types of action to eliminate this obstacle, although, in some cases, the *kampung* have often been overlooked and totally neglected in the planning process. Even in the latter circumstances, the *kampung* may still experience many disadvantages since settings located outside the *kampung* but connected to *kampung* residents' system of settings are gradually transformed into facilities for other groups of people. The range of *kampung* activities thus becomes increasingly narrow.

By conserving the system of activities, this trend may be slowed down or stopped entirely. If this can be realised, the stability of the *kampung* as residential areas will be possible. This will allow for the formulation of urban design in the inner cities that emphasises the settings for people and not just 'urban beautification' or providing attractive environments for the investors.

THE GOLDEN TRIANGLE OF YOGYAKARTA'S INNER CITY

In this era of speculative urban development, the word 'triangle' is widely used by Indonesian developers as a gimmick to attract people to buy or rent properties in a particular area. Jakarta has the Senen Triangle, a huge commercial and accommodation complex that replaced old Chinese shop-houses, and the Kuningan Golden Triangle, a large international office and hotel precinct consisting of high-rise buildings. Like the first, the Kuningan Triangle replaced a large residential neighbourhood which included many *kampung*. Whether it is a triangle, square or other marketing label, the resulting phenomenon is similar: the local people are removed and big business moves in bringing an international ambience with it.

This phenomenon is not only happening in Indonesia's capital city, but also in many other smaller cities around the country. If the trend continues in this way, it is unlikely that the cultural diversity of cities can be maintained. The city of Yogyakarta faces similar problems. The facilities of big businesses are rapidly encroaching upon the land of the *kampung* surrounding the inner city. The presence of old *kampung* as one of Yogyakarta's key townscape images becomes less obvious following the construction of new buildings on former *kampung* land.

Surrounding the Yogyakarta inner city there is a variety of *kampung* which can be roughly classified into three groups. The first group comprises *kampung* where many of the residents' informal economic activities are connected to the Beringharjo Market. Migrants and circulators particularly engage in these activities. Kampung Ratmakan is representative of this category. The second group consists of *kampung* that are being influenced by tourism development in their vicinity. The strong market for low-cost accommodation and the need for inexpensive food provide opportunities for the *kampung* residents to participate in tourism-related business. Kampung Sosrówijayan is an example of such a *kampung*. Finally there are *kampung* situated on the sites of historical sites. Because of the processes of physical deterioration, the monuments were abandoned and the vacant land surrounding them has been gradually transformed into a new *kampung*. Kampung Tamansari is perhaps the clearest example in this category.

Kampung Ratmakan

Kampung Ratmakan is located within a distance of about a 5-minute walk from Beringharjo Market. This short walking distance attracts people who work in the market to stay there although the danger of flooding from the nearby river is problematic. People come from rural areas in groups of ten to forty people, some of them from remote places, to work as labourers or peddlers in the inner city. In Ratmakan, they live in the houses owned by the *kampung* residents. This is a transitory place for them and they go back to the village when the planting or harvesting seasons come.

Kampung Ratmakan is an urban *kampung* located in the inner city of Yogyakarta. The population density is almost 18 000 people per square kilometre (46 620 per square mile). This is higher than the rate of population in Yogyakarta, which is about 12 000 per square kilometre (31 080 per square mile). Historically, Ratmakan used to be the site of a Javanese cemetery but it was inhabited by the servants of the Sultan of Yogyakarta around the year 1800. Over the course of its development, the Ratmakan population became a mixture of different groups of people, including artisans who worked as the rifle-repairers for the Dutch soldiers living in and around a Dutch fort located near the *kampung*. But gradually, the Dutch settlements encroached upon the *kampung* area, especially along its main streets. A number of Chinese merchants were also living in this area, as well as a few wealthy Javanese people. At the rear of the buildings along these main streets were houses belonging to the indigenous Javanese, as shown in Figure 10.6.

The variety of ethnic groups who used to live or still live in the *kampung* is reflected in the range of house types in Ratmakan. Among them are Dutch houses that have been influenced by the local culture and climate and incorporate *pendapa* (verandas or the front part of the house) showing the influence of Javanese architecture. There are also Chinese houses of the shop-house type characterised by inner courtyards. Inside this *kampung*, many old traditional Javanese houses are also found, indicating the presence of wealthy Javanese in this place in earlier days. These houses stand on large lots and have complete sets of traditional housing components such as *pendapa, dalem* (the main building at the back of the *pendapa*) and *gandok* (two rows of long buildings located to the left and right sides of the *dalem*).

Even in this narrow area, there are social differences among the indigenes, those who live along the main path in this *kampung* usually having higher social status than the average resident living to the back of them. Many of those who live in the main path are the descendants of Javanese merchants who came many years ago from Kotagede, the old traditional city situated to the south-east of Yogyakarta. These merchants looked for a place that was close to the Beringharjo Market in order to have convenient access for their trading activities. As they sold rice and sugar in a large quantity, this location was more vital to them than for the others who sold food or became labourers in the market for smaller amounts of money. Because of their high economic status, their houses are bigger and several lots are very large in size. Nowadays, their descendants have different occupations and work as University lecturers, teachers and government employees or have private means.

The social differences between the Javanese who live along the main path and those who live at the back of them also exist in other *kampung*. In his dissertation, Guinness (1985) identifies a similar phenomenon in another *kampung* in Yogyakarta, named Jogoyudan. He claims that people who live behind the big establishments along the main street look down on those who live along the edge of the Code River banks. Indeed they believe that the people who live along the river banks do not belong to their community, considering them people with the deviant forms of behaviour associated with criminal activities. With this label, it is difficult for them to develop good relations with other *kampung* residents.

During a participatory planning exercise in Kampung Ratmakan, the local government made an effort to reduce this social gap by introducing physical improvements into the area. In Ratmakan, the construction of river embankments and sidewalks along these embankments stimulated an improvement in the condition of houses in the river bank area. Apparently, this was due to the sense of security that grew following the development project.

Unlike the merchant descendants who live along

the main path of the *kampung*, many other residents and migrants are still working actively in the market and the surrounding areas. This indicates the dominance of the market and its surroundings as settings for the daily activities of many *kampung* residents. From time to time, the people who engage in such business may change but the interrelated system between *kampung* and market with its associated work settings always persists, showing clearly the importance of conserving the linkage. However, as noted, Ratmakan is facing problems as a result of the rapid development which is now occurring in the Beringharjo Market and its surroundings. Evidently such development does not consider the linkage that has been established between Beringharjo market and the surrounding *kampung* to be important. The development is not locally oriented, but rather neglects the *kampung*.

Kampung Sosrowijayan

Sosrowijayan is a *kampung* experiencing the impact of tourism development in the inner city. The needs of tourists for low-cost accommodation and inexpensive food and souvenirs provide opportunities for the *kampung* residents to convert their houses into accommodation facilities, restaurants and art shops. This *kampung* is located in the inner city near the Malioboro main street. It is also very close to Yogyakarta's main train station.

Like Ratmakan, its population density is very high. Many of the houses are temporary structures and

Figure 10.9   Malioboro, Yogyakarta's commercial axis and major tourist precinct. Market stalls line the building arcades the entire length of one side of the street. (Source: W.S. Logan)

Figure 10.10   Colonial Dutch influences mix with modern in Malioboro. (Source: W.S. Logan)

located at the rear of the large enterprises along Malioboro Street (Figure 10.9 and 10.10). The *kampung* is attracting foreign tourists, many of them backpacker tourists who come to Yogyakarta by train. Their presence is changing the ambience of this neighbourhood which used to be dominated by prostitution activities. It is changing into a more lively place, in the visual sense at least. People are beginning to decorate their restaurants using Western images, such as flags from foreign countries, large photos of cowboys and their horses, the wheels of carriages and replica guns. Several restaurants now provide space for Western dancing. Even the names of restaurants are not local, the most famous one being the Old Superman restaurant.

Foreign tourist interest in this *kampung* started about a decade ago when tourism became one of the main business activities in Yogyakarta. Malioboro Street is the main tourist destination in Yogyakarta, its 24-hour activities creating a unique atmosphere. Formal and informal economic activities mix together here. Beside the big businesses, there are peddlers, hawkers, vendors as well as musicians, storytellers, magicians and *lesehan* (eating places) where people sit on the sidewalk in front of the shops. The *lesehan* usually start operating at night when the shops are beginning to close.

These vibrant activities are stimulating the development of tourism facilities in the area at the back of Malioboro shopping street. Tourists like to stay in this place because of its proximity to Malioboro and the many other attractive places in the inner city as well as the abundant tourist facilities such as public

transport, travel agents and telecommunication facilities. In addition, the accommodation in Sosrowijayan is very cheap, mostly rooms in *kampung* dwellings which have been converted into simple lodging houses. The cost for renting such a room is about $US3 for one night. Eating is inexpensive too. Since most of the guests are foreign tourists, the restaurants serve mainly Western food such as hamburgers, pizzas and steaks, together with a variety of refreshments including beer, wine and soft drinks.

Many *kampung* residents believe that these tourism activities have the negative impact of encouraging deviant behaviour among some of their members. However, on balance, they think that Sosrowijayan is undergoing a beneficial transformation process resulting in a better environment than when poverty and prostitution dominated the *kampung*. In those days, houses for *kampung* residents mixed with the red-light facilities and it was very hard for parents to keep their children from negative influences. Even though the practice still continues there, at this moment, the current number of prostitutes has decreased sharply and the practice is now restricted to only a few houses in the *kampung*.

As with Ratmakan, this *kampung* is not free from the pressure of large enterprises, especially hotel developers. Rich people are competing to buy land in this area and build cottages for tourist accommodation. In several areas, the *kampung* morphology characterised by the maze of alleyways and closely packed dwellings is transformed into islands of buildings separated from their surroundings by high walls. If this trend continues, it is likely that the *kampung*'s traditional characteristics will soon disappear. In addition, many small-scale shop-houses along the Malioboro Street are being replaced by department stores, plazas and big businesses needing large amounts of space. The only available space is located at the back, in the *kampung*.

Kampung Tamansari

Tamansari is the name of a water castle, located in the western part of the Sultan's palace. Formerly, this castle was used by the Sultan for a retreat and there were facilities for contemplation, religious and recreational activities (Figures 10.11 and 10.12). Because of a severe earthquake that destroyed the main building and triggered off the deterioration process, the old buildings which used to be parts of the Sultan's palace were abandoned and have remained with no clear prospects of rehabilitation. The vacant land surrounding the ruins was gradually occupied by newcomers, some of them are migrants from the villages. Many houses were built on this site resulting in the emergence of a *kampung* surrounding the old ruins (Figure 10.13).

Compared to the two *kampung* previously described, Tamansari seems to enjoy more protection from the outside pressures. As the *kampung* is located in the Kraton compound, the Sultan must be consulted before any plan can be implemented and this makes it more difficult for outsiders to establish certain new activities here. In 1989, Tamansari was chosen as one of the cultural conservation districts

Figure 10.12   The central pools of the Tamansari complex, now unused and in need of restoration. (Source: W.S. Logan)

under a decree of the Governor of the Special Province of Yogyakarta. Under this decree, people in the *kampung* are asked to protect its architectural heritage and may seek the support of the provincial government to do so.

Both environments - the monument and the *kampung* - are attractive cultural settings, especially the latter. Many *kampung* residents are batik painters, working on the porches in front of the houses, drying the batiks along the alleyways and hanging the paintings on the walls of their houses. In addition, people also engage in other forms of cultural production, including arts and handicrafts. They teach *gamelan* orchestra, classical dance, *keroncong* music, Javanese song and *kethoprak* performance, and they produce leather puppets, wooden dolls and music tools. Situated at the north-eastern corner of

Figure 10.11   Tamansari or the Water Palace, one of Yogyakarta's key historical images. From this tower the sultan had a view of the pools below. (Source: W.S. Logan)

Figure 10.13 Kampung *dwellings crowd around* *Tamansari's decaying monuments.* (Source: *W.S. Logan*)

the *kampung* is a traditional bird market that attracts many people. As it is the only bird market in this city, visitors are attracted from every corner of the city and even from other cities, coming to buy birds or just to watch and listen to the songbirds.

This *kampung* is unique. If, in the two formerly discussed *kampung*, the development of big enterprises is encroaching upon their land, what is happening in Kampung Tamansari is the opposite: bit by bit, the residents are illegally acquiring the land in the former Sultan's water castle. One of the decree's objectives is to stop this encroachment process. Besides this law, there is also a drastic plan to renovate the water castle entirely and to remove the whole *kampung*. This will, of course, endanger the *kampung* and may not be wise either. Preserving this *kampung* without endangering the old monuments will reinforce the attractive ambience of the place.

These three *kampung* - Ratmakan, Sosrowijayan and Tamansari -are considered by many people to represent the precious images as well as historical settings of the Yogyakarta city and efforts must be made to conserve these environments. This means that settings outside the three *kampung*, but interrelated with them within the framework of systems of settings, must also be conserved. Consequently, approaches to urban planning and the design of the inner city which emphasise the creation of facilities for large enterprises while neglecting the *kampung* should be abandoned. As an alternative, urban planning and design should be based on the conservation of systems of activities and settings linking

kampung and settings outside the *kampung*. In such an approach, development efforts outside the *kampung* will be evaluated according to their relationship to the *kampung* and, gradually, the *kampung* will be strengthened functionally and their physical condition will improve. Instead of creating modern triangles consisting of high-income facilities at the expense of *kampung*, a quite different golden triangle could be developed based on *kampung* improvement: a Ratmakan-Sosrowijayan-Tamansari Golden Triangle.

YOGYAKARTA'S GOLDEN TRIANGLE - A STARTING POINT FOR INNER CITY CONSERVATION?

To approach urban design through the conservation of *kampung* may not be attractive, especially for conventional planners and investors, since it gives little indication of physical improvement or economic benefits. If economic growth is considered the prime criterion for the success of development, then *kampung* conservation may not be a satisfactory answer. However, if development means strengthening the cultural integrity and improving the quality of life of people, then the conservation of *kampung* is most appropriate. In this case, there must be a shift in the development paradigm and, for this to happen, it will depend on the resolve of the decision-makers. In a period when economic growth is still the major goal, investors will still be the main actors in the development process and many of them may consider *kampung* conservation a strange or, worse than that, useless concept. In these circumstances, *kampung* people can only wait until the inevitable day when they have to move. However, if the trend could be reversed, *kampung* conservation may get to a starting point.

It is impractical to think of conserving all the *kampung* in Yogyakarta at once for this would require an excessive amount of resources. However there must be a way to stimulate the conservation process so that it can commence and continue. One possibility is to select several sites as demonstration projects. It is expected that these sites will stimulate other sites to follow in a snowballing manner. Ratmakan, Sosrowijayan and Tamansari are potential sites for this conservation effort and other sites are expected to reap the benefits from their experience. Hopefully, this will be a learning experience that could be replicated elsewhere in the city so that, eventually, conservation of all the inner city *kampung* could become a reality.

The possibility of conserving the Golden Triangle of Yogyakarta depends on the way future development will be implemented. Past experience with development that emphasises the economic aspect rather than increasing the people's quality of life has been disadvantageous to many *kampung*. If the establishment of large enterprises which could yield economic profit is given priority in order to promote Yogyakarta's economic growth, the *kampung* will undoubtedly suffer. Hence such development needs to be re-evaluated and a new concept of development that considers the *kampung* as an alternative and viable form of living environment must be introduced. The *kampung* should be considered as a resource to be preserved; its sustainability should be secured. If these were the planner's principal considerations, the concept of sustainable development will be more appropriate.

SUSTAINABLE DEVELOPMENT

The concept of sustainable development emphasises the balance between development and conservation. In this concept, development is not merely associated with growth but, more importantly, is linked to the view that the people's quality of life must be improved through a development project or plan. Development that stimulates growth but puts many people in a position of disadvantage is inappropriate and unacceptable. Sustainable development also recognises the importance of conserving resources, natural and human. If *kampung* constitute 80 per cent of the residential areas in Indonesia and represent the social and physical resources that dominate the lives of the majority, then the arguments to protect them gain greater weight.

Improvement of the quality of life of the *kampung* does not always mean directing action towards improvement of the *kampung* itself; rather, an improvement in the settings outside the *kampung* could effectively improve the *kampung* in many cases. Hence an understanding of the system that links *kampung* and other outside settings could be one of the points

of departure for general *kampung* improvement. By contrast, improvement efforts which fail to consider the inter-relationships between settings could well destroy these links causing other settings to suffer. The process that affected the Kuningan Triangle in Jakarta is an example of this and the Yogyakarta Triangle could learn from this costly experience.

Several beneficial measures could be suggested related to the conservation of specific resources in each *kampung*. The link between Kampung Ratmakan and work places outside the *kampung* must be conserved. This means that the development of Beringharjo Market and its surroundings must allow for the maintenance of the work places of *kampung* residents. In addition, the impact of this development on the surrounding *kampung* must be positive stimulating improvements and not the opposite, eradicating them. The development of large-scale tourist accommodation facilities inside Kampung Sosrowijayan must be discouraged to avoid the loss of *kampung* character. A similar discouragement must be directed towards the development of department stores, plazas and large commercial facilities which encroach upon the land in *kampung*. The conservation of Kampung Tamansari's historical heritage and the residences surrounding the monuments should go hand in hand. Resettlement will sharply reduce the neighbourhood's vibrant activities, while neglecting the historical artefacts will ultimately eliminate the historical meaning of this place.

With these suggested measures, it is expected that the conservation of Yogyakarta's Golden Triangle will also become an effective weapon in the battle to prevent *kampung* eradication.

REFERENCES

Atman, Rudolf 1975, 'Kampung improvement in Indonesia', *Ekistics*, no.238, pp.216-20.

Baross, Zsa Zsa 1984, 'Prospek Perubahan Bagi Golongan Miskin Kota', in Parsudi Supalan (ed.), *Kemiskinan di Perkotaan Jakarta*, Yayasan Obor Indonesia, Jakarta.

Geertz, Clifford 1965, *The Social History of an Indonesian Town*, MIT Press, Cambridge.

Guinness, Patrick 1985, *Hierarchy and Harmony in Kampung*. Unpublished dissertation. Published in 1986 as *Harmony and Hierarchy in Javanese Kampung*, Oxford University Press, Singapore & New York.

Haryadi 1989, *Residents' strategies for coping with envi-*

ronmental stress: relation to house-settlement systems in Yogyakarta kampung, Indonesia. Unpublished dissertation, University of Wisconsin-Milwaukee, Milwaukee, Wisconsin.

McGee, T.G. 1967, *The South-East Asian City,* F.A. Praeger, New York.

Rapoport, Amos 1977, *Human Aspects of Urban Form,* Pergamon Press, Oxford.

—— 1983, 'Development, culture change and supportive design', *Habitat International,* vol.7, no.76, pp.249-68.

—— 1986, 'The use and design of open spaces in urban neighbourhoods', in D. Frick (ed.), *The Quality of Urban Life,* Walter de Gruite and Co., Berlin.

Sullivan, J. 1980, *Back Alley Neighbourhood Kampung as Urban Communities in Yogyakarta,* Monash University Centre of Southeast Asian Studies, Melbourne

United Nations Centre for Regional Development (UNCRD), Directorate General of Human Settlement, Ministry of Public Works, Republic of Indonesia, Government of Special Province of Yogyakarta 1989, *International Training Workshop on Strategic Areal Development Approaches for Implementing Metropolitan Development and Conservation,* Department of Architecture, Gadjah Mada University, Yogyakarta

Williams, David 1975, 'Jakarta's kampungs', *Architectural Design,* vol.6, pp.339-45.

ACKNOWLEDGEMENTS

Part of this chapter, notably sections dealing with Kampung Ratmakan, is based on the author's doctoral dissertation at the University of Wisconsin-Milwaukee, written under the supervision of Professor Amos Rapoport. The other parts are based on the author's work with the United Nations Centre for Regional Development (UNCRD) Team during the 1991 workshop on 'Urban Development and Conservation'. Thanks to Professor Rapoport and those at the UNCRD for their support. The invaluable contribution from local people in the Yogyakarta *kampung* must be acknowledged: they inspired the writing of this chapter - without them it would not have been possible.

11

Denpasar, Bali: triumph of the profane

Don Townsend

In traditional Bali, all aspects of life were codified, regulated, conscientiously practised and progressively improved. Central to that way of life are the 'three respects': respect for Hindu spiritual belief; respect for human relations; respect for environmental relations. Material and behavioural phenomena which support the three respects could be labelled as 'sacred', whereas those which erode are labelled as 'profane'. The profane is not considered as abnormal or unwarranted as it is in some societies with compulsive ideology or religion; rather, it is regarded in Bali as a necessary but controllable factor in living a full life.

By any measure, the people of Bali have had a 'full life' over the past century. Change has supplanted continuity, global has displaced local, gain has overwhelmed character, noise has fuddled prayer, jobs have defaced work, money has spawned skills and arts, and Balinese, young and old, dance on the asphalt which covers tracts of their former rice fields. The Dutch colonial system suppressed and then chipped away at the politico-religious systems; a national government system with secular education and administration brought mobility, pluralism, new loyalties, demands and rewards. The dazzling tourist age in Bali has brought a party, a prolonged feast with new rituals which change continuously and which progressively assert the success of the profane.

This chapter will describe the interaction of cultural change and urban character in Bali's major urban place, Denpasar.[1] This city has been the main centre of change and profanity in the most transformed of the precolonial regencies, Badung. From a settlement clustering in 50 hectares (124 acres) around the Raja's Palace in 1880, Denpasar grew to 400 000 people in 1980 in a proclaimed urban area of 11 000 hectares (42 square miles). By the year 2000, the contiguous population and built-up area will have reached 600 000, and 100 000 motor vehicles per day will cough against the Palace walls. Vendors' bells and hawkers' shouts block out the prayers and music, as each day, 10 000 foreign and domestic visitors arrive to consume that which entrepreneurs call the 'tourist product'.

Profanity succeeds, and many of the tourists now come for what profanity itself has wrought. Is it possible that the sacred will be shielded behind the dykes and levees of profanity's distractions?

DIMENSIONS OF CHANGE OVER A CENTURY

Badung is the southern and most populous of the eight *kabupaten* (districts) which were based on the

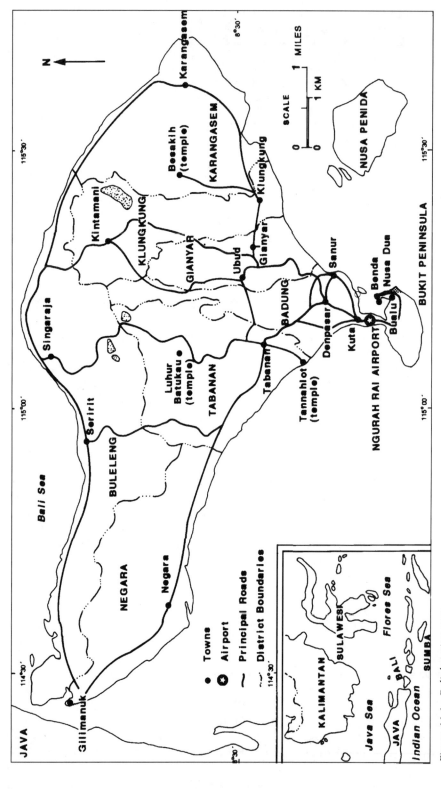

Figure 11.1   Bali: location map

pre-Independence regencies. In the late eighteenth century, leading families of the south organised their regency out of the declining Kingdom of Mengwi, and centred their authority in the rich rice fields where the Badung, Mati, Tego and Ayung rivers change slope and form their coarse sand delta (Putra Agung 1986, p.29). Although the sea and its resources were generally unimportant to the prosperous agricultural society of Hindu Bali, the particular location of the Badung regency with sea access to the east, south and south-west has had profound consequences for the history and cultural change of all of Bali (Figure 11.1).

The Klungkung regency, in the eastern quarter of Bali, was the dominant kingdom in the eighteenth and nineteenth centuries. But foreign influences were encroaching on Bali, most strongly through the trading and fishing ports of southern Badung, north central Bali (Singaraja) and the western villages facing Islamic Java. Through the nineteenth century, the Badung families gained significantly in power and influence. They gathered from the southern half of Bali the power which the Dutch would usurp and replace in 1906, and so shape the physical, political, economic and cultural life for ever.

The sea-oriented migrants and traders from middle Indonesia had been tolerated in small settlements along the southern coast, particularly at Benoa, Tuban and Kuta. People from Java, Madura, Lombok ('Sasaks') and Sulawesi ('Bugis') were the media of innovations, and sometimes a vital factor as mercenaries in the inter-regency wars of the nineteenth century. Perhaps of more profound effect on the

Figure 11.3   'Old Denpasar' (Source: I.K. Neben)

economic and physical form of Badung were the migrants and traders of Chinese and Arab origin, since they settled in clusters and set about capital formation. The migrants and traders influenced but did not much penetrate or join with the introspective, agricultural, religious and severely hierarchical regencies of Bali. When the Dutch decapitated Badung in 1906, they were easily able to demarcate a settlement for the Chinese to the west of the Palace, a settlement for the Arabs around Pasar Badung (Figure 11.2), and a settlement for the Islamic population around 'Java village' which later became Wanasari village (Putra Agung 1986, p.14).

The original though much damaged authority of the major families continued well into the colonial period. Around the home areas of three major clans, there emerged the *kecamatan* (municipality) demarcations which in the 1970s were secularised as Kecamatan Denpasar West, East and South.

The population of this area was around 40 000 in 1912, of whom more than 80 per cent were agriculturalists (Information Bureau [IB] 1939, p.217). There followed a gradual transformation of both land and livelihood as secularisation of administration, production and trade was advanced by the Dutch and other outsiders. Putra Agung (1986, p.12) argues that even though the population grew to 93 000 in 1932 and to 131 000 in 1959, the ecology of the Denpasar area was still predominantly original or *keasliannya* (traditional).

Foreign influences had been very much confined; production for export, for instance, had not been widely nor deeply adopted by the Balinese. Infrastructure for rural development was not greatly ad-

Figure 11.2   Pasar Badung, Denpasar's central market, on Badung River (Source: I.K. Neben)

vanced by the Dutch. Of more importance in the long term was their expansion of education, an activity much respected in the Balinese culture. The communal unit, the *bandjar*, remained robust, vital and self-sufficient. The Hindu religion, the Hindu system of rules governing people's lives and the Hindu social caste system remained strong.

Three great secular forces became evident in the 1960s and enabled profanity to triumph in this garden of culture. The Republican government with a developmental mission exercised unprecedented power over people and resources. Secular education was harnessed to the mission. International tourists, abetted by the technology of modernisation, came in swelling numbers to consume the fruits of a 500-year old garden nurtured in ancient beliefs and practices. In one generation, the garden around Badung River has been obliterated by a polluting and self-strangling city of 500 000, with buildings which cast shadows over sacred temples and engine smoke which blankets the incense of offerings.

That farmer who was growing rice beside the airport when the 'jumbo jet' was first flown, would now have to make a long day's walk north through Denpasar towards revered old Mengwi before seeing a rice field ('Land Use Map' in Departemen Pekerjaan Umum [DPU] 1989).

The farmer would walk through the signs and lights and rules which replace the customs and beliefs by which they once interacted with others. At the midday hour, they might be buffeted by the swarms of blue-and-white students on bicycles; in the late afternoon they would experience the tide of traders, tourists and clock-timed workers. Music louder than the Dutch cannon would blast the ungreened gullies and canyons of hot walls; and not one soul might call their names and bless their families. They would see the new guardians of what is important, well-fed men in uniforms at the fortified entrances of banks, offices and exclusive housing and hotel precincts. At the *desa* (village) on the edge of the city, they would find their grandchildren watching television from the government-sanctioned producers, the proper signals bounced off heaven to that flickering, winning authority. Yet they would have their salve, as they see grand daughters practising their dances, and aunties weaving coconut leaves and flowers into tomor-

row's offerings for the guarded gates and seething schools.

GOVERNMENT, GROWTH, SECULARISATION AND STRUCTURE

Five great waves of change have moved across Bali, and there is perhaps a sixth now appearing. The first was of the Hindus, transforming the landscape as they built hierarchical, largely self-sufficient societies of agriculture, religion, scholarship and art. Then the Dutch, late and, after subjugating the island, relatively unforceful and on the whole beneficent in changing the local society and economy. Republican government from Jakarta has been the principal designer and agent of change. It has enabled and promoted successive changes in livelihood, use of resources and physical structures. Republican government has been influential in two subsequent waves: in trade, industry, wage employment and agriculture; and in large-scale international and, lately, domestic tourism.

Each of these waves has had profound effects on all aspects of the Denpasar area. The latest wave might come to be seen as the wave of decentralisation, as a process of physical, economic and psychological evasion of an unacceptable and culturally offensive way of urban living.

The regency

The lasting consequence of the regency in matters of physical form was the location of the major temples and the tolerance and spatial concentration of the traders and immigrants. Beholden to the favours of the *raja* and the heads of major *bandjar*, the traders were sited at a convenient yet respectful distance from the places of religious and political power. Social rules were prescribed or adjusted to protect the sacred objects and practices from the materialist traders and manufacturers. The trading paths to the east, south and south-west eventually became the main arteries of traffic and business in and around Denpasar.

Colonial changes

The Dutch formalised the incipient structure and organisation. They also confirmed the profanity of colonial government by building some of their offices and residences on land and in relative locations which contradicted some Balinese beliefs about propriety and harmony (Putra Agung 1986, p.2). The first hotel was built on the site of the 1906 killings (Vickers 1989, p.2).

The advent of steamships strengthened the importance of the well-protected Benoa port and, after 1920, the Dutch moved the main business of government and traders from Kuta in the south-west to Benoa. Today's tourist and tourist entrepreneur would see that as a far-sighted decision, since it left white-sand Kuta to the beach hedonists and the grey-mud Benoa area to the mangroves, swamps, prawn farms and by-pass roads (Figure 11.4).

There were several other significant innovations in the colonial period. A museum for Balinese culture was established in 1910. European scholars and artists, most notably Spies and Bonnet, helped in the recognition and promotion of Balinese art and artists of various media (Noronha 1977, p.180). The establishment in 1933 of Museum Le Mayeur at Sanur focussed the interests of Balinese and foreigners. The 1930s saw the confirmation, amongst the European and North American elites of scholars, artists and philanthropists, of Bali as a rich and enviable culture based on religion, community and ethics (Covarrubias 1974, p.400; Picard, 1990, p.4).

A regular package tour was established by shipping lines in 1924, and in 1928 Hotel Bali was built in Denpasar to serve government, business and the incipient tourist trade which the Dutch were then systematically but cautiously promoting. For purposes of government administration, an airport was built at Tuban in 1933, thus introducing the single most important instrument of cultural and economic change in Bali. The roads in and around Denpasar and to the urban centres of Gianyar regency, Tabanan regency and the Dutch regional headquarters at Singaraja were upgraded and sealed by 1935.

Although Singaraja was well-located relative to Dutch trading interests and sea-borne power in Southeast Asia, and was the centre of Buleleng regency, it was a town with a declining agricultural hinterland, whose population was a small and fast-declining proportion of the Bali total.

Perhaps the most important means of dissolving and secularising the well-integrated and hierarchical Balinese village society was by educating its members . Literacy and learning have always been highly respected activities in Balinese life. The colonial education facilities were expanded rapidly, so that by 1940 there were seventy schools and training institutions around Denpasar. This deliberate centralisation of services set a base which, in the Republic period, contributed greatly to the secular growth of Denpasar, particularly through in-migration from surrounding regencies and through the retraining of the agricultural children of south Badung.

The Japanese had a short but telling occupation of the colonial government's residences, offices, the Hotel Bali and surrounding districts. They organised several political cadres, and trained and armed many young men. The organisation, the consciousness of power, the training and the weapons were used against the returning Dutch - but they also had a longer lasting effect in fostering a challenge, direct and indirect, to the traditional and hierarchical power of the Hindu social structure.

The Republic

The victory of the Republic greatly advanced the non-local and secular power in Balinese life. For the first 10 years or so, the Republic was advanced through administration and education, and no rapid changes were evident although commercial farming expanded for domestic trade. The critical act of the Republic was in 1958, namely the replacement of Singaraja by Denpasar as the *ibukota* (main city) of Bali Province.

Physical, economic and social innovations rapidly ensued. Around 10 000 families of government and military staff moved in over the next few years. The far-reaching decision to upgrade Tuban airport was taken in 1959. University education was set up from Universitas Airlangga (Surabaya) in Denpasar in 1958. Four faculties comprising the new Universitas Udayana were established in 1962, and the institution grew to 4000 students and staff by 1969.

Work was started in 1962 on the Hotel Bali Beach (307 rooms and 1000 staff) at Sanur. This massive institution was financed with Japanese grants and located where the Japanese soldiers had invaded. It was organised mainly by national government agencies, designed in a very alien fashion, and made with

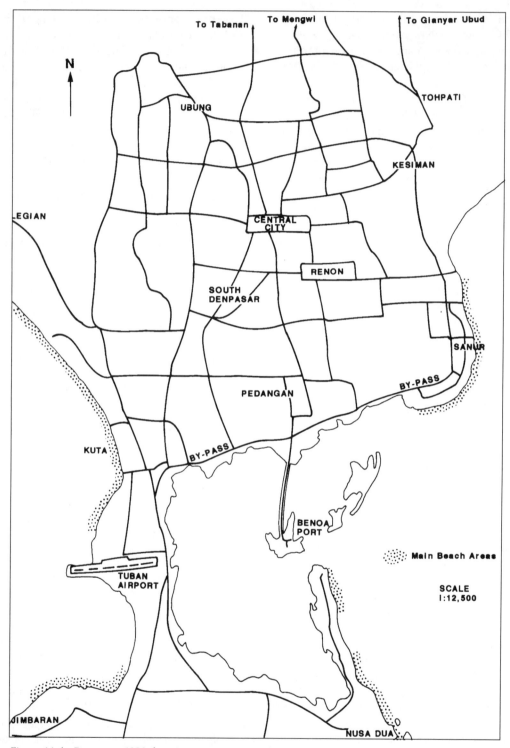

Figure 11.4   Denpasar, 1993: location map

much non-local material and labour. It dominated the skyline for a hundred kilometres of sea and coast, its sea walls reshaping the beach, looking out over the vital cultural *bandjar*, temples and settlements of Sanur. In sum, this was an innovation of profound material and psychological significance to the Balinese. Materially, it was the base for a burgeoning package tour industry, with powerful economic and employment spread effects. Psychologically, it influenced the Balinese thinking about the scale and style of tourism, and about the ability and threat of outside entrepreneurs and regulators to shape their culture and society. It symbolised the determination of the Sukarno government to gain more international respect and developmental opportunity through Bali's attractions.

In the 1960s, education services in Denpasar were rapidly expanded. The colonial base of seventy educational centres was raised to 200 by 1975, 600 by 1989 and is expected to be 800 in the year 2000 (Table 3.2 in DPU 1989). Furthermore, private schools and training centres have grown significantly in the 1980s, reflecting the diversity of demands in a fast-changing economy.

The Republic's influence on urban form has been profound. Through investment, law, regulation, planning and promotion, it has gradually shaped four 'regions' within the urban area (Urban Structure Map in DPU 1989). Business, commerce and shopping are concentrated in west Denpasar; government administration and education in east Denpasar, around the suburb of Renon; recreation, entertainment, hotels, tourism and arts in south-west Denpasar, particularly the Kuta area, and again along the east coast of Sanur (Kecamatan Timur). As will be shown in the following discussion, the Republic government has also shaped the relationship of Denpasar to the rest of Bali and Indonesia, and to the forces and main locations of tourism sector.

TRADE AND PLURALISM

The generosity of Bali's environment and the introspective character of Hindu belief and society obviated the need for intensive or widespread trading or exploitation of marine resources. Primary loyalty and predominant concern was always for the *bandjar*, usually a section but sometimes the whole of a customary village. Activities of the *bandjar* and affiliation with village and district temples were always more important than administrative organisation, an attitude and practice which has persisted well into the Republic period (Noronha 1977, p.178). Noronha continues:

> Beyond the village only a common creed is shared: a pragmatic Hinduism. This sharing, however, is not action oriented. It is merely an adaptation to the numerous cultural intrusions on the island and is based on a common heritage and worship of common symbols in a hierarchy of temples.

And in response to the forces of tourism, Noronha (1977) poses the question:

> ...whether the Balinese can be induced to cooperate with each other when there is no cultural precedent for cooperation beyond the confines of the village.

Dramatic cultural, economic and political intrusions have swept the island since those ideas were formed in the mid-1970s. Cooperation has been required, even demanded, by the pressures and rewards of administrative government, by the strange allegiances of new political parties, by new forms of resource use, by commercialisation of land and labour and by the attractiveness of many aspects of outsiders' lifestyles. A dynamic and disturbing cultural pluralism has entered and spread across the homogeneity characterised in the period of the regencies.

Minorities

The Rajas allowed entry to the immigrants associated with trading, fishing and marine resources, inevitably demonstrating new products, activities, social organisation, values in life and religious beliefs. The Chinese and Arabs were in some ways helpful in providing material goods and technology, and the other Indonesians showed potential from the marine environment and sometimes were deployed as mercenaries. Each of the outside groups had wider contacts than the Balinese leaders and more experience of interacting with the Europeans.

Cultural disturbance was not profound while the Hindu leadership ruled and while the economic system remained as village agriculture. The immigrant component was almost certainly less than 2 per cent of the Hindu population in 1906. Under the Dutch hegemony, Chinese and Islamic Indonesians settled in greater numbers, with a strong concentration in Denpasar and Singaraja (Covarrubias 1974). The immigrant trend has continued under the Republic, particularly with staff of government and army, parastate organisations and private investors moving into south Badung and other main commercial centres at Gianyar, Tabanan and Singaraja. By 1978, the minorities around Denpasar made up about 12 per cent of population (Putra Agung 1986, p.14), and rose to 15 per cent by 1990 (DPU 1989, pp.3-14). They were virtually uninvolved in the agriculture sector (Sudibia 1992, p.28), but they had strong influence in commerce, industry, services and finance. Resentment of outsiders' control, wealth, allegiances and connections was one of the complex of factors in the numerous and terrible killings of 1965.

Trade

Trade in commodities provides some indirect evidence of economic and social change and of the waxing influence of outsiders. Total port trade in the late 1930s, indicated by the schedule of ships, probably did not exceed 20 000 tonnes (IB 1939). Port of Benoa trade in 1960 was around 20 000 tonnes (pers. comm., Port Controller, Benoa, Dec. 1991). It has grown to 100 000 tonnes in 1975, 230 000 tonnes in 1980, 330 000 tonnes in 1990 and is forecast to reach 900 000 tonnes in year 2000 (Benoa Port Authority 1989, 1990, 1991).

Benoa is competing with the road and ferry trade via Gilimanuk. A very rapid growth in traded goods has been experienced at Gilimanuk, since the upgrading of roads and ferry services from and to Java in the 1980s, and almost all of that trade is directed to, from or through Denpasar. Freight through Gilimanuk was 400 000 tonnes in 1980, rose to 1.9 million tonnes in 1990, and is forecast as 3.5 million tonnes in year 2000. Realisation of the last figure will depend very much on road capacity in Bali and East Java, and on the operations and relative pricing of shipping to Benoa. In 1990, 2.7 million passengers and 650 000 vehicles used the Gilimanuk ferries; by year 2000, the figures will be around 6 million and 1.2 million respectively.

Production

Traditional agriculture was subject to significant changes from the 1960s. Commercial cropping of rice, corn, peanuts, beans, vegetables, fruit, coffee, coconuts and animals was adopted by many farmers, and productivity was raised mainly through new knowledge and technology. Real income per household increased at 5 per cent per year in the period 1965-90, mainly due to fertiliser-responsive plants. Thus labour was released at a time when the non-agricultural economy was expanding and diversifying, and when schools were providing more and more capacity for secular learning and training. There was also an increase in sales of land, and an increase in conversion of land for shops, factories, storehouses, houses, roads, parking areas, schools, playgrounds, offices and entertainments. The processes of commercialisation, land sales, land conversion and work conversion were most intense around Denpasar.

Figure 11.5 shows the expansion of the built-up area during the period 1948-89. The urban area was about 700 hectares (27 square miles) in 1948, 1200 hectares (4.6 square miles) in 1960 and 1600 hectares (6.2 square miles) in 1970 (Putra Agung, 1986, p.145). However, the Department of Public Works Outline Plan of 1970 indicated a water supply service area of 800 hectares (3.1 square miles), projected to 1000 hectares (3.9 square miles) in 1980 and 1400 hectares (5.4 square miles) in 1990. The actual extent of the contiguous built-up area exceeded 3000 hectares (11.6 square miles) in 1989, and was forecast to reach 5000 hectares (19.3 square miles) in year 2000 (DPU 1982, 1989). Although the overall density of the Administrative City of Denpasar was twenty-five persons per hectare (6400 per square miles) in 1986, it was over 200 (51 800) in the central business area (Table 2.8 in DPU 1989). There has, however, been some dispersion to the cheaper lands and the thriving commerce in the south, around Kuta, resulting in displacement of agricultural families.

From 1970 to 1990, the quantity of agricultural production for Bali increased at an average of 5 per cent per year; the value increased at around 7 per cent in real terms; rural population increased at around 2 per cent; while around 5 per cent of prime rice land was converted to non-agricultural uses. In the Denpasar area, the conversion of land from agri-

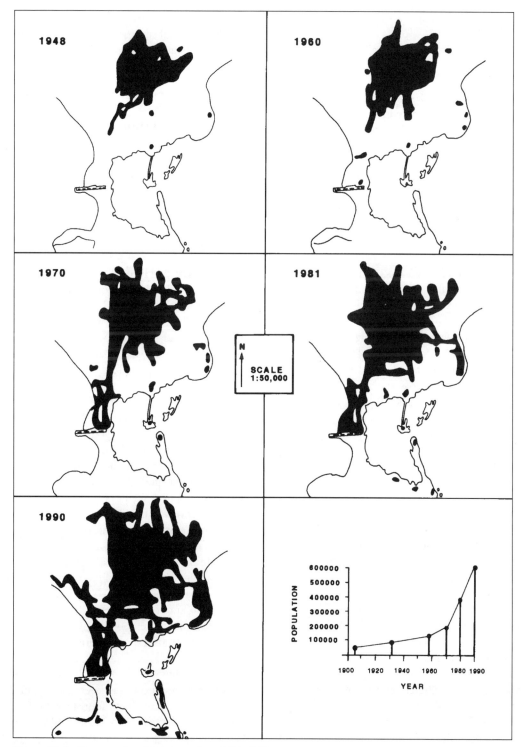

Figure 11.5   Denpasar's urban expansion, 1800-1990

culture in that period appears to be around 40 per cent (Putra Agung 1986, pp.144-6, maps; Table 2.25 on Land Use in DPU 1982; 'Land Use Map' in DPU 1989).

The massive shift in workforce and employment was also concentrated in south Badung. Thirty thousand jobs were created there in small-scale processing and manufacturing, much of it for export markets. Of 1700 industrial establishments surveyed in 1986, 74 per cent had five or less workers. Another 30 000 jobs were added to government, and 50 000 in services, particularly in small trading, commerce, transport and tourism. Education enrolments increased by 30 000 in the period 1970 to 1990 (Government of Bali, *Statistical Yearbooks* 1980 to 1990; *Sensus Penduduk* 1980).

The construction industry has been one of the most influential forces in the economy, and in cultural pluralism. Though varying through waves of investment, the construction sector has provided around 30 000 equivalent permanent jobs in building hotels, houses, shops, offices and infrastructure. The majority of workers have been contracted recruits from the more experienced and lower cost workforce of Java, and they have gradually established their settlements and supporting services around south Badung (Sudibia 1992, p.29).

Diversity

The recipe for dissolving the Hindu 'state' now seems formidable - decapitated leadership; confined authority; secular administration from a national centre with control over many staff and large budgets for infrastructure and services; changes in land use and resource management; wide variations in land values and conversions and consequent control by outsiders over use of resources; shifts in workforce and types and locations of work; new social organisations with demands on time and loyalties; secular and vocational education; infrastructure, buildings, services, machines and vehicles which impose on and transform the physical environment; and outsiders from a hundred different cultures mingling with the Balinese, especially the young with their secular education and interest in novelty. Driving all this change has been the developmental mission of the Republic, and the tourists' desire to experience

Balinese nature, history, culture and art. The undoubted material success in these drives, particularly around Denpasar, has produced an exciting 'party' of cultural diversity, but a serious loss in the quality of the living environment, and in the harmony and sanctity of social life.

SELLING CULTURE AND NATURE

The previous section outlined changes in agriculture and employment which contributed to the urbanisation and economic and cultural diversification around Denpasar. This section will show that the engine of growth - and the prime cause of some serious social and environmental problems - has been tourism.

Growth by curiosity

Foreign tourists in the colonial period increased slowly to several thousand per year in the 1930s (Picard 1990, p.4). A trade by steamships continued in the 1950s and 1960s, to around 10 000 per year in 1965. The number was small in relation to world tourist flows, but the effect on markets was huge. The two largest groups or types of international tourists to Bali in the 1960s were the artists-and-scholars, and the hedonist-adventurers. The former are well known around Sanur and Ubud particularly; the latter provided Kuta with the term 'hippie', spawned a demand for low-cost *losmen* and 'homestay' facilities, and propagated around the postcolonial societies of North America, Europe and Australia a curiosity and reverence for the Balinese way, the artefacts, the tolerance and the natural beauty. Bali gave access to fashionable 'Eastern mysticism' in a beautiful, clean, non-malarial, uncrowded and undemanding situation, and the message permeated rapidly through the restless young people who were entering an era of affluence and experimentation in the West. Among the younger people, less troubled by the contests of the generation of decolonisation around the world, Bali was perhaps seen as the likeable face of the Sukarno Republic, whose negative and threatening aspects had been widely publicised.

In 1968, there were thirty tourist establishments in Bali, and this increased to 116 establishments with 3072 rooms in 1975 (Noronha 1977, p.183). The small but excellent Hotel Tanjungsari built at Sanur in 1963 had demonstrated the potential of high value tourism, and was followed in 1966 by the Hotel Bali Beach. With Hotel Hyatt Sanur in 1973 and Hotel Sanur Beach in 1974, the Sanur area had 1286 rooms of international standard. There were another 1500 rooms in Denpasar and Kuta, spread among ninety establishments and catering mostly for government, businesspeople and low-value tourism. So capacity was available, but tourism had been restrained by the political and social violence of 1965-66 and the rudimentary facilities available to the more demanding market.

Growth by design

The surge in the number of tourists was facilitated by a return to political stability and the upgrading of Tuban airport to long-distance jet standard in 1969. There were concerted promotions by Indonesian government agencies, package-tour operators, airlines and Bali-based service industries. Tourist arrivals grew from 47 000 in 1969 to 200 000 in 1975, at an annual growth rate of 27 per cent.

The government's first Five Year Plan (REPELITA I), in 1968, had targeted the policies and actions in planning and infrastructure to ensure that the tourism sector would make a much greater contribution to national growth and development. The strategy was that tourism would promote a more favourable image of Indonesia, and that tourism sector earnings would finance the development of particular areas of Indonesia. Bali was given first and strongest emphasis. The very close link between large-scale private investment and government policy and spending is a feature of Indonesian planning and development, and has been clearly demonstrated in the tourism sector for Bali.

Supplementary to the airport investments, there were some large and critical developments in the tourism sector, particularly through approvals for hotel investment. The far-reaching Master Plan For Tourism in Bali (the SCETO Plan) was researched and composed in 1969-71, and developed a strategy for maximising higher value tourism while limiting the direct interaction of tourists and Balinese (Societe Centrale pour l'Equipment Touistique Outre-Mer 1971, vol.1, Plan Summary). So the unproductive and relatively unoccupied Bukit Peninsula with its long

Table 11.1   Traffic arriving at Denpasar Airport 1975-2000

Year	Aircraft		Passengers (x 1000)	
	Domestic	International	Domestic*	International
1970	3 558	262	170	20
1975	6 175	450	202	88
1980	8 903	762	278	146
1985	9 241	1954	366	271
1990	10 663	3884	587	490
1995	15 067	5620	979	765
2000	20 000	6837	1493	1024

* includes foreign visitors having officially entered Indonesia at other ports (mainly Jakarta).

(Sources: *Government of Bali Province,* Statistical Yearbooks, *1980 to 1990; Pacific Consultants International [PCI] 1990; Department of Tourism 1992.)*

beaches and cheap land was designed as the location for large hotels with an emphasis on recreation and seclusion. The cultural experience of Bali was to be made available mainly through shows, dances, music and artefacts 'imported' to the resort hotel precincts, and through programmed day tours to the cultural heartlands (including Besakih, Kintamani, Gianyar, Ubud, Mengwi, Tabanan, Tanah Lot and Bedugul). To avoid the narrow, congested, uncomfortable and unhealthy streets of Denpasar, a high capacity by-pass was planned to link Bukit with the airport, Sanur, the north-east rice lands and the cultural heartlands mentioned above.

Although SCETO was pessimistic about cultural preservation in the face of greatly increased tourism, the strategy has been very successful in facilitating orderly development of tourism and controlled exploitation of the tourist product. Its implementation was not smooth, and large loans from World Bank and major government spending were necessary in the 1970s and 1980s to achieve the critical mass of services and market acceptance. Also, changes were made to visa requirements and airline landing rights so as to facilitate flows and access. By 1985, there were nine hotels with 2400 rooms in Bukit, concentrated around Nusa Dua. By 1990, there were twenty hotels and 5820 rooms, there having been significant investment at Jimbaran on the west side of Bukit. The latest projections for 1995 are forty hotels and 15 655 rooms, a rate of investment based on assumptions about higher quality/higher value package tours and demand for resort hotels.

So fast was the rise in demand in the 1970s and 1980s that hotel and related investment continued in other areas, although much slower than at Bukit. Sanur and Kuta areas lost their relative importance in the 1980s following a national government restriction (1975) on construction of hotels outside of Bukit.

The tourism product at Sanur could not compete well with the new and luxurious facilities at Bukit, especially as the Sanur investors had very much damaged their beaches and coastal waters. By 1990, the Sanur area had 2930 starred rooms and 814 non-starred rooms, for a total of 3744. Sanur will have about 5000 rooms by 1995.

Kuta experienced something of a degradation in the 1980s, partly because of vehicle and pedestrian congestion, and partly unprofitability of the many small establishments. However, there has been a resurgence of hotel investment around Kuta, accompanied by public sector work on traffic control, roads, the beach, drainage, water supply and waste management. In 1990, Kuta area had 4800 starred and 4900 un-starred rooms. Current planning projections are for a total of 12 000 rooms by 1995.

Another critical policy change stimulated international tourism. Faced with declining national revenue following oil price falls in 1983, the government sought an even faster increase in the export earnings from tourism. Gradually a change in aviation policy was achieved despite some resistance from domestic operators, and five foreign airlines were allowed to fly into Bali. The airlines and their associated companies promoted package tours and some invested in Bukit hotels, and brought about significant increases in tourists from Germany, France, Italy, Spain and other European countries. A similar lift is expected in the early 1990s as the airport is further upgraded and permits for scheduled flights are extended to ten foreign airlines.

The average annual growth of tourist arrivals has been sustained at around 14 per cent for 15 years. Tourist spending has been growing at least at that level, although it is recognised in Bali that there is a very high degree of 'leakage' in that spending. A large proportion of package tour payments are made outside of Bali. There is a large import content in many of the services and facilities supplied to tourists. There is increasing control by outsiders on the pricing of goods and services supplied by Balinese artists and entertainers and an increasing non-Balinese proportion of the hotel workforce, which could add to remittances from Bali. Investment in tourism sector and the disposal of profits are increasingly controlled from outside of Bali, or by outsiders resident in Bali. There is a fear that the tourist product, while contributing much to the national interest, is not being adequately protected or improved.

Response to growth in tourism

Certainly the Balinese have responded very positively to the opportunities offered by the tourism sector (Vickers 1989, p.12). There were some successful cultural brokers in the 1920s and 1930s, particularly in painting and dance; but the great flourishing in the 1970s came from the *bandjar* themselves, as they formed arts groups in order to improve their skills and styles in both the sacred and the 'vulgar' arts, and to provide services to the hotels and tour groups. There is evidence of arts recovered from history and propagated through Bali and overseas on the tourist stream of demand. The formal organisations for the promotion of arts and culture, and public and private academies of training, have developed into powerful and prestigious institutions. The Bali Arts Festival, established in 1979 in order to present a more coherent image to the world, has been a successful enterprise for both culture and tourism, and is 'first and foremost a showcase where the Balinese celebrate their culture on a grand scale' (Picard, 1990, p.22).

There has been a huge growth in production of artefacts and of exports to widening markets. Some of the labour released from agriculture has found good paying work in sculpting, painting, weaving and carving. Noronha (1977, p.185) reported that woodcarving was already employing 4000 workers in 1973, and that the most suitable timbers had risen to prices which carvers could not manage without some external credit in the line of sale. A conservative estimate based solely on growth in international tourist arrivals would suggest that there are now around 25 000 people making all or part of their living from woodcarving. The Balinese have tried thousands of small businesses associated with tourism - in Denpasar alone in 1986, there were 300 small restaurants and 400 art shops.

Culture, economy and urban character

Picard (1990, pp.9-25) has examined the contest of ideas and opinions about Bali's response to tourism. The current consensus in Bali is that commercialisation has brought revitalisation. It has also brought some profanity to the spiritual and religious aspects of saleable artefacts, ceremonies and objects of reverence. After careful consideration of opinions on this matter at the height of investment for tourism, Noronha (1977, p.201) concluded that:

> income gained from a performance and sale of crafts is channelled back to strengthen the religious and temporal bonds that are the sources of strength for the Balinese: the *bandjar* and the village temples. Tourism has thus affirmed these most important ties which link the past with the present and the future and which form the boundaries through which no outsider can penetrate, not even Balinese who are not members of the same *bandjar*.

Such was the positive note of the mid-1970s. Noronha (1977, p.202) gave warning of a trend which would damage this happy condition:

> The threat to Balinese culture and way of life comes not from numbers as such but from the way in which tourism is organised in Bali today...[and] the Balinese response is increasingly determined by outsiders. The Balinese have been relegated to roles of functionaries and employees...Non-Balinese tourism enterprises

grow in strength and in their ability to dictate...and to play one *bandjar* off against another. It is possible to envision the gradual loss of control by the *bandjars* over their members. Once this link is broken, tourism income will cease to be channelled back to strengthen the *bandjars* and the village temples that give the Balinese their sense of identity and uniqueness.

From personal research and observations, it can be said that the trends have been realised, but 'this link' has not been broken. Seventy per cent of the population of Bali is still rural; 70 per cent of the urban population is concentrated in the Gianyar-Denpasar-Tabanan crescent. Perhaps the village practices in and around Denpasar have been rendered profane beyond caring, but 20 kilometres (12 miles) out from the Raja's Palace, there is a conscientious practice of the rituals, culture and social behaviour which make Bali distinctive. Similarly, along the roads to the cultural heartlands are continuous levees of shops, showrooms, workshops, restaurants, travel agencies, freight agencies and offices... traps to the flows of tourists and traders but a thin slice off the rice fields. At the front door is the tourist bus and the placards for credit cards; at the back is the household temple, tools, trees and fields of old Bali.

Perhaps what the despairing and less optimistic observer might see is the overlay of secular business, government and services, the large and concentrated ethnic minorities gradually dominating the secular and profane, and the great numbers of immigrants who are not socially, culturally nor economically integrated.

Balinese people have tried to mitigate the negative effects of tourism and economic change. Their leaders have consistently improved and restated the customary rules, rights and duties in relation to *telajakan* (environment) and in personal behaviour (*awig awig*) within the *bandjar*. The following list of prominent decisions shows the struggle between culture, economy and form, and imply some points of quiet contest with central authorities.

Table 11.2   Interventions 1970-91

1970	Governor's decree requiring notification of land sales within 200 metres (219 yards) of the shoreline.
1971	vice as a basis for comprehensive physical planning.
1971	Office of tourism services set up in a National Government establishment in Bali.
1971	Publication of the Master Plan for Development of Tourism in Bali (SCETO Report).
1972	Master Plan for Urban Development of Denpasar adopted.
1972	Governor persuaded Kabupaten Badung to distribute 30 per cent of its tourist tax revenues to other Kabupaten.
1972	Bali Tourism Development Board established.
1972	The Master Plan for the Development of Tourism in Bali decreed by National Government despite its over-centralising tendencies and the loss of Bali-based control over resources and infrastructure.
1973	The Bali Tourism Development Corporation established to mobilise investment at Nusa Dua.
1973	Governor decreed that migrants must have a confirmed job and residence before coming to Bali - a matter which was unconstitutional and unenforceable.
1974	National decree for Bali as a centre for cultural tourism.
1974	Governor published the social foundations for the regulation of tourism, with particular reference to the behaviour of visitors in relation to sacred and valued aspects of Balinese life.
1974	Governor decreed that tourist guides must wear national traditional dress during their working times.
1974	Governor declared as a 'green belt' the areas contiguous to the tourist route from Denpasar to Ubud (the arts region).
1975	Badung leaders tried unsuccessfully to break the hotel and tour operators control by forbidding *bandjar* cultural performances at hotels.
1975	The National Government restricted the building of new rooms outside of Nusa Dua, so as to raise the investment returns to Bukit developers.
1975	The Department of Tourism established in Bali Provincial Government.
1975	The National Government amalgamated Tourism Board and Tourism Corporation.

1976	'Listibiya' established, as a board of leaders in arts and culture, to watch over standards and to approve performances designed for tourists.
1976	The Academies for dance and for physical arts were established.
1976	Laws passed against drug trafficking and consumption, directed mainly at users in the Kuta area.
1977	The National Government through the Director General for Tourism introduced a national classification of hotels with regulations and gradings according to standards.
1977	The Provincial Government published detailed building codes, covering such matters as height of buildings (15 metres/ 49 feet), and setbacks from roads and important objects.
1978	Denpasar area declared a 'Kota Administratif', hence regulated as a national responsibility.
1978	Appointment of a leading Balinese scholar and distinguished national civil servant as Governor.
1979	National government delegated some responsibilities in tourism to regional governments, but retained all of the most important functions.
1979	Bali Arts Festival established.
1979	Formal statement of the separation of *bandjar* matters and local administrative ('*camat*') matters.
1981	Decree to restrict coral extraction from reefs to traditional uses and technology.
1982	Physical Plan for Denpasar published (DPU).
1988	Intensive public debate on change and continuity in the Balinese culture and belief.
1989	Restatement of the building and town-planning codes.
1989	Revised Physical Plan for Denpasar published (DPU).
1990	Governor 'froze' applications for new hotels, but allowed some investments outside of Badung.
1990	Adoption of 'kawasan' plan, intended to restrict tourist sector investment to fifteen designated areas around Bali.
1991	Regulation 3, Article 16, referring to the use of Balinese traditional architecture for the outside of all public and commercial buildings; and for regulating building around strategic tourist objects, particularly distance of separation and height in relation to holiness of sites.
1991	Bali Tourism Management Project established, funded by the United Nations Development Program.

There may well be other decisions and regulations which have shaped the Balinese response to the immense pressures of change over the last 20 years. However, the list given in the preceding text is elaborated so as to demonstrate the 'eclectic pragmatism' of the Balinese (Noronha 1977, p.198), even though they could see the erosion of local control over resources, services and infrastructure. Balinese have recognised that, in order to raise their standard of living and to be part of the Republic, they have had to tolerate some violation of their rules of life (Picard, 1990, p.17). It seems that their overall strategy has been to strengthen both the distinctive religious culture and those manifestations which the tourism product requires, whereby success and income from the latter shields further secularisation of the former.

Prospect

Tourist demand has continued to increase rapidly, especially from Europe, Japan, and East and Southeast Asia. The East Asian market is the fastest growing in the world, and there is huge potential to emerge from Hindu India. Bali can reasonably expect sustained increases in arrivals, perhaps with somewhat different demands to be serviced.

Domestic tourism, migration, visiting and trading are having a large impact on Balinese resources, services and economic activity. The number of domestic visitors rose sharply after the improvements to air services, and to roads, bus and ferry services in the early 1980s (see Table 11.3). In the period 1981-86, domestic visitors classified as tourists to Denpasar, Sanur and Kuta increased from 76 000 to 123 000, an annual growth of 11 per cent. Of the increase of 47 000, 25 000 stayed at Kuta and 14 000 stayed at Sanur.

Despite the strong general market predictions, it is difficult to forecast that the very fast growth of domestic and international arrivals can continue for another decade, if only because crowding at favoured locations and facilities will detract from the tourist experience. The latest Bali Government forecast is for an average 6 per cent growth through the 1990s, to reach about two million foreign and two million domestic visitors in year 2000. Job creation, particularly in construction and services, will probably not be repeated on the 1980s scale, thus slowing the rate of influx from Java and Lombok. There is al-

Table 11.3   Domestic arrivals in Bali, 1980-90 (in thousands)

Year	By air*	By sea	
		From Lombok	From Java
1980	278	52	510
1985	366	125	948
1990	587	310	1367

* includes foreign visitors who officially entered Indonesia through other ports.

(Sources: *Government of Bali Province,* Statistical Yearbooks; *Heads of Port Management Offices, Department of Communications at Benoa, Padang Bai, Gilimanuk*)

ready evidence of serious lags in provision of urban services and of degraded environments, which may deter some urbanisation.

The critical question for migration is about the rate of job creation in Java, Lombok, Sulawesi and Sumatra. The critical question for the condition and livelihood of Bali is whether sufficient public and private revenue from tourism is being raised and retained in Bali to maintain the standard of living and to protect and enhance the product which tourists are demanding. If the latter cannot be maintained, then cultural tourism will give way to hedonist and recreational tourism, probably with a lower per capita yield to businesses in Bali and thus a declining capability of maintaining public and private standards. The following discussion will outline the urban form and infrastructure which is straining to support an urban area of 500 000 serving a hinterland of 2.5 million, and as many as three million non-Balinese visitors per year.

THE MATERIAL OVERLAY: INFRASTRUCTURE AND URBAN FORM

Slow growth

The Raja's Palace was set almost in the middle of a plain of 10 x 15 kilometres (6 x 9 miles), bounded by sea to east and west, the 40 metre (131 feet) contour line in the north and the Benoa-Tuban swamps in the south (Scott & Furphy 1971, p.10). Agricultural productivity declines towards the south, as there is an increasing proportion of coarser sands with high porosity and salinity. The growth of the southern suburbs (Kuta and Tuban airport area) detracted little from agriculture, but northwards from Kuta the loss has been large and almost complete.

The central areas of Denpasar were laid out with lanes of less than 7 metres (23 feet) width to serve the pedestrian, porterage, handcart and horse-and-cart traffic of the 1900-40 period. The grid pattern suited the north-south drainage and the Balinese and European sense of proper form. Balinese associate 'north' with the better, the sacred, the proper aspects of life, and their temples and important public buildings are oriented to the Mother Temple at Besakih. The north-south dominance of circulation has been increasingly emphasised since 1970 by the growth of Kuta, the port and airport, investment in Bukit and the By-Pass Highway.

When Denpasar was designated as the main city of Bali in 1958, there was no formal limit of boundaries. The declaration of an urban area for planning purposes was made in 1970, to an extent of 11 300 hectares (43.6 square miles) (SCETO 1971, p.15; Table 1 in DPU 1989). One of the most dynamic areas, Kuta, was not included in the declared planning area.

At that time, the contiguous built-up area of Denpasar was 1600 hectares (43.6 square miles) containing 84 000 people, in a broad average density of fifty persons per hectare (12 800 per square mile). The declared planning area contained 185 000 people, at a broad average density of sixteen per hectare (4144 per square mile). Agricultural and 'green' space made up 80 per cent of the planning area.

Turbulent growth

In the 1960s, population growth maintained 3 per cent per year in Denpasar area, including Sanur and Kuta (Scott & Furphy 1971, p.8). For the next decade, population growth averaged 4 per cent per year, slightly lower in the crowded business and trading area of Denpasar West; higher in the education, government and tourist sector of Denpasar East (Renon and Sanur); and up to 5 per cent in Denpasar South, towards Kuta and Tuban. While the planning area

recorded an increase of 100 000 people in the decade (Table 2.9 in DPU 1989), the 'greater Denpasar' area including Kuta and Tuban showed an additional 200 000 people (Putra Agung, 1986, p.11).

After the build-up of government departments had been achieved, and with the slowdown of national oil revenues and the suspension of new hotel construction outside of Bukit, population growth slowed to 2 per cent or less in the 1980s decade. Growth was slowest in the east (0.6 per cent) and fastest in the south (2.7 per cent). In that decade, population in 'greater Denpasar' and Bukit grew by around 150 000.

Thus in the 30 years since the declaration of Denpasar as the main city of Bali, its functional population increased by 400 000. Since the rest-of-Badung growth rate was less than 2 per cent over the period, it seems that migration and urbanisation accounted for 300 000 of the increase. Extrapolating from the estimate of non-Balinese in 1978 as 12.5 per cent of total (Putra Agung 1986, p.14), and allowing for the influx to construction work, it can be suggested that the non-Balinese made up around 15 per cent of the urbanising stream, or around 50 000 people. Roughly 250 000 Bali residents, about 12.5 per cent of the total, moved into the Denpasar region in that generation.

Services

They came to an area which was already inadequately serviced. Less than 20 per cent of households had electricity before 1980. In 1970, around 20 per cent of the population was served by bulk water connections and sewers (Scott & Furphy 1971, p.7). Service targets were set at 60 per cent supplied by 1984 (Scott & Furphy 1980, p.49), with an assumption of nine persons per connection. There was some gain in the period 1972-84, as population grew by 4 per cent per year and new water connections by 12 per cent. The water main was extended to Sanur in 1979; but in the burgeoning Kuta area, 80 per cent of people did not have connection to a piped supply. By 1990, broadly 300 000 out of 600 000 in the region were officially connected to the mains supply.

The changes in work, lifestyle and industry practices were reflected in increasing daily demand for piped water - from a planning standard of 86 litres (19 gallons) per person per day in 1940, to 150 litres (33 gallons) in 1980 and 200 litres (44 gallons) in 1990. For hotels, assuming 1.5 guests per room plus 1.5 employees per room and 2.5 persons per staff family, the consumption was estimated at 1140 litres (250 gallons) per room per day (Appendix B.3 in Scott & Furphy 1971). The number of hotel rooms has grown from around 1000 in 1970 to 20 000 in 1990, adding about 25 per cent to the total resident demand for water. Even though the total demand has been constrained by the restricted coverage by mains supply, upstream extraction has reduced the flows in the southbound rivers, and contributed to their degraded condition.

There are about two hundred factories in greater Denpasar, the great majority of which discharge directly to drains and water courses without treatment (JICA Report, 1991). The discharge of dyes from garment factories is a particular concern.

Sewerage systems have lagged well behind demand. No public sewerage system exists in Denpasar, Sanur or Kuta, with no prospect of connection before 1996. Of the 350 hotels in the area, only three have packaged sewerage treatment plants. All of the restaurants and commercial premises drain wastes to septic tanks. It is reported that around half of the septic tanks are in less than good condition, and half have not been desludged over the last 10 years. The environmental and health risks of dependence on septic tanks in a crowded and fragile ecosystem are quite high.

Research for the Wastewater and Sewerage Master Plan (JICA Report) in 1991 showed significantly bad pollution in the six rivers from Ayung at Sanur to the Mati at Kuta. Seawater quality was also poor off Kuta Beach. There was significant organic pollution of ground water in central and southern Denpasar. Wastewater disposal and septic tank leakage were the major causes of groundwater pollution.

Work

To visitors and residents, the most obvious signs of overurbanisation and cultural degradation are in the unemployment, and the traffic. The traditional subsistence system hosted considerable underemployment, and even today many Balinese in paid employment remain very much involved in the subsistence economy as well. In 1972, Badung reported as fully employed 31 per cent of its labour force, and 69 per cent unemployed or underemployed (Noronha 1977, p.189). The employment rate in 1987 was reported as 61 per cent, indicating a transformation in economic activity (DPU 1989, pp.3-15). In the generation of rapid transformation (1960-90), it seems that around 15 per cent of the Balinese agricultural workforce left agriculture even while total production increased at around 5 per cent per year.

Broadly described, an additional 100 000 paying jobs (employed and self-employed) and 30 000 education enrolments were created in the region, while population increased by 400 000. In 1990, 30 per cent of the employed people were in the primary sector, 30 per cent in government, 10 per cent in industry, 10 per cent in trading and commerce, and 20 per cent in other services. A large number of jobs were taken up by 'proletarianised' agriculturalists resident in the region, and by Balinese commuting from surrounding villages of Badung. Construction jobs were very much taken up by short-term migrants from Java. It is estimated that around 250 000 Balinese people migrated to the region in the 1960-90 period, of whom perhaps 150 000 were adults able to work. It would seem from the broad description of job growth that perhaps half of them did not obtain paid work outside of the household.

Migrants from other islands probably experience higher rates of unemployment than Balinese migrants, because of their weaker knowledge of the job market and weaker access to capital and land (Sudibia 1992, p.27). Since a large proportion of migrants do not show in the official population and workforce statistics (Putra Agung 1986, p.12), they are not included in official estimates of unemployment. They are now prominent as street vendors and hawkers, whose activities are being subjected to increasing surveillance and regulation by urban authorities.

Traffic

Motorised transport spread slowly in Bali until 1965, and since then has grown at an astonishing rate. There were 1000 vehicles in 1939 (Putra Agung 1986, p.22) and around 10 000 in 1960. Table 11.4 sets out growth and forecasts for the 1980-2000 period.

Table 11.4   Estimates of motor vehicle registrations 1980-2000 (in thousands)

Year	Bali				Badung only			
	M/cycle	Car	Other	Total	M/cycle	Car	Other	Total
1980	60	8	12	80	35	5	5	45
1985	132	13	18	163	80	9	9	98
1990	249	37	38	324	130	27	17	174
2000*	556	86	68	710	250	60	45	355

* Estimated

(Source: *Direktorat Lalu Lintas Polda Nusra, Bali 1991.*)

Total registrations in Bali have been growing at 12 per cent per year in the period 1970-90, including a rate of 14 per cent per year extending from 1985 to 1992. The first wave of mobilisation has been by means of motorcycles, with an increase in registrations from 60 000 in 1980 to 250 000 in 1990. The second wave is by means of cars and utility vans, where registrations are currently growing at twice the rate of motorcycles, reflecting increasing affluence, improved main roads, longer travel distances and larger loads to satisfy needs, consumer preference in response to images of success and power, increasing danger in traffic and increasing number of non-Balinese investors and workers.

Over 50 per cent of registrations are in Badung, and around 75 per cent of all motorised transport

Figure 11.6   Road widening to 'solve' traffic congestion
(Source: *I.K. Neben*)

use and service is consumed in the Denpasar-Sanur-Bukit region (Government of Bali Province, *Statistical Yearbook* 1990). The viable service area of Denpasar businesses has been progressively extended since 1980 by road widening and upgrading, and by intense competition in inter-*kabupaten* bus services. However, the very success of private and public motorised transport is bringing serious penalties to users and non-users, as congestion and pollution become very serious.

Pedestrian and vehicle traffic now compete in unpleasant combat for space, progress and safety, both in the urban centres and shopping places, and along the intervillage arterials. One-way systems and parking controls have been applied to most urban areas where wall-to-wall widths are typically 10 metres (33 feet). In Denpasar, Sanur and Kuta, there has been a ten year program of setting back properties and buildings in order to improve access to businesses and services which originally were designed for high-density flows of pedestrians and handcarts. Narrow buses, three-wheelers and motorcycles provide a huge amount of inner-city service, without which many businesses would probably not have survived.

Congestion and relocation

According to the 1986 surveys for the DPU Second Regional Cities Urban Transport Project, peak-hour traffic had already exceeded road capacity at nine of the thirty observation points on the roads of 'Greater Denpasar', resulting in long delays. Based on forecast traffic growth and public infrastructure investment, it was expected that traffic/capacity ratios would exceed 1.0 at twenty-five of thirty points, including twenty points with a ratio exceeding 2.0. Average daily vehicle flows had reached 50 000 in the central business area in 1986, and with some investments and improvements in traffic management, were expected to exceed 100 000 in 1990 (Table 3.7 in DPU 1989).

Improvement and widening of arterial roads in and around the city have been proceeding for 15 years, enabling growth of central traffic and business (Figure 11.6). Completion of the Sanur By-Pass and the Northern Ring Road have removed through traffic and allowed a higher flow of city business traffic. However, the erosion of the relative dominance of

*Figure 11.7   Houses on Denpasar's periphery encroaching upon green spaces (*sawah*) (Source: I.K. Neben)*

central Denpasar in regional business has probably accelerated since the late 1980s. Direct consumer services have shown a tendency to follow the new consumer power towards Renon and Sanur in the east, and towards the tourist-dominated spending power around Kuta, Tuban and Bukit in the south. There are new offices and large shopping centres at Renon, Sanur, Ubung in the north, on the northern edge of Kuta, and lately in south Kuta and Nusa Dua. Congestion, parking, land price, appearance of premises and environment have been the main determining factors in the relative shift away from central Denpasar.

Denpasar has always lacked parking space, given the origins of its form, the dominance of small trading and processing businesses, the restrictions on building heights and the cost of land (Budiartha 1992, p.20). The actions of searching, parking and depart-

Figure 11.8   Canalised Badung River. Recent efforts by the authorities have now reduced the level of pollution in the river (Source: I.K. Neben)

ing greatly retard moving traffic in the narrow streets and, in the dense grid pattern of intersections, have combined to reduce peak-hour travel speeds in central Denpasar to less than 10 kilometres per hour (6 miles per hour) (Figure 5.2 in DPU Transport 1987).

Many businesses and institutions have extended or varied their operating hours to spread the demand for access, but it seems that the limits have been reached for many users, and that traffic flow in the central area will tend to level off. A greater share of the new owners of private vehicles, having different shopping and business habits and preferences, will probably choose to make more use of the peripheral business centres. However, the shift will certainly be insufficient to restore an attractive living and working environment to the central business areas. Increasing competition from the periphery and increasing costs in the centre could reduce central profitability and public revenues, with consequent deterioration in standards and appearance. Profanity will have reached its self-sustaining level, but without the capacity to improve its environment nor make compensation for the lost green and sacred places.

THE SHIELDED STRENGTH?

Most of the built-up area of Denpasar appears like many other business and trading towns of Southeast Asia which grew around small family organisations, initially low-capital investment, porterage and animal transport and low capacity infrastructure. There is no garden appearance in Denpasar, no celebration of the sacred. The things which have transformed the city - tourists enjoying the culture and environment - do not appear in the centre. The Hindu culture and authority here was decapitated and then over-run by the profane and secular forces propelled firstly by the subjugating mission of the colonials, then by the developmental mission of the Republic, and then by international and domestic tourists. Tourists and diverse profane practices have taken over the beaches of Sanur and Kuta, where Balinese used to symbolically cleanse their gods (Covarrubias 1974, p.405).

It is around the edges of Greater Denpasar that the admired culture and satisfying environment can still be found - parts of Sanur, despite the damage to the foreshores, beach and reef; on the north-west

Figure 11.9 Low income housing along Badung River banks (Source: I.K. Nehen)

edges of Kuta despite the crowds; on the Bukit Peninsula despite the massive luxury of the resort hotels and shopping facilities. Eighty per cent of Bali's hotel beds are found in these areas; possibly 90 per cent of tourist nights per year are spent here. The tourist spending is here, and then spreads out to the 'real' Bali through remittances and payments for labour, food, fruit, flowers, building materials, offerings, decorations, performances, paintings, sculptures, carvings, artefacts, clothes, shoes, baskets, jewellery and myriad other products from an inventive and adaptive population.

This massive vote of admiration for their culture has surely strengthened the Balinese belief in their values and their sacred temples. The world is paying them to do the things which have always enriched their lives and guided their behaviour. The means to do so is in the domain of the profane, which has overwhelmed the crowded southern corner of the island, and provided rich profits to investors, of whom the biggest are from outside Bali. Balinese pay their way in the Republic, by commercialising some parts of their culture and means of livelihood.

The triumph of the profane in Denpasar, Kuta and Bukit is indisputable. It has built its bars, clubs, dances, food stalls, shops, clothes, imitative arts and artefacts, sports, entertainments and the culturally universal products and brand names. The profane thus has its own power of sustained attraction, with the dangers and damage of a driven materialist culture barely sensitive to the form and style of its urban centre.

Its tendrils reach out along each road and wrap around each tourist object in the cultural heartlands. Not deeply, it seems. The metaphor of dykes and levees of shops, showrooms, workshops, *losmen* and restaurants, along the roads and through the small towns, seems valid. The flow of secular wealth can extend and be tapped, then turned to circulate according to the distinctive beliefs about respect for the gods, the environment and the human relations of the *bandjar*. The rooting of behaviour and the visual and performing arts in that triad has allowed them to be responsive to the new infrastructure, money and adoration of the outsiders, without allowing them to be supplanted by foreign forms. The way in which the majority of Balinese have interacted with the profane has in fact shielded the sacred, and both modified and strengthened its distinctive culture.

ENDNOTES

1 For further details of Bali's economic history, especially the growth of its tourism industry, see Daroesman, 1973; Francillon, 1979; McTaggart, 1980; Jayasuriya and Nehen, 1989. For further discussion of Balinese village structures, see Guermonprez, 1990.

REFERENCES

Benoa Port Authority (BPA) 1989, 1990, *Annual Reports to Department of Communications*, BPA, Benoa.

Benoa Port Authority 1991, *Master Plan 1991*, BPA, Benoa.

Budiartha N. *et al.* 1992, *Masalah Dan Pemecahan Sistem Transportasi Kota Denpasar*, Universitas Udayana Kumpulan Abstrak, Seminar Hasil Penelitian, Denpasar.

Covarrubias M. 1974, *Island Of Bali*, Oxford University Press, Jakarta.

Daroesman, R. 1973, 'An economic survey of Bali', *Bulletin of Indonesian Economic Studies*, vol.9, pp.28-61.

Departemen Pekerjaan Umum (DPU) 1982, *Rencana Umum Tata Ruang Kota Denpasar 1982* [Physical Plan], DPU, Denpasar.

_____ 1989, *Kantor Wilayah Propinsi Bali*, DPU, Denpasar.

Department of Tourism 1992, *Tourism Forecasts*, Department of Tourism, Denpasar.

Francillon, C. 1979, *Bali Tourism Culture and Environment*, UNESCO, Paris.

Government of Bali Province 1977, *Tata Ruang Untuk Pembangunan* (Building Code), Governor's Office, Denpasar.

_____ 1980, *Sensus Penduduk, 1980* [Educational Census, 1980], Governor's Office, Denpasar.

—— (series 1980-1989), *Buku Statistik* [Statistical Year-book], Governor's Office, Denpasar.

—— 1989, *Rencana Umum Tata Ruang Daerah* [Planning Regulations], Governor's Office, Denpasar.

Government of Bali Province, Direktorat Lalu Lintas Polda Nusra 1991, *Motor Vehicle Registrations*, Governor's Office, Denpasar.

Guermonprez, J.F. 1990, 'On the elusive Balinese village: hierarchy and values versus political models', *Review of Indonesian and Malaysian Affairs*, vol.24, Summer, pp.55-89.

Information Bureau (IB), Government of East Indies 1939, *Guide to Travellers*, IB, Batavia.

Japanese International Cooperation Agency (JICA) 1991, *Master Plan for Wastewater and Sewerage for Denpasar*, DPU, Denpasar.

Jayasuriya S.K.W. & I.K.Nehen 1989, 'Bali: economic growth and tourism' in H. Hill (ed.), *Unity and Diversity*, Oxford University Press, Singapore.

McTaggart W. 1980, 'Tourism and Tradition in Bali', *World Development*, vol.8; pp.457-66.

Noronha R. 1977, 'Paradise reviewed: tourism in Bali' in *Tourism - Passport to Development?*, UNESCO, Paris.

Pacific Consultants International (PCI) 1990, *Master Plan for Ngurah Rai Airport*, Department of Communications, Denpasar.

Picard M. 1990, 'Kebalian orang Bali: tourism and the uses of Balinese culture in New Order Indonesia', *Review of Indonesian and Malaysian Affairs*, vol.24, pp.1-38.

Putra Agung A.A.G. 1986, *Sejarah Kota Denpasar 1945-1979*, Direktorat Sejarah Dan Nilai Tradisional, Departemen Pendidikan Dan Kebudayaan, Jakarta.

Scott & Furphy Pty. Ltd. 1971, *The Water Supply System in Denpasar*, Department of Foreign Affairs, Canberra.

Société Centrale pour l'Equipement Touristique Outre-Mer (SCETO) 1971, *Master Plan for Development of Tourism in Bali*, UNDP, Paris.

Sudibia I.K., Rimbawan, N.D. & Mariah, E. 1992, *Keterkaitan Hubungan Antara Migran Kelahuran Kuta*, Universitas Udayana, Denpasar.

Vickers A. 1989, *A Paradise Created*, Penguin, Melbourne.

ACKNOWLEDGMENTS

The reader will observe in this chapter frequent references to the ideas of Noronha and the comprehensive survey by Putra Agung. Their contribution thus reaches a wider audience in a comparative collection.

The author is grateful for the ideas and suggestions provided in numerous discussions with members of the Bali Tourism Management Project and the Comprehensive Bali Tourism Development Plan, particularly Dr Ketut Nehen, Dr Anggan Suhandana and Dr I. Nyoman Erawan of Universitas Udayana; and Mr Eka Prayuda and Ir. Lambertus of Gadjah Mada University. The latter was particularly helpful in follow-up research.

Other helpful informants included Dr Wayan Rendha, Chairman of the Regional Planning Board of Bali, Ir. Cok. Gede Wiratama of Dinas Bina Marga, Ir. Ida Bagus Sidharta of DPU, I.B.G. Wiyana of PT. Upada Sastra, and Dr T. Isada of Pacific Consultants International.

The author hopes that they will be as gracious in their assessment of this essay in their field of practice and their geographical domain, as they have been generous and helpful in its preparation.

Index